PRAISE FOR *BLOOD BROTHERS*

"An absorbing and provocative new book."
—David Margolick, *Wall Street Journal*

"It fills a gap in our understanding of one of the most fascinating relationships in American history."
—Allen Barra, *Boston Globe*

"In all it touches—the far-flung but interconnected worlds of race, religion, politics, sports, cities, organized crime, and the news media—this sober and detailed book, a dual biography that alternates between protagonists like a suspense novel, renders profound service. The authors unearth reams of new evidence, shine light on long-overlooked episodes, and hack away at the barnacles of mythology, thereby giving us the finest portrait yet of the doomed relationship that transformed Cassius Clay into Muhammad Ali."
—James Rosen, *National Review*

"In convincing detail, *Blood Brothers* traces Ali's rise to international celebrity while Malcolm was stalked and harassed by the 'Fruit of Islam,' the paramilitary group that enforced obedience to the church."
—*Los Angeles Times*

"In the most detailed account to date of this fascinating bond, professors of history Randy Roberts (Purdue) and Johnny Smith (Georgia Tech) unveil a story few Americans know, arguing that Ali and Malcolm were much more than mere acquaintances; their symbiotic relationship, with Ali as pupil and Malcolm as mentor, was deeply important to each man. . . . From beginning to end, *Blood Brothers* is a story of transformation."
—*Dallas Morning News*

"Electrifying history."
—Peniel E. Joseph, *Reuters*

"[*Blood Brothers*] is shedding light on the secret friendship between boxing great Muhammad Ali and civil rights leader Malcolm X."—*Washington Times*

"The authors give us a thorough examination of the relationship between the two icons in the context of the black experience and the turbulent 1960s. White America blamed Malcolm for Cassius Clay's transformation to Muhammad Ali, but the truth is more complicated, involving the split between Malcolm and the Nation of Islam. We're brought back to the champ's early boxing days and see how the brash Ali whom America came to know developed."

—*New York Post*

"This may well be the most important sports book of 2016."

—**Allen Barra**, *TruthDig*

"Thanks to Randy Roberts and Johnny Smith's enthralling narrative we now have a better understanding of how a complex relationship was born, and how it fell apart." —*The Times* (UK)

"[Roberts and Smith] provide a story that unfolds like a dramatic tragedy. All the classic elements are there: emotional bonds, tortured choices, betrayal, death, denial, remorse." —*Sunday Times* (UK)

"Though their individual lives have been explored through previous books and movies, *Blood Brothers: The Fatal Friendship Between Muhammad Ali and Malcolm X* delves into the close kinship these men shared, and the reasons it ultimately fell apart." —*Economist*'s **Prospero blog**

"The broad outlines of the Ali/Malcolm drama are well known, but Roberts and Smith emphasize how crucial each was to the other's destiny—Ali's as a global figure of black pride and Malcolm's as a martyred black visionary. They provide more exhaustive detail than previously available, aided by newly released FBI files and personal papers. And they infuse the tale with sharp insights and an impending sense of tragedy. . . . *Blood Brothers* reminds us of a time when a heroic image of Ali would have seemed as unlikely as the idea that Cassius Clay could beat Sonny Liston—or that a big-budget Hollywood film would someday venerate the life of Malcolm X." —*City Journal*

"Historians Roberts and Smith have written the first book examining the complex bond between the two men, who met in 1962 as the young Louisville boxer Cassius Clay was making a name for himself."

—*Louisville Courier-Journal*

"*Blood Brothers* comes alive and crackles with tension. . . . The story is gripping and told with particular drama." —Thomas Hauser, *The Ring*

"Roberts and Smith portray both of these courageous and controversial, inspired and inspiring men with fresh, stinging clarity, and extend our perception of the interconnectivity of race, religion, sports, and media during this violent and transformative era, which is so very germane today."
—*Booklist*, starred review

"This book offers a significant contribution to serious studies of Malcolm X, Muhammad Ali, and the Nation of Islam."—*Library Journal*, starred review

"[Roberts and Smith] sharply detail Malcolm's growing disillusionment with Elijah, his heartbreak at the loss of Ali's allegiance, and the ugly dynamic within the Nation that left the defiant minister murdered. A page-turning tale from the 1960s about politics and sports and two proud, extraordinary men whose legacies endure." —*Kirkus Reviews*, starred review

"A provocative history. . . . Roberts and Smith map the relationship between the troubled icons in painstaking detail and debunk long-held assumptions about their break. . . . Roberts and Smith bring a fresh perspective to the story in the civil rights movement, and capture the ferment of the broader era."
—*Publishers Weekly*

"Well researched and spritely written, *Blood Brothers* is, by far, the most complete and detailed account of the friendship between Muhammad Ali and Malcolm X, and how black nationalist politics profoundly changed how black athletes saw big-time sports in America. *Blood Brothers* fills in important gaps for those who know the story and provides a gripping, informative history for those who do not."
—**Gerald Early, editor of the *Muhammad Ali Reader* and author of *A Level Playing Field: African American Athletes and the Republic of Sports***

"In earlier works, Randy Roberts and Johnny Smith have used their skills as professional historians to pierce the veil of myth, hero worship, and hype that mars so much sports journalism. In this illuminating joint effort, *Blood Brothers* tells the story of a strange friendship marked by initial affection, cold manipulation, and ultimate estrangement. They show that Muhammad Ali and Malcolm X, so brave and assertive in their public lives, shared another bond stronger than friendship: fear of assassination by their spiritual mentor, Elijah Muhammad."
—**Howell Raines, former executive editor of the *New York Times***

"There's brilliant history in this crackling story of two men whose tragic brotherhood changed America. Absorbing and essential reading."

—Robert Lipsyte, former sports columnist for *The New York Times*

"Deeply researched and compellingly written, *Blood Brothers* makes clear that the lives of Muhammad Ali and Malcolm X were intertwined. Each needed the other, and as their relationship careened from tenderness to tragedy, each became a global icon. Their story just pops off the page."

—Aram Goudsouzian, author of *Down to the Crossroads: Civil Rights, Black Power, and the Meredith March Against Fear*

"Randy Roberts and Johnny Smith's *Blood Brothers* is a brilliantly conceived narrative linking the Day-Glo legacies of Malcolm X and Muhammad Ali. At heart, it's the story of a fast friendship that rocked the Cold War world and forever changed the destiny of African American history. A towering achievement!" **—Douglas Brinkley, author of *Rosa Parks***

BLOOD
BROTHERS

BLOOD BROTHERS

THE FATAL FRIENDSHIP BETWEEN
MUHAMMAD ALI
AND MALCOLM X

RANDY ROBERTS
AND JOHNNY SMITH

BASIC BOOKS
New York

Designed by Jeff Williams

"Harlem (2)" from *The Collected Poems of Langston Hughes*, by Langston Hughes, edited by Arnold Rampersad with David Roessel, Associate Editor, copyright © 1994 by the Estate of Langston Hughes. Used by permission of Alfred A. Knopf, an imprint of the Knopf Doubleday Publishing Group, a division of Penguin Random House LLC. All rights reserved.

Library of Congress Cataloging-in-Publication Data
Names: Roberts, Randy, 1951–author. | Smith, Johnny.
Title: Blood brothers : the fatal friendship between Muhammad Ali and Malcolm X/ Randy Roberts and Johnny Smith.
Description: New York : Basic Books, [2016] | Includes bibliographical references and index.
Identifiers: LCCN 2015043982| ISBN 9780465079704 (hardcover : alk. paper) | ISBN 9780465098637 (ebook)
Subjects: LCSH: Ali, Muhammad, 1942—-Friends and associates. | X, Malcolm, 1925–1965—Friends and associates. | African Americans—Biography. | Black Muslims—Biography.
Classification: LCC GV1132.A44 R64 2016 | DDC 796.83092—dc23 LC record available at http://lccn.loc.gov/2015043982

ISBN: 978-0-465-09322-9 (paperback)
ISBN: 978-0-465-09323-6 (paperback ebook)

10 9 8 7 6 5 4 3 2 1

For Marjie, Alison, and Kelly, the loves of my life.

—RWR

For my loving wife, Rebecca.

—JMS

CONTENTS

PREFACE: A DREAM DEFERRED

Malcolm X and Ali were like very close brothers. It was almost as if they were in love with each other.

—FERDIE PACHECO, MUHAMMAD ALI'S PHYSICIAN

"What happens to a dream deferred?" Langston Hughes asked in one of his most moving and insightful poems. "Does it dry up like a raisin in the sun? . . . Or does it explode?"[1] We ask the same questions about the lives of two extraordinarily gifted men, both born in a segregated land and raised amidst pain and discrimination to face a violent world. What happens to a dream deferred? Does it snake toward hopelessness, despair, drunkenness, addiction, and poverty? Or does it explode in rage? A dream deferred, Malcolm X knew, could become an American nightmare.

Our story begins with two questions: Who was Cassius Clay? And how did he become Muhammad Ali? As much as has been written about him, he remains enigmatic, a silent sphinx. He has meant different things to different people at different times. It has become increasingly difficult to know the Muhammad Ali of the 1960s. Since the end of the Vietnam War, liberal writers have manufactured an image of him as a hero of social causes, a unifying force of goodwill. He is no longer seen as controversial, threatening, or anti-American. His legacy has become distorted and trivialized.[2]

In a tragic irony, Parkinson's disease has robbed him of his verbal gifts. Once known as the Louisville Lip, Ali no longer boasts, rhymes, or raps. His silence has been filled by corporate sponsors, movie producers, and writers who have created a new voice for him, a voice that neither preaches racial separation nor acknowledges his past with Malcolm X. A minister in the Nation of Islam (NOI), Malcolm espoused racially charged rhetoric about "devilish white men," "brainwashed Christian Negroes," and "bloody revolution." Many feared that he might organize the opening battle of an impending race war. Muhammad Ali called this man his brother, leading critics to vilify him as a disgrace to boxing.

At first, Cassius Clay, as he was known until 1964, hid his relationship with Malcolm. A master of deception, he proved infuriatingly elusive for journalists. "Figuring out who or what is the *real* Cassius Clay is a parlor game that has become unrewarding even for experts," commented Jack Olsen, a white writer who gained unprecedented access to the fighter.

> Clay's personality is like a jigsaw puzzle whose pieces were cut by a drunken carpenter, a jumbled collection of moods and attitudes that do not seem to interlock. Sometimes, he sounds like a religious fanatic, his voice singsong and chanting, and all at once he will turn into a calm, reasoning, if confused, student of the scriptures. He is a loudmouth windbag and at the same time a remarkably sincere and dedicated athlete. He can be a kindly benefactor of the neighborhood children and a vicious bully in the ring, a prissy Puritan totally intolerant of drinkers and smokers, and a teller of dirty jokes.[3]

In 1966, when Olsen began writing *Black Is Best*, a lengthy profile of the boxer, piecing together the jigsaw puzzle of Muhammad Ali seemed impossible. Yet what Olsen and other writers have failed to recognize is that the *real* Muhammad Ali can only be seen when his many masks are uncovered. From 1960 to 1965, the half decade that framed his relationship with Malcolm X, he appeared convincingly as four different personalities, packaged and expressed at different times for different audiences.

He first emerged on the world stage as Cassius Marcellus Clay Jr. of the 1960 Rome Olympics—wide-eyed, talkative, enthusiastic, and likable, a defender of the glacial progress being made in American race relations. In Rome, Cassius proudly told a Soviet reporter who asked him about the American color line, "We've got qualified people working on that problem, and I'm not worried about the outcome. To me, the U.S.A. is still the best country in the world, counting yours." As Cassius Marcellus Clay Jr., he was the quiet southern "Negro," downplaying racial conflict, and avoiding controversy.[4]

After turning professional toward the end of 1960, he became the Louisville Lip—boasting loudly, spouting poetry, belittling opponents, and advertising himself. As the Louisville Lip, he became the booming athletic equivalent of Little Richard and Elvis Presley, echoing the raucous notes of rock 'n' roll and the television antics of professional wrestler Gorgeous George.

As the civil rights movement escalated from 1962 to early 1964, he evolved into Cassius X—the loyal follower of Elijah Muhammad, the Supreme Minister of the Nation of Islam. As Cassius X, a name he adopted only for a brief time, he imitated Malcolm, appearing angry and outraged by racial injustice. Behind the walls of the Nation's mosques, he stood up as an outspoken defender of the Black Muslim philosophy, one that promoted racial pride, self-determination, and complete separation of the races. As an acolyte of Elijah Muhammad and Malcolm X, he defiantly opposed Martin Luther King's approach to the civil rights movement and the ideals of racial integration.

Finally, after winning the heavyweight title in February 1964, he became Muhammad Ali—renamed by Elijah, pried apart from Malcolm, and the new front man for the Nation of Islam. As in his other personas, he inhabited the role of Muhammad Ali, often wearing the somber, stone-faced mask of Elijah's paramilitary followers. As Muhammad Ali, he instantly became the most politically controversial athlete in the country's history.

Cassius Marcellus Clay Jr., the Louisville Lip, Cassius X, and Muhammad Ali—the boxer played all these roles, wearing the different masks as the occasion dictated. He *was* all of these characters, and sometimes more than one at the same moment. "I don't have to be what

xii | PREFACE: A DREAM DEFERRED

you want me to be," he once announced. "I'm free to be who I want." Yet some of the men closest to him had trouble understanding exactly who he was free to be. "They say there's fifteen sides to Clay," his ring physician Ferdie Pacheco said. "To me he's just a thoroughly confused person. Sure, he has sides, but they don't mesh."[5]

Only by examining Cassius Clay's early years in Louisville and his relationship with Malcolm X can one hope to discover Muhammad Ali. Central to his life, relationships, and career was deception. Disguise and dissemblance, of course, have been integral to African American culture since the first moments of contact between blacks and whites. From the stories of B'rer Rabbit's trickery and indirection to such novels as Richard Wright's *Native Son* and Ralph Ellison's *Invisible Man*, the ability of black Americans to wear disguises and assume multiple identities has been crucial in navigating the boundaries and pathways of the color line in America.

But beyond African American culture, the volatile circumstances of young Cassius Clay's home life created an atmosphere conducive to disguise. That he entered a profession that rewarded violence and deception, a trade that trafficked in feints, fakes, and pain, indicates how ingrained those qualities were in his life. If Olsen, Pacheco, and others could not figure out "the riddle of Cassius Clay," that attested to how well he had learned to hide himself.[6]

LIKE MUHAMMAD ALI, Malcolm X was also a man of many masks. The seventh son of an itinerant Baptist preacher, Malcolm Little inherited his father's rage against white supremacy. As a young man in the 1940s, he came of age as Detroit Red, a street hustler strutting in a zoot suit, peddling drugs and prostitutes. In the smoky pool halls and jazz clubs of Boston and New York, he developed the swagger of a trickster, cultivating the cool pose of the "hip cats" he admired.[7]

Behind the mask of Detroit Red, he buried the pain of his past. In prison for larceny, his fellow convicts called him Satan. Voraciously reading history, sociology, and theology, he transformed himself into a puritanical follower of Elijah Muhammad, the self-proclaimed Messenger of Allah. From his cell, he absorbed and memorized Muhammad's writings and speeches, accepting his message of separatism and strict morality. By the mid-1950s, the former convict had become the

Messenger's protégé—Malcolm X—an outspoken minister saving lost souls in bars, nightclubs, and back alleys.[8]

As Malcolm X, he was a model of redemption, preaching a doctrine of abstinence from drugs, alcohol, and crime. The "angriest black man in America" divided the country with his sharp tongue and brutal honesty, openly condemning whites for terrorizing black Americans. Ultimately, the internal politics of the Nation of Islam and his own crisis of faith led him on a journey toward the universalism of Sunni Islam. In Africa and the Middle East, he was known as El-Hajj Malik El-Shabazz, but he would forever be remembered in America as Malcolm X.[9]

Malcolm may have changed his name, but at his core he remained the same dedicated freedom fighter. Fiercely uncompromising, he carried himself with imperial restraint, striking a cool posture that could intimidate the most self-assured white man. For Malcolm, coolness meant speaking his mind, refusing to submit to white authority. Being cool meant being completely free.

In many ways, Malcolm X and Cassius Clay seemed the product of the same DNA. Both thrived on center stage surrounded by an audience. Standing beneath the spotlight—at Malcolm's pulpit or in Clay's ring—they responded to the thundering sound of applause and the deafening chorus of boos. Neither man could resist a platform, an interview, or a debate. Both enjoyed sparring with words and manipulating other men's fears with sensational language. They were both fighters.

Before Cassius X became Muhammad Ali, Malcolm saw something in the young boxer that no one else did. "Not many people know the quality of the mind he's got in there," he told writer George Plimpton in 1964. Like Malcolm, he was absolutely self-assured, proud, and defiant. He carried himself with boundless confidence, boldly professing his own greatness the way that Malcolm fearlessly denounced white America. Studying Clay's interactions with reporters, the way he spellbound audiences with his performances, Malcolm realized that he could become something more than an athlete. As the heavyweight champion of the world, Clay possessed the kind of far-reaching cultural power that could unify black people. Recognizing Clay's global fame, Malcolm exploited him, envisioning a new movement that fused together Clay's world and his into one built around celebrity and politics.

A MYTH HAS ENSHROUDED the encounters between Malcolm X and Muhammad Ali. The stories are told and retold, fashioned in ways that obscure the reality. An anecdote here, a quote there, and before you know it a fabricated "truth" has emerged. Drawing on a few unsubstantiated observations by writer Alex Haley and a couple of self-serving comments by Malcolm X and Muhammad Ali, historians and biographers have manufactured a convenient morality play involving two men who came together, formed a deep relationship, and then suddenly and dramatically broke apart. End of story. It was almost as if the two larger-than-life figures were planets, swinging close to each other in their orbits and then moving apart on separate paths.

But it was never that simple. Although their respective biographers have neglected to show that Ali and Malcolm were much more important to one another than previously acknowledged, we have uncovered and interpreted previously unexamined documents that reveal the personal and political dynamics between them. The complex friendship between Malcolm and Ali is interred in a labyrinthine jungle of sources—the private papers of Malcolm X, Alex Haley, and others; FBI files and surveillance reports; State Department records; archived news footage and television programs; long-unexamined interview transcripts; new interviews with people who knew Ali and Malcolm intimately; the daily press; and a variety of other published and unpublished materials.

Investigating their relationship, we have reconstructed the lives and movements of Ali and Malcolm, focusing especially on the period from the time they met in June 1962 through February 1965. Plotting their daily activities provided a key to deciphering redacted FBI files, revealing the events and conversations recorded in the Bureau's records in a new light. Using these unique sources, we tracked their movements and, in the process, discovered how historians and biographers have misread the complicated relationship between them.

In the generally accepted narrative, writers maintain that Ali severed his friendship with Malcolm the moment Elijah renamed him. These authors have relied on a quote that Ali allegedly gave Alex Haley during an interview in Harlem, one that Haley excluded from the published account in *Playboy*. In fact, nowhere in the *Playboy* interview is there any mention of Malcolm or why Ali turned his back on him in allegiance to Elijah Muhammad. In the epilogue of *The Autobiography of*

Malcolm X, however, published seven months after Malcolm's death, Haley recounted his memory of the interview with Ali. According to Haley, Ali said, "You just don't buck Mr. Muhammad and get away with it. I don't want to talk about [Malcolm] no more." It is likely that during his research for the epilogue, Haley read a nearly identical quote Ali gave *Ebony* in September 1964, when he said, "You just don't buck Mr. Muhammad and get away with it."[10]

Using Haley's quote, several accomplished biographers and historians have mistakenly suggested that Ali made this statement to Haley during the week after Elijah Muhammad renamed him on March 6, 1964. But Ali was not in Harlem at that time, and more importantly, Haley conducted the interview *after* the boxer returned from Africa on June 24, 1964. Accepting his chronology of events, writers have simplified the complex feelings Ali had for Malcolm. Yet in Haley's unpublished notes from the *Playboy* interview, he scribbled on an index card a comment from Ali that revealed the champ's hidden feelings, contradicting the epilogue in *The Autobiography of Malcolm X*. Haley's index card indicated that Ali told him that although he followed Elijah Muhammad, Malcolm was "still my brother, [and] my friend."[11]

According to Haley, shortly after the interview, he mentioned his meeting with Ali to Malcolm. Curious, Malcolm asked what the champ had said about him. Haley wrote that he pulled out the index card with Ali's comments about Malcolm and handed it to the minister. After leading readers to believe that Ali had only cross words for Malcolm, Haley wrote in the *Autobiography*, "Malcolm X stared at the card, then out of the window, and he got up and walked around." It was "one of the few times I ever heard his voice betray his hurt." Sadly, Malcolm said, "I felt like a *blood big brother* to him." Taking a deep breath, he added, "I'm not against him now. He's a fine young man. Smart. He's just let himself be used, led astray."[12]

Under great financial stress to make *The Autobiography of Malcolm X* a publishing success, it appears that Haley manipulated Malcolm's broken relationship with Ali in order to present a more sensational historical account. Throughout the epilogue, Haley selected and excluded events that fit into *his* agenda. In some cases, he tampered with the facts. But the truth was more complex than Haley let on. Only by carefully following the day-by-day activities of Ali and Malcolm can one

see how intertwined their lives became and how their brotherhood un-raveled, leading inexorably to Malcolm's assassination at the Audubon Ballroom.[13]

WE HAVE TRIED to rescue a story that has fallen into the hands of ha-giographers. *Blood Brothers* explores the importance of two of the most important black men of the 1960s. By following their lives, we have discovered that Cassius Clay had begun attending meetings organized by the Nation of Islam well before any reporter caught wind of it. Even before he became a professional boxer, Clay became infatuated with the teachings of Elijah Muhammad and Malcolm.

What follows is the story of how Cassius Clay became Muhammad Ali and the central role Malcolm X played in his life. It is a tale of friendship and brotherhood, love and deep affection. It is also a story of deceit, betrayal, and violence—inside and outside the ring—during a troubled time.

When Malcolm's life was in danger, when Elijah Muhammad threat-ened to cast him outside the Nation of Islam, Clay became the central figure in his world. For the first time, *Blood Brothers* reveals that the in-stant Malcolm realized he might be murdered, he tethered his future—his very survival—to the life of a boxer who most people figured would never win the heavyweight championship. Malcolm had no doubt that someone inside the Nation wanted him dead. He also knew that none of Elijah's disciples would risk Clay's life. As long as they were together, Malcolm figured, he was safe. Cassius was the perfect shield. However, only ten days after they celebrated the boxer's championship victory over Sonny Liston, Cassius stopped taking Malcolm's phone calls. Sub-mitting to Elijah, the champ accepted a new name and the Supreme Minister's edict that all Muslims cease contact with Malcolm. Once Muhammad Ali sided with Elijah, Malcolm knew that he could no longer hide behind him. At that moment, he recognized that losing Ali's cover might cost him his life.

Ali understood the violent world Malcolm inhabited. Boxing re-flected a violent society. "Violence and hate," explained former heavy-weight champion Floyd Patterson, were "part of the prizefighter's world, Clay's world and mine." Boxing promoters paid prizefighters "to get in

the ring and act out other people's hates." Only in that ring of hate could a black man assault a white man with impunity.[14]

Like many young black men born into segregation and contained by white supremacy and the threat of mob violence, Ali channeled his fears and frustrations into the ring. In boxing gyms, he released his anger, sweating out his bile against a system of racial oppression, pummeling men who stood between him and his dreams. Ali fought not only because boxing offered him a way to make a name for himself but also because the gym offered a sanctuary from the dangers lurking outside. The gym became the one place where he could unleash his frustrations on speed bags, heavy bags, and sparring partners. At a time when black men yearned for power, he confronted the dangers of a violent world by retaliating with violence himself.

"What white America demands in her black champions," Black Panther Eldridge Cleaver insisted, "is a brilliant, powerful body, and a dull bestial mind—a tiger in the ring and a pussycat outside the ring." Black boxers' lives, Cleaver maintained, were "sharply circumscribed by the ropes around the ring." But Ali completely rejected the worn-out role. By redefining the political boundaries of sports, he ushered in the beginning of a new era: the revolt of the black athlete.[15]

The seeds of the revolt were planted in the cities that transformed Cassius Clay into Muhammad Ali. Between 1960 and 1965, he traveled widely, fighting in Rome and London, New York and Los Angeles. When he left Louisville as a teenager, he entered a new world, one that exposed him to the possibilities of freedom beyond the American South. Yet the world beyond Louisville also taught him that no matter how famous he became, some white people would hate him just because he was black or because he was a Muslim.

In gyms and mosques across the country, he matured into a man influenced by the discontent in black America. In Chicago and Detroit, Miami and New York, he heard frustrated black men denounce the crimes of white men. Listening to Elijah Muhammad and Malcolm X led him to change more than his name. When he won the heavyweight championship in February 1964, he broke free from the political constraints of the sports world, declaring that he would define himself on his own terms. When he boldly proclaimed, "I'm free to be who I want,"

he became a source of inspiration for others who would later challenge the sports establishment. In 1969, about a year after sociologist Harry Edwards organized black athletes in an Olympic boycott movement, he observed that Ali had been the central hero in the political "revolution in sports." Ali, he proclaimed, was "the warrior saint in the revolt of the black athlete in America."[16]

That revolt began the moment young Cassius Clay had his first talk with Malcolm. Once Clay met Malcolm—once the personal narrative became a political one—the ring and the playing field were no longer sacred spaces. The relationship between Cassius Clay and Malcolm X signaled a new direction in American culture, one shaped by the forces of sports and entertainment, race and politics. When Clay befriended Malcolm and adopted his ideology, he became the most visible, politically conscious athlete in America. More than anyone else, Malcolm molded Cassius Clay into Muhammad Ali. Under Malcolm's tutelage, he embraced the world stage, emerging as an international symbol of black pride and black independence. Without Malcolm, Muhammad Ali would have never become the "king of the world."

PROLOGUE: BEHIND THE VEIL

> Through a veil I could perceive the forbidden city, the Louisville
> where white folks lived. . . . On my side of the veil everything was
> black: the homes, the people, the churches, the schools, the Ne-
> gro park with Negro park police. . . . I knew that there were two
> Louisvilles and, in America, two Americas. I knew, also, which of
> the two Americas was mine. . . . I was a Negro. An act of God had
> circumscribed my life.
>
> —BLYDEN JACKSON, *THE WAITING YEARS*

H e never lifted the veil, not when he was Cassius Marcellus Clay Jr.
or after he became Muhammad Ali. Some things he would talk
about incessantly—his greatness, his beauty, and his rendezvous
with destiny. Other matters he would discuss in more serious moods—
the history of the black man in America, Black Muslim theology, and,
after he became an orthodox Muslim, universal peace. Yet he seldom
whispered a word about the discord in his own family. "There was a lot
of trouble, bad trouble, between his father and his mother," recalled one
of the boxer's early advisers, "but Cassius would bite his tongue before
he mentioned it."[1]

IT WAS A dime-a-dozen domestic battery, out in "the colored district"
of Louisville's West End. On the hot night of August 8, 1957, Officer
Kalbfleisch took the call. When he arrived at 3302 Grand Avenue, an

older man took off running, darting between houses and into the night. Two young boys huddled close to their crying mother, whispering to her in a comforting manner. One of the youths was bleeding from a knife wound. Years later Kalbfleisch couldn't remember if the boy had been cut on his ass or on his thigh, but "it was in the meat" and bleeding pretty good. When asked about the gash, the teenager said that he had cut it on a milk bottle.[2]

It was an unlikely story. The father had bolted when he saw the police car. The mother, the policeman later told a reporter, was causing trouble—"you know how women are." Kalbfleisch got the picture: The father got drunk. Began to beat his wife. Her son tried to protect her and got cut for his efforts. It was not the first time that Mrs. Odessa Clay had called the police. Nor was it the last.

The injured son, only fifteen years old, identified himself. "My name is Cassius Clay," he said. "I'm a boxer under Joe Martin."

The name Cassius Clay meant nothing to Kalbfleisch, but he knew Joe Martin. A patrolman who in his spare time trained young boxers at Columbia Gym, Martin produced a local television program called *Tomorrow's Champions*. Not many of the kids who fought each other on the weekly telecasts ever won titles, but the mere fact that they were seen on TV granted them a certain local celebrity. And Cassius was one of them, a kid from the tough side of town whose transitory fame still proved no defense against a drunk, angry father.

Kalbfleisch could have filed a formal report at police headquarters, but he let it slide. "I said to myself, 'Well, there ain't gonna be no prosecution anyway.' So I said to the mother, 'Now look, take him to your doctor or take him to the hospital, and if you want to, go up and take out a malicious cutting warrant.'" But the officer knew that the incident would end there. Mr. Clay would return soon enough, and life would go on as before.

All that remains of the episode is a few lines in the duty record book: "August 8, 1957—10:32 p.m., Mrs. Clay, cutting INV. [investigation] 330[2] Grand. NA [no arrest]."

CASSIUS MARCELLUS CLAY JR. grew up living in fear—fear of his father's raised fist, the smell of alcohol on his breath, and his rising, angry voice bursting through the front door. He also feared what would

happen if he did not heed his father's warnings about the dangers lurking outside their home. Repeatedly, the man exhorted his boys: Don't leave our neighborhood. Don't go into white people's stores. Don't contradict a white man. Don't look at white women. Don't disobey policemen. And most importantly, don't get arrested. "Our parents taught us to be safe," said Bob Coleman, a childhood friend of Cassius Clay. "And they knew that if I got arrested by a policeman, there was nothing they could do to help me. It would be like I was lost to them. I would be on my own. That scared them as much as me."[3]

Cassius Clay Sr. told parables that taught young Cassius and his brother Rudy about the world. All the stories had the same general theme: black men die after seemingly harmless encounters with white men. The murders, Clay Sr. insisted, were "legal lynchings." They happened all the time, he said. "When I was a boy, seemed like every darned day you'd read in the paper about something like that: a lynching, a burning of a Negro, every day. Now wouldn't that turn you against the white man? Nine or ten or twelve or fifteen cases like that a week?"[4]

The past haunted Clay Sr., and it lived on in the stories he told his sons. Living in a world of intolerable racism and violence, Clay Sr.'s frustration manifested in outward rage and loathing for the white man. As James Baldwin wrote in 1962, "The Negro's past [was one] of rope, fire, torture, castration, infanticide, rape; death and humiliation; fear by day and night, fear as deep as the marrow of the bone; doubt that he was worthy of life, since everyone around him denied it; sorrow for his women, for his kinfolk, for his children, who needed his protection, and whom he could not protect." In the words of Baldwin, this "hatred for white men [ran] so deep that it often turned against him and his own, and made all love, all trust, all joy impossible."[5]

Clay Sr. threw his entire body into the stories he told, twisting, snorting, huffing, and punctuating key points with a loud "Ummmmhm-mmma" or an inopportune laugh. A natural storyteller, he moved gracefully from humor to tragedy, carrying the listener along with him.

He was an exasperated artist who earned a living as a sign painter. A wiry, dark-skinned man, opinionated and outspoken, he was not much of a fighter, except when he was drunk. Then he was apt to turn on his family. But he was also a teller of tall tales, most of which centered on his fantasy life. Given his mood of the moment, he might claim to be

a Mexican, a Hindu, or an Arab. During his Mexican phase he wore a serape and took siestas. During his Arab period he called his second son Rudolph Valentino, after the actor who portrayed the Hollywood sheikh. A friend recalled that during Clay Sr.'s time as an Arab, he observed certain rituals. "At noon he used to get down off his painting ladder and in his little box he had a carpet and he'd put the carpet down and bow to the east and then bow to the west."[6]

All his life Clay Sr. struggled. A friend of the family said he "enjoyed life," by which he meant he took his pleasures where he found them and didn't worry excessively about propriety and consequences. But a streak of anger, a sense of opportunities denied, ran like a river through his life. Had he been white, he thought, he would have been famous and wealthy. His murals on walls and churches in the West End of Louisville attested to his talents, and he could sing any song in his thin baritone. Yes, sir, he said, he could have been a great artist or recording star. Like the other greats, all he needed was a little more training. "Nat King Cole was nothing when he started out," he said. "And Dean Martin was nothing. Frank Sinatra was sickening. Frank Sinatra was *sickening*!"[7]

CASSIUS CLAY JR. was a mama's boy, handsome, sweet, and well liked. He feared his father, avoided violence, and abhorred alcohol. But in fundamental ways he *was* his father's son, and he would become more so as the years passed. His father's stories made all too much sense of the violent world inside and outside his home.

Two events were enough to confirm all of his father's gruesome tales of horror. The first happened within a four- or five-minute drive of Clay's home on Grand Avenue. In 1954 Andrew Wade IV, an African American electrician, and his wife, Charlotte, arranged for a white couple to purchase a house for them in an all-white suburban neighborhood. Their new neighbors immediately and angrily reacted, insisting that the Wades sell their house and move. When the Wades refused, they received ominous threats followed by a cross burning on their lawn. Later someone fired a rifle through a window in their house. Still, the Wades stayed put. Finally, on the night of June 27, 1954, while the Wades were gone for the evening, someone dynamited the house.[8]

There was no justice in the case. The person who ignited the bomb was never identified. And the Wades were forced to move into the segregated West End. It was another example of what Clay Sr. told his son: the white man doesn't want you around. He explained that in America, the black man could never get ahead. Cassius asked why. If he worked hard, why couldn't he become a rich man? Why couldn't he share in the American Dream? His father pointed to the skin on Cassius's arm: "Look there, that's why you can't be rich."[9]

The second event—and for Cassius the more emotionally searing—occurred the following summer. Emmett Till's mother had packed him off to visit family members in Money, Mississippi, and not long after his arrival in the small town, he and his cousin and several local boys went to Bryant's Grocery and Meat Market to buy some candy. While in the store, Till whistled while speaking to Carolyn Bryant. It may have been a wolf whistle, as some recalled, or perhaps due to his problem pronouncing "b"-words, he whistled before asking for bubble gum. Regardless, Bryant later told her husband that Till had made a pass at her. Enraged, Roy Bryant and his half-brother J. W. Milam went after Till. They pulled him from his uncle's home, pistol-whipped him, beat him, and finally shot him in the head. Then they attached a heavy cotton-gin fan to his neck with barbed wire and dumped him into the Tallahatchie River.

In a sensational five-day trial, held in a packed courthouse and attended by nationally prominent reporters, Bryant and Milam were tried for kidnapping and murder. After listening to all the evidence, the all-white jury deliberated for sixty-seven minutes before voting to acquit the two men. "If we hadn't stopped to drink a pop," commented a juror, "it wouldn't have taken that long."[10]

The trial, along with Till's shocking open-casket funeral in Chicago, energized the civil rights movement and stood as a stark confirmation of what black males had long been taught. Justice was not color-blind. That lesson was not lost on young Cassius Clay. Twenty years after the event, he recalled looking at the pictures of Till's mutilated face in the pages of *Jet* magazine, horrified by the sight of "his eyes bulging out of their sockets and his mouth twisted and broken." He would never forget those images or the grizzly stories his father told him about the crime.[11]

MISSISSIPPI JUSTICE WAS not confined to the South. Malcolm Little felt trapped by the same realities that pained Blyden Jackson, frustrated Clay Sr., frightened Cassius Jr., and killed Emmett Till. Writers often asked Malcolm when he first experienced racial inequality, as if he were a test subject whose anger could easily be reduced to some isolated incident. In March 1964, shortly after Clay won the heavyweight championship, a Swedish television reporter inquired about the psychological scars that Malcolm carried from his youth. When did segregation first hurt him? Irritated, he quipped, "When I was born. I was born in a segregated hospital of a segregated mother and father."[12]

Intrigued by his provocative answer, the writer pressed further. "The first was when we were living in Lansing, Michigan, in an integrated neighborhood." One evening, when Malcolm was only six years old, he "woke up and found the house on fire. The good Christians of the neighborhood had come out and set the house afire. The second was when my father was found under a streetcar where he had been thrown by the good Christians—that's my second." Grinning derisively he paused, looking directly into the television camera. "You want my third and fourth and fifth and sixth and seventh?"[13]

He never knew for sure how his father ended up under the streetcar—the coroner ruled Earl Little Sr.'s death accidental—but growing up fatherless, all but certain that white supremacists had killed his dad, Malcolm was embittered from an early age. He often told white journalists, "Your father isn't here to pay his debts. My father isn't here to collect. But I'm here to collect, and you're here to pay."[14]

Burdened by their fathers' broken dreams and shattered lives, Malcolm Little and Cassius Clay transformed the deep pain and anger that they felt into an unshakeable pride. Tormented by the past, they resisted the brutality of America, relentlessly pursuing redemption. One man was scarred by his father's absence, the other by his father's presence. They shared the kind of anguish and love that only a brother could understand.

THE MOTHER SHIP IN MIAMI

As a kid in Louisville, the city seemed so big to me. New York seemed so big. Chicago seemed big. And London, England, seemed far away. Africa was far away. I was Cassius Clay then. I was a Negro. I ate pork. I had no confidence. I thought white people were superior. I was a Christian Baptist named Cassius Clay.

—MUHAMMAD ALI

Clay is a product of our times. The minute he got back from Rome, the saga started.

—MILTON GROSS, *NEW YORK POST*

———

Three hundred and four mostly flat, cornfield miles after it departed Chicago's Union Station, the *South Wind* passenger train rolled into Louisville's Union Station. There, on December 17, 1960, a young man stepped aboard, toting a worn suitcase and a pocketful of dreams.

Cassius Marcellus Clay Jr. was eighteen, tall and slender, with a handsome unmarked face. His body was deceptively lithe, like a dancer's, but he was a professional prizefighter. His electric smile could light up an arena, though he was haunted by fears real and imagined. He had won a gold medal in the Rome Olympics, charmed the press corps and fellow athletes in the Eternal City, and signed a lucrative promotional contract with a collection of white Kentucky movers and shakers known as the Louisville Sponsoring Group (LSG). It was that group, most of whom were millionaires, that had paid for his train ticket.

After the brief stop in Louisville the *South Wind* chugged over the rolling hills of Kentucky, through a narrow, river-veined section of

There had never been a heavyweight boxer like Cassius Clay. He had the fresh, unmarked face of a teenage matinee idol and a smile to match. In a division often dominated by ponderous sluggers, his jitterbug style ushered in a new age for the sport. Getty Images

Tennessee, and then across the border into Alabama. Looking out the window as evening turned into night, Cassius saw mile after mile of the cotton South as the train made its way through the heart of the old Confederacy, stopping to pick up more passengers in Decatur, Birmingham, Montgomery, and Dothan.

It was those sections of Dixie, those cities ruled by King Cotton, where the civil rights struggle would soon turn bitterly violent. There, many white southerners stood armed and ready to defend their way of life, certain in their conviction of black inferiority. While in Italy, however, Cassius had felt a freedom that he had never experienced growing up in the segregated West End of Louisville. As a member of the United States Olympic team, he had witnessed black excellence. Rafer Johnson had carried the American flag in the opening ceremonies and then won the prestigious decathlon. Oscar Robertson had led the basketball team to the gold medal. And the incomparable Wilma Rudolph, who ran as gracefully as water being poured out of a pitcher, fired the imaginations

of people around the globe. Together, Rafer, Oscar, Wilma, and Cassius reigned in Rome like ebony gods. If there was royalty at the Olympics, they were it.

After Alabama, the *South Wind* passed through the southwest corner of Georgia and entered Florida, stopping briefly in Jacksonville in the early morning before continuing its crisscrossing route through the state, stopping more often now to drop off tourists at such resort towns as Orlando, Tampa, St. Petersburg, West Palm Beach, Delray Beach, Fort Lauderdale, and Hollywood before reaching its destination of Miami.

There, roughly twenty-four hours after boarding the train, Cassius got off. It had been a long trip, but to his way of thinking, riding the train was infinitely preferable to flying. And it had given him some time to plan and dream. He was in the Deep South, a place where white residents still generally regarded Jim Crow as the accepted code of life and believed that a "Negro" should know his place. Even so, Cassius Clay had glimpsed an alternative reality, and he knew with every fiber of his being that he was destined to leave his mark on the world. "I am a Man of Destiny," he had said less than a year before. "I'm gonna win the heavyweight championship of the world, earn a million dollars and get me a chauffeur-driven, tomato-red Cadillac with a built-in hi-fi, television and telephones." And that was only for starters. There would be more. Later he admitted, "I guess some sort of divine power must have been with me."[1]

He had come to Miami to learn a trade that would make him rich. What he did not anticipate was that a divine message would set him on the path to becoming Muhammad Ali.

WAITING PATIENTLY FOR the boxer was trainer Angelo Dundee. His name, an alias that mixed the hills of Calabria with the grime of Scotland, said more about his profession than his personality. His real name was Angelo Mirena, but Dundee was such a popular name in prizefighting that his older brother Chris adopted it when he entered the profession. Soon, Angelo followed Chris and took the same name. After World War II, Chris began to promote fights in New York City, and Angelo apprenticed as a trainer.[2]

In 1951, when the boxing business became sluggish in New York, Angelo followed Chris to Miami, where the older brother had established a promotional arrangement with the recently built Miami Beach

Auditorium. By the mid-1950s, Angelo had been around boxing for a decade and had learned the craft of training boxers from the tobacco-crusted floor up. His was a hands-on education, learning by talking to and watching the very best trainers in the sport.

By the end of 1960, just short of his fortieth birthday, he had carved out a place for himself in the fight game. He had trained welterweight and middleweight champion Carmen Basilio as well as a stable of fighters who would soon win other titles. Short and round-faced, with bulging dark eyes, floppy ears, and thinning black hair, Dundee liked his pants high-waisted, his trainer's bag well-ordered, and his life as peaceful as his chaotic profession allowed.

Like that of many men in his world, his personality did not seem to fit the boxing profession. Fiercely loyal to his fighters and capable of all sorts of chicanery in the pursuit of victory, he was in all other ways a gentle, gracious man who sought nothing more than tranquility. He readily chatted with strangers, he was open and friendly with sportswriters, and he did his best to please everyone. The model of discretion, he refused to get involved in marital scraps, religious controversies, or political differences. Over the years he had learned to smile, listen, and mind his own business.

Keeping his mouth shut around Cassius, Angelo learned, was easy. No sooner had Clay stepped off the *South Wind* than he began singing his own praises. "People say Cassius Clay fights like Sugar Ray," he told Angelo, as well as anyone within an earshot. Dick Sadler, Archie Moore's trainer, who had worked with Cassius for a short time in San Diego, had told Angelo if he trained the kid he deserved a Purple Heart with seven clusters. It did not take Dundee long to understand the cryptic warning.[3]

From the train station Angelo drove to "Colored Town," where he had arranged for Clay to share a room at the Charles Hotel with a Jamaican heavyweight. Dundee thought that there were two beds in the room, but there was only a double bed for two heavyweight boxers. Furthermore, since Angelo received a discount on the room, the management recouped some of its loss by not installing an air conditioner.[4]

The spartan, low-rent condition of the room was matched by the neighborhood. Ferdie Pacheco, who would soon become Clay's "fight doctor" and had a medical practice close to the Charles Hotel, called the

area "a hellhole of pimps, hookers, drug dealers, winos, and general bad guys." It was a no-man's-land that slept till late in the morning, took a siesta in the afternoon, and then came alive with an adrenaline rush at night. Its after-midnight scene offered a thousand temptations—marijuana from the islands that could knock a smoker on his ass, heroin so pure that it was lights-out with one shot, long-legged "sisters" wearing short, glove-tight dresses, and any sort of alcohol, sex, or adventure that could be dreamt up. This was a place that would test the dedication of any innocent, handsome young man.[5]

Cassius struggled to get to sleep that first night. He later complained that the worst times of training in Miami were the lonely hours after dark. "I just sit here like a little animal in a box at night," he told a sportswriter in 1961. "I can't go out in the street and mix with the folks out there 'cause they wouldn't be out there if they was up to any good. I can't do nothing except sit. . . . Here I am, just 19, surrounded by show-girls, whisky and sissies, and nobody watching me. All this temptation and me trying to train to be a boxer. It's something to think about."[6]

The next morning Clay made his way to the 5th Street Gym, where Dundee trained his fighters. In the glory days of prizefighting, four training gymnasiums stood above all the others—Gleason's and Stillman's in New York, the Main Street Gym in Los Angeles, and the 5th Street Gym in Miami. Located in South Beach at the corner of 5th Street and Washington Avenue, it was in a neighborhood where nothing good was happening. Increasingly, the money and development were flowing into North Beach, leaving whole sections of South Beach for the derelicts and the druggies. The dilapidated second-story facility featured rotten floors, cracked mirrors, accumulated grime, and the stench of sweat, jock straps, and cigarette and cigar smoke.[7]

In addition to its foul smell and crusted dirt, the gym suffered from other maladies. Clogged drains in the showers, holes in the plasterboard walls, and chipping paint lent a certain grungy charm to the place, but an infestation of hungry termites threatened the entire structure. They attacked floors, walls, rings, and even chairs and desks. Possibly they were angered, or encouraged, by the heat. Hot and sweltering under its tin roof, fighters training in the gym soon realized that the place had no air conditioning, and large floor-to-ceiling windows added to everyone's discomfort. Many of the best fighters who trained there were from

Cuba and accustomed to such temperatures, but boxers from the North considered the conditions inside the gym inhumane, if not entirely illegal. But to Angelo Dundee, the place was "my little slice of heaven."[8]

For the fighters, the gym offered not so much a "slice of heaven" as the chance for salvation. With the windows open, the hot and stale air from the inside mixed with the humid blasts from the outside and the noise of the streets harmonized with the sounds of the gym—men skipping ropes; punching speed bags, heavy bags, and each other; and yelling encouragements and good-natured barbs in English and Spanish. In the 5th Street Gym, white, brown, and black men met in complete equality, fleeing from poverty and even persecution in the pursuit of a dream.

SOME OF THE finest boxers of the early 1960s trained alongside Clay under Angelo's guidance. In 1961, the revolutionary government of Fidel Castro outlawed professional boxing in Cuba, sending dozens of skillful Cuban boxers into exile in the United States, and especially Miami, where they added to Dundee's pool of talent. Willie Pastrano won the light-heavyweight championship in 1963, the same year that Ralph Dupas captured the junior middleweight title, Ultiminio "Sugar" Ramos the featherweight crown, and Luis Rodríguez the welterweight belt. Every week, it seemed, Angelo and one of his contenders headed to some world capital for an important match. It was a heady time, with talk of big-money title fights and the smell of success cutting through the malodorous, low-rent atmosphere of the 5th Street Gym.

But at the center of the action was young Cassius, just beginning his professional career and fighting in small-money preliminary matches, but with an ego and energy that filled the gym. Observing the action inside the facility, sportswriter Myron Cope wrote, "Cassius reigns over the gym's white, Negro, and Cuban fighters like the leader of a street gang who has established his authority merely by talking his subjects into submission. He jabbers away at the Cubans in homemade, simulated Spanish, and they throw up their hands and walk away, shouting, *'Niño con boca grande!'*—the baby has a big mouth." There was no resentment in the comment, just a statement of fact.[9]

In Cassius's case, trainer and fighter were ideally matched. Dundee saw immediately that by the standards of classic boxing Clay was a deeply flawed fighter. He kept his hands too low, often avoided

punches by moving straight back, and was a dyed-in-the-wool head-hunter. He did not even faintly resemble Joe Louis or Sonny Liston, hard-punching heavyweights with wonderful balance, great left jabs, and knockout power in both hands.

But for all his deficiencies, Cassius had assets. Most obviously, he had extraordinary hand and foot speed. When he arrived in Miami, he was a small heavyweight, weighing only 182 pounds, but his quickness was more than just the result of size. Probably no heavyweight had ever been as fast as Clay, certainly none in the early 1960s, when most, with the exception of Floyd Patterson, tended to be orthodox plodders.

Less readily apparent, Clay's sense of distance was nearly perfect. This ability is crucial in boxing. Throw a punch from too far away, and it falls short of its target. Throw it too close, and it loses its full leverage. In addition, a fighter who moves too close to an opponent is easier to tie up. Clay's speed allowed him to dart in and out; his sense of distance permitted him to throw a punch at the ideal moment, when it could reach its target with maximum force. Almost no fighter could snap out a jab as quickly or accurately as Clay, and none could deliver a faster right-hand lead. Furthermore, his quickness and sense of distance allowed him to dodge his opponent's punches, sometimes by mere inches.

Many trainers would have winced at Clay's glaring flaws and attempted to teach him proper technique. Dundee, however, focused on Cassius's magnificent assets. To be sure, he tried to refine Clay's unorthodox style, smoothing his herky-jerky movements. He worked on his balance, convincing him to throw more flat-footed power punches, and advised him to get his weight behind his blows. But crucially, Angelo did not seek to fundamentally change Cassius's style. He believed that every fighter was unique and should be treated that way. "There's not two alike," he noted. "You don't say, 'This guy fights like this guy.' They don't. They're all individuals. They all got their own idiosyncrasies, got their own rhythm."[10]

Much as Cassius may have imagined himself as another Sugar Ray Robinson, Dundee's primary job was to train Cassius Clay to box like Cassius Clay. After listening to Clay talk and watching him spar, Dundee told his fighter, "You, my friend, are neither Sugar Ray Robinson nor Archie Moore, and you've got a long way to go before you will even resemble them. Who you are is Cassius Marcellus Clay Jr., and that's the man

I'm going to teach you to fight like. A guy is never going to get anywhere thinking he's somebody else."[11]

Angelo quickly realized that, for all his bluster, Cassius was a dedicated athlete. He came to the gym on time, trained tirelessly, and learned quickly, as long as the lessons were packaged correctly. Dundee seldom told Clay what to do; rather, he made Cassius feel like he was the source of every improvement. "I didn't train him," Dundee recalled. "I advised him. He'd be in the gym and I'd say, 'You're really putting your left hand into that jab. You're really snapping it.' Then, when I'd see him doing something right again, I'd say, 'Oh my God, I've never seen a heavyweight throw a left uppercut so perfectly. Oh boy!' Then he'd throw it again. And again."[12]

Confronted with Clay's ego, Dundee discarded his own, becoming the ideal second banana. If Cassius said, "I'm going to run five miles," Angelo responded, "That's good for your legs." If Clay changed his mind and said, "No, I'm gonna rest," Dundee instantly added, "Good, you need your rest." This way the fighter was in charge even when he was not really in charge.[13]

On the one critical aspect of the pace of Clay's career, Dundee had the final word. Clay repeatedly told reporters that he wanted to break Floyd Patterson's record as the youngest heavyweight champion of all time (twenty-one years and ten months), which meant that he had to capture the title by December 12, 1963. But that was Cassius's obsession, not Angelo's, who was more concerned with advancing his fighter cautiously. He had seen too many fighters pressured into a mismatch. For the first few years at least, Dundee would only take sure-bet contests for Clay, matches that he could win on his worst day. In the language of the fight game, Angelo arranged for Cassius to box "opponents," men who had virtually no hope of reaching contender status, or one-time contenders on a steep slide down the rankings.

Beginning in the last week of 1960, Cassius began to fight a string of set-ups. The fights were not fixed, but it would have taken a virtual act of God for him to lose. Herb Siler was a drunk who had no boxing talent; Clay took him out in the fourth. Anthony "Big Tony" Esperti had just gotten out of the can on an unlawful entry conviction and was in no condition to fight; Cassius ended the match in the third. "Sweet Jimmy" Robinson had a razor cut on his cheek and no business in a

prize ring; the referee stopped the fight halfway through the first. In just over a month in Miami, Cassius had improved his record to 4–0.[14]

Still, matches against set-ups were little help when it came to persuading boxing fans to accept Clay's claim that he was a great fighter. For now, what happened in a sparring match was more important. In February 1961, a handsome Swedish heavyweight and former world champion, Ingemar Johansson, came to Miami to train for his upcoming title fight with Floyd Patterson. Needing sparring partners, the Johansson camp told promotional coordinator Harold Conrad to hire a few. Conrad went to the 5th Street Gym and asked Dundee for recommendations. Calling Clay over, Dundee said, "Hey, Cash. You wanna work with Johansson?"[15]

The question was a switch, lighting up Clay. "I'll go dancin' with Johansson," he said, repeating, "I'll go dancin' with Johansson." Conrad just looked at Angelo. "You ain't seen nothing yet with this crazy bastard," Conrad recalled Dundee saying.

And he hadn't. "Johansson had a great right hand but two left feet," Conrad said. Once the former champion and the preliminary fighter were in the ring together in front of sportswriters and two thousand spectators, Cassius literally danced circles around Ingemar, hitting him with light jabs as if he were fighting a rematch with Big Tony. "Cassius Clay, 19, advanced on Ingemar Johansson," wrote the *Miami Herald*'s John Underwood. "Whap! His jab bounced off the Swede's headpiece. Whap-Whap! Two more jabs. Clay danced lightly, shifted feet, led with the right. Zing! Ffrap! Whap! The combination explored the celebrated Johansson profile, above and around the dimpled chin." And so it continued, Johansson, a miffed lumbering bear, chasing "the bee who had stung him."

Talking while he moved, Clay exhorted, "I'm the one who should be fighting Patterson, not you. Come on, here I am; come and get me, sucker. Come on, what's the matter, can't hit me?" It was like Jack Johnson fighting Tommy Burns, like Clay was the champion and Johansson the trail horse.

"Johansson was furious," Conrad recalled. "I mean, he was pissed." He chased Clay around the ring, throwing amateurish punches, missing by feet, and looking, at last, "ridiculous." After two rounds he was exhausted, and the session was stopped.

"He made a monkey out of Johansson," remembered *Sports Illustrated* writer Gil Rogin. When he returned to New York he told the editors at the magazine, "This guy is going to be heavyweight champion someday. You have to write about him." For Rogin, Underwood, and other sportswriters, this was Clay's true Olympian moment; they recognized the emergence of a star.

The Johansson session showed Dundee that it was time to match him against more experienced boxers. Clay stopped Donnie Fleeman, a good club fighter, in the seventh round. Then he fought LaMar Clark, who possessed a gaudy 46–2 record that included a streak of forty-four straight knockouts. Against Clay, however, the heavy-punching Clark was outmatched. Cassius took him out in the second round.

Marv Jenson, Clark's manager, was impressed. "This guy isn't very many fights away from a championship as far as I'm concerned," Jenson said. "He has the fastest hands of any heavyweight I've seen any place, including Patterson." Black sportswriters were even more generous. Evoking the near-sacred "L" word, a *Pittsburgh Courier* scribe compared Clay favorably with the legendary Joe Louis. And for the first time in his professional career, *New York Times* feature writer Arthur Daley devoted a "Sports of the *Times*" column to Clay. Describing him as "a compulsive talker with the engaging personality of a youthful Archie Moore," Daley wrote, "This good-looking boy is a charmer and is so natural that even his more extravagant statements sound like exuberance instead of braggadocio. On him they look good."[16]

WITH COMPARISONS TO Louis and notice in the *New York Times*, Clay's career was bounding forward ahead of schedule. After a month's vacation in Louisville and road trips to visit Wilma Rudolph and other friends from the Olympics, in the late spring of 1961 he once again boarded the *South Wind* for Miami, where Dundee waited to resume his education. And that was fine with the fighter who viewed any gym as safe territory—an oasis away from the nation's racial problems and the traps and temptations that waited around every corner of the urban South.

"It's either get rich in three hours or get poor in eight," he liked to say: train hard for three hours (or four or five) or get a manual day job for pennies an hour. He had chosen the path to wealth and applied himself totally, and the Louisville Sponsoring Group made sure that,

unlike most other fighters, Cassius did not have to get a job to make ends meet. Train and dream, dream and train, from busy days at the 5th Street Gym to lonely nights at the Charles Hotel—these formed the physical and emotional parameters of his life in Miami. Boxing, however, could not satisfy his spiritual life.[17]

THERE WAS NO avoiding the world outside his hotel and the boxing arena. After all, Cassius was in the South, the land of Emmett Till's murder and his father's gruesome tales.

Since he did not own a car, he jogged more than five miles from his hotel to the gym at the south end of Miami Beach. He ran in blue jeans and old military boots. As he crossed the Julia Tuttle Causeway, with the Miami skyline in the distance and a cool breeze blowing across the bay, Clay shadowboxed.

It was a strange sight to the white policeman who thought that a black man running across the highway, furiously punching the air, must be crazy or a thief—or both. In Miami, police frequently harassed blacks on the streets and raided black pool halls and bars. The officer stopped Clay to question him. Sweating and excited, Clay explained that he was running to Angelo Dundee's gym. The police then called Dundee to verify his story. The trainer explained that "the kid" was his boxer. "That's Cassius Clay," he said.[18]

The episode offered an important lesson for Clay. White policemen didn't know his name and didn't care to know it. To them, he was just another "Negro" living across the tracks in the "colored" district of Overtown.

After Clay returned to Miami from his visit home, Dundee upgraded him from the low-rent living quarters at the Charles Hotel to the Sir John Hotel on Little Broadway, a vibrant strip of nightclubs, theaters, diners, and shops. Some of the most famous black entertainers and athletes in America stayed at the Sir John Hotel and the Mary Elizabeth Hotel, including Ella Fitzgerald, Duke Ellington, Louis Armstrong, Nat King Cole, Sammy Davis Jr., and Sugar Ray Robinson. These celebrities did not choose to stay at the Sir John or the Mary Elizabeth because these establishments offered the finest accommodations. They had little choice. Blacks could not enter the best downtown hotels unless they waited tables, prepared meals, scoured toilets, or hauled white peoples'

bags. Not even Joe Louis could check into the Fontainebleau Hotel on Miami Beach.[19]

Since the early twentieth century, real estate developers had promoted Miami as "the Magic City." Beautiful beaches, luxurious resorts, and exotic entertainment attracted wealthy investors, tourists, and dreamers. But the city's black citizens were barred from the beaches, restaurants, golf courses, schools, and theaters of Miami's tropical paradise. In 1959, civil rights activists defied white supremacists, sponsoring dozens of sit-ins at department stores, drugstores, and diners. By August 1960, just before Clay arrived, their persistence and shrewd backroom negotiations with white leaders had led to the complete desegregation of the city's downtown.[20]

Yet Clay quickly learned that the city's culture of racism remained intact. In August 1961, Flip Schulke, a white photographer from *Sports Illustrated*, visited Miami for a photo shoot with Clay. Schulke was a serious photojournalist who had traveled the world and taken memorable photos that appeared in leading American publications, but he had never photographed a boxer. Shopping at Burdines department store, Clay picked up a short-sleeved shirt while Schulke snapped pictures. When a white store clerk saw the tall, lean black man touching the shirts, he informed him that store policy prohibited blacks from trying on clothing. Schulke fumed. It shocked him that Cassius Clay—an Olympic champion—could not try on a shirt in an American store. But Clay was not surprised. He wasn't even angry. This was the South. As a southerner he outwardly accepted second-class citizenship as a way of life. "Come on, Flip, don't worry about it," he said. "I don't want to make a big mess here. It's not a big deal."[21]

Clay may have been a boxer, but he was not a fighter. He disliked confrontations and avoided violence outside the ring. He preferred Overtown, where he felt safer among his own people. Throughout the neighborhood blacks greeted him warmly and made him feel important. And soon enough, one man in particular standing at the corner of Northwest Second Avenue and 6th Street, in front of Muhammad's Temple of Islam, caught Cassius's attention.

Sam Saxon, a burly, thirty-year-old, light-skinned black man with the arms of a blacksmith, waved a copy of *Muhammad Speaks*, the Nation of Islam's newspaper. The two men started talking about the

teachings of Elijah Muhammad. As he listened to Clay speak, it was clear to Saxon that he had already heard of the Nation's leader, though he had never seen or met Elijah before. "Hey, you're into the teaching," Saxon said. "Well, I ain't been to the temple, but I know what you're talking about," Clay replied. Then the boxer introduced himself as he always did: "I'm Cassius Clay. I'm gonna be the next heavyweight champion of the world." Saxon, a boxing fan, recognized the name. "I know you, man," he said, "I followed you in the Olympics."[22]

The fact that Saxon knew his name engendered a level of trust from Clay. A former gambler and poolroom hustler turned missionary, Saxon had become a devout Muslim. When he was not selling copies of *Muhammad Speaks* or teaching in the temple, he ran concessions at the Miami racetracks and worked as a bathroom attendant, handing towels to white men and shining their shoes. But his primary objective in life, his real love, was fishing for converts.[23]

Wherever there were large concentrations of "so-called Negroes," as the Black Muslims called them, those "lost souls" in the Kingdom of Allah, Elijah Muhammad's ministers cast their lines. On Sundays, young Muslim men, clean-shaven and hair close-cropped, dressed in dark suits, waited outside churches, inviting Christians to hear the truth about God at the local temple. On weeknights, Muhammad's foot soldiers, armed with Muslim literature, canvassed the streets of the ghetto, "fishing for the dead," those "deaf, dumb, and blind—brainwashed of all self-respect and knowledge of kind by the white Slavemaster." In nearly every large American city, Muslim officers trolled in bars, liquor stores, pool halls, barbershops, and diners. Standing on soapboxes and stepladders, Muhammad's articulate followers preached, captivating the curious.[24]

In their meetings at Temple No. 29, a vacant storefront converted into a makeshift mosque, Saxon noticed that Clay was curious about the Muslim faith. In Miami, most blacks viewed the Muslims with skepticism, rarely entering the temple. When Clay first started attending meetings there were only about thirty members. In his first visit, he heard a preacher named Brother John deliver a sermon on the history of the black man. Cassius learned that white slave owners stripped the black man of his identity, his heritage, his language, and his true name and replaced it with a slave name, a name that belonged to the white

man. According to the Muslims, the word *Negro* derived not from the Latin *niger*, meaning "black," but rather from the Greek *nekros*, meaning "corpse." Thus, the man who called himself a "Negro" remained spiritually dead, buried in the grave.[25]

Brother John's sermon helped Cassius make sense of his family's history and his own identity as a black man. He later recalled, "I could reach out and touch what Brother John was saying. It wasn't like church teaching, where I had to have faith that what the preacher was preaching was right. And I said to myself, 'Cassius Marcellus Clay. He was a Kentucky white man who owned my great-granddaddy and named my great-granddaddy after him. And then my granddaddy got named, and then my daddy, and now it's me.'"[26]

For the first time in his life, Clay's name didn't sound so magical. At that moment, when Cassius began questioning the origins of his name, Sam Saxon knew that he had hooked a big fish.

DEPENDING ON THE day of the week and the whim of the moment, Cassius claimed to have first learned about the Nation of Islam in Atlanta, Chicago, or New York in 1958, 1959, or 1960. Over the years, whenever reporters asked him about his conversion to Islam, his answers were inconsistent. In his stories, Clay created an origin myth based on his scattered memories and affection for tall tales. There were hardly any witnesses who could testify about his accounts, creating a sense of mystery about his activities with the Nation. In all of his anecdotes about meeting the Muslims, one thing remained constant: whenever he left Louisville and found freedom from supervision, he gravitated toward the temples. No one understood this better than Clay's own mother. "The big mistake was when [the Louisville Sponsoring Group] sent him to train at Miami all by himself," she said. "That's when the Muslims got him. That's how Sam Saxon got him and talked that Muslim stuff to him every day."[27]

Odessa was unaware that her son had started listening to the Muslims long before he ever met Sam Saxon. As a teenager, when Cassius traveled for amateur boxing tournaments, he came across Muslim preachers proselytizing for the teachings of Elijah Muhammad. In October 1958, Clay and his brother Rudy traveled to Atlanta for a vacation. At the time, the FBI had assigned Special Agent Robert R. Nichols

to investigate the activities at Muhammad's Temple No. 15 in Atlanta. Nichols set up wiretaps on the temple's phones and hired college students to record the minister's speeches.[28]

Nichols learned that Clay had talked with the Muslims outside the Atlanta temple on Piedmont Avenue. At the time, the information seemed unimportant. After all, Cassius was just a sixteen-year-old kid from Louisville. Yet that day in Atlanta marked the beginning of his indoctrination. That was the moment, he said, "I was fished off a street corner."[29]

When he traveled to Chicago for the Golden Gloves tournament in March 1959, he once again ran into the Muslims outside their temple. Near the Nation's headquarters, the Muslims gave Clay a record that they said would explain everything he needed to know. When he returned to Louisville, he played the record repeatedly. Performing "A White Man's Heaven Is a Black Man's Hell," Louis Eugene Wolcott, a charming and talented calypso singer, crooned over piano and guitar. Wolcott, who was then known as Louis X and would later become recognized as Louis Farrakhan, became so popular singing the song at the Nation's rallies that it became the anthem of the Muslim movement.[30]

Clay played the record over and over, memorizing the lyrics and absorbing the message. In Miami, Sam Saxon and the other members of the mosque echoed the song's central theme, reminding him that there was no heaven or hell after death. While the black man lived in hell, they said, white Christians enjoyed heaven on earth. For a young man who dreamed of riches, Cadillacs, and mansions, the lyrics made him question his Baptist upbringing. As early as 1961, he began talking about what he had learned from the Muslims, though he was careful to ensure that not even the sharpest reporter could recognize that he was sharing what the Muslims had taught him.

When Clay started telling *Sports Illustrated*'s Huston Horn what he thought about heaven and hell, the writer had no idea that the boxer's interpretation of the afterlife came directly from the Black Muslims. "Like last Sunday," he said, "some cats I know said, 'Cassius, Cassius, come on now and let's go to church; otherwise you won't get to Heaven.' 'Hold on a minute,' I said to them, 'and let me tell you something else. When I've got me a $100,000 house, another quarter million stuck in the bank and the world title latched onto my name, then I'll be in

heaven. Walking around making $25 a week, with four children crying at home 'cause they're hungry, *that's* my idea of Hell."[31]

Clay already knew from experience that merely talking about the Muslims could jeopardize his future. During his senior year of high school, he had written a paper about the Nation for his English class. At night, he and his brother Rudy sometimes listened to Elijah Muhammad's national radio address. On the streets of Louisville, Cassius noticed black men dressed in dark suits, similar to the men he had seen in Atlanta and Chicago, selling copies of *Muhammad Speaks*. Yet when he wrote his paper, his teacher was so alarmed that she threatened to fail him, though the principal ultimately overruled her.[32]

Clay continued his education about the Nation in Miami. His most important teacher was Ishmael Sabakhan, minister of the local temple. Nearly once a week, he visited with his spiritual mentor. At their meetings, he listened more than he talked. Sabakhan taught him the basic tenets of the Nation, an esoteric religious movement fabricated from Black Nationalism, Christianity, Islam, and cosmology. He explained that God was a black man—a real man on earth—and that the devil was a white man, who also inhabited the earth. Blacks and whites must separate because there could be no peace between God and the devil.[33]

The Muslims' views about God and the devil, heaven and hell, helped Cassius understand the cruel world his father had described. Clay Sr. had told him how whites had segregated, abused, and tortured his people, and the history lessons Cassius learned from the Muslims offered further proof of the white man's wicked ways. The devil, they said, had kidnapped, shackled, and enslaved his ancestors. When the slaves arrived from Africa, whites forced them to abandon their native culture. Being black, the whites preached, was a curse; they convinced the slaves to hate everything that was black, including themselves. The devil imposed Christianity onto their slaves, manipulating them into worshiping the white man and the white man's God—a "God having the same blond hair, pale skin, and blue eyes as the slavemaster."[34]

It all made sense to Cassius. Growing up he never understood why everything associated with blackness was considered bad. "When I was a little kid, I always knew something was wrong," he said. "Everything good was supposed to be white. And I'd ask my mom, why is Santa Claus white? Why is Jesus white?" He continued, "Miss America was

white. The good cowboy always rode on a white horse. Angel food cake is white and devil's food cake is black . . . even the President lived in a *white* house."[35]

Listening to Muhammad's radio addresses, Cassius heard something that he had never heard before, a message that he would begin repeating over the course of his career: blacks were the strongest, most intelligent people in the world. The black man, Muhammad proclaimed, was *the greatest*. "The Black people in America have for many years been made to feel that they were something of a Divine Curse," he preached. "You must not think that about yourself anymore. We the Black Nation of the Earth are the NUMBER ONE owners of it, the best of all human beings. You are the Most Powerful, the Most Beautiful, and the Wisest."[36]

THE SON OF A poor sharecropper turned Baptist preacher, Elijah Poole was born in 1897 in south-central Georgia. Raised on his father's fiery sermons, he became enraptured with scripture, though he struggled to read the Bible after dropping out of school around the fourth grade. Laboring on farms, at a sawmill, and as a bricklayer, he matured into a frustrated young man, disillusioned by meager wages, harsh employers, and the humiliation of Jim Crow. Seeking relief from discrimination and poverty, in 1923 Elijah followed the Great Migration north, settling in Detroit with his wife, Clara, and dreaming of a better life.[37]

Failing to find work in Detroit's auto factories, he found himself living on the dole, drinking away his misery. A tiny, light-skinned man with a pinched face and sad, almond-shaped eyes, Elijah found salvation in 1931 when he heard Wallace D. Fard (pronounced FA-rod) deliver a lecture at an old lodging hall. A year earlier, Fard, an ex-convict turned door-to-door silk salesmen, had founded the Nation of Islam. He claimed that he was a Muslim from the Holy City of Mecca, Saudi Arabia, and began using a variety of names: Wali Farrad, Professor Ford, Farrad Muhammad, and Wallace Fard Muhammad. He lectured on the history of the black man, biblical prophecy, and an unorthodox doctrine of Islam. Preaching out of basements and rented halls, he emphasized self-help and racial pride. Gradually, with Poole becoming his most devoted apostle, he built a sect with a few thousand members. Fard rewarded Poole by appointing him "supreme minister" and bestowing upon him a new name: "Elijah Muhammad." But in 1933, Fard vanished amid accusations that he had

ordered a human sacrifice. Shortly afterward, Muhammad proclaimed Fard's deification as Allah incarnate.[38]

After Fard's disappearance, Muhammad anointed himself the Messenger of Allah and continued to build the Nation, despite dissension and death threats against him from some members. Muhammad preached about the "Original Man," Allah, a black man who created the universe. The Muslims believed that the "so-called Negro" was a descendant of the Original Man, who belonged to the Tribe of Shabazz, an ancient group that founded the Holy City of Mecca and eventually migrated to Africa.[39]

According to Muhammad, the origins of the white man could be traced back to Yacub, an evil "big head scientist." Nearly 6,600 years ago, Yacub began preaching a dangerous version of Islam in the streets of Mecca. When authorities learned about his distortion of true Islam, he and his 59,999 followers were exiled to the island of Patmos in the Aegean Sea. There, Yacub sought revenge by creating a "devil race" that would dominate the Black Nation through tricks, lies, and deception. Mutating the germs of the black man, Yacub produced "pale-faced, blue-eyed" men who were weaker morally and physically. He planned for these devils to rule the earth for more than six thousand years, testing the strength of the Black Nation.[40]

Muhammad prophesied that the white man's rule would end in 1970 after the "Battle of Armageddon." Destruction of the white man, he foretold, would be carried out by the Mother Ship, a wheel-shaped spacecraft a half-mile wide. Piloted by the most intelligent black men, the Mother Ship would carry fifteen hundred bombers. The plane could not be attacked, of course, because it could disappear behind the stars. In the days leading up to the resurrection, the Mother Ship would litter the earth with pamphlets printed in English and Arabic, telling Allah's followers where to hide when the planes attacked. When the battle was over, the white man would be eliminated from the planet and the black man would rise up from the smoldering ashes. In the 1960s, purported sightings of unidentified flying objects startled many Americans, but for followers of Muhammad, the presence of flying saucers portended that the Day of Judgment was near.[41]

Cassius Clay began reciting Muhammad's lessons, leaving his friends at a loss as to what he was talking about. Ferdie Pacheco recalled driving

around in his vintage Cadillac convertible on a muggy Miami night with Clay and two women. Suddenly, Clay tapped the doctor on the shoulder and told him to pull over to the side of the road. He stood up and pointed toward the stars.[42]

"See that?" Cassius asked, his arm extended toward the sky. "It's the spaceship."

"What spaceship is that?" one of the women asked.

Clay stared at her, dumbfounded that she did not know about *the spaceship*. Then he launched into a lecture on Nation theology.

"One day, 'bout six thousand years ago, a bad, mad scientist named Dr. Yacub created the white race off the black. . . . The mad doctor made the whites superior, and pushed the blacks down into slavery. That period is coming to an end now."

"What's that got to do with the spaceship?" the young woman asked.

"Well, a spaceship took off with twenty-six yellow families living on it, circling the globe. They called it the Mother Ship. The non-white races are being oppressed by the whites, and soon they will come down and wipe out the white race."

"What they been waiting for, chile?" asked the older woman.

Clay, ignoring the question, rambled on in a serious tone. "Once a year they come down from the North Pole, put down a big plastic hose, and scoop up enough oxygen and ice to last them a year," he said.

Then, he just pointed toward the sky, looking in awe: "The Mother Ship."

For Cassius, the Muslims' tales about a big-headed scientist, mythical spaceships, and the coming of Armageddon were more than the stuff of fantasy. Muhammad's prophecy offered Clay a means of survival in a hostile country. Cassius's own belief in prophecy developed as a youth living in segregated Louisville. A schoolteacher explained,

> If you can't stand the world you live in and you can't change it, you've got to believe in magic, in predictions. That's Cassius when he was growing up, living with that wild father and all that crazy talk around the house. You've got to believe that things are gonna change. So predictions have a great charm and appeal. 'Next year the white man's gonna lose his power,' . . . '1966'll be a bad year for the white man.' That's great news to some people dumb enough to believe it. Believing

in predictions is a way of warding off evil in the present when you can't ward it off any other way. You can bear living miserable if you accept a prediction that tomorrow will be better. That's why you get so much predicting and prophecy in the Negro churches. That's why you get so much predicting and prophecy from Cassius Clay, too.[43]

For Clay, the Black Muslims offered security, a sanctuary from the violent world that surrounded him, and he steadily gravitated toward the Miami temple as a result. His frequent visits excited Sabakhan and Saxon, who alerted Jeremiah X, minister of the Atlanta mosque and the chief organizer of the Nation in the Deep South. Jeremiah visited Cassius in Miami, teaching him about the Muslims' moral code. He explained that they prayed five times a day, at sunrise, noon, midafternoon, sundown, and before bed, and that all Muslims prayed facing east, toward Mecca. But before Clay prayed, he had to make the proper ablutions: rinsing his mouth and washing his hands, feet, and arms. Cleanliness, inside and out, Jeremiah reminded him, was absolutely essential. Furthermore, Muslims were required to attend at least two temple meetings each week, though because of Clay's schedule—and his celebrity—the minister made an exception.[44]

Clay learned that Elijah Muhammad instructed his followers to live a "righteous life," prohibiting extramarital sex, gambling, dancing, attending movies, taking long vacations, lying, stealing, defying civil authority, and disobeying ministers. Muslims, he commanded, should refrain from consuming alcohol, tobacco, and drugs, and from overeating. An overweight Muslim could be fined until he lost the excess weight. And pork was strictly forbidden. The hog was a "parasite," "dirty, brutal, quarrelsome, greedy, ugly, foul, a scavenger which thrives on filth," just like the white man.[45]

In the process of educating Clay about the laws of the Nation of Islam, Jeremiah cultivated a personal relationship with him and later his brother Rudy, who was even more eager to join the Nation. The more Cassius learned, the more he questioned. Jeremiah recognized that Clay's presence in the movement could create potential conflicts for the boxer and the Nation alike. The minister understood that if the public learned about Clay's association with the Nation, the boxer might be vilified. It could ruin his career. So Jeremiah sought the counsel of John

Ali, the Nation's national secretary and adviser to Elijah Muhammad. When Jeremiah called Ali on the telephone and informed him that a fighter had attended their meetings, Ali "roundly condemned" the minister "for being involved with a boxer." Elijah Muhammad himself later told Jeremiah that he'd "been sent to the South to make converts, not to fool around with fighters."[46]

Muhammad disapproved of sports, especially boxing, which he maintained was just another avenue for the exploitation of black youths by white, mostly Jewish men. He associated boxing with the evils of gambling, drunkenness, and crime. In his *Muhammad Speaks* column, he argued that sports encouraged blacks to throw away their money on the white man's "games of chance." The only reason the white man allowed blacks to participate in their sports, he claimed, was to distract them from their real problems. Sports were just another tool to keep the black man down.[47]

Yet perhaps Clay's pursuit of a righteous life was not as incompatible with boxing as Muhammad believed. In many ways the ritual and regimen of the Nation's strict code of behavior mirrored the boxer's spartan training. The Muslim ministers dictated when Clay prayed, what he ate, and how he spent his leisure time. Similarly, Angelo Dundee created his training routine: he told him when to rise in the morning, when to run, when to eat, when to spar, and when to go to bed. Clay's spiritual mentors and boxing instructors required hard work, sobriety, and proper nutrition. Both worlds—boxing and the Nation of Islam—demanded physical fitness and a purity that rewarded resistance to temptation.[48]

In Miami, Clay chose to occupy both worlds. There were two places where he felt most comfortable, two sanctuaries that provided shelter from outsiders and antagonistic white men: Muhammad's Temple No. 29 and the 5th Street Gym. One hardened his body, the other nurtured his soul. Yet he had no idea what would happen when those two worlds collided.

Chapter Two

GOD'S ANGRY MAN

I have no last name. Just a name some white man gave one of my
ancestors a long time ago. I'd rather be called nigger.

—MALCOLM X

———————

On a cold April evening in 1957, a fight broke out between two black
men at the corner of 125th Street and Lenox Avenue in Manhat-
tan, the heart of Harlem. Swiftly, police cars arrived at the scene,
sirens wailing, and officers jumped out of their vehicles. White patrol-
men broke through the crowd, gripping their nightsticks, demanding
the onlookers disperse. As the policemen thumped a suspect, the crowd
watched in horror. "Why don't you carry the man to jail?" Johnson
Hinton asked. In Harlem, patrolmen routinely subjected black men to
random searches and brutal force. The officers ignored Hinton's protest,
ordering him to move on. But he just wouldn't listen.[1]

Growing bolder and louder, he shouted: "You're not in Alabama!
This is New York!" Enraged, Officer Mike Dolan knocked Hinton to
the ground. The officer unleashed his baton, cracking Hinton in the
skull until blood gushed onto the sidewalk. While the police stuffed
his limp body into the squad car, black and brown faces looked on in
disgust, complaining in hushed tones. It seemed that there was nothing
that they could say, nothing that they could do. The one black man
who had challenged the police found himself behind bars, silenced by
a bloody baton.[2]

In Harlem, the black man's anger toward the white man had long
simmered. Everywhere he turned, the white man embarrassed, exploited,

"My hobby," Malcolm X said with a sly grin, "is stirring up Negroes." A provocative orator, he stirred crowds with his quick wit and sharp tongue. Malcolm's fearlessness and his scathing critiques of white men made him a hero in Harlem and the subject of FBI surveillance. Associated Press

and emasculated him. The white man arrested him. The white man raised the rent. The white man got the job. The white man cut his wages. The white man denied his loan application. The white man had better schools, nicer homes, and more money. The goddamn white man.

"To live in Harlem," Ralph Ellison wrote in 1948, "is to dwell in the very bowels of the city; it is to pass a labyrinthine existence among streets that explode monotonously skyward with the spires and crosses of churches and clutter underfoot with garbage and decay." Black families lived in crowded tenements, crumbling buildings infested by vermin and cockroaches. In the shadows of dark alleys and on crowded street corners, men sought relief, drinking, smoking, and gambling away the little money that they had. Poverty, addiction, and violence plagued black neighborhoods. "Overcrowded and exploited politically

and economically," Ellison observed, "Harlem is the scene and symbol of the Negro's perpetual alienation in the land of his birth."[3]

As the squad cars pulled away from the scene, a woman who witnessed the assault rushed to the Nation of Islam's Shabazz Restaurant at 113 Lenox Avenue. She told the men that one of their Muslim brothers—Johnson X, as he was known—had been severely beaten by the police. Immediately, Joseph X, the rugged captain of the local temple's Fruit of Islam (FOI)—the Nation's "secret army"—organized more than fifty men using a phone chain. Every temple had a security unit made up of an elite group of men who were held to a higher standard of discipline than other members. Trained soldiers, the FOI was responsible for enforcing the laws of the Nation and protecting Elijah Muhammad's followers. They defended the temples and regularly drilled in paramilitary tactics, boxing, and judo, though they were forbidden from carrying arms.[4]

When the Muslims arrived at the 28th Precinct on 123rd Street, the police feared that they were hiding guns under their heavy coats. The temple's minister, a lean, copper-skinned man with a long face and square jaw, wearing thick, black horn-rimmed glasses, marched right into the station. Standing nearly six feet three inches tall and sporting a camel-hair coat, Malcolm X spoke forcefully but calmly, requesting to see Hinton. The police denied that any Muslims were held inside their jail, but as an angry throng of nearly two thousand black people gathered in front of the station, they allowed the minister to check on him. Lying on the cold cement floor of the jail, Hinton could hardly speak; an officer had struck him across the jaw with his baton when he began praying inside his cell. Containing his rage, Malcolm demanded that the lieutenant in charge take the concussed prisoner—who was actually suffering from subdural hemorrhaging—to a hospital. Fearing a riot outside the station, the police called for an ambulance.[5] When the minister walked out of the precinct, he directed the brethren to follow him to the hospital.

Outside of his congregation, few people in the crowd knew much about Malcolm. They had never seen him lead a march or a picket or a boycott. The Muslims rejected the American democratic system, refusing overt political action. They didn't even vote. Instead, the Nation occupied an insulated world of complete separation.

Elijah Muhammad taught his followers to respect civil authority and avoid confrontations. "Be polite, courteous, and respectful so that you may inspire respect from the police officers," he preached. "If you are attacked when peaceful, God comes to our rescue. If you are aggressive, you must fight your own battle without Allah's help." Yet nonviolence had its limits, as Muhammad acknowledged: "If attacked the Holy Koran says fight back."[6]

Tired of wanton police violence against blacks, Harlem itched to fight back. In Harlem, most black men never dared to question a white man in uniform. So when Malcolm strode into the 28th Precinct, challenging white authorities, he inspired black Harlem. From there he marched at the front of a solid line of nearly one hundred Muslims and the sympathetic onlookers who had gathered at the precinct, leading them to the hospital.

As the Muslims advanced down Lenox Avenue, Harlem's busiest thoroughfare, more than two thousand blacks clustered closely behind them. Shortly after they arrived at the hospital the doctors treated Hinton, but then inexplicably released him and he was taken back to jail.[7]

Surging back toward the police headquarters in a fury, within an hour more than four thousand people stood in solidarity with the Nation outside the 28th Precinct. Standing in rank formation, "God's angry men" stared straight ahead, arms crossed, waiting for the minister's orders. Inside the station, Malcolm negotiated with the police, securing the release of two other Muslims who were arrested with Hinton. But the commanding officer refused to send the injured prisoner back to the hospital because he had to be incarcerated overnight to appear in court the next day.

By two thirty a.m., Malcolm sensed a stalemate and an opportunity to demonstrate his authority. The police pleaded with him to break up the crowd, promising that Hinton would continue to receive medical care. Fearing a violent confrontation between the police and his followers, he walked outside, turned toward one of his lieutenants, and whispered in his ear. Then he raised his fist, signaling for the Muslims to disperse. Without a word, the minister's troops drifted into the darkness, as did the other blacks who had gathered in the street.[8]

The police had never witnessed a man control a crowd the way that Malcolm X did that night. Stunned by the scene, an officer looked at

James Hicks, a reporter for the *Amsterdam News*, and said, "No one man should have that much power."[9]

IN THE AFTERMATH of the Nation's protest against police brutality, Malcolm X became a Harlem folk hero. "For the first time," he later recalled, "the black man, woman, and child in the streets were discussing 'those Muslims.'" The New York City Police Department instantly became interested in "those Muslims" too, urgently seeking more information about "Mr. X." Undercover agents in the NYPD's surveillance program, the Bureau of Special Services (BOSS), sat in parked cars monitoring the activities of the Harlem temple. Malcolm's increasing visibility in New York concerned the FBI too, and about a year after BOSS began its surveillance, the FBI designated him "a key figure." For the rest of his life, government agents would track his movements, document his speeches, and record his telephone calls. Malcolm could hardly smile, frown, or smell a flower without the FBI knowing about it. Meanwhile, public curiosity led increasing numbers of blacks to visit Malcolm's temple. Before the Johnson Hinton episode, the New York temple had only a few hundred members; afterward, several thousand became followers of Elijah Muhammad at Temple No. 7.[10]

Benjamin Goodman was one such visitor. A tall young man with an angular face, Goodman was raised in the Christian churches of Virginia. After moving to New York, he bounced between unfulfilling jobs until he found a position in the shipping department of Vanguard Records. One of his friends at work insisted that he visit the temple at the corner of 116th Street and Lenox Avenue to hear "the Minister."[11]

Inside the paper-littered doorway of the storefront temple, a red hand-painted sign greeted visitors: "Welcome to MUHAMMAD'S TEMPLE NO. 7. Every Wed. & Fri. at 8:00 P.M. Sun. at 2:00 P.M. Elevator Service 4th Floor." When Goodman arrived for his first meeting, two sharply dressed men acknowledged him: "Welcome, brother." Climbing three flights of creaking, rotting stairs, he could hear the echo of black men's voices. When he reached the fourth floor, which was much cleaner than the others, two large men directed him into the men's room, where four other men stood bolt upright, eyes forward, lips closed. A stocky man in a dark suit, standing only a foot away from him, leaned in close enough to smell his breath and firmly asked, "Do you have any weapons, alcohol,

cigarettes, or drugs in your possession?" Had he answered affirmatively or reeked of liquor, he would have been asked to leave. After Goodman emptied his pockets, the security guard frisked him thoroughly. When the inspection was over, the guard thanked him for his cooperation and informed him that he could enter the auditorium.[12]

Goodman walked inside the lecture hall and sat on a metal folding chair on the men's side of the aisle, across from women dressed in white floor-length gowns and wearing head coverings. While he waited for the meeting to begin, he studied the blackboard, which was divided into two sides: one representing Christians, the other representing Muslims. On the left side, he saw an American flag framed by a cross and a silhouette of a black man hanging from a tree. In the corners of the flag, painted in bold letters, were the words *Christianity, slavery, suffering,* and *death.* On the opposite side, the corners of a red Muslim flag included the words *Islam, freedom, justice,* and *equality.* Beneath both flags, the congregation read the central question of the Nation: "WHO WILL SURVIVE THE WAR OF ARMAGEDDON?"[13]

As Goodman pondered the question, an assistant minister named Brother Henry walked to the front of the room and welcomed the congregation in Arabic: "*As-Salaam-Alaikum*"—"Peace be unto you." The visitors replied in unison, "*Wa-Alaikum-Salaam*"—"Peace also be unto you." Only during the greetings did the Nation's Muslims use Arabic. Not even Elijah Muhammad—the Messenger himself—spoke or wrote the language.

While Brother Henry lectured, a tall, rail-thin, bespectacled man wearing a dark blue suit, white shirt, and red tie sat at a small table studying three-by-five index cards. Occasionally he pushed his glasses up the bridge of his nose while he penned notations. When Brother Henry introduced him, Malcolm X unfolded his body like a three-part extension ladder, rising from the chair. He gathered his index cards, the Bible, and the Koran, and walked toward the podium.[14]

Malcolm surveyed the packed auditorium, grinning. Then he began, "*As-Salaam-Alaikum.*"

"*Wa-Alaikum-Salaam.*"

Malcolm lectured on a variety of topics that day: the history of slavery, "Negro" ministers who preached the "white man's religion," the Bible—that "book of poison"—and the evils of consuming pork. He did not say

much about the Johnson Hinton case, but he promised that if the police ever attacked another Muslim brother or sister, then they would "be dealing with Malcolm X." Goodman had never heard a black man speak with such unbridled confidence and authority. Malcolm talked plainly in a language that everyone in the audience understood, with a directness that bordered on open rebellion.[15]

At the end of the meeting, visitors were invited to join the Nation. Malcolm asked them to raise their hands if they believed what he said was true. Goodman raised his hand. If a visitor could not commit to the teachings of Elijah Muhammad, Malcolm asserted, the Muslims would not persecute him. "You are among the deaf, dumb, and blind," he explained in a friendly voice. Returning to the temple for further study about "the teaching of the devil," he said, would reveal hidden truths.[16]

After visiting the temple twice more, Goodman penned an initiation letter—the same letter that every convert wrote. After reading the letter, the applicant copied it verbatim by hand:

Date
Mr. W. F. Muhammad
4847 So. Woodlawn Avenue
Chicago 15, Illinois

Dear Savior Allah, Our Deliverer:
I have been attending the teachings of Islam by one of your Ministers, two or three times. I believe in It, and I bear witness that there is no God but Thee, and that Muhammad is Thy Servant and Apostle. I desire to reclaim my own. My slave name is as follows:

Name
Address
City and State

In Chicago, Muhammad's lieutenants carefully examined the applicants' letters. If the letter was written without errors, then the truthseeker received a questionnaire regarding his or her marital status, dependents, and employment. Upon completing the application process, new members immersed themselves in the world of the Nation, submitting completely to the teachings of Muhammad. Every follower

was supposed to give up dope, tobacco, alcohol, profanity, and vice of all kinds. In return, the believer was no longer a wandering "Negro," ashamed of his or her skin color, weakened by Christianity. After initiation, new disciples proclaimed their loyalty to the Supreme Minister. In exchange for their devotion, the true believer received a new life, a new identity, and a new name.[17]

All true believers retained their first name and accepted an *X* in place of their surname—their *slave name*. For example, in the New York temple, Joseph Gravitt, the FOI captain, became Joseph X. Benjamin Goodman, the second man named Benjamin to join Temple No. 7, became Benjamin 2X. Black people, Muhammad taught, did not know their true last name; it remained a mystery. The *X* was a temporary replacement until the Messenger gave the follower an Arabic name, their "original name," such as Ali, Muhammad, Sharrieff, or Shabazz, though many of his disciples went years without replacing the *X*. In rejecting one's slave name, the *X* signified crossing over and erasing the past, the legacy of slavery, and the life of self-loathing. It meant that a black man denounced what he was before he became a Muslim: an "ex-slave."[18]

In two years, Benjamin 2X became one of Malcolm's assistant ministers. During a weekly seminar, Malcolm quizzed his assistants about religion, history, geography, politics, philosophy, economics, and current events. For every class, he required that each student bring a notebook, dictionary, thesaurus, and library card. When Benjamin and the other ministers were not working at their day jobs, they diligently studied the Bible and the Koran; they read the *New York Times*, the *London Times*, and a variety of news magazines; and they prepared for debates. Wasting time on television, movies, parties, and sports was unacceptable. Once his assistants convinced Malcolm that they were ready to do God's work, he took them out fishing on the streets of New York.[19]

Standing on congested street corners and stepladders, outside churches and drugstores, Malcolm courted lost souls, inviting them to hear the truth at Temple No. 7. Armed with a Bible and handbills, he worked the streets, talking to men who reminded him of a younger version of himself: hustlers, gamblers, and bottom-feeders, men searching for a way out of the ghetto. He understood these men, their frustrations, their anger, and their language. He spoke directly, never wasting a word, appealing to their experiences—experiences that he had lived.

And anyone who listened to Malcolm was invariably transfixed by his stories of his own reinvention.

The path that led Malcolm to the Nation of Islam was a tortuous one. After bouncing around predominantly white reform schools and foster homes, Malcolm, three months shy of his sixteenth birthday, with only an eighth-grade education, eagerly boarded a Greyhound bus in Lansing and traveled to Boston. There, under the care of his twenty-six-year-old sister Ella, Malcolm gravitated toward the "hip" swindlers standing on the street corners, the gangsters and bookies, dope dealers and pimps. These men educated him on the life of a "hustler." An older man who called Malcolm "homeboy" taught him the importance of performance when he was shining the white man's shoes. Kneeling at a foot stand, Malcolm mastered the art of polishing, brushing, and shining shoes, snapping the rag across the leather, making it "pop like a firecracker." That popping sound was pure "jive noise," worth two extra bits.[20]

Whether he was shining shoes, cleaning dishes, or serving diners on Pullman cars, Malcolm hustled. He earned generous tips from white men by shucking with a sly smile, ingratiating customers with compliments. When Malcolm finished work he rushed to the nightclubs, where he danced and drank the night away, gambling his tips while he dreamed of hitting the jackpot.

Eventually he settled into the underworld of Harlem, where he came of age as "Detroit Red," a small-time hustler sporting conked red hair and brightly colored zoot suits. His burglary spree ended in 1946 when the police nabbed him and his partner, Shorty Jarvis, and their white girlfriends. The judge gave the twenty-one-year-old offender concurrent eight- to ten-year sentences. He wound up serving his seventy-seven-month incarceration at three Massachusetts penitentiaries. At the Charlestown State Prison, a dank, century-old fortress without running water, Malcolm festered in a dirty, cramped cell, lying on his cot, staring at the ceiling. In his misery, he yearned for the pleasures of the past: the rush of a robbery, the high from snorting cocaine. "Big Red" bragged about his criminal exploits and offered to acquire whatever the other prisoners needed: reefer, tobacco, liquor. He would later claim that he was an obstinate prisoner, a devout atheist nicknamed "Satan" for his mutinous behavior.[21]

After Malcolm transferred to Concord Prison, he received a startling letter from his brother Philbert, who explained that he and other members of the family had converted to "the natural religion for the black man": Islam. Soon, he read more letters from his brothers and sisters, educating him about the movement "designed to help black people." In 1948, after Malcolm transferred to the Norfolk Prison Colony, his younger brother Reginald, a former hustler, visited him. He told Malcolm that there was a man who knew everything. "Who's that?" Malcolm asked. "God is a man," he answered, and "His real name is Allah." Reginald explained that Allah had come to America and taught everything he knew to his disciple, Elijah, "a black man just like us." Allah had instructed Elijah that the devil was also a man—the white man.[22]

Malcolm thought about all the white people who had hurt him and his family: the white supremacists who killed his father; the white doctor who diagnosed his mother as "crazy"; the white social workers who broke up his family; the white kids who called him "nigger" on the playground; the white schoolteacher who told him that he was foolish for thinking that a "nigger" could ever become a lawyer; the white judge who took *ten years* of his life away; and all the other white folks who had done him wrong.[23]

His siblings continued to educate him through correspondence and their visits. They urged him to trust the teachings of Elijah Muhammad, the "Messenger of Allah," a "small, gentle man" who possessed "the true knowledge of the black man." Reginald advised him to purify his body and avoid cigarettes, alcohol, drugs, and pork. Malcolm followed his instructions, accepting Muhammad's strict rules of morality.[24]

Like many of Muhammad's prison converts, he idolized the Nation's patriarch. After sending Muhammad a letter he'd revised twenty-five times, they enjoyed a regular correspondence. Malcolm could not wait to meet Allah's prophet and serve his cause. On August 7, 1952, about a month after the Massachusetts Department of Corrections transferred his parole to the State of Michigan, he walked out of prison a new man, wearing a cheap suit and shedding the cloak of Big Red.[25]

Shortly after his release, Malcolm rode a bus to Detroit. Canvassing the neighborhoods of Black Bottom, he shared his story of self-emancipation, crediting Elijah Muhammad for his liberation from a life of destitution and delinquency. "Before hearing of [Muhammad]," he admitted, "I

had nothing, knew nothing, and was nothing. I was addicted to and enslaved by all the evils and vices of this white civilization—dope, alcohol, adultery, thievery, and," he added hyperbolically, "*even murder.*" Without Muhammad's grace, he had "very little hope, desire, or intention of amounting to anything."[26]

After Malcolm served as an assistant minister for the Detroit temple and proved himself an effective organizer, in late 1953 Muhammad rewarded his protégé with his own ministry in Boston, where Malcolm established Temple No. 11. Shortly thereafter, Muhammad sent him to Philadelphia to further build the movement's membership along the East Coast. In just three months, Muhammad promoted his charismatic disciple once again, naming him minister of Temple No. 7 in New York. Muhammad recognized that no one could relate to the "bottom-of-the-pile Negroes" the way that Malcolm did. Those beaten-down, dead-end blacks trusted Malcolm because he also knew life in worn-out shotgun houses and rancid tenements.[27]

In the tenement neighborhoods of Harlem, Malcolm persuaded many blacks to hear him preach at the temple. But not everyone was easily convinced that Islam was the path to righteousness. When people heard him talk about the Nation's theology, many just shook their heads in disbelief. One man yelled, "You niggers are crazy!" and marched right past him. On another occasion, when Malcolm tried to convince a Baptist into converting to Islam, the man asked, "What are the rules of your organization?" Malcolm replied, "Well, my brother, you'll have to stop drinking, stop swearing, stop gambling, stop using dope, and stop cheating on your wife." The man thought for a moment. "Hell," he quipped, "I think I better remain a Christian."[28]

In the mid-1950s, during the Nation's ascendance in the impoverished black neighborhoods of northern cities, Malcolm was fast becoming the most important symbol of the movement. The New York minister served as living proof that through the Messenger, anything was possible. If Muhammad's message could cleanse a depraved, atheist criminal and transform him into a minister of God, a man who respected himself and his people, then Muhammad could save the most immoral degenerate. "Malcolm redeemed," observed literature professor Michael

Thelwell, "was the word incarnate, the message made flesh, the living metaphor and exemplar of the redemption of an entire race."[29]

As Muhammad's most prized minister and one of his closest confidants, the minister's presence was felt everywhere: Atlanta, Atlantic City, Buffalo, Jersey City, Newark, Pittsburgh, and Washington, DC. In the seven years after he left prison, the number of temples increased from ten to thirty. "I thank Allah for my Brother Minister Malcolm," Muhammad proudly declared.[30]

They became like father and son. Some of the Messenger's aides believed that he cared more for Malcolm than for his own children. They forged a familial bond, speaking on the phone nearly every day, Muhammad advising him on all matters, professional and personal. "Anywhere you will find me," Muhammad said, "you will find him." In Malcolm's devotion to Elijah, he offered blind obedience. There was no one he trusted more.[31]

Whenever possible Malcolm visited Chicago. A mutual friend recalled, "I sat in Elijah Muhammad's home one Saturday morning while he was lecturing a group of ministers. The doorbell rang, and a servant came in and announced that Malcolm had come. Elijah's eyes lit up as if the prodigal son was home. He leaped from his seat and when Malcolm appeared they embraced and kissed." Muhammad had no doubt that Malcolm would take a bullet for him. Malcolm had said as much: "I would give my life so that he may live. He has done so much for me."[32]

Yet Muhammad was not the only one closely following Malcolm's growing influence within the Nation. In late 1958, a black FBI informant assessed the New York minister's rising power: "Brother MALCOLM ranks about third in influence"—behind Muhammad and his son-in-law, Supreme Captain of the Fruit, Raymond Sharrieff. "Outside of the Messenger's immediate family he is the most trusted follower. He is an excellent speaker, forceful and convincing. He is an expert organizer and untiring worker. . . . MALCOLM has a strong hatred for 'blue eyed devils,' but this hatred is not likely to erupt in violence as he is much too clever and intelligent for that. . . . He is fearless and cannot be intimidated by words or threats or personal harm. He has most of the answers at his fingertips," and, the informant warned, "he should be carefully dealt with."[33]

MORE THAN ANY other event, the documentary *The Hate That Hate Produced* brought Malcolm into the country's national consciousness. In New York, journalist Louis Lomax and news anchor Mike Wallace sensed that the rising popularity of the Black Muslims in Harlem and the surrounding controversy over their beliefs would spark great interest. In the summer of 1959, Lomax gained Muhammad's cooperation through Malcolm. In a sensationalized narrative, Wallace told viewers that they were watching "a story of black racism." The documentary portrayed the Muslims as adversaries of the civil rights movement. The growing "black supremacist group," it declared, taught their "anti-white" and "anti-American" doctrine in more than fifty cities and claimed more than 250,000 members, an exaggerated figure that only enhanced viewers' fears about the Nation.[34]

In the documentary, Muhammad's heir apparent, the younger, more charismatic minister Malcolm X, overshadowed the Nation's leader. Almost overnight, Malcolm appeared on news broadcasts across the country. The national media's reaction to the documentary convinced Muhammad that the press deliberately distorted his teachings in an effort to undermine him.[35]

Widespread attacks on the Nation convinced Muhammad that Malcolm should respond directly to critics, despite accusations from some Nation officials who blamed the New York minister for seeking too much publicity. Yet Muhammad insisted that Malcolm should become more visible. If Malcolm became famous, he explained, "it will make *me* better known."[36]

Over the next year, Malcolm began traveling more, giving interviews on television and radio. He visited college campuses, delivered lectures, and engaged in public debates. His life became "a blur of planes and trains, speeches and sermons." His frequent appearances on television shaped a public perception that Malcolm *was* the Muslims, creating envy inside the Nation's headquarters. Muhammad warned him, "You will grow to be hated when you become well known. Because usually people get jealous of public figures."[37]

Given his recent heart attack and chronic bronchial asthma, Muhammad could never have taken on the demands of traveling as Malcolm did. The frail sexagenarian's deteriorating health led him to move to the drier climate of Phoenix, Arizona. Separated from the national

headquarters, he empowered Raymond Sharrieff, John Ali, and his sons, Herbert and Elijah Jr., to run the daily operations in Chicago.

Muhammad's physical decline and heightened sense of mortality led him to tighten his grip on the world around him. He carefully monitored his ministers, requiring them to record their weekly sermons and send tapes to Chicago, ensuring that they did not deviate from his message. He especially depended on Sharrieff and his network of temple informants to report any conflicts or subversive activity within the Nation.[38]

The more hostile attention the Muslims received from outsiders, the more paranoid Muhammad became. "He has tremendous faith in himself and Allah," a minster told journalist William Worthy. "He trusts his subordinates to a degree, but essentially he thinks that no one is his friend. He alone is going to run the Nation of Islam and he is so strong right now that a split in the organization would be impossible at this time."[39]

In the spring and winter of 1960, thousands of college students in dozens of cities settled on a new tactic for forcing change to the civil rights landscape: the sit-in. This nonviolent direct action movement was aimed at desegregating southern lunch counters. Yet the sit-in was of little use in the North, where black people could eat at any coffee shop or lunch counter. There, the blurred color line of *de facto* segregation, hardened by history and custom, created separate and unequal neighborhoods, poor public schools, dilapidated housing projects, and persistent unemployment. Trapped in a cycle of poverty, blacks lived as second-class citizens, fatigued by empty promises of a better life. "The mood of the Negro, particularly in New York City," Louis Lomax asserted, "is very, very bitter. He is losing faith. The Negro on the streets of Harlem is tired of platitudes from white liberals."[40]

On a mild Saturday afternoon in May 1960, about three months before Cassius Clay departed New York for the Rome Olympics, an estimated ten thousand Harlemites, standing shoulder to shoulder, attended an outdoor "freedom rally" at the intersection of West 125th Street and Seventh Avenue. The large assembly of people, most of whom were not Muslims, attested to Malcolm's growing popularity as a political figure. Responding to the urban unrest, he offered a broad message of solidarity.

"As black people we must unite," he insisted. He exhorted the masses to follow "fearless black leaders who will stand up and help the so-called American Negro get complete and *immediate* freedom." While civil rights activists challenged segregation in the South, a temper of defiance swept through northern cities like an epidemic. Radicals tried to cure the disease by pressing for full citizenship, equal rights, and racial justice. Well before "Black Power" became a rallying cry, the belief in self-determination and racial pride blossomed as northern black activists fought for better jobs, quality education, and open housing.[41]

No one articulated black rage against American hypocrisy and the failures of democracy more strongly than Malcolm did. Despite his calls for unity, he could hardly resist criticizing civil rights leaders who advocated integration. Although he did not call anyone out by name, he made it clear that black people wanted "leaders who are not afraid to demand freedom, justice, and equality. . . . We do not want any more Uncle Toms."[42]

Many admired Malcolm for his fearlessness. He was willing to debate anyone, anytime, anywhere. Malcolm debated the way Clay fought, swinging from the opening bell, hitting his opponent with hard cuts and fierce jabs. Unrestrained by the "conventional niceties of debate," he played by his own rules, on his terms. He cultivated a combative style, bobbing and weaving, pivoting the conversation in the direction that he wanted. Malcolm was not interested in simply scoring points and landing a few punches. Decisions were not his goal. He swung for the knockout. Alex Haley recalled, "He would turn a radio or television program to his advantage in a way he credited to the boxing ring's great Sugar Ray Robinson, who would dramatize a round's last thirty seconds. Similarly, Malcolm would eye the big studio clock, and at the instant it showed thirty seconds to go, he'd pounce in and close the show with his own verbal barrage."[43]

Photographers popularized a fiery image of him lecturing at the podium, fist clenched, face masked with a snarl. Yet Malcolm's behavior on stage belied the provocative image of the angry black man. Dressed in a conservative suit with his tie perfectly knotted, he appeared more like an intellectual than an itinerant preacher. Before responding to a question, Malcolm looked back at the moderator or his opponent,

holding their full attention. Then, after calculating his response, he thoughtfully answered. Joseph Durso interviewed Malcolm, expecting "more of a platform speaker, somebody who was very militant." But "he was more cerebral than physical. He reasoned. He was almost like a college professor."[44]

On multiple occasions Malcolm matched wits with Bayard Rustin, the veteran civil rights activist and close friend and adviser of Martin Luther King. In January 1962, they debated at Manhattan Community Church, a liberal congregation made up mostly of whites. In the past two years, they had become friendly rivals, fully aware of each other's tricks and strategies. Rustin, an advocate of racial cooperation and direct action against segregation, argued that separatism failed to address the problems facing black people. It left them powerless to change the oppressive conditions of the society they inhabited. Without any clear plan, Rustin charged, Malcolm resorted to emotionalism.[45]

"When a man is hanging on a tree," Malcolm snapped, "and he cries out, should he cry out unemotionally?"

> When a man is sitting on a hot stove and he tells you how it feels to be there, is he supposed to speak without emotion? This is what you tell black people in this country when they begin to cry out against the injustices that they're suffering. As long as they describe these injustices in a way that makes you believe you have another one hundred years to rectify the situation, then you don't call that emotion. But when a man is on a hot stove, he says, "I'm coming up. I'm getting up. Violently or nonviolently doesn't even enter the picture—I'm coming up, do you understand?"[46]

Pleased by his decisive blow, Malcolm flashed a sardonic smile—the same satisfied grin that eased onto Jack Johnson's face after the black boxer knocked his white opponents to the canvas.

As Malcolm's celebrity grew, he became empowered, speaking more independently about politics. The less time he spent inside Mosque No. 7, the less he spoke about Muslim theology. Privately, Malcolm became convinced that the Nation needed to engage "in more *action*." As Muhammad read news clippings and transcripts of Malcolm's speeches and

debates, he grew suspicious about his popular minister's motives. In Chicago, Muhammad's lieutenants whispered that Brother Malcolm was "trying to take over the Nation."[47]

Muhammad suspected that Malcolm aspired to lead the Muslims into the front lines of protests, though he feared such involvement would only attract greater scrutiny from the government. On February 15, 1962, the Messenger wrote Malcolm, reminding him not to "go too much into details on the political side; nor into the subject of a separate state here for us." The Nation's patriarch ordered him to speak only about what "you yourself have heard me say." He insisted that Malcolm avoid discussing political issues, an impossible request as long as Malcolm engaged civil rights activists.[48]

Less than a month after he received Muhammad's edict, Malcolm debated James Farmer at Cornell University. Speaking first, Farmer, leader of the Congress of Racial Equality (CORE), shrewdly borrowed the minister's standard speech about the white man's crimes against blacks. He explained that everyone already knew that racism poisoned America. Then he aggressively criticized the Nation's theology and separatist doctrine.

"The time has passed when we can look for pie in the sky, when we can depend upon someone else on high to solve the problem for us," he said. "What we want Mr. X, the representative of the Black Muslims and Elijah Muhammad, to tell us today, is what his program is, what he proposes to do about killing this disease?" Turning toward his opponent, he attacked Malcolm's flank, demanding an answer: "We know the disease, physician, what is your cure?"[49]

The question haunted Malcolm. Farmer had set the perfect trap. Malcolm slowly rose from his seat and took the microphone. He rambled for a few minutes, searching for the answer that the black masses were waiting to hear. But he could not give them what they wanted, not as long as Elijah Muhammad was listening.[50]

Chapter Three

"WHO MADE ME IS *ME*"

I'm a boxer, and I really don't want anything to do with the civil rights program right now.

—CASSIUS CLAY

———————

The morning definitely did not show Gorgeous George in his most gorgeous light. Born George Raymond Wagner in 1915, the forty-six-year-old performer showed up at the Las Vegas radio station looking hung over and worn out. His skin had a sickly pallor; his famous platinum blond hair hanging uncharacteristically loose without his "Georgie pins." The most famous professional wrestler in America was less than one and a half years away from retirement and two and a half away from dying of a terminal liver condition brought on by decades of heavy drinking. But at showtime, George could still muster enough energy to please the crowds.

Clay arrived in Las Vegas on the evening of Wednesday, June 21, 1961, and the next morning he met the wrestler at the station. They both had tickets to peddle. George had a grudge match—they were all grudge matches with him—scheduled for June 23 at the Las Vegas Convention Center against Freddie Blassie. Clay was fighting Kolo "Duke" Sabedong, a six-foot-seven Hawaiian of Samoan ancestry, at the Convention Center on Monday the twenty-sixth.[1]

Turning first to Clay, the show's host asked about his chances with the experienced, hard-punching Sabedong. The Hawaiian had a mixed career that included wins over club fighters and losses against better boxers. He had also fought contenders, though he usually did not finish those

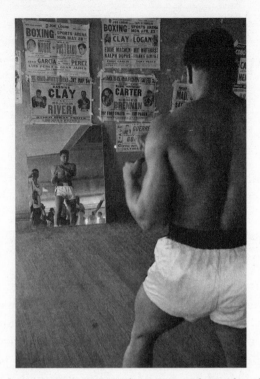

"Who made me is me," *Cassius Clay announced. But his identity was subject to interpretation. He was like a magician, revealing only what he wanted his audience to see and hiding the secrets behind his tricks.*
Associated Press

fights on his feet. When the host asked Clay about his own chances, he was circumspectly confident. "I can't say I was humble, but I wasn't too loud," Clay later recalled.[2]

The host then turned to George. In the early years of television, Gorgeous George practically invented the persona of the flamboyant, bombastic villain. After observing that the untalented "freaks, baboons, and foreigners" who passed themselves off as professional wrestlers attracted the largest audiences and purses, he asked himself, "What if a guy had a flair for showmanship *and could also* wrestle—would he go over?"[3]

George Wagner reinvented himself as Gorgeous George, a villain of the first order. He dressed effeminately—long, dyed hair; gold-plated, sequined "Georgie pins"; satin outfits; reportedly an ermine jockstrap;

monogrammed towels; and robes that looked like they had been lifted from Liberace's closet—and swished down the aisle to the ring to "Pomp and Circumstance." Once inside the ropes, his valet sprayed a fine, sweet-smelling mist from an atomizer on the robes, canvas, and, stealthily, on the referee and opponent. The Gorgeous One performed other pre-match rituals with great solemnity and formality, but once the bell sounded he was capable of committing any vile trick or underhanded tactic to win a match. Gorgeous George was, in short, the very negation of the American male athlete; the persona he originated was equal parts drag queen, aristocratic prig, and lowdown cheat. And audiences in arenas across the country and on television could not seem to get enough of him.

The host asked George, what would be the outcome of his upcoming match? "I'll kill him; I'll tear off his arm," Clay recalled George saying. "If this bum beats me, I'll crawl across the ring and cut off my hair, but it's not gonna happen because I'm the greatest wrestler in the world." Floating on a sea of self-endorsement, he continued to wax eloquently about how great and beautiful he was. "And all this time," Cassius remembered, "I was saying to myself, 'Man, I want to see this fight. It don't matter who wins or loses; I want to be there to see what happens.'"[4]

Clay closely watched the match, noting the wrestler's grand entrance illuminated by a spotlight and covered by a red velvet gown lined with white satin. George moved imperiously toward the ring, shouting that the spectators who booed him were "ignorant peasants." It was a sensational act, and afterward Clay vowed, "[Although] I'd never been shy about talking . . . if I talked even more, there was no telling how much money people would pay to see me." He later told Dundee about George's performance, concluding, "This is a gooooood idea."

"*Niño con boca grande!*" the Cubans in the 5th Street Gym had called Cassius. But in Las Vegas his mouth, like the Grinch's heart, seemed to grow three sizes bigger. A few days later he told sportswriter George King what to expect in the fight: "Someone's got to go before the 10th—and you can bet it won't be me." There was no way he would lose, he explained. Losing a fight against a big Hawaiian just was not a possibility.[5]

Sabedong made his most pointed statements with his fists in the ring. From the first round it was clear that Clay was faster and infinitely superior in boxing ability. But the Duke had a few dirty tricks that

would have shocked even Gorgeous George. When he got a chance he hit Clay low, on the breaks, and after the bell, and he used his head as a third fist. "I threw a couple of low punches just to let him know I was there," he later said. "The first time I hit him low, his eyes went as big as saucers. I was going to bite his ear. You know when you are in clinches you get the guy's ear between your teeth and give it a little tug, that usually would bring water to their eyes."[6]

Sabedong's problem was that he rarely got close enough to Clay to hit low, butt, or bite. Constantly moving, Cassius peppered him with jabs and hooks, landing harder punches occasionally but not often enough to take him out. The fight went the distance, but for Clay it was a learning experience. Professional boxing was not like the amateur version of the sport, where referees passed out penalties for the slightest infractions. In the pro ranks you had to expect the unexpected and protect yourself at all times. Clay departed the Convention Center a wiser boxer. And he left Las Vegas with a new bag of verbal tricks.

BEFORE GORGEOUS GEORGE departed Las Vegas, he talked briefly with Cassius. Clay had gone to the wrestling match, watched the packed house scream insults at the foppish athlete, and met with him afterward in the dressing room. "Boxing, wrestling—it's all a show," he told Clay. "A lot of people will pay to see someone shut your mouth. So keep on bragging, keep on sassing, and always be outrageous."[7]

Clay got it. He understood that most beat reporters were less interested in the truth than a good tale. Every day or so they needed a story to file, and they spent their lives scrounging for copy—digging for leads, tracking down facts, conspiring for quotes. "Trouble with boxing today," Cassius told a reporter after the Sabedong match, "is most boxers don't want to talk. Say, 'Yeh, no, yeh, no.' You writer men ain't got nothing to write about. . . . Look at *Ring Magazine*—it loaded with stuff about John L. Sullivan and all them old-timers. Nothing else to write about."[8]

He knew the solution to the sport's woes—it was him. And he expressed it with candid specificity.

> Boxing need fighters who talk a lot and *kill*. Fighter today, he bring two
> or three girls with him to the fight and go into the ring with his hair all

waved silky. In the olden days a fighter go back in the woods and train and drink tea without sugar in it, getting *mean*. Today, temptation is abroad in the land. There's more pretty cars these days, and you can get 'em cheap. Everything's a dollar down, and a liquor store on every corner. Rock 'n' roll show in town every week. But Cassius Clay go to bed at *nine*. I'm eating them lima beans, collard greens, okra and tomatoes, and spinach. Man, them are things that stick to your kidneys. Most guys eat crackers and soda pop and expect to stay in shape. But Cassius Clay, he a determined young man. When he lay down on a guy, that guy supposed to go *down*. So as I see it today, I should be champ when I'm twenty-one. You writ that?[9]

After his short exchange with Gorgeous George, Cassius became the most vocal and opinionated athlete in America. He sounded off on topics ranging from boxing and diets to music and foreign policy, though rarely did he address racial issues or domestic politics. When he said, "The trouble is boxing's dying because everybody's so quiet," he meant it, and he made it his personal mission to pump some noise into the sport. He lectured on his personal growth—"I'm mature. I'm growing a mustache. I shaved yesterday for the first time." He rendered an opinion about his similarity to the leaders of communist nations—"Man, the way I been talking, if I didn't back up my talk I'd have to leave town. I'd have to leave the country. Take a man like Feedel Castro. He say, 'I gonna do this, I gonna do that.' Next morning, rat-a-tat-tat—six people die. He *do* it. . . . So I talk big and that just makes me fight harder." And, of course, he mentioned his importance to the Fourth Estate—"I'm the best friend a reporter ever had because I always give good quotes, changing them around so everybody gets a fresh one."[10]

Some sportswriters thought he was charming and refreshing; others found him conceited and bombastic. When Huston Horn of *Sports Illustrated* met Clay in 1961, he noted that the boxer was "irrepressible, impish, cocksure and sometimes utterly unbearable." But it mattered little how they felt about him because they all wrote about him.[11]

Clay became for the early 1960s what Joe Louis had been for the mid-1930s, a singular, transcendent force in the world of sports. In the Depression, sportswriters had competed to pin a tag on Louis, coining

such monikers as the Dark Destroyer, the Tawny Tiger, the Chocolate Cobra, the Ebony Assassin, the Saffron Sandman, and, of course, the Brown Bomber, among scores of others. Virtually all referred to his skin color and destructive power. Clay's nicknames included the Louisville Larruper, the Mighty Mouth, the Mouth That Roared, the Marvelous Mouth, Claptrap Cash, Cash the Brash, and, most famously, the Louis-ville Lip. They suggested neither his race nor fighting ability but alluded to the tenor and volume of his verbiage. In an age of celebrity, when fame was conferred on the loudest self-promoters, Cassius Clay was reaching for the moon.[12]

He even dressed the part. Aware of his audience, fashion was im-portant to him. "If the women come, the men got to follow, ain't that so?" he asked a reporter. So his ring attire was clean and light—white shoes with three coats of polish, white satin trunks, and a white satin robe. To complete the look, he spread a thin coat of Vaseline on his arms and torso "to make me look real musclely." He appeared almost ethereal as he danced, light-footed, in his corner before the bell and glided toward an opponent. As much as possible he tried to take the pain out of fighting—at least the pain he suffered. "Women don't like the sight of blood . . . so I make sure they don't see none of mine by not getting hit." For him, boxing was a sport of speed and grace, not shuffling and slugging.[13]

He was a self-made product, and he knew it. Frequently, he said, people he knew approached him saying, "Cassius, you know *I'm* the one who made you." Maybe all they had done was give him a lift to the gym or a piece of advice. But they wanted to make sure that Cassius did not forget them when he started to write his name on the back of large checks. Number one on the list of the claimants was his father, who talked endlessly about the sacrifices *he* made and privations *he* suffered to allow his son to reach his dreams. Cassius understood his father's motivations: "If I had a child who became rich and famous, I know I'd want to cash in too, like my daddy, and I guess more teen-agers ought to realize that they owe their folks."[14]

Yet the truth of the matter was that his father did not make him. "When you want to talk about who made me," he told a reporter, "you talk to me. Who made me is *me*."[15]

"There's only one Cassius Clay," Dundee said. "Thank God." Cassius was as unique as Coca-Cola, and like the Atlanta soft-drink maker, he branded and marketed himself. Often when fighters trained they advertised the training camp or a hotel where they worked out. Sonny Liston frequently wore Thunderbird Hotel T-shirts, giving a plug to the Las Vegas hotel. Grossinger's, the popular Catskills resort, was another favorite of boxers in training, and the name adorned such heavyweights as Floyd Patterson and Ingemar Johansson.

Shortly after he began training at the 5th Street Gym, Cassius started wearing crisp white T-shirts with his name printed in the front in bold red Spencerian script, reminiscent of the Coca-Cola logo. No other athlete in America exercised, ate, and slept in a shirt branded with his own name. Clay was years ahead of his time. The shirts revealed a conscious effort not only to market his name but also to inscribe that name onto the landscape of American popular culture through the art of self-promotion.[16]

He had a genius for marketing himself. In September 1961 *Sports Illustrated* started work on their first feature about Clay, assigning Huston Horn to write the piece and Flip Schulke to contribute a full-page photograph. For most of a week Schulke trailed Clay, snapping pictures of him training in the 5th Street Gym, eating with friends, and mingling with the residents of Overtown. During a lunch at the Famous Chef Café, Cassius told Schulke that he wanted to broaden his base of appeal. "I want to get into *Life*," he said. Schulke, who had recently shot some underwater photos for the magazine, replied, "I really don't know how I can get you into *Life*."[17]

The next day when Schulke arrived at the Sir John Hotel, Cassius jumped into the pool, splashing around and throwing punches in the water. The photographer was intrigued by the trail of bubbles the punches made. They looked like the tail of a comet and reminded him of the underwater waterskiing photos that had appeared in *Life*. When he mentioned it, Cassius immediately invented a story telling the photographer that the underwater work was part of his training regiment. It increased his punching power and hand speed. He had learned it from an old trainer, he said.

Schulke came to the Sir John Hotel the following morning carrying scuba gear and an underwater camera to photograph Clay's unusual

workout. Standing on the bottom of the pool in a perfect fighter's pose, throwing punches that created contrails of bubbles, Cassius smiled and mugged for the camera. The results were terrific, and *Life* published them in the September 8, 1961, issue of the magazine, several weeks before the *Sports Illustrated* feature appeared.[18]

Clay's ability to take Gorgeous George's shtick and make it his own, his intuitive understanding of precisely what reporters wanted and needed, and his ingenuity in breaking into *Life* magazine all attested to his decision not only to reinvent himself but also to redefine how others saw him. He would not be another Floyd Patterson, quiet, dignified, fearful of making a false step or offending white America. Nor would he be another Jackie Robinson, speaking out about civil rights. His search was for autonomy in a country that had historically denied black men that basic freedom.

In this sense he identified with James Baldwin, the black writer who defied every simple definition. "I did not intend to allow the white people of this country to tell me who I was, and limit me that way, and to polish me off that way," he wrote in his personal manifesto, *The Fire Next Time*. "And yet, of course, at the same time, I *was* being spat on and defined and described and limited, and could have been polished off with no effort whatever. Every Negro boy—in my situation during those years, at least—who reaches this point realizes, at once, profoundly, because he wants to live, that he stands in great peril and must find, with speed, a 'thing,' a gimmick, to lift him out, to start him on his way. *And it does not matter what the gimmick is.*"[19]

Cassius's gimmick—and his mask—was the Louisville Lip persona. "I'm the boldest, the prettiest, the most superior, most scientific, most skillfullest fighter in the ring today," he told Howard Tuckner of the *New York Times*. "Man, it's great to be great." Tuckner responded by calling him "a professional loudmouth" and a "windbag." But it was Clay who determined and defined the conversation, "aware that the world may despise, but never ignore, a braggart." Since, as Cassius said, "Floyd Patterson's got nothin' to say, and Sonny Liston can't say anything," he would determine the future of boxing. Whatever Americans, white or black, desired, he would be the man in the glass booth. All eyes would follow him.[20]

That is, as long as he continued to win.

THE BOMBAST OF Clay's pronouncements were not reflected in his matches, which he won in a workmanlike, unspectacular fashion. On July 22 he fought Alonzo Johnson in a *Fight of the Week,* out-pointing the slick, defensive boxer in a sleepy ten-round contest. Defeated but unimpressed, Johnson told reporters who asked if Clay was ready to take on contenders, "He won't beat them boys."[21]

Dundee agreed, at least for the time being, he wanted nothing to do with "them boys." On October 7 he put his fighter in the ring against Alex Miteff, an overweight, worn-out journeyman in the twilight of his career. Making Clay's chances even more certain, Miteff, in the argot of the trade, was a bleeder. "The slightest blow to his nose or eyes taps a stream of blood which cannot by damned by Vaseline or medicated cotton swabs," noted a sportswriter.[22]

Dundee expected that Clay would win a sanguinary victory, and he wasn't disappointed. Not long after the fight started, Clay's punches opened old scars on Miteff's face. By the sixth round the Argentine fighter was having trouble seeing through the blood and swelling around his eye, leaving him practically blind to Clay's punches. Then midway through the round, Cassius landed a short, hard right—the hardest of his career, he said after the match. Miteff fell, rolled over once, struggled to his feet, and stumbled toward a corner "in the determined important walk of a drunk." As Clay moved forward, the referee stepped between the boxers and stopped the fight.[23]

After the Miteff fight, Dundee looked for another old, slow, and unimaginative opponent for his young, swift, and creative prodigy. Willi Besmanoff was perfect. The squat German heavyweight had survived internment in Buchenwald as a youth during World War II. After turning professional in 1952, he engaged in almost fifty matches before coming to America four years later. Soon *The Ring* ranked him among the top ten heavyweights. However, by the late 1950s he was losing more than he was winning, and by 1961 he was well advanced into the twilight of his career.

Clay realized as much. To make the fight more interesting he added a new wrinkle—a prediction. "Besmanoff must fall in seven," he told a reporter. It was an audacious statement, an earthquake moment in the history of self-promotion. When asked to predict an outcome of a match, fighters usually mumbled that they would do their best. Some,

of course, predicted victory, which, after all, was just an indication of confidence. But Clay predicted a round, a show of specificity that bordered on crystal-ball soothsaying.[24]

And Cassius fully understood the power of his prophecy. It was magic, imbued with supernatural power, and as such magnetically charged. Why did people come to watch him fight? "They want to see that *round*. People are superstitious. It's the *round* that gets them. They don't come to see me win. They come to see that *round*." It was, he believed, an example of man's mystical hunger. "People run to priests. They pray and shout in church. People is spooky-minded. They look at the moon. They wonder about numbers. Preachers say Jesus called them but they got no proof. I got proof. The round I call is the round they must fall."[25]

The fight certified Clay's sagacity. It was no contest. By the sixth round Besmanoff was bloody and disoriented, looking "like a man caught in the middle of a busy street," wrote one reporter. Cassius could have finished the German off in the fifth or sixth round, but he carried him to the seventh. Then, in the predicted round, he knocked Besmanoff out cold.[26]

The fight was over, and so was Clay's time in boxing's minor leagues. In the year since he traveled to Miami to train with Dundee, he had put on muscle and weight, honing his technique and learning his craft. He had fought in preliminary matches and main event bouts before small to medium-sized crowds and on television. His record was a perfect 10–0, with seven ending in knockouts or technical knockouts. He had fought half of his matches in his hometown, but now it was time to move on.

In a feature article, *The Ring* called him the "Bonus Boy of Boxing," claiming he looked like the "Rookie of the Year." "Right now he has shown that he has the ability to handle the top grade men, but how he would do against the ranking fighters, is something which has to be answered." To be sure, some critics assailed his boxing style and promotional antics, but perhaps no pugilist had risen as quickly and as spectacularly. He had appeared on the pages of *Sports Illustrated* and *Life*, been the subject of hundreds of newspaper stories, and appeared in a feature film. He was ready, Dundee now felt, for "THE BIG TIME."[27]

BY JANUARY 1962 Cassius had become impatient, veering in a more independent direction. Increasingly his rhetoric mixed humor with mean-spirited jabs at other heavyweights. He complained to reporters that he was frustrated by the slowness of his advancement up the heavyweight division. He grumbled, "I'm tired of being fed on set-ups. I can't get a title shot by knocking out a bunch of has-beens and novices, mostly fighters who are over the hill."[28]

Although Dundee was in no hurry, for the right opportunity, he was willing to take a modest risk. In February he accepted a fight against a tall southpaw from Detroit named Lucien "Sonny" Banks. Normally, Angelo would have avoided a boxer like Banks. Too inexperienced to be predictable, awkward, left-handed, and hard-hitting, he was the sort of boxer who made anyone he fought look bad. In his stumbling, free-swinging style, he recalled legendary trainer Whitey Bimstein's description of another untutored fighter: "Nobody never learned him nothing." And because of his elbows and head advances, he often cut opponents.[29]

Angelo accepted the fight because it would give Clay national television exposure and would be staged at Madison Square Garden. The Garden was the summit for a boxer, as holy to the sport as Jerusalem and Mecca are to the faithful. Its landmark marquee jutted out between 49th and 50th Streets on Eighth Avenue like a square chin waiting to be punched. In its prime in the 1930s, the Garden was just a few blocks away from Stillman's Gym and the Neutral Corner saloon, as well as a seedy collection of drugstores selling bandages and wrapping gauze, hock shops trafficking in fake diamonds and watches, and a few fleabag hotels that rented rooms by the half hour. Even more rundown by 1962, these blocks on Eighth Avenue still reigned as the undisputed center of the world of pugilism, although the sport was falling out of favor with younger sports fans.

Undaunted by the shabbiness of Eighth Avenue and the state of boxing, Cassius was determined to restore the Garden and the sport to its glory days. A publicist's dream, he was like a windup toy: just give the key a turn and point it in the right direction. A few days before the fight he addressed a crowded luncheon of the Boxing Writers Association, boasting that he would save the sport as Joe Louis once did. As

for his upcoming fight, he promised, "If I don't beat Banks I'll take the first plane out of the country." There had never been a heavyweight who looked so young, talked so fast, and smiled so brightly. To writers new to Cassius's shtick, it had the feel of a perfect New York spring day, fresh and scrubbed with a hint of naughty fun.[30]

Enticed by the fact that Clay wrote poetry and was thus a "fellow-littérateur," A. J. Liebling, the fabled chronicler of the demimonde, ventured down to West 28th Street, where Cassius was training. The writer had seen Clay box in the Rome Olympics and did not give him high marks. "Clay had a skittering style, like a pebble scaled over water," he observed. But the fact that Clay was a man of verse who could recite his poetry while doing sit-ups without breaking cadence astounded him. "He is probably the only poet in America who can recite this way," he speculated. "I would like to see T. S. Eliot try."[31]

Liebling captured Clay's light, whimsical quality—the way he glided through his training regimen, skipping rope without a rope, toying good-naturedly with his sparring partners, talking nonstop at record speed. Nothing about Cassius smacked of a traditional pugilist. He even dressed like a nineteenth-century man of letters from the school of Oscar Wilde. After his workout he retired to the locker room and reappeared in a snuff-colored suit and lace-front shirt, the sort Liebling had seen in shop windows on Broadway but had never "known anyone with nerve enough to wear." The overweight, sharp-eyed journalist had spent much of his life around boxers and their retinues and had lived in France and England, but he had not met anyone quite like Cassius Clay.[32]

Clay, he judged, might just be the fighter who could save boxing, a "new Hero," coming along "like a Moran tug to pull it out of the doldrums."[33]

A COLD FEBRUARY wind lashed New York on the night of the bout, making it feel even colder than the fifteen-degree temperature. And for all of Clay's ballyhoo, only a smattering of people showed up at the Garden—Liebling wrote that the attendance was "so thin that it could more properly be denominated a quorum. . . . Only fans who like sociability ordinarily turn up for a fight that they can watch for nothing on

television, and that night the cold had kept even the most gregarious at home."[34]

As Clay moved to the center of the ring for the referee's instructions, he saw a boxer very different from the ones he had been fighting. Unlike Miteff or Besmanoff, Banks carried no excess weight around his middle. He was as tall and as heavy as Clay, and only a year and a half older. But where Cassius's face was round, Banks's was thin, with a long pointed chin. His body was hard and muscular, with "the kind of inverted-triangle torso the pro-proletarian artists like to put on their steelworkers," wrote Liebling. His record was 10–2, and his career was on the upswing.

At the bell, Clay glided across the ring like a ballet dancer, his high, white buckskin boots seeming to barely touch the canvas as he moved toward Banks, who fought out of a crouch, advancing toward Cassius like a crab with one pincer out front and the other close to its body. "Wrapped in certitude," Clay circled, jabbed, moved, and talked, nimbly avoiding Banks's slow maneuvers. For a minute or so it looked like a contest between a skillful matador and an awkward bull.

Then, for only a moment, the matador took his eyes off the bull and the fight took a sudden, dramatic turn. Forcing Banks into a corner, Cassius carelessly left himself open and Banks lashed out with a hard left hook. It was a solid punch, knocking him to the canvas for the first time in his professional career. In Clay's corner Dundee turned pale, as if he had just dropped an heirloom Ming vase.

At the count of two, Clay got up, appearing more embarrassed than hurt. At that moment, when it was most needed, he demonstrated his professionalism. He was cool. He didn't charge Banks in a fit of anger or back away from him. Instead he boxed smartly, "cuff, slap, jab, and stick, the busy hands stinging like bees," observed Liebling. It was Banks who became overly excited, throwing wild punches and receiving punishment for his efforts. By the end of the round he was spitting blood and was bone-tired from throwing and missing haymakers.

For the rest of the fight Clay was in complete control. His speed frustrated Banks, who fought defensively, "like a man trying to fight off wasps with a shovel." As Banks's legs tired, his face became his primary defensive weapon. Near the end of the second, Clay floored him with a

hard right hand. And in the third, Cassius continued the punishment, cutting Banks's eye so badly that the ring doctor had to examine it at the end of the round.

The physician permitted the fight to continue, but it did not last long. Clay had predicted he would end it in round four, and so he did. A quick flurry of punches staggered Banks, rendering him defenseless. That was enough to convince the referee to stop the contest. Afterward, Banks tried to explain what had happened: "Things just went sour gradually all at once. . . . You got to respect a boxer. He'll pick you and peck you, peck you and pick you, until you don't know where you are."[35]

Ringsiders had booed Cassius throughout the match, taking particular objection to his "hospital-white shoes," which they thought no self-respecting fighter would wear. And the sportswriters were more impressed by Clay's antics than his ability. "Cassius Marcellus Clay has the personality of a Roman candle and the potential to light up the drab skies of boxing," wrote Milton Gross, "but the brilliance of the young heavyweight's tongue still outstrips his talent."[36]

THE BANKS VICTORY earned Clay his first top-ten ranking. The National Boxing Association and *Boxing Illustrated* ranked him tenth, and *The Ring,* ninth. He still had not fought an active contender, but he had climbed into the elite group. Some sportswriters insisted that he belonged near the top, while others thought that he was a loudmouth fraud. But they all wrote about him. The combined strategies of Dundee and Clay had succeeded almost effortlessly.[37]

By spring 1962, Cassius Clay had become one of the leading draws in boxing. He fought only has-beens and never-has-beens, none ranked among the contenders, without taking substantial risks, and his reputation soared. His appeal was so great that promoters vied to put him in yet another sure-bet match. In Los Angeles, matchmaker Joe Louis arranged for Clay to headline a card of contenders.[38]

Louis selected George Logan, a battered veteran fighter from Idaho, to fight Cassius. In contrast to Clay's flawless face, which gave no hint of his profession, Logan's displayed grim souvenirs of his ring wars. He was a fighter, columnist Jim Murray wrote, whose "face makes him look like he wasn't born, he was knitted. . . . He has taken more punches than a time clock because he fights with the unorthodox style of a dart

board." Everyone involved in the fight understood that Logan was included because he moved ponderously, bled freely, and had no chance of harming Cassius's record or face.[39]

Cassius was the show. "I'm fighting the main event on Louis' first show," he said. "And what's the secret?" Stretching his mouth wide with his index fingers, he said, "Boca Grande."[40]

Fight night was a booming success for the promoters, but the actual contest was less spectacular. Clay made a royal entrance, accompanied by the house organist's rendition of "Pomp and Circumstance." Preening and mugging for the cameras, he actually looked more like popular singers Chubby Checker and Sam Cooke than a professional prizefighter. Jim Murray wrote, "The love of Cassius for Clay is so rapturous no girl could come between them. Marriage would be almost bigamy."[41]

Logan was less interested in aesthetics. He climbed into the ring with a large gob of Vaseline smeared over his eyebrows and had the look of a man being taken to the woodshed for a beating. Once the match began he gamely went to work, stolidly pursuing his elusive opponent. But he had no answer for Clay's speed. He could not get close enough to hit him or stay far enough away to avoid getting socked. "He had less protection than a guy facing a Castro firing squad," wrote Sid Ziff.[42]

By the end of the first round Logan's face looked like "raw hamburger," and by the end of the second spectators called for the referee to stop the slaughter. It was gruesome. Clay's punches sliced into the soft scar tissue above Logan's eyes like a hot knife into butter.

Blood ran down Logan's chest, stained his trunks, and soaked the canvas. His cut man worked feverishly between rounds to stop the flow, putting an astringent into the wound then smearing it with Vaseline, but the fix only lasted until Clay went back to work. Finally, midway through the fourth round, Logan's manager threw in the white towel of surrender. Logan protested the decision, not knowing how bad he looked. "It couldn't have been much worse if Clay had used knives," wrote a reporter. In his corner seconds later, Logan realized his condition and tried to hide his face while the ring doctor examined it.

"I'm trying to keep my pretty looks," Clay told writers in his dressing room. Then his mind flew away from the mundane present and landed in the fabulous future.

HE CONTINUED TO talk long after the fight had ended and most of the reporters had left to file their stories. He chatted about himself—his plans and his future. More interesting was what he wasn't talking about. Only days before a major racial conflict in Los Angeles, Clay had still said nothing about the civil rights movement or the plight of black Americans. Far from reflecting a lack of interest, he kept much of who he was hidden away from reporters, buried inside himself.

In April 1962, one could still only glean kernels of that hidden self. Publicly, he emphasized his Christian virtues. "I live by the Bible," he told *Los Angeles Times* reporter Paul Zimmerman. "My mother and father taught me to live right. 'No stealin', no cussin', no drinkin', no smokin',' the Bible says that he who reads the good book will understand to tell the truth."[43]

But other times he hinted that his religious beliefs were not exactly the ones he had learned in Louisville. Even when he was not in Miami, he pondered what he had learned at the mosque and in his conversations with Sam Saxon and the Black Muslim ministers. During several talks with reporters he addressed the subject of pork. Once at dinner during a long train ride, Clay witnessed sportswriter Myron Cope cut into a roast pork loin. Cassius shuddered: "Poke give me a headache. . . . Doctors tell me poke ninety percent live cell parasites. Poke ninety percent maggots. . . . You let that poke lay two days, it get up and crawl. The hawg is an unclean animal. Cat, rat, dog, hawg—add 'em up." It was the language not of his Baptist mother or his father but of Elijah Muhammad and Malcolm X.[44]

Chapter Four

IN COLD BLOOD

Because a man doesn't throw a punch doesn't mean he can't do so whenever he gets ready.

—MALCOLM X

When Cassius Clay answered the telephone one day in early June 1962, he had no idea that the call would change his life. It was Sam Saxon, calling to invite him and his brother Rudy to Detroit for a Black Muslim rally. Over the past year, Cassius had attended more Muslim meetings outside Miami, but he had not yet heard Elijah Muhammad preach in person. With more than five weeks until his next scheduled fight, Clay could afford to spend a weekend with Saxon. So Cassius eagerly accepted his invitation, and a few days later, Sam picked up the Clay brothers in Louisville and drove them to Detroit. There was someone very important Saxon wanted Cassius to meet.[1]

When they arrived on Sunday, June 10, they stopped at a luncheonette crowded with black patrons. Sitting at a back table where he could watch the front door, surrounded by Muslim officers and an assortment of supplicants, Malcolm X noticed Sam Saxon accompanied by two handsome, athletic men walking straight toward his table. Malcolm could see that they were anxious to meet him. One of the brothers, a confident young man with the face of a matinee idol, pumped the minister's hand and announced, "I'm Cassius Clay," which he assumed said it all.[2]

For more than two years Cassius had been repeating his name, usually adding that he was "the greatest" and "the prettiest fighter" who had

ever laced on a pair of gloves. When Malcolm met the Clay brothers, however, he did not realize that one of them was famous. He had not followed boxing, bet on matches, or read the sports page since he left prison. "Up to that moment . . . I had never heard of him," he said later. "Ours were two entirely different worlds." They spoke only briefly, as Malcolm had only a few minutes to finish preparing his opening remarks for the rally. But Clay had already made an impression on him. There was something about the young fighter—some "contagious quality . . . simply a likeable, friendly, clean-cut, down-to-earth" charm— that intrigued Malcolm. He did not know it yet, but he would soon understand that there was a place for Cassius Clay in his world.[3]

IN THE EARLY 1960s, as the civil rights movement intensified, so, too, did Malcolm's violent rhetoric. The Muslims, he claimed, lived by *lex talionis*. "We believed in a fair exchange," he said. "An eye for an eye. A tooth for a tooth. A head for a head and a life for a life. If this is the price of freedom, we won't hesitate to pay the price." When anyone questioned the Nation's willingness to retaliate, he replied that a Muslim was like a boxer in the ring with his fist cocked, just waiting for the right opening. He warned, "You might see these Negroes who believe in nonviolence and mistake us for one of them and put your hands on us thinking that we're going to turn the other cheek—and *we'll put you to death just like that*."[4]

The time had arrived for the Muslims to punch back. On April 27, 1962, about six weeks before Cassius Clay met Malcolm X, a melee broke out between police officers and members of the Nation's Los Angeles mosque. It all began when two black men standing behind the open trunk of a car were stopped by white policemen in a parking lot a few doors away from the mosque. As the officers frisked them, a crowd of angry Muslims gathered. In a matter of minutes, chaos erupted, shots were fired, and the Muslims retreated for safety. Squad cars of backup officers rushed to the scene. Policemen raided the mosque and randomly struck black men with nightsticks. The next morning, the *Los Angeles Times* announced in bold print: "'MUSLIMS' RIOT: Cultist Killed, Policeman Shot."[5]

When the gun smoke cleared, one Muslim—Ronald Stokes, the secretary of the mosque—was dead, another was paralyzed, and five others had been wounded. All but one of the policemen's bullets hit

the Muslims in their backs. The LAPD booked fourteen black men on suspicion of assault with intent to kill. The *Times* described "the blazing gunfight" like it was the shootout at the O.K. Corral. Beneath the newspaper headline was a picture of Stokes, handcuffed and lying facedown in a pool of blood.[6]

When Malcolm heard the news, he wept for Stokes, whom he had known since 1960. Enraged, he swiftly buried his sadness and prepared for revenge. In Harlem, he confided to his assistant ministers that he planned to organize vigilantes. But Elijah Muhammad ordered him to stand down. "Brother, you don't go to war over a provocation," he told him. "They could kill a few of my followers but I'm not going to go out and do something silly." Muhammad sent Raymond Sharrieff to Los Angeles, where the Supreme Captain of the Fruit ensured that there was no coordinated retaliation.[7]

Without authorization to retaliate, Malcolm instead escalated his rhetoric. On May 4, a week after the shooting, Malcolm held a press conference in Los Angeles at the Statler Hilton Hotel and accused the police of murdering Stokes. "Seven innocent unarmed black men were shot down in *cold blood* by Police Chief William Parker's Los Angeles City Police," he charged. He thought that Parker, who sometimes pronounced *Negroes* as "Niggras," was guilty of "filling his own men with hatred of the black community" and spreading lies about the Muslims. In Los Angeles, Malcolm argued, blacks lived under a "police state," just like the "Jews in Nazi Germany."[8]

The following morning, Malcolm conducted Stokes's funeral at the two-story mosque, where more than two thousand blacks packed the old stucco lodging hall. Although white journalists were barred from entering the building, black reporters told the *Los Angeles Times* that the minister delivered a moving tribute for the Muslims' "fallen warrior." Outside the mosque, hundreds of mourners lined both sides of Broadway, watching the pallbearers carry Stokes's body in a gray casket. Some men bitterly complained about Elijah Muhammad's warning against revenge. Others were so angry that they renounced Muhammad and left the Los Angeles mosque all together. If the black man was ever going to be truly free, they declared, he had to defend himself.[9]

Standing near the hearse, a tall, lean black man with a shaved head, dressed in a dark suit, faced a photographer from the *Times*. Fixing his

gaze on the camera, he struck a militant pose, raising his fist in what would later become known as a Black Power salute. His clenched fist signified defiance, assertiveness, and liberation. The *Times* didn't identify the man by name, but in his silent rage for justice, his gesture spoke eloquently about a burgeoning movement that had no name.

Muhammad sent word that the Muslims should head out into the street and "begin the war with the devil." But it was not the kind of war his followers expected. They would fight the white man by exposing his crimes, letting the world know that he was the devil by selling newspapers.[10]

Selling newspapers? The men could not believe what they had just heard. What were they going to do with newspapers? Roll them up and swat armed policemen like flies? Edward 2X Sherrill, the captain of the mosque, exhorted, "I want all of you brothers to take at least fifty newspapers! Be sure you pay for them right now at the door."[11]

Malcolm shared the brothers' frustration with Muhammad's passivity. He was even more outraged when an all-white coroner's jury took less than thirty minutes to acquit the LAPD of killing an unarmed black man, claiming his death was "justifiable homicide under lawful performance of duty and in self defense." The police shooting radicalized the black community, galvanizing the movement toward greater militancy and confrontation.[12]

The Stokes case further elevated Malcolm into a national political figure. He began thinking of himself as a leader, a grassroots organizer, and a voice for the masses. He spoke less and less about Muhammad's religious teachings and more about politics and current events. Most importantly, the murder made him reconsider the Nation's role in the larger struggle. Calling for wider racial unity that transcended religion and ideology, he urged blacks to "come together against the common enemy."[13]

The events in Los Angeles deepened Malcolm's internal conflict within the Nation. When Muhammad heard that Malcolm had called for greater cooperation with civil rights groups, he demanded that his minister return home. "Brother, stay where I put you because [the civil rights organizations] have no place to go," he said. Muhammad did not want him leading demonstrations, agitating authorities, or arousing greater attention from the FBI. The risk was too great. Malcolm was the

Nation's most prized asset, and Muhammad could not afford for him to go to jail or get himself killed. The Supreme Minister instructed him to "play dead on everything." *That* was an order.[14]

Malcolm seethed. He felt like a tiger on a leash, reduced to nothing more than an empty roar. His critics complained that he sure talked a good game, but he never *did* anything. In Harlem, people saw him standing across the street from picketers, distancing himself from demonstrations. Sometimes he showed up at civil rights meetings, slouching in the back of the room with his hat pulled low.[15]

Elijah's passive response to the assault on the Los Angeles mosque was an embarrassment. For years, he had been telling his followers that if they were attacked, they must be willing to sacrifice their lives in the name of Allah. Every mosque had captains, lieutenants, and soldiers in the Fruit, preparing for the Battle of Armageddon. Now Muhammad ordered retreat just as the battle was about to begin. "The Messenger," Malcolm bitterly complained to his assistant ministers, "should have done more. People in the civil rights movement have been brutalized, and we haven't done anything to help them. Now we have our own brothers killed and maimed, and we *still* haven't done anything."[16]

FBI agents listening in on Muhammad's phone calls learned that he had become alarmed about his young minister's restlessness. He worried that there was no one who could "control Malcolm," not even the Messenger himself. During a phone call Elijah warned Malcolm, just before he hung up, "I hope Allah will keep you wise."[17]

ON APRIL 26, 1962, the FBI's Chicago office sent a report to J. Edgar Hoover offering valuable information that could be "used to discredit Elijah Muhammad with his followers." Informants divulged that Muhammad had engaged in extramarital affairs with women who belonged to the Nation. Of those, at least seven mistresses, most of them former secretaries, claimed that the Messenger had fathered their children.[18]

Muhammad's harem was the worst-kept secret inside the Nation. Over the past year, the FBI had collected sensitive information about his affairs. Agents noted that Muhammad had strict rules about adultery, forbidding married men from "taking up time with other sisters." A Muslim man accused of fornicating outside his marriage risked facing not only a trial before the Fruit but also complete banishment from

the Nation. Brothers were supposed to respect Muslim women, glorify them, and guard their purity with their lives.[19]

Although Muhammad claimed that Muslim women should be elevated on pedestals, they were also instructed to show absolute obedience to their husbands. Women were segregated from men during rallies and taught domestic skills in comprehensive courses, where they learned about cooking, sewing, and raising children. They were prohibited from wearing cosmetics, short skirts, or pants. Nor did women conduct religious services, organize meetings, or make decisions about the family. If a woman questioned her male partner in any way, she could receive a hard slap across the face.[20]

In some cases, Muhammad made his lovers endure farcical trials, charging them with immorality for bearing children out of wedlock and violating the Nation's moral code. In other instances, he lavished his mistresses with gifts using money donated from the Nation's followers. He promised some of his young paramours that they would raise a family together. But most often those promises went unfulfilled, and bitter women threatened to expose his lies. Some even showed up at his Chicago doorstep, ringing the bell and leaving their babies on the stoop.[21]

The FBI realized that if Muhammad's followers learned about his affairs, the hypocrisy could lead to the downfall of the Nation. The Bureau's agents recommended using "carefully selected informants" who would plant "the seeds of dissension through anonymous letters and/or telephone calls." Specifically, they suggested mailing letters to his wife, Clara, even though she already knew all about his trysts.[22]

So did Malcolm X. Since 1955, he had heard whispers about Muhammad's infidelities. Initially, he discounted them as unsubstantiated gossip, denying any possibility that the Messenger of Allah—his personal savior—would ever betray him and his followers. But the rumors persisted. He heard them everywhere he went, from New York to Chicago. By 1962, increasing numbers of Muslims began abandoning the Nation, forcing him to finally admit what he had suspected for years.[23]

In his solitude, Malcolm's mind drifted to the image of Muhammad groping young women. Some nights he couldn't sleep. Other nights he woke up damp with perspiration, panicked that the world would soon know Muhammad's secret. Scandalous headlines jumped at him in his dreams. At some point, he feared, an investigative journalist would stick

a microphone in his face and ask him, "Is it true, Mr. Malcolm X, this report we hear, that . . ." How would he answer the question? How could he come to terms with the idea that the man he had built up as a moral paragon was actually a fraud?"[24]

"I believed he was divine, divinely taught and divinely guided," Malcolm later admitted. "And it was only when Elijah Muhammad—ah—something in his personal life—he found himself confronted with a moral question which he could not face up to as a man. And his failure to face up to that as a man made me begin to doubt him, not only as someone divine—divinely guided—but it made me doubt him as a man. And in the face of that, I began to analyze everything else he taught."[25]

Malcolm was not the only one concerned about the Nation's future. Inside the Chicago headquarters, Muhammad's closest aides worried that his bronchial asthma and other ailments portended a leadership change. With Muhammad spending most of the year in Phoenix and his son Wallace serving prison time for draft evasion, Raymond Sharrieff, John Ali, and Muhammad's sons Herbert, Akbar, and Elijah Jr. expanded their influence over the sect. The junta enjoyed their growing power and the benefits that came with it.[26]

They lived an extravagant lifestyle while Muhammad's mostly poor followers struggled to survive and pay a weekly duty of three dollars and thirty cents. In some mosques, the Fruit demanded even higher tithes. Destitute blacks were urged to buy multiple copies of *Muhammad Speaks*, frequent the Nation's businesses, and drop donations into collection plates during mass meetings. FBI informants noted that Muhammad's followers were "continually harassed by NOI officials for greater and greater contributions." Muhammad instructed his closest advisers "to purchase expensive cars and homes for him; to provide him with bodyguards and servants; and to give him other manifestations of affluence." He even referred to the Nation's relief funds as "my checking account."[27]

In some ways, Elijah stoked his advisers' fears that Malcolm might reduce their influence in the Nation. In February 1962, at the annual Saviours' Day rally in Chicago, he openly referred to Malcolm as his "heir apparent" and "chief aide." He also gave Malcolm the authority to resolve conflicts between members of different mosques. When

Muhammad ordained him supreme authority by proxy, he gave Malcolm power that no other minister enjoyed, provoking deeper jealousies among his rivals.[28]

Malcolm's enemies charged him with avarice, a baseless accusation. Although he had access to the Nation's treasury, he and Betty, his wife of four years, lived on a strict budget, owning virtually nothing, not even the house they lived in. When he traveled, rather than pay for a taxi ride to and from the airport, he asked fellow Muslims to give him a ride. He avoided expensive restaurants, collected receipts for every expense, and kept meticulous records of his purchases. Whenever he received money for campus lectures, he made sure that the checks were always written out to the NOI and not himself. In his ascetic lifestyle, Malcolm completely rejected his old life as Detroit Red.[29]

Although his austerity made him a more appealing political figure to the black masses, his adversaries resented his puritanical beliefs. With the Nation's businesses thriving, Muhammad's cabinet feared that if he died and Malcolm replaced him, then Malcolm might terminate the spoils system. Benjamin 2X recalled, "There was a lot of money floating around and a lot of people were spending money in areas where it shouldn't have been spent, and Malcolm spoke out against it. And they knew that if Mr. Muhammad had passed on, they would not have their positions anymore, because they were the first people that Malcolm would have gotten rid of."[30]

Malcolm had no aspirations of becoming the Supreme Minister. Uninterested in managing the national affairs of the Muslims or arbitrating disputes between Muhammad's children, he was far more concerned with the direction of the struggle for black freedom. The more he talked about confronting the white man, the more agitated his rivals in Chicago became. But after the Stokes murder, Malcolm no longer cared. He was on a mission, and now he would have to enlist foot soldiers of his own.

IF MUHAMMAD WISHED that Malcolm would avoid further controversy, his hopes were soon dashed. At a rally in Harlem on Saturday, May 26, he disobeyed Elijah Muhammad's order to stand down and suggested that Harlem's civil rights leaders coordinate a coalition against police brutality. On June 6, at a press conference, pressure intensified when

Los Angeles mayor Sam Yorty played a police informant's recording of Malcolm speaking at a Muslim gathering. Referring to a plane crash in Paris that killed white passengers traveling from Atlanta, he declared, "I would like to announce a very beautiful thing that has happened. As you know, we have been praying to Allah. We have been praying that He would in some way let us know that he has the power to execute justice upon the heads of those who are responsible for the lynching of Ronald Stokes on April 27. And I got a wire from God today," he said over a chorus of laughter. "Wait! All right! Well somebody came and told me that he answered our prayers over in France. He dropped an airplane out of the sky with over a hundred and twenty white people on it." Since the Stokes case, he said, many blacks had asked him what the Muslims were going to do. "We call on our God," he answered. "He gets rid of one hundred and twenty of them in one whop . . . and we hope that every day another plane falls out of the sky," he said as the crowd roared with applause.[31]

Malcolm's comments shocked Americans, crystalizing his image as a demagogue who preached hatred. Immediately, civil rights leaders condemned him. In Atlanta, Martin Luther King canceled sit-ins against segregated restaurants and lunch counters out of respect for the city's mourners. "That's my home town," he said. "I knew many of the people who were killed. Many of them believed in progress." When he was asked about Malcolm's comments, he answered, "If the Muslim leader said that, I would certainly disagree with him. Black supremacy is as dangerous as white supremacy."[32]

Facing a firestorm of criticism, Malcolm traveled to Detroit, where Elijah Muhammad was scheduled to deliver a major address at Olympia Stadium on June 10. The "Old Red Barn," as it was known in Motown, was a three-story, Romanesque arena with arched windows, built of steel, brown terracotta, and red brick. By noon, busloads of blacks had congregated outside the stadium at the corner of Grand River Avenue and McGraw Street. Uniformed police officers directed the traffic while several thousand people braved the wind and rain.

Shortly before two o'clock, when the rally was scheduled to begin, Cassius, Rudy, and Sam headed over to the stadium. In the crowded lobby, hundreds of earnest security guards patted down everyone who entered the building. Even Detroit's police commissioner submitted to

a body search. After the Clay brothers passed inspection, the FOI corps, communicating by walkie-talkie, ushered them into a long line of men who were escorted to their seats on the right side of the floor. Cassius had never seen such a spectacle of dignified-looking black people, all the men wearing dark suits and all the women, seated on the left, dressed in immaculate white gowns and shawls. Reporters and cameramen covering the event sat in the very front rows, near the curious blacks who were not members of the Nation.[33]

Cassius stretched his neck as he watched an honor guard escort Elijah Muhammad, Malcolm, and other officials onto the speaker's platform. Standing amid the awestruck silence, he felt the crowd's reverence for the Messenger. After exchanging the traditional greetings, *As-Salaam-Alaikum* and *Wa-Alaikum-Salaam*, Malcolm delivered his opening remarks and defended the Nation's doctrine. "We are not a sect or a cult, nor are we a hate group," he asserted. "We are a group of people who have accepted the Islamic faith and believe that Allah is the Supreme Being."[34]

When Malcolm finished, Muhammad, the featured speaker, rose from his large chair, like a royal descending from his throne, and walked over to the lectern. Cassius listened attentively as the slight man with a receding hairline forcefully asserted that the "so-called Negro" had been enslaved for more than four hundred years, echoing what Clay had heard at the Miami mosque. "That is a long time for a master to mistreat you," he said. For two hours, Muhammad zealously preached while Cassius and Rudy sat well back in the crowded arena, "practically leading the applause."[35]

Flanked by twenty to thirty members of the Fruit, Muhammad declared, "The time to rise is now." It was time for black men to renounce the "games of white men," he urged, time to abandon the struggle for integration and turn inward, looking to Allah's Messenger for salvation. Muhammad condemned the Los Angeles police for murdering Ronald Stokes and reminded his parents, the honored guests, that their son did not die in vain. The white man's day of judgment, he promised, would come before long.[36]

Muhammad demanded a separate state where blacks could live independently from whites. Malcolm sat just a few feet away from him,

nodding with approval as he listened. "We must remember that we are two different people and we must be separate. That is the only way out."[37]

The message Clay heard that day jived with what he had learned from his father—keep your distance from white men; they will never treat a black man fairly. It reinforced what he had read in newspapers and magazines and seen on television—images of the mutilated body of Emmett Till, the bombing of Martin Luther King's Montgomery home, and a white mob assaulting black teenagers outside a Little Rock high school.

That day in Detroit changed Clay's life. There was something about Malcolm—his swagger, the dazzle in his smile, the way that everyone in the diner watched him—that alerted Cassius that the brother minister, who, in the words of activist Dick Gregory, "spoke like a poor man and walked like a king," possessed an unbridled confidence and an audacity to speak his mind in a way that no else did.[38]

"My first impression of Malcolm X was how could a black man talk about the government and white people and act so bold and not be shot at? How could he say these things? Only God must be protecting him," Clay said later. Malcolm was unlike anyone he had ever met. "He was fearless. That really attracted me."[39]

Malcolm had magnetized Clay, drawing him toward the inner circle of the Nation. He had no idea the effect he had on the young boxer that day in Detroit, but he would soon see him again.

AT THE END of the rally, after Clay departed Olympia Stadium, all members of the NOI were required to remain seated. Malcolm read a letter from Supreme Captain Raymond Sharrieff requiring "every Muslim to obtain no less than two subscriptions" of *Muhammad Speaks* "per day for three months." Those who failed to meet the sales quota "would be eliminated from the Mosque."[40]

Since Stokes's death, the captains of every mosque had pressed their members to sell more copies of the newspaper. *Muhammad Speaks* not only offered the Nation an independent platform but also, more importantly, generated significant revenue for the organization. After the Stokes murder, instead of printing the newspaper on a monthly basis, Chicago officials began publishing the periodical biweekly. Supposedly,

the issue that covered his funeral sold more than four hundred thousand copies, a misleading figure since an unknown number of copies belonged to members who were forced to purchase stacks of the newspaper in cash but never actually sold them to others.[41]

On Sunday, July 29, at two p.m., Malcolm attended a fund-raising benefit for Stokes's family at the Boston Arena. In the hours before the rally, Muslims stood on the corners of St. Botolph Street and Massachusetts Avenue, selling a special reprint edition of *Muhammad Speaks* featuring gruesome pictures of Stokes that resembled the images of Emmett Till's disfigured face in *Jet* magazine. An autopsy photo displayed Stokes lying on his back, his bare chest exposed with deep stitches and his skull lacerated and bruised from policemen's nightsticks. Inside the tabloid were pictures of black men tethered to trees and hanging from nooses. In an open letter to five black congressmen, Malcolm argued that Stokes was as innocent as "Mack Parker, Emmett Till, or Isaac Woodard," all victims of southern lynchings.[42]

Despite the propaganda value of the Stokes murder, Muslim men in Boston resented the sales quotas, which were imposed under the guise of raising money for Stokes's family. His cousin, Aubrey Barnette, would later claim that Ronald's wife and baby never received a dime from the Muslims' national or local treasuries. The Nation, he charged, was nothing more than a "money-grabbing scheme feeding on the frustrations and the ignorance of Negroes." When Muhammad's followers failed to bring in money, his lieutenants resorted "to terror, violence, and extortion."[43]

As a secretary of the mosque, Barnette witnessed how Captain Clarence X and "his terror squad" intimidated Boston Muslims into buying more copies of *Muhammad Speaks* than they could sell. If Captain Clarence and his lieutenants could not collect money from the men, they took them for a ride to Franklin Park and taught them a painful lesson about financial obligations. When more than forty men quit the mosque, Elijah Muhammad Jr., Assistant Supreme Captain of the Fruit, visited Boston, reminding the faithful that "in the old days recalcitrant brothers were killed." "And," he warned, "the Messenger fulfills all."[44]

Disillusioned with the Nation, Barnette left the mosque nearly two years later. But no Muslim ever really left the Nation. Captain Clarence made sure of that. One afternoon, when Barnette and another former

Muslim drove past the mosque in Roxbury, a pink Cadillac cut them off. In broad daylight, Clarence and his squad dragged Barnette from the car, punching and stomping on him, fracturing his ankle, ribs, and vertebrae. "I believe," he said later, "we were beaten as punishment for quitting and also as a warning to us to keep our mouths shut."[45]

The fratricidal violence within the Nation usually occurred out of sight, far removed from anything Cassius Clay ever saw in the mosques that he visited. But tales of attacks against obstinate blacks terrified Muhammad's followers. Although he refused to let the Fruit retaliate against whites, Muhammad approved corporal punishment against his own people. Such abuse alienated many members. In Harlem, a street corner speaker complained to Louis Lomax, "Those damn Muslims are too scared to do anything to the white man; all they do is talk and beat up on other niggers!"[46]

IN MID-AUGUST, after Elijah Muhammad delivered a sermon to a disappointingly small crowd in St. Louis, he attempted to tighten his hold on Malcolm. In a private meeting, Elijah told the increasingly disobedient minister that he disapproved of the way that he deviated from his message, talking publicly about politics and civil rights. In the following months, Muhammad reminded him not to make any more appearances on college campuses without receiving his permission. Before agreeing to let Malcolm speak anywhere, Muhammad wanted to "know exactly how" he would "carry out such a program in advance."[47]

For a time, Malcolm decided that he should avoid the spotlight. He declined cover story requests from *Life* and *Newsweek* and turned down a television interview on *Meet the Press*. He also noticed that his name and picture disappeared from the pages of *Muhammad Speaks* after Herbert Muhammad replaced him as editor.[48]

Elijah resented all the attention focused on Malcolm, even though he had made him the Nation's spokesman. He especially disliked the way that people lionized Malcolm for his intellectual superiority and rhetorical eloquence. Muhammad's insecurities festered, fueling his paranoia over comparisons to the younger man, who claimed that he had learned everything from Elijah. But unlike Malcolm, Muhammad made grammatical errors in his speeches and stumbled over words he did not recognize. Lacking any formal education beyond the fourth

grade, he struggled while reading aloud. His sermons rarely impressed or excited audiences the way that Malcolm's did. "To be able to listen to Muhammad for any length of time," one observer commented, "you had to be a believer, convinced in advance."[49]

Muhammad worried that the controversies surrounding Malcolm's public appearances would invite closer scrutiny from the government. On August 15, three days after the St. Louis rally, Congressman Francis E. Walter, chairman of the House Un-American Activities Committee (HUAC), condemned the Black Muslims as a subversive group influenced by communists and announced that an investigation would begin soon.[50]

When he heard about the HUAC probe, Muhammad became agitated. Although the Muslims were ardent anticommunists, the government suspected that a tinge of red ran through their teachings. It did not help that two years earlier, in Harlem, Malcolm had met with Cuban revolutionary Fidel Castro without Elijah's approval. Castro had been in New York to condemn the United States before the United Nations. At the time Muhammad had suspected that the meeting would come back to haunt him. But Malcolm maintained, "We will welcome any investigation, we have nothing to hide."[51]

Malcolm may have believed that he had nothing to hide, but Cassius Clay did. A month after HUAC announced that it would investigate the Nation, the heavyweight contender appeared in a photograph at the bottom of a page in the September 15 issue of *Muhammad Speaks*. Dressed in a dark suit, white shirt, and bow tie, Clay seemed completely comfortable smiling for the camera, as if someone were snapping a picture of him and his brother at a family reunion rather than at a Muslim rally in St. Louis. No one interviewed him for *Muhammad Speaks*, as athletes received little coverage in the paper. He was not yet considered an important figure in the Muslims' national agenda, but for the second time in two months he traveled a great distance to hear Elijah Muhammad and to spend more time with Malcolm.[52]

Clay's fascination with the Nation evolved alongside his growing notoriety as a boxer. At a time when the government planned an extensive, if unwarranted, investigation into the organization, Clay risked his boxing career by associating with the Nation. Remarkably, the blacks

who saw him in Detroit and St. Louis never shared that information with reporters. If a black writer recognized him at one of the rallies or noticed his picture in *Muhammad Speaks*, or a white writer caught wind of him shaking hands with Malcolm X, it could have ended his career.

Chapter Five

THE WINTER OF BOXING

The boxing game was slowly dying
And fight promoters were bitterly crying
For someone somewhere to come along
For a better and different song.

Patterson was dull, quiet and sad
And Sonny Liston was just as bad
Along came a kid named Cassius Clay
Who said, "I'll take Liston's title away."

—CASSIUS CLAY, *EBONY*, MARCH 1963

Cassius Clay's involvement with the Nation was not the only threat to his career. Prizefighting was in a sorry state and was dying in New York. By 1962, everything wrong with the sport—from its endemic mismatches and ring fatalities to its shady characters and fixed fights—was magnified in Gotham. There had been a time when millions of Americans followed the big New York fights of Joe Louis and Rocky Marciano and reporters trumpeted the results on front-page headlines. Now the coverage of boxing had spilled over into the crime pages. The *New York Times*, as well as such national publications as *Sports Illustrated* and *Time*, featured the illegal antics of promoters, managers, and fighters. To make matters worse, Sonny Liston, the most dynamic heavyweight of the early 1960s, had a past so nefarious that he was barred from fighting in the Empire State. Always the bellwether for the sport, the New York fight game pealed as mournfully as a death knell. Boxing needed a heavyweight savior, and no contender was rising more quickly or loudly than the undefeated Louisville Lip.

Liston's face was broad, flat, and impassive, his eyes cold and threatening. Just his look was enough to win most confrontations. But his face suggested something even more sinister. Getty Images

The question was whether he could ascend fast enough to reverse the rapid descent of the sport.

Less than a month after disposing of George Logan in Los Angeles in April 1962, Clay was back in New York for another test. Matched against Billy Daniels, a former Air Force boxer who was 10–0 as a professional, the publicist promoted the contest as a fight between the two finest young heavyweights in America. But Cassius promised to finish him in the fifth round, telling reporters, "I would be embarrassed if he lasted any more."[1]

The match was a disappointment. Only 1,642 spectators attended the bout at New York's historic St. Nicholas Arena, and neither boxer lived up to their hype. Daniels came out in the first and hit Clay with a powerful left-right combination. As the customers "cheered lustily," Cassius "tottered and blinked his eyes," then "went on his bicycle" in an effort to avoid further damage. In the second and third rounds, Clay came back. He bloodied Daniels's nose in the second and cut his right eyebrow in the third. It was a deep, ugly gash, and Daniels's cut man could not effectively stop the bleeding. In the fourth Clay went to work

on the eye, and by the seventh the blood was hampering Daniels's vision. At that point, the referee stopped the fight.[2]

The Daniels contest may have been a slip for Clay, but it was no knockdown. He had won, and his undefeated record stood fast. All he needed to continue his ascent was a convincing victory over a contender. With his keen sense for fighters just beginning their decline, Angelo Dundee accepted an offer against Alejandro Lavorante in Los Angeles.

In November 1961, Lavorante, bare-chested, his fists up in a fighter's pose, appeared on the cover of *The Ring*. In the accompanying feature story, Nat Fleischer made him seem like the future of the division. Pinky George, his American manager, asserted that the twenty-five-year-old was ready to fight anyone. "This is the year of the astronaut," he told the magazine's editor. "Everyone is shooting for the moon. We're doing the same."[3]

It wasn't all hyperbole. Lavorante knocked out highly rated Zora Folley and became a ranked contender. But he fought too often and was brought along too fast. On March 30, 1962, former light-heavyweight champion Archie Moore gave Lavorante a cruel boxing lesson. Struggling to compete, swallowing too much of his own blood, the Argentine boxer absorbed a frightful beating. After the referee stopped the bout in the tenth round, Lavorante slumped to the ropes and had to be taken to his dressing room on a stretcher.[4]

Less than four months after the defeat, Lavorante was back in the ring against a younger, stronger, better-conditioned boxer than ancient Archie Moore. He was at a crossroads. A loss to Clay would be more significant, indicating that his career was sinking, and boxing insiders recognized it. "When two fighters are on the way up, they avoid each other as scrupulously as two women wearing the same dress at a party," wrote Jim Murray. Before the Moore fight, Angelo Dundee would have never matched Cassius against Lavorante. But Archie had exposed him, and it was clear to Dundee that "the tango was over" for the Argentine.[5]

Clay dominated the bout from the opening bell. He staggered Lavorante in the second, opened a cut over his left eye in the fourth, and knocked him down twice in the fifth. Sprawled wide-legged on the canvas after the second knockdown, the Argentine took a full ten count.[6]

Lavorante rose slowly but recovered before heading back to the dressing room. His manager was grim. A few days before the contest, Pinky George had commented that the fight was critical to his boxer's future. "It's back to the minors if we lose," he predicted.[7]

Two months after losing to Clay he fought Johnny Riggins, a preliminary boxer who had lost seven of his previous nine matches. In the sixth round Riggins landed a series of punches, the final one a vicious uppercut that twisted Lavorante's brain stem, causing threadlike veins to hemorrhage. His head swiveled violently and his eyes rolled to the tops of the sockets. He did not so much fall as crumble, finally coming to rest in an awkward sitting position against the lower rope, his head dropping in a sleeping position toward his chest and his arms falling lifeless into his lap.[8]

An ambulance rushed Lavorante to California Lutheran Hospital, and a surgeon operated immediately to remove blood clots and relieve pressure on his brain. But the fighter never recovered. He sank into a coma, and on April Fool's Day 1964, nineteen months after his last boxing match, he died. He had arrived in America just over four years before. An overly ambitious manager had filled his head with dreams of shooting for the moon, but in the ring, Alejandro Lavorante was like "a child playing in traffic, a blind man heading for a cliff." And rather than intervening, "people PAID to see it."[9]

THE FATE OF Alejandro Lavorante epitomized the state of boxing in the late 1950s and early 1960s. In the years between the emergence of Joe Louis in 1935 and the retirement of Rocky Marciano in 1956, the sport luxuriated in a golden age of great fighters and matches, enormous attention and popularity, and million-dollar gates. When World War II ended, television, just in its infancy, fell in love with pugilism, and by the mid-1950s a fight was being broadcast virtually every night of the week. As comedian Red Skelton quipped, "The Monday fight, scheduled for Tuesday this Wednesday, has been postponed till Thursday and rescheduled for Friday this Saturday because Sunday's a holiday."[10]

Then, with an unimaginable speed, it ended. The great fighters retired or, worse, kept fighting after their skills had eroded. Television's romance with the sport resulted in a series of financially rocky divorces. Louis and Marciano were replaced by lesser men who were only willing

to risk their titles against still-lesser boxers. Even worse, a series of exposés and criminal investigations revealed boxing's hideous underbelly of violent mobsters, fixed fights, heartless exploitation, and battered fighters.

The problems of the sport were years in the making, but they crystallized before a national television audience in Madison Square Garden on the night of Saturday, March 24, 1962. That evening, ABC's *The Fight of the Week* pitted Cuban Benny "the Kid" Paret against Virgin Islander Emile Griffith for the welterweight championship. The two had battled for the title twice before, Griffith winning the first in a knockout and Paret taking the second in a close decision. There was also bad blood between them. At the morning weigh-in, when Griffith stripped to his underwear and stepped on the scale, the Spanish-speaking Paret moved in close and grabbed Griffith's ass, whispering, "Hey *maricón* [faggot], I'm going to get you *and* your husband."[11]

That word—*maricón*, which Gilbert Rogin of *Sports Illustrated* called "the most vulgar epithet in that violent idiom"—and the touch enraged Griffith. His high-pitched voice, tight clothes, and former career as a hat designer had started rumors that he was gay. He jerked away from Paret's touch, telling him to "shut up" and to keep his hands off him or he would fight him then and there.

In the early rounds, the fight was close, but by the twelfth Griffith staggered Paret with several devastating blows. The next seconds were unquestionably the most violent in recorded boxing history. Punching "faster than most observers could count," as Robert L. Teague of the *New York Times* wrote, Griffith whaled on Paret, landing punch after punch with deadly force. He connected six or seven times with right uppercuts to the point of the chin, and then landed more lefts and rights to Paret's face and temples. In just a matter of seconds, Teague thought that Griffith landed twenty-five unanswered punches. It might have been more, but the exact number hardly mattered. Paret was unconscious, entangled in the corner ropes, well before referee Ruby Goldstein stepped between the two boxers.[12]

As Goldstein pulled Griffith away from Paret, the Cuban slowly slid from the corner ropes to the canvas. Ringside observer Norman Mailer later wrote that he sensed death in the air as Paret gave an unconscious half-smile and then fell "more slowly than any fighter had ever gone

down, he went down like a large ship which turns on its end and slides second by second into its grave."[13]

The bout ended, and the ring swarmed with activity. The senior ringside physician called for a stretcher while TV announcer Don Dunphy scrambled into the ring to get a statement from Emile. After saying how happy he was to regain the title, Griffith added, "I hope Paret is feeling very good." Ignoring the chaos in the ring, Dunphy decided that the time was right to unveil ABC's newly developed slow-motion replay system. In nightmarish slow motion, with Emile narrating his brutal beating of Benny, the last conscious seconds of Paret's life were replayed, the man who beat him to death providing the color. All Griffith could do was describe inarticulately how he had killed his opponent.[14]

On April 3, ten days after the fight, Paret died without ever regaining consciousness. His death introduced a new vocabulary into the sport. Phrases like "traumatic brain injury" and "subdural hemorrhage" and "edema" sounded like a foreign language to boxing fans but reflected the sweet science's new reality.[15]

The horrible end of the Griffith-Paret fight had both immediate and longer-range consequences. While Paret was still in a coma, journalists and politicians began debating the future of a sport "where the object is to knock an opponent loose from his senses." In the days after the match, politicians demanded that New York governor Nelson Rockefeller do something—form a commission, ban the sport, or at least speak out against it. Ultimately, the state legislature formed a committee to investigate whether prizefighting should be abolished altogether.[16]

Paret died two years before *The Fight of the Week* did, but only because of existing contracts between the network and the sponsors. His death prompted industry executives to reexamine its relationship with the sport. In fact, boxing's television ratings had been declining for years, down from about a third of the available audience to a tenth. One by one, the national weekly shows that had appeared in the 1940s and 1950s went off the air by 1962. All that remained was *The Fight of the Week,* which ABC aired from 1960 to 1964.[17]

The combination of ring deaths, criminal influence, public opposition, and declining ratings made ABC reconsider the renewal of their contract with the Gillette Safety Razor Company, which began sponsoring the show after NBC canceled *The Gillette Cavalcade of Sports* in

1960. The fact that the demographics of boxing were all wrong—that is, its audience was not only dwindling but also generally poorer and older—was as devastating as Griffith's punches. Increasingly, TV executives demanded shows that appealed to the youth market—ranging from *The Addams Family* and *Bewitched* to *Shindig* and *Hullabaloo* to *The Many Loves of Dobie Gillis* and *Peyton Place*—not programs where men were battered bloody and killed. Boxing's core audience of World War II and Korean War veterans, from ethnic, working-class backgrounds, with limited education and disposable incomes, were proving a poor fit for the age of John Kennedy, John Glenn, and the Beach Boys.[18]

Two days before Christmas in 1963, ABC announced that it planned to cancel *The Fight of the Week* when its new season began. The program, which had begun less than four months after the D-Day invasion, ended on September 11, 1964. Harry Markson, director of boxing for Madison Square Garden, predicted that the end of the long-running show would not be fatal to boxing—in fact, he foresaw the very opposite. But his tone sounded off-key. Most critics thought that the cancellation of *The Fight of the Week* was another portent of the slow death of the sport.[19]

WITH BOXING ON its deathbed, Cassius Clay sensed an opportunity. He understood that there was truth in the old axiom: the health of boxing follows the popularity of the heavyweight champion. What the sport needed, he calculated, was a dynamic, entertaining titleholder. In his view, Floyd Patterson and Sonny Liston, the top two heavyweights, were incapable of saving the sport. Only he could remedy boxing's ills.

At the beginning of 1962, Patterson held the title, which he had won in 1956 after Marciano retired, lost in 1959 when he was knocked out by Swedish Ingemar Johansson, and regained in 1960 when he in turn knocked out Johansson. Floyd was a good, compassionate, complex man in a profession normally dominated by men with other attributes, and the crown of Dempsey, Louis, and Marciano was an uncomfortable fit for him, a fact not lost on Clay. Cassius thought that boxing needed a champion who was great, not one who ran from challengers and lost to Scandinavians.

Patterson grew up in poverty in Bedford-Stuyvesant, Brooklyn. As an adult, he was so timid, shy, and withdrawn that even when he became a

successful professional prizefighter, he could not look his opponents in the eyes before a fight. After one match he gently kissed the man he had just knocked out.

Sportswriters accused him of gross pugilistic malfeasance—that is, as a champion he had not defended his title against the best contenders. Most of his defenses were against mid-ranked, smaller heavyweights with overblown records, who, perhaps not coincidentally, were white. He consistently avoided top-rated heavyweights. And he steered widely clear of Sonny Liston, generally recognized between 1960 and 1962 as the top contender in the division. Unlike Patterson, Liston *had* fought and defeated virtually every other major contender.

Sonny, whose nickname seemed singularly inappropriate, had a past, and much of it was bad. The first murky fact about his life was his exact age. When he needed a date of birth on an application to fight in the 1953 Golden Gloves tournament, he gave May 8, 1932. His mother told one reporter that she thought it was January 8, 1932, and another, January 18, 1932. But those dates only set the upper range for the speculations that included 1931, 1930, and back into the 1920s.

Over time, Sonny developed an effective tactic for shutting down questions about his birthdate. When a scribe probed the subject, Liston would throw him a glance as cold as a gravestone at midnight and say, "Anyone who says [I wasn't born in 1932] is callin' my momma a liar."[20]

By his own reckoning, he was one of twenty-five children sired by Toby Liston, a brutal, abusive father who sharecropped a small patch of ground near Forest City, Arkansas. He beat his son so often that if a day passed without a hard whupping, Sonny would wake his dad at night and ask, "How come you didn't whup me today?" Lines of bird-track scars down his back testified to the frequency and severity of the beatings, and by the time he was twelve Sonny had endured enough. As he told sports columnist Jerry Izenberg, one day the family's mule died, prompting Toby to say to Sonny, "Boy, you're the mule now." Not relishing the promotion, he ran away from home early the next morning.[21]

He caught a train to St. Louis, where his mother lived with several of his brothers and sisters. But the reunion did not solve his problems. Instead of attending school—he remained functionally illiterate all his life—he took to the streets and alleys of St. Louis, running with the wrong sorts of people and embracing a life of crime like it was his

calling. As he once said, "I had a tendency to find things before they got lost." "He's a bad man," commented Detective Sergeant James Reddick. He was a bad man who brutally mugged innocent people, held up small businesses at gunpoint, and did not get away with it. In 1950, he was arrested, tried, convicted, and sentenced to five years in the Missouri State Penitentiary in Jefferson City.[22]

In the pen he learned valuable skills that saved his life. Father Alois Stevens, the Catholic chaplain and athletic director at "Jeff City," saw in Liston "a big, ignorant, pretty nice kid" who seemed perfectly suited for the boxing ring. "He was," Stevens remembered, "the most perfect specimen of manhood I had ever seen." At six foot one and a half inches tall and over two hundred pounds, with thick legs, broad shoulders, long, heavily muscled arms, and enormous hands, he had a heavyweight's build. He was also graceful on his feet and had remarkably quick hands. Frank Mitchell, one of Liston's early managers, witnessed the same quickness when Sonny suddenly reached down and scooped a live pigeon off the sidewalk. If ever there was a case of biology being destiny, Liston was it.[23]

After serving just over two years of his sentence, Sonny was paroled in October 1952 to the custody of Father Stevens as well as Monroe Harrison and Frank Mitchell, two men with ties to the St. Louis boxing scene. Under their direction, Liston strung together a few amateur titles and then in 1953 turned professional. An immediate success, by early 1956 he had won fifteen of sixteen fights.

Once again, his problems came from outside the ring, among the "unwholesome influences" in the dark streets and back alleys of St. Louis. Harrison sold his management share of Liston's contract in 1955, but even before then John Vitale had become Sonny's undercover manager. Reputed to be the leader of the St. Louis crime family, Vitale undoubtedly received a piece of Liston's ring earnings and employed him when Sonny was not engaged in his primary profession. Liston did odd jobs for Vitale's construction business. Sometimes he served as his chauffeur, other times he broke legs and cracked heads for his boss.[24]

Although Sonny's face was impassive, it conveyed the pain of his life. But his face also suggested something even more sinister, something buried just beneath the surface of white American culture, struggling to crack the crust. Poet Leroi Jones (after 1968, Amiri Baraka) described

the implicit threat of the boxer: "Sonny Liston was the big black Negro in every white man's hallway, waiting to do him in, deal him under, for all the hurts white men have been able to inflict on his world."[25]

As a result of his various activities and his implicit threat, the police constantly harassed Liston, and he was arrested as often as he fought professionally. On May 5, 1956, he got into an argument with a cop over a parking ticket. The confrontation escalated, ending with patrolman Thomas Mellow lying on the ground with a broken knee and a gash over his left eye and Sonny trotting away with the officer's Colt .38 service revolver. Soon arrested and convicted, he was sentenced to nine months in the city workhouse.[26]

Liston walked out of prison in the fall of 1957, but he was far from rehabilitated. He continued to run afoul of the law, and it seems probable that St. Louis policemen targeted him for special harassment. Soon he was advised to leave the city. As Sonny recalled the episode, a police captain said, "If you don't, they're going to find you dead in an alley." So Liston left, resettled in Philadelphia, and reappeared in the ring under new management.[27]

His career was to some degree always controlled by mobsters, but by 1958 he had become the special project of the leading gangsters in the boxing business. There were layers to his management, with each stratum more secretive and powerful than the one below. On paper, Joseph "Pep" Barone was his manager, but he was merely a front man for Philadelphia gangster Frank "Blinky" Palermo, who in turn took orders from Frankie Carbo. And with such influential friends behind him, Liston's career bounded forward. Suddenly he was able to get fights with leading contenders, and by spring 1960 he was the top-ranked fighter in the division.[28]

His problem, however, was that he had become a focal point for critics who assailed the sport. From the late 1940s to the early 1960s, two men from two organizations had control of prizefighting. The first was initially a legal corporation organized in 1949. Controlled by James Dougan Norris, a Chicago businessman, the International Boxing Club (IBC) soon acquired a stranglehold on the promotion of major fights in the United States. Within a few years, it was a monopolistic octopus of the first order, and in 1957, a federal court ruled it so and ordered it broken up. Two years later, it was disbanded.[29]

But like Liston's managers of record and undercover managers, James Norris was little more than a front man for Frankie Carbo, whose power was virtually absolute, his dictates tantamount to royal commands. Virtually every major boxing manager and promoter worked to some degree with Carbo—his henchmen gave them no choice—and many fighters owed their careers to him, as Sonny Liston did.

Carbo's influence began to wane in the late 1950s, when he was arrested for federal income tax violations and sentenced to twenty-five years in prison. But Liston's career continued to flourish. Sportswriters debated whether Patterson should give him a title shot and whether he was a reformed man or still a back-alley thug, but none questioned that he was the most fearsome, most qualified contender in the division. Even President John F. Kennedy offered an opinion. In January 1962, at a White House meeting with Patterson, he suggested that Floyd not risk his crown against Liston.[30]

Patterson, however, was an honorable man who believed in redemption and second chances. Liston's life, he thought, was not so different from his. Both had bad beginnings and had moved into petty crime, only Floyd had received help and Sonny had not. A devout Catholic, Patterson believed, "There but for the grace of God, go I." Liston had committed crimes, gone to prison, paid his debt, and was now a fellow professional. No matter what Patterson's manager, Cus D'Amato; sportswriters; the NAACP; or the president of the United States thought, Liston had earned a chance to fight for the heavyweight title.[31]

Patterson fought Liston on September 25, 1962, under the lights at Comiskey Park in Chicago. It may have been the most talked- and written-about fight since the 1938 rematch between Joe Louis and Max Schmeling. It was covered by some two hundred sportswriters and a distinguished collection of novelists and essayists. Less than half a year after the death of Benny "the Kid" Paret, they seemed to have come to write boxing's obituary. Norman Mailer had been sent by *Esquire*, James Baldwin by *Nugget*, and A. J. Liebling by *The New Yorker*. They were joined by Gay Talese, Nelson Algren, Budd Schulberg, Gerald Kersh, and a busload of others. Surveying the array of talent, Liebling judged that it was like one of "those highly intellectual *pour-parlers* on a Mediterranean island" and suspected that "placed before typewriters, the

accumulated novelists could have produced a copy of the *Paris Review* in forty-two minutes."[32]

Yet the great struggle to determine which black man would represent the aching hopes and smoldering resentments of black Americans was not much of a contest at all. Instead of staying away from Liston, Patterson advanced toward him, trying to slip under what he thought was a slow jab and get close enough to land hooks to Sonny's body and face. But Sonny banged away with several hard hooks, then he pushed a left to the head that sent Patterson sprawling onto the ropes. As Floyd bounced awkwardly off the ropes, Liston hit him with a left, a grazing right, and a devastating left hook that half lifted him off the ground.

Patterson dropped to the canvas like a man who had slipped on ice, landing clumsily and rolling onto his back. Immediately, he maneuvered to his side, managing to elevate his torso slightly. There he hesitated, shaking his head a few times in an attempt to regain his senses. Finally, he struggled to his feet. But it was too late. Referee Frank Sikora had counted him out at two minutes ten seconds of the first round. Summarizing the match, Gilbert Rogin reconfigured a Churchillian phrase, writing, "Never have so many paid so much to see so little."[33]

Spectators trudged out of Comiskey Park and theaters across the country feeling disappointed, if not cheated. Liebling insisted that Patterson was "a nice young man—kind to children, socially conscious, conscientious about his work"—who did not quit: "he just got licked." As for Floyd, he slunk out of Comiskey wearing a fake beard and mustache and drove through the early morning hours to New York. Still in disguise the next day, he went to the airport and bought a ticket to Madrid, where he stayed for a week or so, limping through the poorer section of town like an old man and eating soup because, he said, that was what an old man would eat.[34]

Liston, "who had once been a tool of mobsters" and who kept running afoul of the police, was the new titleholder. Although Sonny claimed that he planned to prove that he could be a "good and decent champion," few insiders believed he could change his old habits. Boxing, some thought, was dying. The death of Paret and the ascendancy of Liston seemed to seal its fate.[35]

IN THE MINUTES before the Patterson-Liston fight, boxing's two most vocal practitioners were introduced in the ring. The younger man received little attention. He was, after all, still lightly regarded as something of a comic novelty. "Ladies and gentleman, heavyweight contender, Cassius Clay," the announcer intoned. Cassius swung through the ropes wearing a black tie and shouting something, "as insolent as ever," James Baldwin commented dismissively. In Norman Mailer's twenty-thousand-word article on the match, Clay did not even rate a mention. Of more interest to the novelists and fans was the stylish veteran Archie Moore, elegant in a black opera cape and carrying a cane. He entered the ring with the panache of a stage performer, twirling his cape with the flair of a magician.[36]

At that moment, when so much talk was about the death of boxing, neither Cassius nor Archie seemed in a position to change the sport's fate. For all his boasting and predicting, Clay was still young, "a barely discernible figure on the distant horizon," commented Arthur Daley. His record was padded with no-name boxers, over-the-hill fighters, and other assorted paper tigers. And Archie Moore was clearly a boxer on his way out of the sport. Like Liston, his birth date was a mystery, but whether it was 1913 or 1915, it was definitely during Woodrow Wilson's first term. As he neared his fiftieth birthday, the fact that he was still boxing and articulate seemed miraculous. He was a monument to the sport's past, not a cornerstone of its future.[37]

For Angelo Dundee, old, out-of-shape Archie, a former light-heavyweight champion who had been stripped of his crown by sanctioning bodies, was both an ideal stepping-stone and a potentially lucrative draw. Cassius began the buildup for a match minutes after he knocked out Alejandro Lavorante. After slipping out of the ring, he noticed Moore sitting near ringside. Pointing a finger, he scowled, shouting, "You're next, old man! Moore will fall in four." A few days later Moore responded. "That kid's got a lot to learn. And I'm afraid the ole Professor is gonna have to teach him. I've discovered a few chinks in his armor."[38]

Moore understood Clay's showmanship, but he was also keenly aware of the young man's many talents. Cassius had all of the outrageous fortunes of youth—speed, strength, endurance, and the firm belief in his own destiny. Against those advantages, Archie possessed only experience, guile, and a reputation supported by yellowing newspaper

clippings. He no longer had the skills to compete with the best in the young man's sport. But he needed money.[39]

By the fall of 1962, with shrinking television ratings and other boxing cards drawing meager audiences, money seemed to be fleeing the sport. Even the Liston-Patterson match was a bit of a financial disappointment, drawing fewer than twenty thousand fans to Comiskey and a closed-circuit audience forty percent below expectations. With these grim facts in mind, promoters Cal and Aileen Eaton took a cautious approach by staging the Clay-Moore match in the Los Angeles Sports Arena—rather than the larger Coliseum—and initially excluded live radio, television, and closed-circuit-theater broadcasts.[40]

That was before Clay and Moore began drumming up interest. Clay's routine produced good copy, but while he had once been good-natured and humorous, he had now turned edgy and mean. Archie Moore was a beloved and respected West Coast boxer, the sport's elder statesman, and Cassius treated him like a two-bit bum. When the two appeared together on a half-hour television show called *The Great Debate*, Clay came off not so much as an occasional scene-stealer but as a serial scene-mugger. As soon as Moore said "Good evening," Cassius began a spontaneous filibuster, drowning out virtually everything Archie tried to say. Moore considered himself a thoughtful speaker and conversationalist, but it was difficult to engage a rabble-rouser and a shouter. "Don't humiliate yourself," Moore finally said. "Our country depends on its youth. Really, I don't see how you can stand yourself."[41]

As the interest in the bout mounted, the Eatons decided that the fight had blockbuster potential and maneuvered to increase revenues. Although they maintained a television blackout for the LA area, they did contract for a fifty-five-theater closed-circuit broadcast, adding a potential seating capacity of two hundred thousand. By the night of the match, Clay's predictions of his drawing power were confirmed. The fight sold out the Los Angeles Sports Arena—16,200 spectators paid a total of $182,599, both indoor records for California. Closed-circuit venues in New York, San Francisco, Boston, San Diego, Seattle, and Louisville also sold out, adding nearly another $250,000 in revenues. In a year when prizefighting was under attack and revenues were falling off a cliff, the Clay-Moore bout was the glittering exception. The Louisville Lip, the Mouth That Roared, was a certifiable cash cow.[42]

The term "Battle of the Ages," as it was called, was accurate in only its most literal sense. In two years as a professional, Cassius had filled out into a sleek heavyweight of just over two hundred pounds and had entered his prime. His face creased with age, Moore was old and flabby, with a welted scar on his stomach that looked like it was from some primitive operation. Jimmy Cannon wrote that Archie "seemed to be drowning in his own fat." Before the fight began Clay danced lightly in his corner, bouncing gracefully and rolling his shoulders. Moore managed a few knee bends, the limbering calisthenics of an old man getting ready to jog around the block. Cassius had predicted "Moore in four," and nothing about the appearance of the two indicated that the match would not follow the young man's boast.[43]

And so it went. As Al Buck of the *New York Post* summarized, "a 20-year-old youth beat up a tired 50-year-old veteran of too many fights. Ancient Archie was fat and slow. He had nothing left." Once in the ring, Clay demonstrated his superiority. From the beginning of the contest, Cassius circled around Archie, who tried to protect himself with his familiar cross-armed defense. He threw an unusual number of punches for a heavyweight, repeatedly bouncing them off the top of Moore's head. Archie ducked and weaved, avoiding many of the shots, but not nearly enough. "Clay missed 100 punches," said Moore's trainer, Dick Sadler, "but he threw 200."

The punches were not as heavy as Liston's, but they had a cumulative effect. "His speed was too much for me," Moore recalled. "You see, he had a style, he would hit a man a lot of times around the top of the head. And if you hit the top of a man's head, you shake up his thought pattern." By the fourth round, Moore was as disoriented as a man who had just stepped off of a Tilt-a-Whirl. His face, commented Gilbert Rogin, was "as red as a boy who has been in a jam pot," and his body was covered with traces of whiplash punches. Quickly, with a flurry of shots, Clay knocked him down, sending Archie's mouthpiece skipping across the ring like a smooth rock across a pond. Dancing, raising his arms, and admiring his handiwork, he remained above Moore until the referee pushed him to a neutral corner. Moore got up at the count of eight, but Clay knocked him down a second time. Again he struggled off the canvas, and once more Clay knocked him down. The referee waved his arms, signaling the end of the contest.

Sitting at ringside, watching the fight with a benign smile, Sonny Liston seemed gratified with the results. Clay had demonstrated that he could fill an arena as well as shown Liston that he lacked real power. After the bout, Cassius had pointed at Liston, shouting, "You're next. I'll fix you in eight rounds."

"If you can go eight seconds with me, I'll give you the fight," Liston answered.[44]

By the end of 1962, boxing was creaking back to life. "Clay 'Saved' Sad Year for Boxing," headlined the *Los Angeles Times*. It had been an awful year. Paret had died, Lavorante was dying, Moore and Sugar Ray Robinson were limping toward the ends of their careers, and Liston and his gang had captured the heavyweight title. But in a series of matches in Los Angeles, Clay had revealed an ability to attract spectators. He seemed, as he often proclaimed, the savior of the sport.[45]

Boxing's savior he was. He had the golden touch, the Gorgeous George magic that put customers in seats. He displayed his special talent in November in Los Angeles against Moore, and then repeated it in January in Pittsburgh against Charley Powell, an exceptional athlete but not proficient enough a boxer to challenge Clay. A week after his twenty-first birthday, Cassius knocked him out in the third round. Yet in subzero weather, more than eleven thousand fans, a local indoor record, paid to boo the undefeated boxer.[46]

It was just before the Powell match that in a conversation with sportswriter Mort Sharnik, Cassius revealed a different side of himself. Without confessing his ties to the Nation of Islam, he began talking about spirituality. He wondered why he couldn't have visitations from God. Sharnik recalled, "He was saying that Moses spoke to God and the prophets spoke to God, and why couldn't he speak to God?" It was a curious observation. Sitting in a room in Pittsburgh, preparing to fight a powerful boxer whom he had dubbed "Frankenstein," Cassius seemed more interested in his relationship with God. "I had the feeling he sensed he was a special vessel, that he might be ordained for special things," the writer recalled.[47]

Sharnik did not understand the source of Clay's power. He was unaccustomed to athletes speaking so openly about deeply personal matters. But Sharnik had not spoken so intensely with Malcolm X, for

whom profound religious conversations were common. Malcolm knew a man who did speak with God. And in the months since he met Clay, he had followed the boxer in newspapers, watching his career blossom. It was time, Malcolm had decided, to visit Cassius, attend one of his fights, and talk about a new message.

Chapter Six

APOLLO

Coffee is the only thing I like integrated.
—MALCOLM X

I want to integrate my coffee. I don't want to drink it black. Think
I'll have my coffee weak this morning.
—CASSIUS CLAY

Elijah Muhammad's children distrusted Malcolm. They were certain that he coveted the Messenger's throne. In early 1963, they became especially concerned about their father's chronic bronchial asthma. If his health deteriorated, they wondered, who would lead the Nation? Thin as a scarecrow, weighing only one hundred and twenty-five pounds, Elijah couldn't shake a persistent cough. He was so weak that he sent a telegram to Chicago informing his followers that he could not attend the annual Saviours' Day convention, the holiest day in the Nation of Islam. In his place, Malcolm would serve as master of ceremonies, an appointment that drove an even deeper wedge between him and Elijah's children.[1]

In late February, on the eve of the convention, Malcolm met with Elijah's son Wallace to discuss the most urgent problem in the Nation: the Messenger's affairs. Recently paroled after serving more than a year in prison for draft evasion, Wallace arrived in Chicago stunned by rumors of his father's infidelities. He was shocked to see two women standing out in the cold on his father's lawn, holding babies that they claimed belonged to the Messenger. The women said that they would

not leave until Elijah acknowledged the children. Wallace knew the women, he said, and shortly thereafter confirmed to Malcolm that the children belonged to Elijah.[2]

During the convention, Elijah's children complained that Malcolm had taken over. When they asked to hear Wallace speak on stage, Malcolm said that there was not enough time for him to address the assembly. The tension escalated when Malcolm called a family meeting, and announced his plan to confront numerous problems harming the Nation. Undercover FBI agents reported that the family "was especially resentful of [Malcolm's] attempts to advise and tell the family what to do."[3]

When his children grumbled about Malcolm's lingering presence in Chicago, Elijah dismissed their complaints, reminding them that Malcolm was responsible for "boosting us up" throughout the country. On other occasions, though, he admitted that he had always known that Malcolm would breach his trust and that he had no business discussing "a family affair"—*his* affairs.[4]

On March 10, Elijah telephoned his son-in-law, Raymond Sharrieff. Raymond explained that Malcolm had not yet left Chicago and planned to make more public appearances later in the week. Elijah gave Raymond an order: tell Malcolm to go home and check on Betty.[5]

During the flight back to New York, Malcolm mulled over his conversations with Elijah's former secretaries. The women told him that Muhammad had said that he was the best minister in the Nation but that his ambition made him "dangerous." Someday, Muhammad predicted, Malcolm would leave him. It was only a matter of time. Listening to the women, Malcolm learned that while Elijah praised him to his face, "he was tearing me apart behind my back." Just thinking about Elijah's words made it hard to breathe. He felt betrayed.[6]

What Elijah did not know was that Malcolm already had plans to return to New York City so that he could attend the biggest prizefight of the year, a bout involving Cassius Clay. Since meeting Malcolm nine months earlier, Cassius had attended more Muslim meetings, ingratiating himself with the Harlem minister. But no one outside the Nation suspected that Malcolm had taken an interest in the young boxer. Elijah himself had no idea that Malcolm planned to sit ringside at Madison Square Garden during his next match.

When a reporter asked Malcolm what he thought about prizefighting, he called it "a racket." "Commercialized sport is the pleasure of the idle rich," he said. Rich white men exploited poor men who beat up other poor men. "The vice of gambling stems from it." No one appreciated this better than Big Red. He was, after all, a product of the street, a former "sport" who had lived the life of urbanity, gambling, and vice. It was the same world occupied by boxers, promoters, and hustlers who ran the fight game. It was a world of backroom deals, late-night escapades, and easy women.[7]

Malcolm nevertheless understood the cultural power wielded by champions. He had matured during the age of Joe Louis, the most admired and talked-about black man of the 1930s. He recalled that in 1937, when Louis defeated heavyweight champion James Braddock, "all the Negroes in Lansing, like Negroes everywhere, went wildly happy with the greatest celebration of race pride our generation had ever known. Every Negro boy old enough to walk wanted to be the next Brown Bomber."[8]

Malcolm recognized that unlike Joe Louis, Cassius Clay refused to let white men control him. The brash young boxer had shown an independent side, an unwillingness to play by the white man's rules, asserting his freedom in the world of boxing. Sometimes he defied Angelo Dundee's instructions and ignored his advisers in the Louisville Sponsoring Group. Many white fans and sportswriters who disapproved of his gloating in the ring would have preferred that he stand in the corner after he won a match, like Louis, gracious and expressionless.

The fact that Cassius spoke his mind, attended Muslim meetings, and reached out to the minister, risking his career, convinced Malcolm that he was not the white man's puppet. Perhaps, Malcolm thought, he could mold him like a lump of clay, sculpting him into a new kind of black champion—a champion of Black Nationalism. But to do that, to become the heavyweight champion of the world, the Muslim's champ, and a powerful voice carrying Malcolm's message, Clay had to beat Doug Jones.[9]

CASSIUS WAS IN New York City to sell tickets. Scheduled to box third-ranked heavyweight contender Doug Jones in Madison Square Garden on March 13, 1963, he faced a daunting promotional task. Jones was a

very good boxer, small for a heavyweight, though a fine defensive fighter with solid punching power. He had won twenty-one of his twenty-five professional matches, and his three losses and one draw had been by decision to boxers of his caliber. Competent and workmanlike in the ring, he was undistinguished outside the ropes, and he most emphatically was not a drawing card.

Cassius had to do the talking for both men, a task he attacked with relish. On Sunday, February 3, he kicked off his campaign with an appearance on *The Ed Sullivan Show*, a popular variety program. Once a sportswriter and still a boxing fan, Sullivan regularly introduced boxers on his show and plugged upcoming matches.[10]

Sullivan tried to put the boxer at ease by asking him if he had a prediction for the Jones fight. "I understand that Jones likes to mix, but he must fall in six," Cassius replied.

"Suppose I were to box you, how far would I go?" the host asked.

"Well, Ed, if you run, I'll have to cut it to one."

"One round?"

"No, one punch."

Then, for a moment, Clay became nervous and misspoke. "I'm not just a musician in the ring, I'm not . . . ah, ah . . . I'm not just a musician in the ring, I'm the same out of the ring." He meant to say that he was a magician in and out of the ring, and to prove his point he took a blue scarf out of his pocket, waved it a few times, and, presto, transformed it into a cane.

Cassius loved magic, and his trick looked professional, winning instant applause from the audience. But what no one at the time realized—or would recognize for some time to come—was that his life had come to resemble his magic. A good magician makes you see what he wants you to see, concealing from your gaze what he wants to hide. He is like a great boxer who, as former light-heavyweight champion José Torres once suggested, lies for a living. "Champions and good fighters are champions and good fighters because they can lie better than the others. The first thing you learn in the gym is that you have to have a double personality if you are to become a good fighter." Torres understood that to reach a championship level, a boxer had to employ feints and fakes to make his opponent look at one hand when he was about to get hit with the other.[11]

Cassius, too, had a deceptive personality. At the beginning of 1963, Cassius's magic showed the world a buffoonish, loudmouth clown while hiding his growing relationship with Malcolm X and his inner feelings about race in America. In public, he shouted, "I am the greatest!" repeating doggerel and refining his Gorgeous George routine. In private, he attended Nation of Islam meetings and memorized the speeches of Elijah Muhammad and Malcolm X. Inside Cassius Clay was Muhammad Ali, but for the moment the magician kept that identity hidden.

Two DAYS AFTER appearing on *The Ed Sullivan Show*, Clay traveled to Albany, where the movement to abolish boxing in New York had collided with an army of boxers, baseball players, and journalists. Before a joint legislative committee conducting a hearing into the sport, they formed a line of defense against the politicians, moralists, and reformers out to ban the sweet science. Boxing in New York was cleaner than anywhere else in the world, said Melvin Krulewitch, the New York State Athletic Commission chairman. Boxing is safer than baseball, judged Gil McDougald, former New York Yankee infielder. Boxing "is one area of the sports world where equal opportunity is granted to members of my race," commented James Hicks of the *New York Amsterdam News*, adding, "Negroes may not be accepted on the tennis courts of Forest Hills . . . but they are accepted as equals in the boxing ring."[12]

After almost a decade of close scrutiny and a year of hostile attacks, the sport seemed to be slowly rebounding from its lowest point. Dressed in a dark suit and bow tie, Cassius Clay lectured the committee on the history of pugilism. "Boxing is in the winter of its life now. In the time when there were great fighters like Dempsey and Joe Louis, nobody talked against it. When there are no great fighters, people lose interest." Boxing was like the march of the seasons. "In the winter, things are cold, things are dead. Spring will come again, and so will summer."[13]

Clay himself was the warm breeze of spring, he made perfectly clear. "I am here to liven things up. On March 13, I will be fighting in the Garden, and it will be a total sellout." After answering a few of the committee's questions, Cassius concluded his testimony. "When he stepped down," journalist A. J. Liebling observed, "a faint odor of *hubris*, like Lilac Végétal, lingered behind."[14]

The whiff of spring might have lingered in the committee room, but not Clay, who immediately departed the frigid weather of Albany for the sunshine of Miami. On the first leg of the trip, he rode a train back to New York City. Sitting alone, he stared out the window, looking up at the sky and attempting, it seemed, to see beyond the clouds into the mysteries of space. Growing restless and bored, he switched seats, moving across the aisle to sit next to Frank Deford, a junior sportswriter for *Sports Illustrated* assigned to cover the hearings on the off chance that anything of note took place.[15]

Deford assumed that Clay would want to talk about his testimony, the fate of boxing, or his upcoming match against Doug Jones. But Cassius didn't want to discuss his career. Instead, he grabbed Deford's notepad and pen and started drawing what looked like an elaborate solar system "with lines and circles indicating descending aliens and something or other about God." The sportswriter knew nothing about the theology of the Nation of Islam. He had no idea that the boxer sitting three feet away from him was reciting what he had learned from Muslim ministers about the Day of Judgment.

Listening to him, Deford thought that this was just another one of his gimmicks, an amusing tale designed to provoke laughter. As Cassius continued lecturing, though, he realized that this was no joke. Clay sincerely believed this story about a "Mother Ship" descending on Earth, saving the true believers.

When they disembarked at Grand Central Terminal, Deford packed his notepad in his briefcase, shaking his head at the "*very amusing but nutty*" story Clay had just told him. Later, when he returned home, he tore out the drawings of spaceships and tossed them into the trash. He did not realize that he had thrown away the best evidence that any sportswriter had to prove that Cassius Clay had embraced the Nation of Islam.[16]

Later in the day, Cassius took another train to Miami, arriving late Friday night. The next day, he returned to the 5th Street Gym to begin training for Jones. As he sparred in the ring, Sonny Liston sauntered in to watch. Liston, who had also arrived on Friday, had come to town to train for his April 4 rematch in Miami with Floyd Patterson. Unconcerned about that fight—he planned to knock out Patterson even "quicker than before"—he decided to scout a future opponent.[17]

"Get him out of here, that bum is spying on me," Cassius yelled.

The comment prompted an exchange of insults.

"What have I got to spy on you for? You're no fighter," Sonny shot back, and then offered Cassius a job as his sparring partner.

But Sonny was out of his league in the game of the dozens. "You ain't so hot," Clay said. "I could leave both legs at home and beat you." Sonny was nothing but a "big ugly bear," he shouted as he shifted to a more personal assault. "Ugly! I hate him because he's so ugly. I'll murder the bum," he told everyone in the gym. Then he began to climb through the ropes to get closer to the champion.[18]

Liston charged. Clay scrambled back through the ropes to the security of the ring. What had started good-naturedly as a publicity stunt had not gone well for Sonny, and he was angry. "I'm not training for Patterson—I'm training for you," he fumed as he left the gym. Clay smiled. It was a small, early victory in his campaign against Sonny Liston.

ON MARCH 6, a large gathering of reporters and radio and television men greeted Clay when he stepped off the train at Pennsylvania Station. Wearing a brown sports jacket and gray slacks, he looked fresh after a long ride from Miami, but his voice was subdued, at least at first. Was he surprised that the fight had attracted so much interest? a sportswriter asked. "That's only natural," he said matter-of-factly. "The fans know what they want. They're coming to see me—to see the greatest."[19]

It was the beginning of operation hype, but his quips were not covered in the *Times, Daily News, Herald Tribune, Journal-American*, or any other New York City newspaper. The timing of Clay's campaign could hardly have been worse. Cassius, the sportswriter's dream, was silenced by an army of linotype workers, photoengravers, paper handlers, office boys, and other members of Local No. 6 of the International Typographical Union and a patchwork of affiliated organizations. They had gone on strike against the owners and publishers of New York City's seven major newspapers, walking off their posts on December 8, 1962, and not returning for 114 days.[20]

For New York sports fans and gossip devotees, it was like a citywide blackout. The strike cut off the circulation of 5.7 million daily and 7.2 million Sunday newspaper copies in a city where newspapers dictated

the rhythms of millions of lives. No Arthur Daley and Gay Talese (*New York Times*) or Red Smith (*New York Herald Tribune*) with their morning coffee; no Dick Young (*New York Daily News*) or Walter Winchell (*New York Daily Mirror*) for their subway rides to work; no Milton Gross (*New York Post*) for their subway rides home; no Dan Parker and Jimmy Cannon (*New York Journal-American*) or Westbrook Pegler (*New York World-Telegram & Sun*) as they relaxed after dinner. Although on February 28, 1963, *New York Post* publisher Dorothy Schiff abandoned the other owners and resumed the publication of her paper, the rest of the magnates grimly fought the unions.

Of all sports, the strike had the greatest impact on boxing. The major professional and college team sports have their seasons, with game schedules and times readily available and widely distributed. But boxing has no such predictability. Matches are made and scheduled willy-nilly, and promoters depended on sportswriters to promote the contests by visiting training camps, interviewing combatants, and generally creating the sense that each upcoming battle promised to be the greatest grudge fight since the Paleolithic era. It was the sportswriters who awarded the pugilists personality quirks, created heroes and villains, and imbued the sport with drama.

Better than any other fighter, Clay understood the role of sportswriters and sought to give them what they wanted when they wanted it. Arriving in a city where he had an upcoming fight, he acted like he was running for mayor, prepared to talk to every voter and kiss every baby. There was hardly a newspaper, television, or radio reporter whose attention he did not covet. "The only ones I send away," he admitted, "are those guys from the little radio stations—they put you on at 4:30 in the afternoon when no one's at home and no one's listening."[21]

But with New York newspaper writers carrying placards on picket lines, Cassius had to find other ways to spread his message. Before the strike, television news was hardly worthy of the name, mostly providing fifteen minutes of local tragedies, weather reports, and a few game scores. What hard news the telecasters reported was what they read in the morning *New York Times*. The strike presented them with a challenge and an opportunity. WCBS added fifty thousand dollars to its weekly news budget and hired eighteen news reporters. WNBC expanded from

a fifteen-minute newscast to a half-hour. The city turned to television for its news as never before.[22]

Cassius's routine played even better on screen than in print. The week before the fight he appeared on *The Today Show*, *The Tonight Show*, and once again on *The Ed Sullivan Show*. Showing no physical evidence of his profession, he was polite, articulate, and handsome, looking and sounding like the anti-boxer. Since the death of Benny "the Kid" Paret, news reports and documentaries had fed Americans a succession of stories about punch-drunk, broken-nosed, down-at-the-heels fighters. But now here was Cassius Clay, looking more like a movie star than a boxer, talking to Johnny Carson, Hugh Downs, and Ed Sullivan, demonstrating complete poise and humor.[23]

He also made personal appearances designed to attract media attention. On March 7, just before he went on *The Tonight Show*, he headlined a unique media event. Dressed for the occasion, he ventured down to the Bitter End on Bleecker Street in Greenwich Village for a noontime poetry reading contest. He looked as out of place in the legendary coffeehouse as Allen Ginsberg would have appeared in the ring at Madison Square Garden.[24]

In front of an international audience of writers and curious out-of-towners, a group of poets read their verse. Unimpressed with the poets, Cassius read his own predictable doggerel:

The word's been passed around
That I'm a very charming guy,
The greatest fighter that ever lived,
And I'll gladly to tell you why.

My secret is self-confidence—
A champion at birth;
I'm lyrical, I'm fresh, I'm smart—
My fists have proved my worth.[25]

Laughter and applause punctuated his reading, and the *New York Post*'s Pete Hamill acclaimed him "the messiah of the poetry racket," who had "annihilated, with one terrible stroke, the frail world of Beat

Poets, Square Poets, Academic Poets, and Zen Poets, anti-poet poets, jazz poets, and lady poets."[26]

Throughout the week, Clay worked every angle. From TV shows to standing on street corners and singing his own praises, he did not miss an opportunity to promote himself. His one-man publicity campaign demonstrated that he was just as unique as he claimed. There had been "television boxers" before him, but he was the first boxer who belonged to the television age, the first to understand how to use the medium to project an image and sell an event. Like Chubby Checker, father of the twist dance craze, Cassius realized that fame was just a matter of delivering the same message ten thousand times. A. J. Liebling noted, "The more he bragged, the more of a drawing card he became, although he certainly did not understand the mechanics of this phenomenon." But Liebling was wrong. Clay fully understood; he knew that his words created a media buzz that produced a honey jar of cash.[27]

Doug Jones knew it as well. While Clay worked to build the gate, Jones quietly trained. With what one reporter described as "a catfish-style mustache" and another called a "cueball"-shaped head, he had the look of an interesting character, but he said very little to bring attention to himself. Asked if he resented Clay's constant verbal attacks, he shook his head no. "Let that Cassius keep talking. The more he talks the more money I'll make."[28]

By Wednesday, March 13, the morning of the fight, Clay had had his lengthy say. Unable to sleep, he was up and dressed by six thirty a.m. Slipping unobserved from his room at the Plymouth Hotel, he walked two blocks to Madison Square Garden and looked at the large marquee: TONIGHT—BOXING—CLAY VS. JONES. At the ticket booth he saw a smaller sign that read, "Sold Out." For the first time in six years, all of the Garden's 18,732 seats were sold out. It was the first time they had ever sold out ahead of time. It was tangible proof of his assertions that he was the savior of boxing, hard evidence that the sport was not dying. It was the stuff of his childhood dreams of fame and wealth.

As he had said earlier in the week, "That Jones! That ugly man! I'll annihilate him! You know what this fight means to me? A tomato-red Cadillac Eldorado convertible with white leather upholstery, air conditioning and hifi. That's what the [Louisville Sponsoring Group] is

giving me for a victory present. Can you picture me losing to this ugly bum Jones with that kind of swinging car waiting for me?"[29]

Clay walked into the weigh-in that afternoon with a two-inch-wide strip of adhesive tape over his mouth, signaling that he was through talking, though he was not done communicating. When Jones stepped onto the scale, Cassius held up four fingers. Doug Jones, a fighter in his prime who had never been stopped, would fall in four, just like old Archie Moore.[30]

LATER THAT AFTERNOON, as Cassius was resting in his room, he received an unusual visitor. A black man with a mobile face that displayed his every emotion walked into the room, which was easier than it sounds because people were always coming and going around the boxer. He took one look at the cluttered room with clothes, fight equipment, and shoes tossed about haphazardly and began to give orders. "Who takes care of you?" he asked. Clay pointed to a white man seated in the corner, smoking a cigar. The stranger then barked orders at the white man. He said Cassius's shoes needed polish, suggesting precisely the brand of wax to use, and that the boxer's socks needed washing, and that the white man better move fast because "a fighter packing people into the Garden up to the rafters and the seats where before there was nothin' there but *pigeons*" needed to be serviced just right.[31]

The stranger was Drew "Bundini" Brown. Like Clay himself, Bundini was a larger-than-life self-creation. He had walked uninvited into the boxer's world and decided to stay. When Clay left to go to Madison Square Garden in a limousine, Bundini sat in the backseat with him. When the traffic slowed the limo to a crawl, Bundini ordered the driver to maneuver onto the sidewalk. When several policemen came running, Bundini told them that Cassius was in the car and "if it weren't for him, they wouldn't be out there on duty. Sugar Ray, they let *him* park on the sidewalk." Everything he said made sense, and everyone seemed to follow his orders. It seemed only natural that he floated alongside Cassius past the Garden's entrance and into his life.

Unlike Cassius and Bundini, A. J. Liebling did not float into the Garden. He struggled through a throng of people coming in the opposite direction. "They were coming away from it because the house was

sold out—a report that they had refused to believe—and the cops were chasing them out of the lobby, where they were blocking the entrance." Remembering the meager turnout the year before for Clay's first New York match, Liebling reflected on the drawing power of this poet boxer, whom he had dubbed Apollo, the god of truth, prophecy, music, and poetry. "Could Paul Valéry have filled the Vel' d'Hiv," he wondered, "or Keats Her Majesty's Theatre?"[32]

The greatest venue in pugilism bubbled with life, and in the lobby Liebling thought that he saw the life-size bronze statue of Joe Gans, a champion from early in the century, break "into a sweat of excitement." The reporter had not seen such a high time since the up-and-coming Rocky Marciano sent the great Joe Louis into permanent retirement. Arriving early to his seat in the press row, he watched the Garden fill from the rafters to ringside. Sitting nearest the action and pulling hard for Cassius were the elite of Louisville—Ross Todd and his father, Jouett Ross Todd, up from their winter home in Nassau; Mr. and Mrs. Worth Bingham, down from a skiing vacation in New England; and, of course, William Faversham, Gordon Davidson, and other members of the Louisville Sponsoring Group.[33]

Not far from the august group of southerners were dignitaries from black America. Legendary baseball player and activist Jackie Robinson sat near tennis great Althea Gibson, and Nobel Peace Prize winner Ralph Bunche was not far off. Malcolm X was also perched at ringside, though none of the sportswriters commented about how unusual it was that one of the two most recognizable figures in the Nation of Islam attended the fight. Looking around the Garden, Malcolm realized that all of the people there had come to see one man: Cassius Clay. He had never seen so many people drawn to an event because of a single black man. Not even Elijah Muhammad, he thought, could fill the Garden.[34]

Malcolm was joined by athletic luminaries and politicians, including Sugar Ray Robinson, Jack Dempsey, Gene Tunney, and members of the Joint Legislative Committee on Professional Boxing, down from Albany to get a closer look at the sport's nefarious activities. They were all there to see if Apollo, a solid 3–1 favorite, would finish the shaven-headed fighter with a catfish mustache in the fourth round.[35]

It was a curious fight crowd, not so much pro-Jones as anti-Clay. Cassius had played the villain during his promotion of the fight, and

the spectators treated him as such as he made his way to the ring. Jeers trailed him as he slid between the ropes. In what Liebling labeled "the most emphatic anti-poetry demonstration in American history," the spectators registered their disapproval for Clay's act.[36]

The first round began predictably. Clay came out on his toes, circling away from Jones's left leads, flicking out whiplike jabs meant to aggravate more than injure. His head down and protected by his hands, Jones moved straight forward in a direct, no-nonsense fashion, his eyes locked on Clay, looking to land power punches. Both fighters concentrated on head shots, avoiding body punches as if they had been outlawed for the fight.[37]

Less than a minute into the bout, Clay made a critical error. Since his amateur days, conventional boxing experts had criticized his habit of avoiding punches by moving straight back instead of slipping to one side or the other. It was like avoiding a speeding train by backing up on the tracks rather than by jumping off them. Now, as Cassius pulled back, Jones leaped forward with a sweeping right hand, landing with devastating power on Clay's chin. Cassius's knees buckled momentarily as he stumbled back into the corner ropes, hitting them hard and bouncing off into a charging Jones. He was hurt, and, as the over eighteen thousand spectators in the Garden rose out of their seats as if they had been shocked, Jones pressed his advantage.

Cassius grabbed Jones's arms, pulled him close, and hugged him like a long-lost friend, placing his face cheek-to-cheek with his opponent's. The desperate maneuver gave him ten or so seconds to clear his head and steady his legs. When the referee pried them apart, Clay fought like a seasoned professional. He backpedaled, pushed out defensive jabs designed to keep Jones at a distance, and gave himself more time to run a check on his senses. A half minute later he was out of danger and back in control of the fight. Jones had missed an opportunity, and Clay was wiser for the exchange. He had taken Jones's best punch, and now he knew just how fast the Harlem fighter could strike.

After the first round, the fight settled into a pattern. Jones worked to connect with another hard right, and Clay fought from a distance, content to score points and avoid damage. Neither combatant was very aggressive, and Liebling contended that both had "repertories . . . as limited as the club fighters." In the next two rounds Clay landed the most

punches, but when Jones reached Cassius with anything approaching a clean shot, the Garden exploded with cheering. It was the sort of match that the judges had to watch carefully with their eyes so they would not be influenced by their ears.

There was another factor that played against Cassius: his prediction. At the weigh-in he had boasted, "I'm changing the pick I made before. / Instead of six, Doug goes in four." If he did not fulfill his prophecy, the partisan fans would interpret it as a victory for Jones. And although he increased his attack in the fourth, he was unable to hurt, let alone finish, his opponent.

As the big electric clock in the Garden counted down the seconds in the round and Jones remained upright and strong, the jeers and catcalls built like the climax of a Beethoven symphony. The spectators felt cheated, and they rained insults into the ring. "Clay, you're a big bum! Nothing but a bum!" a ringsider shouted. "You can't fight or write poetry!" cried another. The round ended with Clay landing a hard right at the bell, which created another stir of discontent. The round had come and gone, and Doug Jones moved briskly back to his corner with no sign of damage.

In the middle rounds Jones fought Clay evenly, but the unconditional support of the spectators made it seem like he was winning. In Clay's corner, watching the action and listening to the fervor, Angelo Dundee was alarmed. After the seventh round, he felt the fight slipping away. Imploring Clay to action, he told him "he could kiss Tomato Red goodbye." That got Cassius's attention. "Dundee shook me up," he said after the fight. "I came out in the eighth saying, 'So long Dougie, hello Tomato Red.'"[38]

In the last three rounds, Clay consistently landed three or four times as many shots as Jones did. He fought with heart, cutting the distance between Jones and him and taking more chances. Victory, at this juncture, was more important than survival. Following the fight from just behind Clay's corner, Bundini Brown beamed. "When I saw . . . how he bear down . . . and start beatin' the man to death, he made me fall in love. I was with him from that fight on."[39]

The pause between the final bell and the decision seemed interminable. Finally, announcer Johnny Addie approached the microphone: "Both of the judges, Artie Aidala and Frank Forbes, they score it this

way—five, four, one even in favor of Clay." Cassius had won, and boos showered the ring. Undeterred, the unflappable Addie finished his chores, though the booing made it difficult: "Referee . . . referee . . . referee Joe LoScalzo has it eight, one, one even Clay. The winner by unanimous decision, Cassius Clay." And the floodgates of discontent opened wide. Spectators screamed and jeered, held their heads in amazement and looked dumbfounded, protesting with all their faculties what they considered a miscarriage of justice.

Cassius egged them on. He raised his hands, opened his mouth wide, mimicking the booing fans while he mugged for the cameras, and stuck out his tongue. As he began the ring interview with Don Dunphy, the spectators commenced a chant: "Fix! Fix! Fix!" Then: "Fake! Fake! Fake!" As Cassius told Dunphy that he did not want to fight Jones again and that he was ready for Sonny Liston, spectators started to throw bottles, programs, crumpled cigarette packs, cardboard drinking cups, and whatever was at hand into the ring. Some tossed unshelled peanuts; one pitched his switchblade. Cassius smiled as he gathered, shucked, and ate a few peanuts. A short time later he asked a reporter, "Why did those people boo me when I whup him? Why they don't boo *for* me?"[40]

In the packed Miami Beach Auditorium, Liston had watched the match in a theater on closed circuit. He smiled when Cassius said he wanted to fight him for the title. *What did Clay show him?* someone asked. "He can't punch. Clay showed me I'll get locked up for murder if we're ever matched." He added, "He don't know how to duck, he don't even know how to run. He don't know how to do anything." But the packed Garden and impassioned fans showed Sonny something else. Boxing fans, that dying species, had been resuscitated and would pay to see someone close the Louisville Lip.[41]

JUST OVER A week after he defeated Jones, Cassius's notoriety reached a landmark when he was featured in a portrait on the cover of *Time*, the country's leading weekly newsmagazine. The drawing had two main parts: a book and the man. The illustration of the boxer hardly looks like him. The skin is darker, the features more coarse. Above his head two boxing gloves hold open a book of poetry, looking remarkably like a holy text. Together the images suggest that Cassius Clay was a man of action and words, a warrior and a prophet.[42]

The accompanying story portrayed the boxer as a simple athlete with simple dreams: "I'm going to drive down Walnut Street in a Caddy on Derby Day and all the people will point and say, 'There goes Cassius Clay.' Pretty girls will be there, and I'll smell flowers and feel the nice warm air. Oh, I'm cool, then, man. I'm cool. The girls are looking at me, and I'm looking away." This, the author of the piece implied, was Cassius Marcellus Clay, the fresh, innocent savior of boxing, the sum total of his dreams a tomato-red Cadillac Eldorado, the right woman, and a heavyweight crown.

The cover story, however, lacked depth. It laughed at Clay, noting his low IQ and uncomplicated dreams of material success. It bought his magic, seeing only what he chose to reveal. Nowhere in the article is there a mention of the civil rights movement or the Nation of Islam, of Martin Luther King or Malcolm X. There is no sense that he had an inner life, or that he wore a disguise as complete as those worn by the Scarlet Pimpernel, Sydney Carton, or Ellison's Invisible Man. Even in the spring of 1963, he was not who people thought he was or wanted him to be.

Chapter Seven

HIDE YOUR CAT

Every man should have something he'd die for. A man who won't die for *something* is not fit to live.
—**MARTIN LUTHER KING JR.**

Treat me like a man or kill me.
—**MALCOLM X**

S ince Clay turned professional, he had rarely uttered a single political word. Not once had he complained about the slow pace of desegregation, nor groused to reporters about the escalating racial violence in America. His entire focus was on building a boxing career so that he could earn a title shot and enough money to buy a grand house with two swimming pools—one inside for those rainy days—and a garage full of Cadillacs. All he talked about was boxing, his dreams, and himself. If Clay was a spokesman for any cause, it was his own. Yet the day after he defeated Doug Jones, he told a black writer in Harlem, "I will become the first heavyweight champion to fight a benefit for the NAACP."[1]

Clay's statement was completely disingenuous. He didn't really have any plans to fight for the NAACP. What concerned him more than civil rights was status—his status in the world of boxing and his material worth. In some ways, his attitude about social mobility and materialism reflected the temper of his generation, one that came of age in the "affluent society." National advertising campaigns encouraged the millions of young people of his generation to buy rock 'n' roll records,

radios, blue jeans, shirts, shoes, soft drinks, cereal, comic books, magazines, movie tickets, and gasoline for cruising in chrome-covered cars. Clay belonged to a youth culture that celebrated pleasure and instant gratification, a distinct demographic that was told that their opinions about everything, from consumer products to social issues, mattered.[2]

In an age of growing prosperity, black teenagers who identified with this youth movement believed that freedom and living "the good life" should be one and the same. Seeing themselves as first-class consumers, many black youths became increasingly alienated when confronted with the reality of their second-class citizenship. When they entered a diner or a department store and were turned away because of the color of their skin—as Clay was in Louisville and Miami—they were told that the good life was not for them. The tension between full participation in the consumer culture and racial exclusion from society cut deep into the dreams of black youths.[3]

Yet Clay never expressed the same dissatisfaction that tens of thousands of black activists did when they demonstrated against racism during the sit-ins. When he was growing up in Louisville, there were certain places that he could not go because he was black: restaurants, libraries, public swimming pools, and some downtown movie theaters. The one time he joined a picket in Louisville, a woman dumped hot water on him and he never returned to the marching lines again.[4]

But by March 1963, he was a celebrity and, by his calculation, rich. If for any reason he could not eat somewhere, he could always return to the hotel where he was staying and order anything he wanted from room service, or he could ask his private chef to make him a meal at his home in Miami. Wealth helped him escape discrimination, a luxury most blacks could not afford.

Cassius now had more money than most youths ever dreamed of having. He took home $13,500 from selling out Madison Square Garden and earned another $10,000 from the closed-circuit-theater ticket sales. By the end of the year, he'd made $81,000, not too far from the president's $100,000 salary. Donating money to the NAACP, therefore, would have certainly benefited him during tax season, a fact that was not lost on him. He frequently complained that the more money he made, the more he paid Uncle Sam.[5]

When he declared that he would raise money for the NAACP, he never said anything about giving civil rights lectures or joining any marches in the South. Rather, his financial offer reflected his own strategy of dealing with racism. His success as a boxer earned him economic independence, the kind that Elijah Muhammad promoted. Money, Muhammad preached, gave black men freedom from whites.

Most reporters who covered boxing never suspected that Clay had embraced Muhammad's philosophy. Since he rarely talked about race or the civil rights movement, writers assumed that he gave the subject little thought. All they ever heard from him were bombastic proclamations of his own greatness. But in his declarations of preeminence, Alex Poinsett, a black writer for *Ebony*, heard something more. "For when Cassius Clay declares, 'I am the greatest,' he is not just thinking about boxing," he wrote. "Lingering behind those words is the bitter sarcasm of Dick Gregory, the shrill defiance of Miles Davis, [and] the utter contempt of *Malcolm X*."[6]

Poinsett was circling in on the truth, though he had no idea just how much Clay echoed Malcolm or why he had started to sound like him. Hidden behind Clay's clowning, behind the "publicity gimmicks and boyish buffoonery, behind the brashness, Cassius Marcellus Clay is a blast furnace of race pride. His is a race pride that would never mask itself with skin lighteners and processed hair," the way Detroit Red once degraded himself, burning his scalp with a homemade congolene in a quest for straight hair.[7]

Clay possessed "a pride scorched with memories of a million little burns like the paper cup he drank root beer from at a New Orleans stand while his white companion [*Sports Illustrated's* Huston Horn] sipped from a glass." He may not have talked publicly about discrimination, but he projected a more militant, defiant posture, rejecting any notion of racial inferiority. When he boldly shouted, "I am the greatest," he defined his self-worth on his own terms, expressing an emerging attitude of Black Power.[8]

The *Pittsburgh Courier's* Eric Springer viewed Clay as a new kind of black cultural hero, a symbol "of the change that is occurring in our youth," an emblem of racial pride and boundless confidence. In the past, black heroes had been expected to act inconspicuously, humble

and deferential to whites. But Clay ushered in a new age when black youths agitated for change, unafraid of testing the limits of white acceptance. Springer compared him to the courageous black teens who endured daily abuse when they entered Central High School in Little Rock and the brave black college students desegregating southern universities, like James Meredith at Ole Miss.[9]

The moment blacks began embracing Cassius as the personification of youth activism and the struggle for integration, he shed any responsibility for being a leader of his race. "I'm no James Meredith," he told the *New York Post*'s Pete Hamill. "He's got more guts than I'll ever have." Clay had no interest in meeting him or following his example.[10]

He stunned readers when he announced that he did not believe in racial integration. "I believe it's human nature to be with your own kind," he declared. "I know what restrooms to use, where to eat, and what to say. I don't want people who don't want me. I don't like people who cause trouble. I'm not going out there to rile up a lot of people." The civil rights movement, he said, was not like a boxing match. "There's no referee in the street."[11]

Only a few days after he told a black reporter that he would raise money for the NAACP, and after further consultation with Malcolm, he denounced the organization's goals. "I'm a fighter," he claimed, sounding like he had just left Malcolm's mosque in Harlem. "I believe in the eye-for-an-eye business. I'm no cheek-turner. The NAACP can say, 'turn the other cheek,' but the NAACP is ignorant." Then he added a final point, ripped from the rich language of his new teacher: "You kill my dog, you better hide your cat."[12]

For the first time Cassius found himself at the center of a political controversy. When he attacked the NAACP, many blacks hoped that this was just another publicity stunt, but Clay was not performing the role of the self-created villain. His comments provoked fear that one of the most famous black athletes in the country had forsaken the ideals of integration and embraced the separatist ideology of the Nation, an unsettling thought for those who had built him up as a hero. While most New York newspapers did not cover the controversy due to the labor strike, rumors spread throughout the black press that Cassius had spent time with the Black Muslims, though no reporter confirmed his visit with Malcolm after the Jones fight.[13]

In Louisville, Clay's white sponsors worried that he had made a grave mistake, alienating much of the country and one of the most respected civil rights organizations in America. Dr. Maurice Rabb, an executive with the NAACP's Louisville branch, contacted the national office, informing them that Cassius had been "thoroughly exposed to the teachings of Elijah Muhammad." He reported that Clay "sneered at the fact that a Jew is the National President of the NAACP," a questionable accusation given Clay's unsophisticated knowledge about the group's leadership.[14]

The Louisville Sponsoring Group's director, Bill Faversham, arranged for Clay to apologize to Rabb and other local civil rights leaders. Accompanied to the meeting by his brother Rudy and his chauffeur, Cassius denied his verbal assault on the NAACP, but when Rabb invited him to show his support for the organization by purchasing a lifetime membership, he said that the only way that he would join was if they paid him $250,000. Clay left the appointment promising that he would attend the branch banquet and "take a bow" if he was in town.[15]

After the meeting, the controversy faded from the pages of the black press, though Faversham remained concerned about Clay's increasingly defiant behavior. He told Rabb that if the NAACP wanted to influence the boxer, they might try reaching out to Jackie Robinson or Sugar Ray Robinson, two black athletes Cassius greatly admired. But, he advised, don't bet on him listening to them either, because "CASSIUS makes all decisions concerning CASSIUS."[16]

Faversham suspected that Clay had ties to the Black Muslims. Someone must have been advising him and confusing him, he thought, filling his head with dangerous ideas. What he did not know was that Clay was listening to a new mentor who did not trust whites, the NAACP, or Jackie Robinson. This man taught Clay that he was special not in spite of his skin color but because he was black, an empowering message that awakened his political consciousness. For the first time in his life, Cassius said, "I feel free since I learned the truth about myself and my people."[17]

As CLAY CAME into his own, Malcolm hesitated, unsure of his future. Since he had returned from Chicago, all he could think about was the collateral damage from Elijah's affairs. On the streets of Chicago and

Harlem, blacks who were not Muslims told him that they had heard about Muhammad's harem. He pretended that he did not know what they were talking about, but it was no use. He could no longer ignore the truth.

For years, he had built up the Messenger as an honorable man, the moral compass of the Nation. Every time he mentioned the Supreme Minister's name, he referred to him as "the *Honorable* Elijah Muhammad," but Malcolm could no longer call him an honorable leader, knowing how he had disgraced the Nation. He hated to admit that Elijah was nothing more than an imposter hiding under the cloak of divinity because that meant that he, too, was a fraud.[18]

He realized that he had no choice: the only way he could deal with the Nation's calamity and his own personal crisis was by confronting Elijah. He began by writing Muhammad letters, explaining his actions in Chicago. FBI agents listening to wiretapped lines between Chicago and Phoenix overheard NOI officials say that Malcolm was only "seeking, prodding, and prying" under the guise of helping. Muhammad assured the NOI officials that Malcolm would never discuss the "problems" in person, but his younger minister had already decided to fly to Phoenix to confront the issue before it was too late.[19]

When he arrived at Muhammad's home, Elijah embraced him like a returning prodigal son. They walked through his backyard patio and settled into chairs near the swimming pool. "Well son," Elijah asked, "what's on your mind?" Malcolm spoke directly and plainly about what he had heard in Chicago, suggesting a biblical solution that justified Elijah's indiscretions. He explained that he and Wallace had studied the Bible and the Koran for precedents that would justify Elijah's fathering children outside his marriage. If necessary, he said, the ministers could tell the followers that the pregnancies were "the fulfillment of prophecy." Elijah smiled and praised his loyal minister. "Son, I'm not surprised. You always have had such a good understanding of prophecy, and of spiritual things. You recognized that's what all of this is—prophecy."[20]

"I'm David," he declared. "When you read about how David took another man's wife, I'm that David. You read books about Noah, who got drunk—that's me. You read about Lot, who went and laid up with his own daughters. I have to fulfill all of those things."[21]

After their conversation, Malcolm felt unsatisfied. If Elijah had convinced himself that he was David, Malcolm was less sure that the Nation would accept this convenient allegory. Instead of denying his worst fear, Muhammad had confirmed it, leaving Malcolm and the other ministers in the untenable position of having to convince the followers of Elijah's prophecy. Muhammad had instructed him to discreetly inform a few ministers about their conversation, but, he said, under no circumstances should he tell Brother Louis X. Do not tell Louis, he repeated.[22]

Malcolm returned to New York not knowing that Elijah was testing his loyalty. If Malcolm followed his orders, then Elijah would know that he could trust him. But the moment Malcolm attempted to "inoculate" the Nation from the "oncoming virus," his enemies in Chicago would charge that he, not Elijah Muhammad, was the untrustworthy one.[23]

IN WASHINGTON, DC, where Muhammad had recently assigned him to build up the Muslims' presence, Malcolm watched news footage of white police officers unleashing attack dogs on black teenagers who marched for freedom. He admired the courage of Birmingham's youth, but he could not believe that Martin Luther King would allow them to march on the front lines, unable to defend themselves. Teaching nonviolence, he insisted, sedated blacks into passivity. For Malcolm, King's willingness to turn the other cheek made him weak and cowardly, a message he shared with Cassius Clay. A real black man would never let a white man put a hand on him or "put their children on the firing line." If a white man turned "his dogs on your babies, your women and your children, then you ought to kill the dogs, whether they've got four legs or two."[24]

Despite Malcolm's position on the outskirts of the civil rights leadership, his violent rhetoric shaped the contours of the movement. In the public mind, he became King's foil, a dark and menacing alternative to the Christian philosophy of brotherly love. Malcolm's public criticisms of King's nonviolent philosophy moved him to the center of the national civil rights debate. The fact that reporters interviewed him, seeking his opinion about the Birmingham crisis, gave him further credibility and elevated his national profile.

Increasingly, journalists simplified the struggle as a rivalry between two political movements: the nonviolent integrationists and violent

Black Nationalists. In the aftermath of Birmingham, journalists wrote that the black freedom struggle had reached a crossroads. According to most writers, the struggle could either embrace the moderate leadership of the Southern Christian Leadership Conference and the NAACP or turn toward the "extremism" of Malcolm and the Nation of Islam.[25]

In mid-May, after the Ku Klux Klan bombed Birmingham's A. G. Gaston Motel, King's organizing headquarters, rumors spread that Malcolm might visit the battered southern city, but he never did. Elijah Muhammad would not allow it. Instead of traveling to the South, Malcolm criticized Jackie Robinson and Floyd Patterson for going to Birmingham. He claimed that Robinson and Patterson were being used by white liberals to pacify angry blacks.[26]

For a boxer who admitted to being scared in the ring, nothing frightened Patterson more than going to Birmingham. When Robinson invited him to speak, he prepared for the worst: jail, beatings, even death. He had told Jackie that he could only afford to stay behind bars for three days, but when a television reporter asked him what he would do if the police turned on the hoses or unleashed the dogs, he answered, "I'm not used to standing by like the people in the South, who are much stronger than I am when it comes to this type of thing. I can't stand around and let an animal bite. So," he declared, "I will have to do something."[27]

Not every boxer shared Patterson's views. Heavyweight champion Sonny Liston scorned Martin Luther King's nonviolent ideas and the strategies of the NAACP. Several years before, he had called the Freedom Riders "stupid," explaining, "That ain't no way to do things. You have to fight for what you get. It's like boxing. No use being in there if you just catch punches, because you're not going to get the decision. . . . Now, if some sucker comes and blows up my house, then someone else's house is going to be blown up. And the next time this sucker ain't going to be in no hurry to go blow up houses." It was all a matter of fighting back, trading punch for punch. He was not going to participate in any nonviolent protests. When a white reporter asked why he was not going to Birmingham, Liston answered, "I ain't got no dog-proof ass."[28]

But Patterson was committed to a cause that Liston refused to join. When he and Robinson arrived in Birmingham on May 13, they learned that white vigilantes threatened their lives. Protected by a police escort,

they toured the ravaged city, visited with ministers and citizens, and spoke at rallies. The next night, they accompanied King to the Sixth Avenue Baptist Church. After Patterson spoke briefly about his admiration for the grassroots activists, Wyatt Tee Walker, the executive director of SCLC, introduced Robinson, a man who needed no introduction.

As the graying baseball legend rose from the pew and walked pigeon-toed toward the podium, leaning on his cane, the congregation cheered even louder than they had for King. They never forgot all the abuse—the beanballs, the vile epithets, and the death threats—that he had endured to prove that blacks belonged in the national pastime. His presence at the church demonstrated that he did not believe that his fight against segregation had ended when he hung up his baseball cleats. When Robinson spoke, the congregation drew strength from a "race man," a proud, fearless black man who had stared down Jim Crow without blinking.[29]

Malcolm remained unimpressed with Robinson's politics, calling him a traitor for working with white politicians. Over the next year, they sparred through the press. Robinson claimed that he respected Malcolm's intellect, but he insisted that the Nation of Islam's Black Nationalist philosophy "set back the cause of the Negro."[30]

Later in the year, Robinson indicted Malcolm for failing to risk his life fighting injustice the way that other activists did in the South. "Whom do you think you are kidding, Malcolm, when you say that Negro leaders ought to be 'thankful' that you were not personally present in Birmingham or Mississippi after racial atrocities had been committed there? The inference seems to be that you would have played some dramatic, avenging role."[31]

Robinson did not believe Malcolm would have ever retaliated against white supremacists because he had never done so before. "I think you would have done exactly what you did after your own Muslim brothers were shot and killed in Los Angeles. You left it to the law to take its course."[32]

Apparently Robinson did not realize how eager some Muslims were to retaliate against those who had crossed them. After the former baseball star wrote a searing editorial denouncing Elijah Muhammad, two Muslim officials brought a copy of the *Amsterdam News* to the Nation's Harlem restaurant. When a gang of Muslims overheard the lieutenants

condemning Robinson, they figured that it might be worth their trouble if they hurt him. The only problem was that the avengers confused the former baseball player with a boxer. They staked out the offices of the *Amsterdam News*, looking for *Sugar Ray* Robinson, but when he didn't appear they went to his house. Fortunately for him, he never came home. Eventually the Muslims drove away and both Robinsons escaped Allah's vengeance.[33]

Even if Malcolm disagreed with Robinson's views, he recognized the power of famous black athletes who engaged the freedom struggle, making Cassius Clay all the more valuable to his political aims. Before the early 1960s, most black professional athletes avoided overt political demonstrations, fearing negative consequences to their careers, while others evaded social action as a personal choice. Most black athletes let their performances on the field do the talking.

Yet in 1963, in the aftermath of the Birmingham crisis, some of the most prominent black athletes became important actors in the struggle, but most of them, like Robinson and Patterson, advocated integration as a racial ideal. So when Clay spoke out against the NAACP, he not only renounced the goals of the civil rights movement, he also rejected the accepted expectations for "Negro" athletes. The more time he spent with Malcolm, the more he began to sound like him. For now, though, reporters did not question the origins of his evolving political views. But soon the world would know that Cassius Clay had befriended Malcolm X.

As a subject, writer Alex Haley found Malcolm X more fascinating than anyone he had ever interviewed. Everything he did seemed "dramatic and it wasn't that he was trying to be," Haley later recalled. "It was just the nature of him." In the early winter of 1963, before Malcolm flew to Phoenix to confront Elijah, he met Haley at the Muslims' Harlem luncheonette for a lengthy interview, which was later published in *Playboy*. Malcolm, as was his custom, sat facing the door, sipping coffee, while his aides occasionally whispered messages in his ear.[34]

The interview covered Malcolm's redemption story, and the Black Muslims' ideological beliefs. When Haley asked him if he regretted his comments about the plane crash that killed 120 white Atlantans, he replied, "Sir, as I see the law of justice, it says, as you sow, so shall you

reap. The white man has reveled as the rope snapped black men's necks. He has reveled around the lynching fire. It's only right for the black man's true God, Allah, to defend us—and for us to be joyous because our God manifests his ability to inflict pain on our enemy."[35]

Malcolm knew that some of his answers would frighten people. He didn't trust that Haley or the editors at *Playboy* would publish his comments verbatim, as they had agreed, though the editors kept their word. He also knew that whatever he said would be read by Elijah and other officials in the Nation, so when Haley suggested that he was "the real brains and power of the movement," he immediately corrected him: "Sir, it's heresy to imply that I am in any way whatever even equal to Mr. Muhammad. No man on earth today is his equal." He insisted that no one, including himself, was worthy of replacing the Messenger.[36]

His answer must have pleased Muhammad. In May, after the magazine appeared on newsstands, Haley pondered something that Malcolm had said to him: "You wouldn't believe my past." Perhaps, he thought, the minister would talk more about his life, his evolution, how Malcolm Little became Malcolm X. When the writer asked him if he would consent to an autobiography, he looked stunned. "It was one of the few times I have ever seen him uncertain," Haley later recalled. Malcolm told him that he would need to think about the offer.

After considering it, Malcolm told Haley that he would agree on two conditions: first, every penny of his royalties would go directly to the NOI; second, Elijah Muhammad must approve the project. When Haley visited Muhammad in Phoenix, he explained that the book would help spread his message. Nodding, Elijah answered, "Allah approves."[37]

After Haley returned to New York City, he and Malcolm signed a contract with Doubleday, which included a twenty-thousand-dollar advance for them to split equally. After planning their next meeting, Malcolm handed him a handwritten dedication: "This book I dedicate to The Honorable Elijah Muhammad, who found me here in America in the muck and mire of the filthiest civilization and society on this earth, and pulled me out, cleaned me up, and stood me on my feet, and made me the man that I am today." As promised, Haley filed away the dedication, oblivious of how much Malcolm's life would change by the time he finished the manuscript.[38]

ON FRIDAY, JUNE 14, 1963, an all-white Los Angeles jury rendered its decision in the Stokes case. It convicted nine of thirteen Black Muslim defendants, finding them guilty of assaulting police officers during the raid on the West Coast mosque. Two of the Muslims were acquitted, and the jury could not reach unanimous verdicts on two others. Four of the convicted men received prison sentences ranging from one to five years, one served time in the county jail, and the others received probation.[39]

Ten days later, WNDT in New York televised *The Negro and the American Promise,* a series of interviews Dr. Kenneth Clark conducted with Malcolm, King, and James Baldwin. Clark, a prominent psychology professor at City College in New York, taped the interviews separately and focused his questions on the future of the black man. Still carrying the burden of Birmingham on his shoulders, King looked exhausted on camera, as if he had just returned from a funeral. In a quiet, gentle voice, he recalled his experience in jail, unwavering in his commitment to nonviolence. Malcolm, angered by the Stokes ruling, spoke forcefully and bitterly, repeating his criticisms of King.[40]

James Baldwin sympathized with King but feared that America's blacks were exasperated with his message. Sitting cross-legged, smoking a cigarette, the slight, "dark splinter of a man" with bulbous eyes spoke in contemplative, almost theatrical tones. Wearily, he vented, "You can only survive so many beatings, so much humiliation, so much despair, so many broken promises, before something gives." He warned that although King possessed great moral authority in the South, his message did not resonate with blacks in northern cities. "Poor Martin has gone through God knows what kind of hell to awaken the American conscience," he said, "but Martin has reached the end of his rope."[41]

Baldwin's comments echoed the sentiments of his book *The Fire Next Time,* a searing indictment of America's history of racism. Writing in labyrinthine sentences, he fiercely articulated the anger and alienation of black America. "The so-called American Negro," he wrote, "remains trapped, disinherited, and despised, in a nation that has kept him in bondage for nearly four hundred years and is still unable to recognize him as a human being."[42]

His message carried overtones of Malcolm's speeches and Elijah Muhammad's sermons. In the second of the book's two essays, Baldwin recounted his Sunday afternoon visit with Elijah at the Chicago mansion

in the summer of 1962. Before his meeting with the Black Muslims, many Americans thought of Baldwin as an integrationist, though he never embraced such a label. In the age of television, he emerged as a celebrity writer turned activist, *the* literary voice of the black experience, a poet of the blues.

At the mansion, Baldwin sat nervously at a large dining table for nearly thirty minutes, chatting with Elijah's aides while they waited for him to arrive. When Muhammad entered the room, everyone rose from the table. "Something came into the room with him—his disciples' joy at seeing him, his joy at seeing them," Baldwin wrote. Studying Muhammad, Baldwin recognized that the "central quality in Elijah's face is pain, and his smile is a witness to it—pain so old and deep that it becomes personal and particular only when he smiles." That agony etched onto his face derived from the haunted memories of his boyhood, growing up with eleven siblings in a poor family of sharecroppers in rural Georgia, hearing frightening stories about slave drivers abusing his grandparents, and seeing a bloodied black teenager "dangling from a tree limb" when he was just ten years old.[43]

As Elijah lectured on American history and the affliction of blacks at the hands of whites, Baldwin realized that he couldn't refute him. When Kenneth Clark asked him about the appeal of the Nation, he admitted, "When Malcolm talks or the Muslim ministers talk, they articulate for all the Negro people who hear them . . . their suffering, the suffering which has been in this country so long denied. That's Malcolm's great authority over any of his audiences."[44]

In Baldwin's view, what made Malcolm so potent politically, so sinister, was that when he spoke, he told black people the brutal truth. Malcolm made them confront their fears about whites, about the source of their powerlessness. Without acknowledging their past, he said, they could never sustain meaningful change. When he talked about the solution to ending their suffering, black people believed him because they had lived his words.

For the first time, Baldwin declared, America had legitimate reason to fear the Black Muslims. If whites failed to eradicate the conditions that created the Nation, if they failed to cleanse the country of hatred, then America might not survive. "A bill is coming," he warned, "that I fear America is not prepared to pay."[45]

Chapter Eight

THE GREAT PRETENDER

One forgets that though a clown never imitates a wise man,
the wise man can imitate the clown.

—MALCOLM X

———————

I n November 1961, Roy McHugh, a young reporter from the *Evansville Sunday Courier and Press*, finally got the assignment he wanted—a feature story on undefeated Kentucky boxer Cassius Clay. He left town early, driving 120 miles from Evansville, Indiana, to Louisville. At the local hotel where Cassius and his group were lodging, McHugh called Angelo Dundee from the house phone. "Come on up," Dundee said. "Cassius is here. You can get acquainted."[1]

When he got to Clay's room, the boxer was nowhere to be found. Dundee was the picture of contrition. Cassius had left to avoid the interview, he said. "He's shy, you know. Newspapermen scare him to death." Almost before McHugh could digest the news, Clay rolled out from under a bed and bounced to his feet laughing like "a smooth-cheeked adolescent prankster."

McHugh spent the rest of the day with Cassius, listening to his unconventional "trash talk" and wild predictions. The reporter was so captivated that he returned to Louisville a year later to gather material for a longer feature for *Sport* magazine. Again he spent the day with Cassius, riding in the backseat of his pink Cadillac while Cassius's brother Rudy chauffeured the two around the town. They stopped for gas and a car wash, a haircut, a bite at his parents' home, an evening outing at a bowling alley, and a late-night snack at Big Boy. McHugh watched Clay

In 1963, the Louisville Sponsoring Group, Cassius Clay's management team, sent him to England to fight heavyweight contender Henry Cooper. By shipping him to London, they also hoped to distance Cassius from Malcolm X and the Nation of Islam. Clay came off the canvas to win the fight, but the LSG lost their bid for control over his personal life. Associated Press

mooch money (mainly from him) for gas and food, flirt with women, and work a crowd at the bowling alley—greeting diners, shaking hands, and kissing babies. "'Listen folks,' his body language said, 'I'm running for heavyweight champion, and I'd appreciate your vote.'"

It was a delightful adventure for the sportswriter. Cassius seemed to be genuinely open and friendly, as transparent as a picture window. But there were several disquieting moments. Rudy was clearly uncomfortable driving a white man around the black section of Louisville. He was solemn, seldom speaking to McHugh unless he was asked a direct question. Even then, his answers straddled the line between brevity and rudeness. Whenever they got out of the Caddy, at the parents' home in

Mont Clair Villa or the Champion Lanes bowling alley, Rudy would disappear into another room.

Rudy's attitude toward the day's activity was an easy read. Only once, silently and secretly, did Cassius reveal his inner thoughts. Twice during the day, Clay ordered stops at the San-Se-Re—"Sanitation, Service, Relaxation"—barbershop, where he put coins in a jukebox and chattered with a barber whom he called "Country Girl." At one point, when McHugh was looking in another direction, Cassius and Rudy made "derisive gestures" toward him, pantomiming their true feeling about the white reporter. In a room full of mirrors, however, McHugh had eyes in the back of his head.[2]

Deception, of course, was essential to Clay's profession. It was what separated contenders from ham-and-eggers. The moves Clay made in the ring—all the feints and shifts and creation of openings and avoidance of punishment—were the results of deception. Even outside the ring, deception was essential to Clay's rise to prominence. His outrageous acts, his poetry routines, and his constant boasting hid more than they revealed. As long as he was talking, no one asked what he was thinking. As long as he spent so much time in public, few people wondered what he did in private. He showed only what he wanted others to see—but gradually, what he wanted others to see was changing.

In the weeks after Clay defeated Doug Jones, the Louisville Sponsoring Group became steadily more concerned about reports of his political activities. It was bad enough that he had told Pete Hamill that he had no use for the NAACP and no desire to meet civil rights icon James Meredith. But even more alarming, he used language reminiscent of the Nation of Islam to justify his opinions. It was, he argued, just "human nature to be with your own kind." These views contrasted sharply with the benign message of the LSG. While Bill Faversham, the leader of the group, claimed that Cassius's "idea of a big time is four scoops of ice cream and a double orange juice," Clay was beginning to take controversial social and political stands. The group's leaders believed that he was advancing into dangerous territory at the same moment that he was reaching his biggest paydays.[3]

Although Faversham knew little about the Nation of Islam, the few things he did know rang like a fire bell in the night. Most white

Americans regarded the Nation as a hate group, a weird cult that believed in spaceships and "blue-eyed devils." Clay's association with the organization seemed as dangerous as playing with matches in a munitions factory. It threatened to blow up the LSG's investment and Cassius's title plans.[4]

Faversham and LSG lawyer Gordon Davidson refused to intervene in Clay's personal or religious beliefs. They managed his career and business affairs, not his life, but they agreed that a change of scenery was a good idea. A match outside the United States would remove Cassius from the gaze of suspicious reporters and the influence of his Black Muslim associates. Although there had been negotiations for matches against Floyd Patterson and George Chuvalo in the United States, on April 10 Clay unexpectedly accepted a deal to fight British heavyweight Henry Cooper in London on June 18. For months he had claimed there were only two greats in the world: Britain and himself. Now the two could take stock of each other.[5]

Clay invaded England on May 27. From the moment his TWA flight touched down and he made his way through customs, he confirmed all the worst British notions of brash, overconfident Americans. Soon after his arrival, he verbally attacked his popular opponent. "Cooper's a tramp, a bum and a cripple not worth training for. If he talks jive I'll take him in five," he announced.[6]

His bombast helped him achieve his goal: building interest in the match. Whatever else they thought of him, British sportswriters agreed that "Gaseous Cassius" was a breath of spring for a sport suffering through a long winter. Peter Wilson, the famed *Daily Mirror* columnist, noted, "There has never been anything quite like it. He came, he saw . . . and he talked." Contributing a stanza of his own, he wrote:

> Boxing poet Cassius Clay
> Hit the City yesterday,
> Posing, shouting, full of action
> Selling Clay, the big attraction.[7]

Moving from one publicity stunt to the next, Clay received front-page treatment. Not even the sensational sex-spy scandal involving Secretary of State for War John Dennis Profumo and "showgirl" Christine

Keeler was able to best Cassius's show. With his combination of charm and genuine wit, he dazzled British reporters. But every so often he stopped clowning and jiving and became serious. At those moments, the teachings of Malcolm X—indeed, his very words—rolled effortlessly off Clay's tongue.[8]

The depth of his political opinions and awareness surprised some reporters. "I know wise people," he said quietly to a group of reporters. "I learn from them." He took what his mentors taught seriously. All the public saw was an act. The role he played was not *who* he really was. "A wise man can act a fool. But a fool can't act like a wise man," he mused.[9]

But what manner of a wise man was Clay? Certainly he was different from other American athletes and entertainers. He eschewed marches and integration, and argued for the complete inequality of the sexes. "The word man means master," he said. "The animals, the trees, the chickens, everything was put here for man. Woman is for man. I see women leading men to the dance floor. That's wrong. The man should lead the woman. The man is master." And, he claimed, he knew who God was and when the world would end. "You're a tough man to cope with if you know that."[10]

The serious Clay mystified reporters more than Cassius the clown. Who was he? Who were the wise people with whom he spoke? What were the sources of his beliefs, if in fact he believed what he said? The journalists had interviewed Floyd Patterson, Sammy Davis Jr., Sidney Poitier, and other black celebrities, but they had not heard any of them speak like Cassius Clay.

NOR HAD THEY seen antics quite as flamboyant as his. Days before the weigh-in, he had already overstayed his welcome. "Cash has run out of gas," headlined the *Daily Mirror*. Even the normally laconic Cooper, whose comments had the hard edge of oatmeal, observed, "Surely by now Clay knows that everyone in Britain, including me, hates his guts." But just in case he had a circle of silent supporters, he alienated them too with his weigh-in performance at the London Palladium. Before two thousand curious spectators who had queued up for the event on a chilly, rainy day, he made a mock-royal entrance wearing an ankle-length red-and-white satin robe with "CASSIUS CLAY THE GREATEST" stitched on the back. Strutting about the stage, he

opened his hand wide, displaying five fingers, the number of rounds he predicted the fight would last.[11]

Unquestionably, Clay had offended, angered, and outraged millions of Britons. "There won't be more than a handful of people hoping to see him win," judged Wilson. "Yet this astonishing young Negro has done more to restore world-wide interest in boxing than any individual . . . since the palmist days of Joe Louis."[12]

Clay's entrance for the match in Wembley Stadium was even more elaborate than the weigh-in. Preceded by a band of Coldstream Guardsmen and an assortment of British and American soldiers and wearing an ornate crown, he entered the ring to the sound of trumpets and boos. It was a circus act. A stunned BBC announcer chirped that it was "ridiculous"; the American had "cheapened the game." But Clay only smiled at the waves of jeers and heckles. "The noise he heard was in direct proportion to the number of tickets he sold (35,000) and his take of the gate (about $60,000)," wrote Huston Horn of *Sports Illustrated*.[13]

The temperature was in the low sixties, and although the rain had stopped, a thick band of low clouds hung in the bruised sky above Wembley. There were no stars visible in the heavens, but there were dozens at ringside. The most famous was Elizabeth Taylor. At the height of her fame and beauty—*Cleopatra* had just premiered in New York—she attended the match with her lover and costar Richard Burton and received what appeared to be a personal bow from Cassius.[14]

Clay's opponent, Henry Cooper, had spent his career fighting a perpetual battle against the inevitable. He was a fine boxer, with knockout power in his left hand, but the sharp features of his face—prominent cheekbones, deep-set eyes—and tissue-thin skin rendered him chronically susceptible to cuts. "That's why the people who live off Clay selected Cooper," wrote Jimmy Cannon. "The flesh on his face is lined with the scribbling of old scars. A hiccup reopens them." Sooner or later in any competitive fight, Cooper's face would resemble a scene out of a slasher movie. His goal was always the same: win before the referee stopped the contest.[15]

Knowing that Clay's punches were of a peculiarly surgical nature and that he better score while his eyes were clear of his own blood, Cooper began the fight like he had an early curfew. He rushed Cassius, threw lunging punches, and held and hit in the clinches. Cooper's fans

reacted with delight. After one "unclean clinch" Clay emerged with a smear of blood on his nose, and the blood this time was not Cooper's. Wembley exploded with cheers. Clay appealed to the referee "for justice," but on this night, the 148th anniversary of the Battle of Waterloo, he found no sympathy.[16]

Between rounds Dundee scolded Clay, telling him to stay out of clinches and fight from the outside. In the second, Cassius did just that, moving and jabbing. By the middle of the round a dark smudge, like a small grape, appeared under Cooper's left eye. After several more pinprick jabs, the grape split open and a trail of blood trickled down his face. A round later, another cutting punch above the left eye turned the trickle into a river. The BBC's blow-by-blow man, Simon Smith, informed his listeners, "Cooper's left eye is beginning to look a little bit bad now. This is the sort of thing, of course, that Cassius Clay does. He scientifically and systematically cuts up his opponent and that's why he stops so many inside the distance." But Cooper's eye was more than a "little bit bad." It was literally spurting blood, as if an artery had been sliced open, splattering onto reporters at ringside.

In full control of the contest, with still more than a round before the fifth, Cassius virtually stopped punching and began mugging and clowning, shouting boasts to the spectators close to the ring and sneaking glances at Liz Taylor. He extended his gloves to keep Cooper at arm's length and popped his gloves in the English fighter's face. He jutted out his chin and challenged Cooper to hit him. "Contemptible cheek," one ringsider muttered. "A show of bad taste and worse sportsmanship," Horn wrote. Sitting at ringside, Bill Faversham was furious. After the round ended, he stormed to Clay's corner, telling Dundee, "Make him stop clowning."[17]

But Clay was determined to coast until the fifth and then fulfill his prediction. Ignoring Faversham's orders, he continued his act, dancing and talking and treating Cooper like a bit player in his Cassius Clay Show. In the meantime, Cooper continued to bleed, pawing at his eye like a wounded bear. He looked to Wilson like "a red-rimmed Cyclops." The British champion could already sense that it was bad. "You don't actually feel a bad cut," he said later. "It just stings and goes numb. What tells you it is a bad one is when you feel the warm blood dripping on your body. This one felt like a tap pouring on my chest."[18]

Just before the end of the round, Cooper saw an opening. Perhaps, as Clay later said, he had taken his eyes off Cooper to "look at Cleopatra." Regardless, Cooper lunged at him with a sweeping, rising left hook that landed solidly on his cheek. Clay bounced against the ropes, then crumbled to the canvas. His face was blank, like he had just come out of a powerful anesthetic. He rose to his feet quickly but moved like a drunk, unsteady, uncomprehending, his hands at his side. But the bell sounded immediately. Dundee leaped into the ring and escorted Clay to the corner.

"You OK?" Dundee asked.

"Yea, but Cooper's getting tired," Cassius answered.[19]

Dundee noticed a small tear in the seam of Clay's left glove. While he lobbied the referee and the British Boxing Board of Control for new gloves, his second broke a vial of smelling salt under Clay's nose, dropped ice cubes into his trunks, and massaged his legs. Later the legend would grow that Dundee's rant to the authorities gained valuable seconds—even minutes—for Clay to recover before the fifth round. Not so. Clay had recovered fully in the sixty seconds between rounds, and he was ready to make good on his prediction.[20]

As Clay threw punches, small tufts of horsehair spit out of the tear in his glove like spent cartridges, noted one reporter. A punch or two and blood was flowing from Cooper's eye in "sobbing, pulsing spurts," splattering referee Tommy Little. Dressed all in white, the referee looked like he had been working in an active army field hospital. "Blood from the red ruin which was the left side of Cooper's face splashed yards out of the ring and on to the paper on which I was writing," wrote Wilson. A reporter for *Time* magazine said Cooper "looked like a man who had just gone through the windshield of a car." Spectators chanted, "Murder! Murder!" and "Stop it! Stop it!" as they threw wadded-up newspapers into the ring. Liz Taylor jumped out of her seat crying, "No, no, no." She could not watch any longer. Finally, at the same time as Cooper's corner threw in the towel, Little halted the contest.[21]

Back in his dressing room, Cassius praised Cooper. He wasn't a bum and a cripple, he admitted. "He shook me up. He hit me harder than I've ever been hit. . . . I was a little numb." With his performance in England officially over, he was gracious and soft-spoken, almost as if he

were auditioning for another role. But more than anything he wanted to return to America and talk with the wise men he so admired.[22]

THE DAY AFTER he fought Cooper, Clay returned to the United States. His victory did little to improve his reputation among boxing scribes. Jimmy Cannon summed up the prevalent opinion: "It was clear after the close fight with Doug Jones that Clay didn't qualify as an opponent for Sonny Liston. There is no doubt about it now that Cooper has exposed him as a gabby amateur." But he knew that after Liston dispatched Floyd Patterson in their rematch, Clay would get a title shot. Cannon's only suggestion was that the match be held in an emergency ward, saving Cassius a ride in an ambulance.[23]

"I don't need Liston," Clay told reporters when he landed at Idlewild Airport, which would be renamed John F. Kennedy Airport at the end of the year. "He needs me." He now fancied himself a world figure, the sort of man who could be plopped down any place on the globe and attract adoring crowds. "I'm very big in those foreign countries. They love me over there," he said.[24]

Clay knew he was the draw. The gates for the Archie Moore, Charlie Powell, Doug Jones, and Henry Cooper fights had proved it. But he was reckless in the ring. If Cooper had caught him early in the fourth, rather than just before the bell, Cassius might not have survived the round. The thought gave pause to his sponsors. Clay was now ranked second in the world, and he would advance to first after Liston defeated Patterson. The Louisville Sponsoring Group saw no reason for him to face another contender. The risk was just too great. Besides, before the end of the year, LSG lawyer Gordon Davidson wrote a sponsor, Clay "could earn somewhere in the neighborhood of $100,000 through public appearances and exhibitions." It seemed that every week he received an offer to perform on a television variety show or make some other appearance. Frank Sinatra wanted Cassius for a major part in a movie. For the small screen, Jack Benny promised to write an entire script about him if he appeared on his show, the producers of *Mr. Ed* promised similar star treatment, and executives for *Talent Scouts* and other television programs requested his services.[25]

To be sure, Davidson did not want any of the appearances "to prevent Clay from stepping into the ring with Liston with the best possible

conditioning and training, and thereby give him the best possible opportunity to defeat the 'Ugly Bear.'" But he supported marketing "the boy's national image" as a show business personality. Should Liston defeat him, Davidson argued, Cassius could still make money as "a comic star."[26]

But Cassius was living two lives. Publicly trained by a white man and managed by a consortium of white millionaires, he was also privately advised by Malcolm, Rudy, and a small group of trusted Muslims. His career demanded that he work with the one group, while his psyche depended on him living with the other. Whenever a reporter probed near the heart of the matter, he asserted his independence. Tom Wolfe recalled hearing a phone conversation in New York between Cassius and some man who wanted to set up a business deal. When the man asked to talk to Clay's manager, Cassius exploded: "I don't have no manager. I got a trainer and he's in Florida. I'm my own boss. I got backers, they put up the money, but I'm the boss, I'm the *onliest* boss."[27]

This theme—"who made me is *me*"—was nothing new. But since moving closer to the Nation, Clay had grown more inwardly self-confident and outwardly self-aware. In a conversation with Alex Haley, Malcolm took credit for Cassius's maturation. "In general," he said, "I taught him that ninety percent of success would depend upon how alert and knowledgeable he became to the true natures and motives of all the people who flocked around him."[28]

Clay absorbed these lessons well. After spending time with the fighter for an *Esquire* profile, Wolfe concluded that Cassius's "chief mental asset" was that "he is quite aware, even supersensitive at times, to other people's motives. He is aware of the newspapermen's motives, his backer's motives, his trainers' motives, autograph hunters' motives, and even the social motives of sophisticated white New Yorkers he has seen only at a glance."[29]

Suspicion of white men colored Clay's awareness. When he returned to Louisville a week after the Cooper match, he avoided his white sponsors and spent time on the West Side, entertaining black youngsters and joking with old friends. When a white reporter asked him why he didn't follow Dundee's instructions and try to knock out Cooper in the third round, he replied angrily, "I'm the boss in the ring, not Angelo or my backers. They're boss outside the ring, handling money and that stuff. They've got the easy job."[30]

Without an upcoming match consuming his time, Clay was free to travel with Rudy and attend more Nation of Islam functions. Doing so, he risked that a journalist might see him at a mosque and reach the obvious conclusion, and it was only a matter of time until the inevitable came to pass.

On July 2, Bruce Hills, a reporter for the *Chicago Sun-Times*, spied a tomato-red Cadillac convertible in an alley behind the Nation's University of Islam. He waited, and soon Cassius, Rudy, and another man came out the back door and got into the car. Clay was dressed in conservative Muslim attire and wearing a star-and-crescent NOI membership pin. Since Cassius's Kentucky driver's license had been suspended for repeated traffic infractions, Rudy got behind the wheel and Cassius climbed into the backseat. Two automobiles filled with "glowering Black Muslims, determined to protect the heavyweight pretender from questions," flanked the Cadillac. But Hills and his driver were determined to get the story, even if it meant a high-speed chase.[31]

Out of the alley onto 54th Street, then to Lake Park and finally to Stony Island, the reporter in his own car dogged Clay, conducting a dangerous, rolling interview. He asked the obvious question: "Are you a Black Muslim?"

For a block, Cassius considered the question before responding, "No," only to promptly amend his answer to, "I don't know." After another second or two he added, "I'm for the Black Muslims."

"Do you believe everything they advocate?" Hills asked.

"Listen, I've looked real hard at every organization that's for the black man. This is the greatest one I've found." Then, raising his voice above the roar of traffic, he emphasized, "The Black Muslims are the sweetest thing next to God."

As the interview continued, Cassius explained that he was in favor of "anything good that can happen for the black man," but that he would not participate in any southern demonstrations. "I don't want anybody to sic dogs on me," he said.

Before Rudy turned onto the Skyway and headed toward the Indiana border, Hills asked another question: "Are you afraid your identification with the Black Muslims might hurt your boxing career?"

"Say, I don't have a record," Clay replied, referring to Sonny Liston's criminal past.

A day later, Cassius was already backing away from his answers. To other reporters, he did not deny that the interview had taken place, but he asserted that he hadn't been wearing a Black Muslim pin and wasn't a member of any organization. He was still searching for a movement under the leadership of a holy man that offered an "eternal solution and not just a temporary one," a statement that was pulled straight out of the teaching of Elijah Muhammad. Besides, he believed that athletes and entertainers did not have the time or experience to lead civil rights groups. Someday he might join an organization, but until then he would "wait to see which is best."[32]

MALCOLM X AGREED, at least publicly, that black athletes and entertainers should not define or lead the civil rights movement. On July 22, 1963, the day of the Liston-Patterson rematch in Las Vegas, Malcolm's fight was in Brooklyn, where more than a thousand protesters were demonstrating against racial discrimination at a hospital construction site. From across the street, where he shook hands and supported the participants, he watched as policeman arrested peaceful protesters and sent them off to the station in paddy wagons. What did a million-dollar contest in Las Vegas have to do with this fight against discrimination?[33]

Robert Lipsyte, a young *New York Times* reporter, asked the question for a sidebar to the Liston-Patterson match. "They'll always give us the opportunity to act like animals," responded a black lawyer on the picket line. "We're beyond the point where we can get excited over a Negro hitting a home run or winning a championship," offered another protester. When Lipsyte approached Malcolm, he received more than a comment. The minister dismissed the reporter's inquiry with a brusque reply: "That's a stupid question." With that, three shaven-headed members of the Fruit of Islam stepped between Lipsyte and Malcolm. They "formed a wall with their chests and walked me into the gutter," the reporter recalled.[34]

"The only stupid question is the unanswered question," Lipsyte shouted. Smiling, Malcolm nodded to his bodyguards to let the reporter through. "I'm pleased to see that the two best men in the sport are black," he said. "But they'll be exploited, of course, and the promoters will get all the bread. They let a Negro excel if it's going to make some money for them."

Ending the conversation, Malcolm said he hoped that Liston would "really shake Patterson up." Floyd had attacked the Nation. Malcolm, the single-minded revolutionary, obviously knew something about boxing.

IN LAS VEGAS, Cassius worked the spectators and sportswriters who were in town for the big fight like he was performing in the showroom. Dressed in a black-and-white houndstooth sports jacket, he strutted around the streets and casinos belittling the other fighters. According to Cassius, Liston would dispose of Patterson and then have to face him. That would spell the end of Sonny's reign of terror. And the world would be blessed with a new titleholder, a pretty champion in stark contrast with the "big ugly bear." As he told several journalists, "That poor ol' man, he's so ugly, his wife drives him to the gym every morning 'fore the sun comes up, so nobody'll have to look at him around home."[35]

Generally Liston endured the verbal assaults, realizing that it was Clay's shtick, part of the promotion scheme to get people interested in a match between them. But Sonny was a violent, unpredictable man who, given his mood of the moment, was apt to take offense. That was precisely what happened a few days before the Liston-Patterson match. Sonny was shooting craps and losing money at the Thunderbird Hotel. "Liston was a mean-tempered son-of-a-bitch," recalled publicist Harold Conrad, "and he was losing, so naturally he's mad. Liston picks up the dice and throws craps and there's a big silence."[36]

Then a sharp voice cracked the hushed stillness. "Look at that big ugly bear; he can't even shoot craps," called out Clay, leaning against a wall close to the game. Liston glared, rolled again, and once more threw craps. Again the insouciant voice: "Look at the big ugly bear. He can't do nothing right." It was the voice of a man about to walk the plank.

Liston had reached the limit of his limited patience. Walking over to Cassius, he fixed him with a dead-eyed stare and said, "Listen, you nigger faggot. If you don't get out of here in ten seconds, I'm gonna pull that big tongue out of your mouth and stick it up your ass." A *New York Times* reporter who watched the confrontation said that Liston also slapped Clay hard across his face, but Conrad swore that there was no slap. Just the hard eyes and violent threat and promise that worse was to come.[37]

Clay walked away. "He scared the shit out of him; you better believe it," Conrad said. Cassius agreed: "[That] big ugly bear scared me bad."[38]

But Cassius returned for the title fight, determined to upstage Liston and Patterson. When the announcer introduced him before the match, he slipped gracefully between the ropes, shook hands with Patterson, and started to walk toward Liston. Halfway there he froze in mock horror, raised his hands in a gesture of surrender, and fled the ring. The pantomime drew laughter and applause.

"'Our boy' stole the show completely," Gordon Davidson wrote a member of the LSG. As it turned out, the fight itself proved no competition for the Cassius Clay Show. In another one-sided match, Liston again knocked out Patterson in the first round. A reporter for *Time* summed up the contest: "Like a man killing a rabbit with a stick, he clubbed the hapless challenger to the canvas—gracelessly and methodically, his sulphur-and-obsidian eyes betraying neither pleasure nor anger."[39]

To the dismay of sportswriters, Liston seemed indestructible, a fighter who was likely to hold the title for years. "He's here for keeps," noted Jim Murray. "It is like finding a live bat on a string under your Christmas tree." And sportswriters believed that there was no one in boxing who could get rid of him. Liston, commented columnist Arthur Daley, was "arrogant, surly, mean, rude and altogether frightening." And "nobody," not even the "Loudmouth from Louisville," had a chance against him.[40]

Cassius, however, did not think that Liston was invincible. After the fight, he was loud and obnoxious, at one point grabbing the TV-theater microphone and announcing his intentions to closed-circuit viewers. It was all, Daley thought, a bit shabby. "The exceedingly likable Clay is lousing up his public relations by his boasting and it's high time he eases off and let his fists serve as his spokesman. Unfortunately, they don't speak anywhere near as eloquently as his vocal cords."[41]

Yet Clay's ongoing vaudeville routine was going exactly as planned. By mid-1963 he thought of himself more as an entertainer than a boxer, identifying with Sam Cooke and Elvis Presley more than Sonny Liston and Floyd Patterson. When Tom Wolfe interviewed him, he referred to himself as a "show-business figure." "I don't feel I'm in boxing anymore. It's show business." When it was showtime, his "150-watt eyeballs" lit

up and he went into his act. "He wants to be thought of as a man who does the clown act consummately well, which is to say, an actor," Wolfe observed.[42]

He aspired not to Liston's title but to Elvis Presley's. He wanted to be the king—king of the world. Pursuing that goal, after attending the title fight he went to Columbia Studios in New York to cut a spoken-word LP entitled *I Am the Greatest.* Cassius claimed that he wrote "everything on the record" and predicted it would outsell comedian Vaughn Meader's enormously popular spoof of the Kennedy family. In truth, the LP was a collaborative production, filled with sophisticated comic material written by Gary Belkin. When they first met, Belkin was shocked by Clay's reading problems. Clay was in fact an undiagnosed dyslexic, and Belkin judged him "a functional illiterate" and set about composing lengthy poems to go with Cassius's basic couplets.[43]

People assumed that Clay wrote such poems as "I Am the Greatest" and "Will the Real Sonny Liston Please Fall Down," and that he actually came up with the line that he was so pretty that his "face should be considered a natural resource" and preserved by the secretary of the interior, as opposed to Liston, whose face "should be appropriated by the Bureau of Wildlife." But he did not create his material any more than Presley wrote the hundreds of songs he recorded. What Clay provided was the Louisville Lip character, and during the production of the record he worked diligently to weave the material into his persona. He memorized poems, questioned the comic material, and helped shape the finished product. That many of the cuts became permanent routines in his repertoire demonstrates how carefully and successfully he played his part.

Away from the studio, accompanied by the ever-present Rudy and a few black friends, Cassius ventured into Harlem. There, he attended NOI rallies and had private meetings with Malcolm. By the summer of 1963, after three years of feature stories about him in *Time, Life, Ebony, Jet, Sports Illustrated,* and other national publications, scores of television appearances, and his photograph in hundreds of newspaper stories, Clay's face was too well known to go unrecognized.

On August 10, he attended an outdoor rally on the corner of 115th Street and Lenox Avenue, where Malcolm spoke to a large audience about the upcoming March on Washington. The Nation, he said, would

not participate in the march, which he suggested had been hijacked by the Kennedy administration. "When the white man found out he couldn't stop [the march], he decided to join it," he claimed. It was just another example of "black men with white hearts," and of the fact that Martin Luther King and his ilk had too cozy a relationship with white politicians.[44]

An undercover agent from the NYPD's Bureau of Special Services spied Cassius Clay at the rally, listening intently to Malcolm. Now the top-ranked heavyweight contender, Clay was far from being an invisible man.[45]

ON AUGUST 28, 1963, the entire country focused its attention on the nation's capital for the March on Washington for Jobs and Freedom. The television networks assigned hundreds of people to cover the march, setting up dozens of cameras between the Washington Monument and the Lincoln Memorial. On the morning of the demonstration, more than two thousand buses, twenty-one special trains, ten chartered flights, and armies of cars converged on the capital. From all over the country, thousands of people, young and old, black and white, came to DC to witness a historic occasion.[46]

Elijah Muhammad had forbidden his followers from joining. In the months leading up to the Freedom March, FOI captains reminded the faithful that there were serious consequences for violating his edict. In Chicago, Supreme Captain Raymond Sharrieff issued a directive: "Let me put it more clearly to you. Do not participate in these demonstrations. If you are caught, you will wish you were dead."[47]

Although Malcolm publicly maintained that no Black Muslim would attend the march, he could not resist being near the center of the action. After Muhammad granted him special permission, he traveled to the capital to witness what he called "the Farce on Washington." In the lobby of the Statler Hilton Hotel, he engaged young demonstrators and reporters, offering political opinions, but never divulged his frustrations with the Nation's disengagement from the movement.[48]

Later that afternoon, sitting in his hotel room, he watched Martin Luther King deliver his iconic "I Have a Dream" speech, an idealistic vision of interracial brotherhood. When reporters asked him what he thought about the Freedom March, Malcolm compared it to a sporting

event—"the Rose Bowl game, the Kentucky Derby, and the World Series"—the kind of event where people went simply to say, "I was there." The Freedom March had done nothing but create false hope for blacks, he insisted.[49]

A few weeks later, Malcolm traveled to Chicago to visit Elijah. Before he arrived at the mansion, C. Eric Lincoln, the author of *The Black Muslims in America*, waited in the foyer to meet the Supreme Minister. He wondered how Elijah would receive him since many Muslims had expressed dissatisfaction with his book. One angry minister told him that he wanted to "burn them as fast as they came off the presses." But Elijah greeted him with a firm handshake and welcoming eyes, though he did not smile. In fact, Lincoln thought, he had never seen him smile—except moments later, when Malcolm entered the living room. Elijah embraced Malcolm, kissing him gently on both cheeks, and asked about Betty and their children. Lincoln never suspected friction between them. "There was genuine affection here between these two," he observed, "not unlike the affection between a father and son who has done well for the family name."[50]

If Malcolm felt uneasy being around Elijah, he masked his anxiety. Lincoln sensed that the bond between them was stronger than ever. After they all sat down, the Messenger lectured the ministers while Malcolm dutifully wrote notes, transcribing his every word. Since their meeting in Phoenix, Malcolm had submitted, "getting [Elijah's] permission before doing anything, like he should have been doing all the time." Lincoln was unaware that Malcolm's faith in the Messenger had already begun to erode.[51]

The next day, September 15, Malcolm learned that the Ku Klux Klan had bombed Birmingham's 16th Street Baptist Church, killing four young black girls. As the father of three daughters and another on the way, he could well imagine the pain the parents suffered. He bristled at calls for turning the other cheek. The bombing was a brutal reminder, he said, that the March on Washington had failed. "The Negroes spent a lot of money, had a good time, and enjoyed a real circus or carnival atmosphere," he told a reporter. "Now that the show is over, the black masses are still without land, without jobs, and without homes. . . . Their Christian churches are still being bombed, their innocent little

girls murdered. So," he asked the writer, "what did the March on Washington accomplish? Nothing!"[52]

SINCE JULY, WHEN a reporter from the *Chicago Sun-Times* caught Cassius Clay leaving Mosque No. 2, writers had been investigating his involvement with the Nation, probing for clues about his relationship with Malcolm. When he was not training, he visited the Nation's mosques, though he never advertised his presence at Muslim rallies in the same way that he did his attendance at Sonny Liston's title fights.

In late September, Clay attended an Oakland conference on "The Mind of the Ghetto," organized by Don Warden, chairman of the Afro-American Association, a Black Nationalist group. Warden invited political figures, celebrities, and athletes, including Clay and Malcolm. Although Malcolm did not attend, John Shabazz, minister of the Los Angeles mosque, represented the Nation. When a reporter questioned Clay about his position on the civil rights movement, he denied interest in joining the struggle. "I don't stand for anything," he said. "I'm not a politician. I don't talk against anything. I'm a peaceful man." After the writer asked him about his affiliation with the Nation, he replied, "It's like I said though, I don't identify myself with anybody—anybody except Cassius Clay."[53]

Much as he might deny his involvement with the Nation, his interviews revealed that he had embraced their philosophy. Cassius puzzled writers with a story about how two flocks of birds in Africa fought each other, became temporarily mixed, and then separated. The moral of the story, he explained, was that the "law of nature" created a world where people "should associate with their own kind."[54]

Listening to Cassius, reporters detected the Nation's influence on his evolving identity. In the past, he had proclaimed that he would save boxing because he was the most talented and entertaining fighter in the world. Yet as he listened to Muhammad and spent more time with Malcolm, Clay began thinking of himself as divine, graced by the power of Allah. "I am the resurrection. I am the prophet," he declared, sent to save boxing. Hearing Muhammad and Malcolm preach about black superiority and the power of true believers affirmed what Cassius had always thought about himself: that he *was* the greatest.[55]

After the conference ended, Cassius traveled to Philadelphia to attend Muhammad's first public lecture of the year. More than six thousand people, including black and white "guests" and reporters, packed the arena at the corner of 45th and Market Streets. Sitting erectly in the third row next to Bundini Brown, Clay listened intently as Muhammad gave a lecture titled "Separation or Death." The Supreme Minister excoriated the white man, who was "created for the purpose of murdering black people." If blacks fail to separate from whites, he warned, "they will die."[56]

At several points during Muhammad's harangue, Cassius leapt to his feet, loudly applauding his wisdom, while the Jewish Bundini slumped in his chair with a quizzical look on his face. As an auditory learner, Cassius was mesmerized by what he had *heard* at Muslim meetings. Since childhood, when his father repeatedly told him tall tales, he had gravitated toward grand stories, legends, and myths. Muhammad's yarns about the big-head scientist Yacub, the Mother Ship, and white devils excited Cassius the same way that his father aroused his imagination. Muhammad's simple lessons—that all white men were evil and all black men were good—echoed his father's rants. Over and over again, he heard Muslim ministers repeat Muhammad's messages. The oral culture of the Nation emphasized preaching and "fishing," memorization and recitation, which suited Cassius's communication style. He did not have to prove that he understood Muhammad's doctrine by reading and writing. He could learn about history, politics, and religion simply by listening and talking, an empowering feeling for a man with dyslexia.

Near the end of the rally, an official asked Clay to rise from his seat so that everyone could see that one of the most famous athletes in America was proud to stand with the Nation. At that moment, even before he won the heavyweight championship, Clay became a propaganda tool for the sect. He was a visible symbol of the movement at a time when the black masses were growing increasingly disenchanted with the Nation's failure to improve the conditions of black citizens.[57]

No one heard these criticisms more often than Malcolm. On the streets of Harlem, blacks complained that the Nation needed to do more; *he* needed to do more. The Black Muslims talked tough, but when it came time to confront the white man, they were nowhere to be found. Malcolm sensed that the disaffection among blacks threatened

the future of the movement. He knew that Muhammad would never change his tactics. What they needed, then, was an infusion of energy and youth, an icon of strong, defiant black manhood, a voice that could be heard above all the noise. So when Cassius Clay received a standing ovation in Philadelphia, a stirring sound that Malcolm had only heard at Madison Square Garden, he knew that he had found the Nation's new symbol, a galvanizing force for the movement.

Yet the boxer was not yet prepared for such a role. After the rally ended, reporters rushed toward him, but he was in no mood to answer their questions. "If you want to interview somebody, interview Malcolm X," he quipped. "He's really got something important to say." The newsmen were stunned that, for the first time in memory, Cassius did not want to talk. He departed the arena without saying much, worried that the media's muckraking might derail his shot at the title.[58]

Clay did not yet realize that Malcolm had bigger plans for him. Nor could he have foreseen that the rally in Philadelphia would be the last time he would ever see Malcolm and Muhammad together. From his third row seat, he witnessed Muhammad bestow a great honor upon Malcolm, naming him national minister. But this was just another test, a challenge for Malcolm to prove that he really was his "most faithful, hard-working minister." What Cassius saw that day was a mirage, a kingdom in harmony. He heard Muhammad close with an eerily prophetic promise. Malcolm, he said, "will follow me until he dies."[59]

BACK TO THE GRAVE

How can you justify being nonviolent in Mississippi and Alabama, when your churches are being bombed and your little girls are being murdered?

—MALCOLM X

"History," *Newsweek* declared, "would mark it: the summer of 1963 was a time of revolution, the season when 19 million U.S. Negroes demanded payment of the century-old promissory note called the Emancipation Proclamation." The revolution of 1963 was rooted in the rich soil of the South, where overworked field hands bristled under a sharecropping system that locked them into permanent poverty. The revolution could be seen in the northern slums, where blacks protested dilapidated housing, police brutality, and substandard wages. It could be heard in the mourners' cries at Ronald Stokes's funeral, in the prayers of Martin Luther King, and in the sermons of Malcolm X. From the churches of Birmingham to the streets of Harlem, a "revolution of rising expectations" swept the country. It was a revolution teetering between frustration and faith, despair and hope, nonviolence and bloodshed.[1]

In Detroit, Malcolm talked about the revolution. Reverend Albert Cleage Jr., a Black Nationalist Christian minister, had invited him to deliver the keynote address at the Northern Grassroots Leadership Conference in November. Organized by the Group on Advanced Leadership (GOAL), the conference attracted a wide range of radicals, militants, Marxists, and socialists who viewed Malcolm as a leader of Black Nationalism.[2]

On November 10, Richard Henry, GOAL president, greeted two thousand blacks, most of whom were not Muslims, into the King Solomon Baptist Church with a grand announcement: "Welcome to the revolution!" At the conference, organizers proclaimed support for the all-black Freedom Now Party, the principle of armed self-defense, and solidarity with "the colored oppressed people of the world." From the pulpit, Malcolm delivered his "Message to the Grassroots," a Nationalist manifesto that would endure as a source of inspiration for Black Power activists over the next decade.[3]

He began by reminding the audience that what united them—with each other and with the dark-skinned people in Africa and Asia—was resistance to racial oppression. History, he said, taught that only bloody revolution would end the long suffering of black people. The nonviolent "Negro revolution" led by King and other integrationist liberals, he insisted, was not a revolution at all. A real revolution "is bloody, revolution is hostile, revolution knows no compromise, revolution overturns and destroys everything that gets in its way."[4]

Marches, boycotts, and sit-ins were not revolutionary tactics. "Whoever heard of a revolution where they lock arms," he asked, "singing 'We Shall Overcome'? You don't do that in a revolution. You don't do any singing, you're too busy swinging."[5]

Malcolm's speech gave voice to the growing anger in black America. It also reflected his evolving global perspective, linking the black freedom struggle in America to the anticolonialist movement in Africa. Between 1960 and 1963, twenty-four African nations wrested independence from Western colonists. For Malcolm, these revolutions were successful because black people demanded land of their own and "engaged in a bloody battle." But, he complained, "Negro" civil rights leaders were not demanding land. "These Negroes aren't asking for any nation—they're trying to crawl back to the plantation."[6]

Listening to him speak that evening, activist Gloria Richardson recognized that Malcolm sounded more like a freedom fighter than a disciple of Elijah Muhammad. He hardly said anything about religion or the Nation of Islam. His speech was not written to build the Nation or praise the teachings of Muhammad. Instead, Malcolm's "Message to the Grassroots" announced his own vision for a mass movement that

unified all black people, regardless of religion. It represented an ideological break from Muhammad, a fusion of Black Nationalism and internationalism, and the declaration of his political independence. That night in Detroit, Richardson "wondered how long it would be before he would break with [the Nation]."7

IF MALCOLM'S LOYALTY to Elijah Muhammad was in doubt, Cassius Clay's was not. Five days after Malcolm spoke in Detroit, Clay was spotted in New York with three burly Black Muslim security guards. A few days before he was scheduled to film an appearance for *The Jack Paar Tonight Show*, the Selective Service notified him that he was required to get a physical examination, which would determine his eligibility for the armed services. But Clay wasn't worried about wearing a uniform or carrying a rifle. "I've just spent four hours with God today," he said after leaving Mosque No. 7. "He's going to fix it so I won't have to serve in the Army."8

Clay found his sanctuary visiting with Malcolm in Harlem at Mosque No. 7, the Shabazz Restaurant, and the Hotel Theresa, where he was staying. Since Clay returned from London that summer, his relationship with Malcolm had deepened. Spending more time in New York, he snuck into meetings with Malcolm. He solicited his mentor's advice about all things, spiritual and professional. "Malcolm," he said later, "was very intelligent, with a good sense of humor, a wise man. When he talked, he held me spellbound for hours."9

In their private moments together, they forged a friendship, a bond, a brotherhood. Clay adored Malcolm and treated him like an older brother. He swelled with pride whenever the minister was near. Malcolm treated him like a man whose thoughts mattered, not like an athlete whose only worth was his body. Cassius, he observed, was "sensitive, very humble, yet shrewd."10

Studying him, Malcolm recognized that the thoughtful boxer had "a plan in his public clowning." That plan was on full display when Clay filmed an appearance for *The Jack Paar Tonight Show*. Before introducing him, Paar mentioned that Clay put on quite "a wild act," but he found him to be a genuinely "well-mannered young man." Paar told the audience that offstage, Clay spoke "very quiet and sensibly." The fighter's clowning, he suggested, was only an act.11

Paar's program was known for pairing disparate characters in humorous settings. When Cassius walked onstage, he met Liberace, the flamboyant musician known for his glittering costumes and outrageous personality. When Cassius shook Liberace's hand, he buckled his knees, feigning injury at the strength of the effeminate musician's strong grip, provoking laughter from the audience.

Clay reminded Paar that not only was he the "resurrection of the fight game" but someday he would also become a "great singer" too. After he told the host about his upcoming album with Columbia Records, Paar suggested that he and Liberace perform a song together. It seemed like an odd pairing—a black boxer and a closeted gay pianist—but the two were perfectly suited to share the stage. Both men thought of themselves as entertainers and they shared a love for audiences. Liberace sat down at the grand piano, then he abruptly rose from the bench and told Cassius to step aside so that the television viewers could see his candelabra. The crowd roared with laughter as Cassius and Liberace exchanged smiles. Finally, the musician deadpanned to the self-promoting boxer, "For a change, do the one about you."

After performing a tune, they delivered an encore:

Clay comes out to meet Liston and Liston starts to retreat,
If Liston goes back an inch farther he'll end up in a ringside seat.
Clay swings with his left, Clay swings with his right,
Look at young Cassius carry the fight.
Liston keeps backing, but there's not enough room,
It's a matter of time till Clay lowers the boom.
Now Clay lands with a right, what a beautiful swing,
And the punch raises the Bear clean out of the ring.
Liston is still rising and the ref wears a frown,
For he can't start counting till Sonny comes down.
Now Liston is disappearing from view, the crowd is going frantic,
But radar stations have picked him up somewhere over the Atlantic.
Who would have thought when they came to the fight,
That they'd witness the launching of a human satellite?
Yes the crowd did not dream, when they put up the money,
That they would see a total eclipse of the Sonny.[12]

CLAY'S PERFORMANCE WON over an audience outside the world of boxing. While reporters hounded him about his association with the Black Muslims, Clay distanced himself publicly from the controversial sect. Instead of talking about his relationship with Malcolm or Elijah, he continued to craft a nonthreatening image—an image of a smiling, jovial "Negro," an entertainer cracking harmless jokes and reciting poems, an act encouraged by his white managers. But the real Cassius Clay—the man who would become Muhammad Ali—could hardly hide his enthusiasm for the most controversial black organization in the country.

Dan Parker, a prominent columnist for the *New York Journal-American*, reported that while Clay was in New York, he visited corporate offices on Madison Avenue proudly wearing an NOI signet ring, a clear "badge of membership," and showed people a picture of himself with Elijah Muhammad. Although Clay maintained that he had not joined the Nation, Parker and other sportswriters no longer doubted the boxer's membership. Since July, when a reporter from the *Chicago Sun-Times* caught him leaving the Muslims' school, Clay's association with the Nation had provoked suspicion that "he had been brain-washed by the Black Muslims."[13]

The Louisville Sponsoring Group shared the reporter's concerns and worked to disentangle Cassius from Malcolm. Job one, they thought, was to get their fighter out of New York City and away from Mosque No. 7. Since Cassius had returned from London, he had been markedly distant from his wealthy, white benefactors, reluctant to return to training under Dundee in Miami. Bill Faversham talked to Clay's mother, Odessa, explaining the need to persuade Cassius to return to Miami. Promoter Bill King pitched in as well, explaining to Cassius that if he didn't train in Miami there would be no Liston fight.[14]

He reluctantly returned south, but he still chafed under the LSG's guidance. W. S. Cutchins, a prominent member of the group and president of Brown & Williamson Tobacco, reported that Cassius wanted larger paydays—"$200,000 after taxes" was the number that he fixed on—and no more television appearances, which he had come to consider undignified. "Fighting, not acting," was his profession, he asserted, and even if the LSG upped his take for TV appearances to 60 percent, he was still not interested. Suddenly, it seemed, Cassius no

longer wanted to jive on stage or sing songs with Liberace. He didn't want to play the clown anymore.[15]

The LSG suspected that the Muslims, one in particular, had persuaded the young fighter to ignore the counsel of his white advisers. The group feared that they no longer spoke for Cassius because Malcolm X did. Malcolm didn't want Clay singing and dancing on television like Stepin Fetchit. If Cassius was ever going to become a freedom fighter like Malcolm, he had to keep his gloves on outside the ring as well.

Cutchins's solution to separating Clay from the Muslims was to schedule nontitle matches for him every few months. Then, between training in Miami and boxing in various cities, he would not have time for Malcolm. Only if they followed that plan could they get "just about 75% back to our normal relationship with him."[16]

Yet Cassius kept slipping away from Miami to New York. There he met with an associate of Malcolm's who would become his new business manager. Archie Robinson, a slight, bespectacled, soft-spoken man not much older than Clay, had first met the young boxer a few months earlier when Malcolm introduced them at the Muslims' luncheonette. Malcolm worried that Cassius needed protection from manipulative white men who exploited black boxers and knew that he could trust Archie to keep an eye on him.[17]

But Archie wasn't interested in wasting his time on the boisterous boxer. A former road manager for The Platters, Robinson did not know anything about the fight game or Clay except that he found him a bit obnoxious. "He's a clown," he said. "I don't play with amateurs." Malcolm's tone turned serious. He was not asking for a favor. He was giving him an assignment. "It's not about boxing," he said. "One day this kid is going to be heavyweight champion of the world, and he's going to embrace the Nation of Islam. Do you understand what that could mean?"[18]

Robinson did. He recognized that the minister believed that Clay could become a unifying force for the Nation. He also understood that Malcolm could not always be close to Clay. He had too many responsibilities and too many appointments. That's why he needed Robinson. When reporters noticed the new adviser escorting Cassius around town, he revealed little about their relationship and never mentioned Malcolm's name. "We were brought together by certain persons who knew us in New York," he cryptically told a writer.[19]

The more time Cassius spent with Robinson and Malcolm, the more he questioned his contract with the Louisville Sponsoring Group. In New York, Clay boasted that he was "going to free himself from the domination of his 12 white managers from Louisville." As he had said in London, "I am my own master." But as long as white men controlled his career and his finances, Malcolm taught him, he would never be truly free. At some point he would have to break the white man's shackles.[20]

His association with the Nation threatened the conservative sports establishment. Dan Parker maintained that the Black Muslims were just using Clay as a propaganda tool and that the boxer did not realize how they might damage his career. But Clay was not the dimwitted fool that Parker made him out to be. He fully understood the risks of associating with the Nation. Ever since he met Sam Saxon in Miami, he'd made sure not to talk about his relationship with the Muslims. If Clay had wanted to promote Elijah Muhammad's message, he could have done so, but he didn't. He knew exactly what he was doing.[21]

Reporters and the members of the LSG were not the only ones interested in Clay's involvement with the Muslims. A day after Parker published his column, the FBI's Chicago field office filed a memorandum justifying the continued surveillance on Elijah Muhammad's mansion. The special agent in charge reported that the surveillance had "proven extremely valuable in covering the overall activities of the NOI." The Bureau had learned about the sect's vulnerabilities and discovered that Cassius Clay, "the well-known heavyweight title contender, had made arrangements to meet ELIJAH MUHAMMAD and to also have his parents meet The Messenger."[22]

Clearly, Malcolm was not the only power broker inside the Nation courting Clay. After seeing the way that his followers responded to Clay at the Philadelphia rally, Muhammad grasped the boxer's propaganda value. Given his interest in recruiting more converts and selling more copies of *Muhammad Speaks*, Elijah relaxed his strict prohibition against Muslim participation in sports, as long as it "remained in its proper perspective" and did not interfere "with the attainment of good education and the building of a strong nation." He also authorized his son Herbert to publish more articles on black athletic achievements in the pages of *Muhammad Speaks*. Wider sports coverage, Elijah reasoned, would generate more newspaper sales and help him disseminate his message.[23]

Previous accounts of this dramatic moment have insisted that Elijah Muhammad had no interest in Clay before he won the heavyweight title. But that story simply isn't true. In fact, Muhammad had set his sights on bringing him closer to the center of the Nation well before he fought Sonny Liston. Of course, he also knew that Clay's value rose in proportion to his feats in the ring. If Cassius defeated Liston, it would prove the power of the righteous and affirm the Messenger's divine authority to bless those who followed him.

MALCOLM WAS SITTING at a back table in the Shabazz Restaurant counseling his lieutenants when the phone rang. A shout went out to Captain Joseph; it was his wife on the other line. He walked over to the phone booth and picked up the receiver. Her voice was frantic. After Joseph hung up the phone, he walked back toward Malcolm's table looking visibly shaken. Then he announced to everyone in the luncheonette: President Kennedy had been shot.[24]

Malcolm asked one of the brothers to retrieve a radio from the back of the restaurant. When they dialed in to a news station, the announcer said, "To repeat, we're confirming that the President has been shot in Dallas, Texas, and at this point we don't know how serious it is." Outside the Harlem restaurant, blacks huddled in front of appliance store windows and crowded inside bars, watching live news broadcasts on television.[25]

By midafternoon on November 22, the whole nation had come to a halt. Americans hovered near their radios or televisions while reporters and producers scrambled for news from Dallas. Shortly after two p.m., ABC Radio announcer Don Gardiner issued a special bulletin: "The president is dead. Ladies and gentlemen, this is a trying moment for all of us. Let us all pause and let us all pray." When Malcolm heard the announcement, he remarked coldly, "That devil is dead."[26]

Muhammad released a short statement expressing shock over "the loss of our President," a surprising comment given his past diatribes against the government. Privately, he worried that the Nation would be implicated in some way over the assassination. He ordered all ministers to remain silent about the president, and on Sunday, December 1, before Malcolm's speaking engagement at the Manhattan Center, he called to again remind him not to talk about Kennedy.[27]

After Malcolm's talk, reporters asked him about the president's assassination. At first, he refused to answer the writers' questions, suggesting that the media wanted to trap him into exclaiming, "Hooray, hooray! I'm glad he got it!" But when the crowd laughed and clapped, it stirred something in him. He relished delivering a memorable line, and with a little more prodding from the press, he finally gave in. The president's murder, he said, was a case of "the chickens coming home to roost." Then, he added, "Being an old farm boy myself, chickens coming home to roost never did make me sad; they've always made me glad."[28]

Malcolm believed that Kennedy and the CIA were behind the murders of South Vietnamese president Ngo Dinh Diem and Congolese prime minister Patrice Lumumba. He also thought that Kennedy had sat passively while whites murdered blacks in the American South. The president's assassination was an inevitable result of America's culture of violence.

Incensed at Malcolm's comments, the Nation's national secretary John Ali immediately telephoned Elijah. Malcolm had disobeyed Muhammad's order, threatening the Nation's reputation. Ali also advised Elijah that Malcolm's comments would provoke closer scrutiny from the FBI.

Malcolm had made a fatal error: he had handed Ali, Sharrieff, and Elijah's sons the wedge they needed to separate him from Muhammad once and for all.

The next day, Malcolm and Ali flew to Chicago for a meeting at Muhammad's home. The morning edition of the *New York Times* quoted Malcolm, exacerbating Muhammad's disappointment in him. After Muhammad and Malcolm embraced, they sat in the living room. Malcolm knew Muhammad so well that he could usually predict what he would say. But this time he had no idea what was coming.[29]

"Did you see the papers this morning?" Muhammad asked.

"Yes, sir, I did," Malcolm answered.

"That was a very bad statement. The country loved this man. The whole country is in mourning. That was very ill timed."

Malcolm agreed, adding that he understood he had made a mistake.

Muhammad stressed that Malcolm's imprudent statement had consequences. "I'll have to punish you for the next ninety days—so that

Muslims everywhere can be disassociated from the blunder." He was silencing Malcolm, muting a man whose voice defined him. Malcolm would rather lose a leg or an arm than his voice.[30]

But Malcolm had no choice. He accepted his punishment without protest. He would continue his administrative responsibilities at Mosque No. 7, but he would refrain from preaching or speaking to the media. Muhammad instructed Ali to release a public statement to the press. Denouncing Malcolm's comments about Kennedy, Ali informed the media that Malcolm was suspended from public speaking for an undetermined amount of time.[31]

In the following days, writers speculated that Muhammad would permanently replace Malcolm as minister of Mosque No. 7. Journalists reported that the Nation would split into two factions: one in Chicago following Muhammad and another in New York supporting Malcolm. A writer called Muhammad to ask when he would lift Malcolm's public speaking ban, but he refused to offer a deadline. "We are still brothers and I still think Malcolm is wonderful worker of mine," he answered. "But . . . we have rules; we must obey them."[32]

Muhammad was not so generous toward Malcolm when he spoke to his closest advisers. He told one aide that Malcolm "should have known better than to talk about the President." But Malcolm gave Elijah no choice after he made him "look like a fool." "Papa," he said, had to "spank his son." If Malcolm disobeyed him again, then he would receive "a worse beating the next time."[33]

MALCOLM BELIEVED THAT if he was contrite, his suspension would not last the full three months. Muhammad had gone so far as to admit that he would have said the same thing about Kennedy—nonetheless, Malcolm had disobeyed him, and now Elijah would reassert his authority.

When journalist Louis Lomax asked Malcolm about reports implicating his break from Muhammad, he snapped, "It's a lie! Any article that says there is a 'minor' difference between Mr. Muhammad and me is a lie. How could there be any difference between The Messenger and me? I am his slave, his servant, his *son*. He is *the* leader, the only spokesman for the Black Muslims."[34]

Yet while Malcolm maintained public confidence in his return to the Nation, he noticed ominous signs. Elijah informed his aides that

Malcolm would be reinstated, but *only* if he submitted, giving his disciples the impression that Malcolm had not capitulated.[35]

Over the course of December, Elijah's suspicions of Malcolm deepened. His sons, Sharrieff, and Ali encouraged him to remind Malcolm, once and for all, who was *the* Supreme Minister. Sharrieff and Ali instructed Captain Joseph and the assistant ministers in Harlem to openly condemn Malcolm for spreading stories about Muhammad. They also reminded Elijah that Malcolm knew things about the royal family that could damage the movement. If he revealed the Nation's secrets—the financial abuses, the promiscuous behavior, and the corporal punishment—the entire kingdom might collapse.[36]

On New Year's Eve, Muhammad called Captain Joseph and the most prominent ministers on the East Coast. He learned that Malcolm had informed them about Elijah's affairs, including Boston minister Louis X, in spite of Muhammad's specific instructions not to tell Louis about their private conversations. When Malcolm had broached the subject with Louis, he had failed Elijah's test of leadership.[37]

Elijah sensed that Malcolm's ambition could not be contained. Malcolm was beyond his reach—Malcolm knew it, Elijah knew it, and soon the world would know it. Muhammad sent word to his most trusted followers on the East Coast to cut ties with the wayward minister. Anyone who took Malcolm's side was his enemy. "I'm going to strip him of everything," he told Louis X. Everything—his mosque, his following, his life.[38]

ELIJAH HAD GIVEN Malcolm a new life and now he intended to take it all back. When Malcolm languished in prison, he gave him hope. When he joined the Nation, Elijah gave him power, promoting him to minister. When he showed him loyalty, Elijah gave him love—the love of a father. But now it was all over.

On January 2, 1964, during a tense phone conversation, Elijah scolded Malcolm. "I've been hearing about Malcolm this and Malcolm that, and even Malcolm being called a leader," Muhammad fumed. "You made an error," he said harshly, referring to Malcolm's conversations with the East Coast ministers.[39]

"I asked your permission in a letter before I said anything and I understood that it was all right," Malcolm said nervously.

"I certainly didn't say such a thing!" Elijah raged. Malcolm couldn't believe that the frail, gentle man who had embraced him with such warmth had turned so cold. Elijah showed him no forgiveness. "How can you take this poison and pour it all over my people? I knew all along that you had some sly scheme or shrewd plan to undermine me, but it won't work, sir, not this time."

"Messenger," Malcolm said, "I'd rather be dead than say anything against you."

"Then how could [Ministers] Isaiah and Lonnie and [Captain] Joseph all have gotten the wrong impression from what you said?" Elijah shouted. "They all wrote to me and said about the same thing." He paused, breathing heavily into the phone. "Why are you checking into my personal affairs?"

Malcolm answered that he'd only begun investigating the adultery charges after Muhammad's son Wallace brought it to his attention. And then, after FBI agents in Boston questioned one of Elijah's former secretaries, he'd become more concerned. When agents had asked the young woman if her newborn baby was Elijah's, Malcolm had suggested to Louis that "it would be a good idea if we told some of our top people about all these rumors so that if they heard about the charges from somewhere else," they would be prepared to deflect them with parables acceptable under Islamic law. He also admitted that he had mentioned this strategy to Captain Joseph and that he'd intended "to write you for instructions on how to deal with the matter."

"I don't need you to protect me," Elijah said. "I don't need you meddling in family matters. I know Wallace is the one spreading these lies. I've warned him about going to you with our troubles . . . you're an outsider."

Malcolm was shattered. He'd never imagined that Elijah, the man who had called him "son," would ever consider him an outsider. Never before had he heard Elijah shout with such vitriol.

Then Elijah cut him again. "I'm suspending you for an indefinite time," he said coldly. "I'm going to be watching you to see if you become stronger, strong enough to resist this poison Wallace is pouring over my people." And with that final message, Elijah slammed down the phone, leaving Malcolm wondering when he would hear from him again.

THE FOLLOWING DAY, Elijah called his trusted confidant Captain Joseph, informing him that James 3X, the head of Newark's mosque, would assume all ministerial duties in Harlem, but Joseph would retain all authority there. Undoubtedly, Joseph's loyalty belonged to Muhammad. Years earlier he'd been one of Malcolm's most dependable lieutenants, yet their relationship had fractured in 1956 when the captain was accused of assaulting his wife. Before the entire mosque he'd faced a trial, with Malcolm serving as judge and jury. Joseph pleaded guilty, and the minister banned him from the temple for ninety days. Humiliated, Joseph never recovered from the ordeal. Although he eventually returned as captain, his relationship with Malcolm remained strained and tense. Since 1961, when Muhammad made all mosque captains accountable directly to Chicago, Joseph had become an independent potentate, untethered to Malcolm's authority and nearly equal in power to him. Malcolm strongly disapproved of the way that Joseph disciplined the congregation and, in November 1963, had quietly petitioned Chicago to replace him as captain, a request that was denied.[40]

With Joseph assuming complete control over the Harlem mosque, the New York Muslims were directed to sever all ties with Malcolm. Muhammad informed the East Coast officials that the censured minister was suspended indefinitely and, through his aides, told his son Wallace that Malcolm had blamed him as the primary provocateur. Then he summoned Malcolm to Phoenix for a decisive trial, declaring, "I'm not through with Malcolm yet."[41]

In Phoenix, Malcolm faced the court: Muhammad, Sharrieff, and Ali. Since they had last spoke on the phone, Elijah had become even more caustic toward him. Sitting across from Malcolm, he looked at him like a stranger. Malcolm sat uncomfortably until he finally confessed that he had told Captain Joseph and various ministers about Muhammad's dalliances. Elijah demanded that he retract everything he said to them. "Go back and put out the fire you started," he said.[42]

After Malcolm returned home, he learned that the Nation's headquarters had made it known that no one in the sect could speak to him. Elijah had effectively quarantined him from his people, from his center of power. In Harlem, he learned that a mosque official told members of his congregation, "If you knew what the Minister did, you'd go out and kill him yourself." When Malcolm heard that the brothers in his

own mosque had started talking about his death, he knew it "could have been approved of—if not actually initiated—by only one man."[43]

In isolation, Malcolm considered a new reality, a life without Elijah, one divorced from the Nation. He had built his entire world around the teachings of Muhammad, committing himself to his mission. Without the Messenger, he'd preached, he was nothing. Elijah was the one who woke him from the dead. But now he had been cast outside the Nation, and he feared that his worst nightmare was coming true: Elijah intended to bury him and send him "back to the grave."[44]

MALCOLM ENDURED HIS exile in a daze. He tried ignoring the death talk, but he couldn't. His headed pounded relentlessly, day after day. It hurt all the time, as if he suffered from *dementia pugilistica*. "I felt like my brain was damaged," he told Alex Haley.[45]

His doctor examined him and recommended rest, but he didn't know how to slow down. His life had become a blur. Everything was out of focus. On January 14, he met Haley on the fourth floor of the International Hotel at the JFK Airport. For seven hours, from seven p.m. to two a.m., Haley sat at his typewriter, listening to Malcolm as he paced around the room, sitting only to scribble notes to himself on napkins.[46]

Malcolm could hardly concentrate. He knew what happened to insubordinate Muslims. He had seen gruesome images of black men bludgeoned at the hands of Muhammad's avengers. No one survived Muhammad's wrath. He could well imagine stalkers from the Fruit attacking him at any moment.

Even when he was inside the hotel room, he did not feel safe. He suspected that the FBI had bugged the room, a fear exacerbated by a radio broadcast he had heard just before the meeting claiming, falsely as it turned out, that the FBI and Rochester police considered him a suspect in an assassination plot against President Lyndon Johnson. He continued to agonize about what would happen if Elijah never reinstated him. Without his position, he would lose his monthly salary and his family's home in East Elmhurst, Queens. He had no savings, no insurance, and no property. He had even signed a contract donating his future book royalties to the NOI.[47]

This was no time to write a book. Haley wanted Malcolm to focus on the stories from his past, but all he could think about was his future.

What had first been only a vague idea began to take shape. He had long considered how he could benefit from the unique talents and fame of Cassius Clay, but mostly his musings had come from within the structure of the Nation. Now, if Elijah forced him out of the NOI, banished him from the organization that had given him sustenance, and made him move forward alone, Malcolm needed to consider how he could take Clay with him. How could he pry the boxer away from an organization and a theology that Malcolm had taught him was the foundation of all truth and reality? How could he convince Clay that everything Elijah preached was wrong?

Malcolm decided what Clay needed was a dose of political reality. He wanted Cassius to see the dark side of the movement and its leader. Malcolm fully understood that Elijah had ordered him not to talk with reporters and had commanded other members of the Nation not to associate with the defrocked minister—a directive that certainly applied to Cassius Clay. Yet instead of moving a step behind Elijah, reacting to the Supreme Minister's edicts, Malcolm chose to take the lead and compel him to follow. If Malcolm went to Miami and flaunted his friendship with the boxer, he would challenge Elijah to either pull Malcolm back into the fold or punish Cassius. Either way, Malcolm thought, it would strengthen his relationship with Clay.

Chapter Ten

TROUBLE IN MIAMI

Where do you think I would be next week if I didn't know how to shout and holler and make the public sit up and take notice? I would be poor, for one thing, and I would probably be down in Louisville, Kentucky, my hometown, washing windows or running an elevator and saying "yes suh" and "no suh" and knowing my place.

—CASSIUS CLAY

S portswriter Robert Lipsyte, sent to Miami to record the all-but-certain destruction of Cassius Clay, wrote Sonny Liston's comment into his notebook in red ink: "He's a fag, I'm a man.".[1]

Liston was not the first member of the boxing fraternity to question Clay's manhood. Since 1960, when he began training in Miami, rumors had persisted that he was gay, mostly because he defied simple stereotypes of boxers. From his first professional contest until the Liston match, he showed only a passing interest in women. To be sure, he talked about "foxes," spent hours observing them, and engaged in good-natured, nonthreatening flirting, but that was about as far as he went. At this stage in his career, Cassius was "old school," believing that any sort of sex drained strength and weakened fighters. "Masturbation is the curse of mankind," *The Ring* editor Nat Fleischer wrote in his influential book *Training for Boxers*. By extension, sex while training was tantamount to career suicide. Determined to win the title and all the fame and money that went with it, Clay accepted the common beliefs and for the most part pushed women to the far corners of his life.[2]

151

Cassius Marcellus Clay Sr. was a frustrated artist who was convinced that white men had stunted his career. His rage shaped the man that his son became. But the father also resented the influence the Nation of Islam had over his eldest child. Getty Images

His androgynous behavior added to the rumors. Like Emile Griffith, who designed women's hats and spoke in a wispy, breathless voice, Clay's actions defied the conventional masculinity. He seemed obsessed with how he looked inside the ring. His polished white shoes and white satin trunks, Vaseline-coated body, and sleek defensive style seemed dictated more by his sense of aesthetics than any athletic imperative. And no boxer in a sport that almost guaranteed facial cuts and a flattened nose talked more compulsively about his appearance. Choosing feminine adjectives, he repeatedly asked before and after every match, "Ain't I pretty?" or "Ain't I beautiful?" Seldom, if ever, did he refer to himself as handsome.

Liston might have sensed that, like Benny "the Kid" Paret did with Griffith, he could belittle Clay's masculinity by calling him a "fag" or "bitch." But although Griffith was sensitive about his sexual identity, Clay was not. Paret's taunts were on target, causing Emile to respond

violently. But Liston's vulgar labels never reached Cassius's heterosexual core.

Clay's psychological warfare against Liston was dramatically more effective. He began his campaign in earnest on November 5, 1963, at about three a.m. outside Liston's home in Denver. Fleeing police harassment in Philadelphia and looking for a "new start" and a quiet life, Sonny had moved to Denver and bought a home in an upscale neighborhood filled with well-established bankers, lawyers, physicians, and businessmen. *Sports Illustrated's* Huston Horn claimed that the week after Liston moved in, thirty-two for-sale signs sprouted in neighborhood lawns, but Sonny wanted peace, not war, with the other homeowners.³

Liston may have desired a quiet suburban existence, but Clay had other ideas. While Sonny slumbered peacefully, Cassius, aboard a red-and-white thirty-passenger 1953 Flxible bus, was headed in the champion's direction. There was nothing incognito about his approach. The slogans "CASSIUS CLAY ENTERPRISES," "WORLD'S MOST COLORFUL FIGHTER," and "SONNY LISTON WILL GO IN EIGHT" decorated the side of the bus, which bounced and rumbled with a circus-coming-to-town festivity. Inside, Cassius, Rudy, Bundini Brown, photographer and friend Howard Bingham, and a few other merry pranksters joked as they planned their assault on Liston's domicile. To guarantee an audience for his performance, Clay had already alerted local reporters that something was about to happen at Sonny's place.⁴

Outside the house, Clay hit the horn: *"Oink! Oink! Oink! Oink!"* Lights blinked on in the surrounding houses. "You know how them white people felt about that black man just moved in there anyway, and we sure wasn't helping it none," Cassius later remembered. "People was hollering things, and we got out with the headlights blazing." Bingham had a mild stuttering problem, so of course Cassius insisted that he knock on the door and talk to Liston.

About the time he reached the door, Sonny, wearing short nylon pajamas, cracked it open. "What do you want, you black motherfucker?" he greeted Bingham. And if his point was not made quite strongly enough, he fixed him with his infamous stare, as if the intruder were a bug about to be pinned in his insect collection.

While Bingham beat a hasty retreat, Cassius advanced into the yard, "screaming and hollering about how he was gonna whup Liston bad,"

as Bingham later recalled. "Come on out of there! I'm going to whip you right now! Come on out of there and protect your home! If you don't come out of that door, I'm going to break it down!" Cassius raged. Sonny, however, stayed put. Finally, seven squad cars arrived and the police sent Clay and his band on their way.

Liston was trapped by his past and his police record, and Clay knew it. If the police were called out and he was involved in a scuffle, even one he did not provoke, he knew he would get arrested. Furthermore, Cassius's actions confused Sonny. "You know, if a man figures you're crazy, he'll think twice before he acts, because he figures you're liable to do *anything*," Clay said.

He had planted the seed in Liston's mind. Initially Sonny assumed Cassius's stunts were just that—harmless acts to build the gate. But as one stunt led to the next, he found it difficult to separate the act from reality. "A man with Liston's kind of mind is very funny. He ain't what you would call a fast thinker," said Cassius. "He's got one of them bull-dog kind of minds. . . . Once he ever starts to thinking something, he won't let hold of it quick." Once he had believed that, like virtually every other man, Clay was afraid of him. Now he did not know what to think.

Clay continued his campaign on the afternoon of November 5, when he met with Liston in a Denver hotel to sign contracts for a title match. "I don't want to sit by him," he said when he arrived, and throughout the proceeding he shouted insults at the champion. Liston swatted away the verbal attacks, occasionally laughing at Cassius's performance. "I'm the champ of fighting," he told Clay, "but you the champ of talkin'." There were reasons for his good cheer—his 40 percent of ticket, concession, closed-circuit, television, and radio revenue would amount to several million dollars. Toward the end of the meeting, as Liston was speaking and Clay was digging into a plate of chicken, the champ looked over at his next opponent and said, "You eat like you headed to the electric chair."[5]

LISTON AND CLAY had signed on to fight, but the contest still needed a home and a date. For a while it seemed that the world of boxing was divided between promoters who did not want any part of Liston and his underworld ties and promoters who worried that Clay would fare no better than Patterson did against the powerful champion. They feared

involvement in a congressional inquiry, a shameful mismatch, and a financial fiasco.

Liston understood what constituted an attractive contest: "A boxing match is like a cowboy movie. There's got to be good guys, and there's got to be bad guys. That's what the people pay for: to see the bad guy get beat." He understood his role—"I'm the bad guy." Yet between Sonny's nefarious past and questionable present and Cassius's incessant patter and Black Muslim connections, there was no cowboy to wear the white hat.[6]

The December issue of *Esquire* attempted to put the white hat on Liston—actually, photographer Carl Fischer shot him in a red-with-white-trim Santa Claus hat. The cover close-up of Sonny's face—his expressionless mouth, flattened fighter's nose, and eyes that projected all the pain of his unhappy life—suggested that there would be no Christmas in 1963, an appropriate metaphor for a nation still morning the death of President John Kennedy.

In Miami, however, there was another Santa. "William B. MacDonald needs only a snowy beard to pass for Santa Claus," wrote *Miami Herald* reporter Edwin Pope. Shortly after *Esquire* appeared on the newsstands, Uncle Willie, as businessman and sportsman MacDonald referred to himself, bought the dubious rights to stage the Liston-Clay fight in the Miami Beach Convention Hall. Perhaps it took a gambler and promoter like MacDonald to agree to pay the enormous sum of $625,000 for the live gate of a match that had sent so many other established boxing promoters fleeing for the doors.[7]

Why take the chance? He had the answer: "For kicks. I'm in it for kicks." But beyond the sheer fun of the action, he sought to promote the image of America abroad. During the 1950s and 1960s, the Soviet Union openly ridiculed what it considered the hypocrisy of America's claims of freedom and equal opportunity. MacDonald thought "it would be great to show the world that two colored boys like Liston and Clay could fight in a Southern city and be treated like kings."[8]

Although paternalism streaked through MacDonald's discussion of race, he praised Liston and Clay, emphasizing their gentlemanly qualities. But his liberalism stopped short of tolerance for the Nation of Islam. A MacDonald associate said, "Don't invite Uncle Willie and Malcolm X to the same party."[9]

THE IDEA OF Malcolm running into Uncle Willie at a cocktail party in Bal Harbour or the Fontainebleau Hotel seemed unlikely. But he would have found a warmer welcome there than in New York, where his troubles with Elijah Muhammad weighed heavily on his mind. Malcolm needed to get away. His phone rang nonstop with press calls dogging him with questions about his future. The man who had always had an answer for reporters was now unsure what to tell them. Tortured by his separation from the Nation, his mind randomly jumped among Elijah, Captain Joseph, President Kennedy, his mosque, the press, and the death threats. It was all too much.

On Wednesday, January 15, the morning after his late-night writing session with Alex Haley, he reached for the phone to call a friend. But before he could dial the number, it rang. Joseph K. Ponder, an FBI agent from the Buffalo field office, was on the line with a few questions: Where were you last night? Do you know anything about a plot by the Black Muslims to assassinate Lyndon Johnson? How long will your suspension from the Nation last? Ponder seemed especially interested in Malcolm's future with the sect.[10]

After the call from Ponder, the phone rang again. A reporter from the *New York Times* also wanted to know if there was any truth about the plot to kill the new president. "The whole idea is ridiculous!" Malcolm declared. For an hour, reporters from all over the country dialed his number, inquiring about the assassination rumors and his suspension. Finally, the phone stopped ringing. After being badgered for an hour, Malcolm turned to a personal matter and called a friend in Miami to tell him that he was bringing Betty and their children to visit. "That's the best news I've heard all day!" Cassius Clay said. "Me and Brother Archie will pick you up."[11]

After the call ended, an FBI agent listening to their conversation contacted the Miami field office and instructed agents to tail a 1963 Chrysler with Florida license plate 1E-16521. The New York agent stressed that it was important that they follow the car to the airport the next day and "determine" the purpose of the "subject's activities" in Miami.[12]

The next morning, Cassius and Archie Robinson greeted Malcolm and his family at the airport. Smiling as he shook Malcolm's hand, Clay showed no fear of being seen with the suspended minister, whom he

called his "brother." After he hugged Sister Betty and lifted her three lit-
tle girls up into his arms, Cassius, Archie, and Malcolm's family packed
into the Chrysler and headed to Brownsville, a segregated, middle-class
black neighborhood.[13]

Sam Saxon, the Miami mosque captain since the late 1950s, was a
little surprised to see Malcolm. Clay's fight against Liston was still more
than a month away. Malcolm told the brothers in Miami that he and
Betty were celebrating their first vacation in more than six years. But he
wasn't on vacation. Malcolm, Saxon soon realized, "had another agenda
in mind."[14]

Malcolm and his family checked into the Hampton House Motel on
Northwest Twenty-Seventh Avenue. A popular retreat for black tourists
and locals, some of the most famous figures in America had booked one
of the balconied rooms. Considered more glamorous than the black
hotels in Overtown, the Hampton House was a resort, featuring valet
parking, a courtyard swimming pool, a restaurant, and a jazz club fa-
mous for its mixed-race sessions lasting until sunrise.[15]

When he was not training, Clay visited the Hampton House and
played with Malcolm's daughters, teasing them like a big brother.
Watching Cassius entertain them made Malcolm smile and, for a mo-
ment, forget all about his troubles. "I liked him," Malcolm later admit-
ted. "Betty liked him. Our children were crazy about him." Watching
her husband interact with Cassius, Betty could see that Malcolm "loved
him like a younger brother."[16]

Cassius brought out Malcolm's warm, playful side. The minister
laughed as he snapped pictures of the boxer clowning for his camera.
But the pictures Malcolm took were not for a family photo album.
In a private notebook, he began constructing photo captions and a
narrative he entitled, "The Other Side of Malcolm: The Family Man."
The notebook and accompanying photos of Cassius, Malcolm, and his
daughters, which were published in two black newspapers, the *Chicago
Defender* and the *New York Amsterdam News*, suggest that he had begun
to fashion a less threatening image of himself, one of a loving father and
husband and an older brother to Cassius, someone more acceptable in
the mainstream civil rights movement. It was also no coincidence that
the pictures were published in the two cities where his enemies in the
Nation could not miss them.[17]

In the early evenings, Malcolm walked with Cassius on the streets of Brownsville while FBI agents trailed closely behind. In all the time that they had spent together, in storefront mosques and crowded temples, in private meetings and family gatherings, Malcolm had learned that Cassius was an impressionable, inquisitive youngster who absorbed everything that he taught.

Cassius, he recognized, was perfect for his plan. He was a one-man publicity machine, capable of attracting Malcolm's desired audience: young, idealistic, angry black men. Cassius, Malcolm told a reporter, "[has] as much untapped mental energy as he has physical power." He possessed incredible potential to be something much more than a boxer. Studying Cassius with a crowd of journalists and a mob of black admirers, Malcolm could imagine him as a political force—someone "who should be a diplomat," traveling the world with him, galvanizing a human rights movement at home and abroad.[18]

Whether Malcolm returned to the Nation or not, Cassius was ideally suited to follow him, to use his platform as a boxer to mobilize poor, disfranchised black Americans. Cassius, Malcolm noticed, "knows how to handle people, to get them functioning. He gains strength from being around people." He could draw people in, shape their perceptions, and make them believe what Malcolm wanted them to believe.[19]

Nothing seemed to rattle Clay. "He has tremendous self-confidence," Malcolm observed. "I've never heard him mention fear." Perhaps he did not realize the depth of Malcolm's problem. His public relationship with Malcolm irritated the Nation's officials in Chicago, especially Elijah Muhammad. The Supreme Minister had directed all followers to avoid the censured minister, but Cassius had disobeyed him.[20]

In Miami, Malcolm became convinced that his future with the Nation depended on Clay winning the heavyweight championship. While most doubted his chances of beating Liston, Malcolm bolstered Clay's inner strength, telling him that he was too smart, too fast, and too big to lose the fight. And Allah, he preached, had ordained that Clay would win. He believed in Clay so much that he called Alex Haley in New York and told him that if Haley bet on his friend, the underdog, he would win big. This fight was more than just another athletic contest; it was part of his larger plan. Clay would not just win, he would deliver a message—a message inspired by Malcolm.[21]

Malcolm's message sounded to Clay like a voice from a burning bush. At a moment when the world seemed to doubt him, the man Cassius greatly admired never lost faith. Malcolm filled him with confidence. And if he said that Allah had ordained a victory, then it must be true. Malcolm, Cassius believed, only spoke the truth. But he'd told him a lie, the same lie that he told reporters and himself: that he would be reinstated within ninety days.[22]

Malcolm was living in the past. At some level, he must have realized that he would never return to the Nation, but he still held out hope that he would reconcile with Elijah. He desperately wanted to believe it, and he convinced Cassius. Throughout January and early February, he wrote the Messenger, pleading for reinstatement, but he received only silence from Chicago. Most likely, Malcolm's enemies intercepted his letters before they ever reached Elijah. The silence troubled him, making him even more desperate to do something to restore his place in the Nation.[23]

THE ONLY THING that Angelo Dundee knew about Malcolm X was what he had read in the papers, and he mostly read the sports pages. He knew that Malcolm had said something incendiary about President Kennedy, but he did not realize that the man reporters described as "the violently anti-white New York chief of the Muslims" would be in Miami celebrating Cassius's twenty-second birthday. Seeing him in the flesh made the trainer nervous. Malcolm wore a broad, casual smile that never touched his eyes, a mask that seemed more threatening than friendly. But nothing startled Angelo more than when he saw Cassius "involved in a deep conversation with Malcolm X."[24]

Sam Saxon was similarly surprised to see Malcolm hanging around the gym. He knew that the suspended minister was not there to trade small talk. Earlier, Malcolm had asked him, "If I go over to the gym, would I hurt Brother Cassius?"

"Hell, yeah, man. Everybody knows you," Captain Sam replied. He suggested that Malcolm go nowhere near 5th Street. Malcolm said nothing, but a few hours later he showed up at the gym. Saxon noticed that whenever reporters came around to see Cassius, Malcolm talked to them. And anytime a photographer snapped photos of the contender, Malcolm maneuvered in front of the camera.[25]

Malcolm knew exactly what he was doing. If Elijah never accepted him back into the Nation, then he had to consider an exit strategy that would force Cassius to walk in his shoes. Talking to reporters while photographers took his picture with Cassius violated the terms of his suspension. More importantly, he understood that all Muslims, including Cassius, were prohibited from speaking with him. If anyone in Chicago learned that Clay had disobeyed the Messenger, perhaps Elijah would have no choice but to punish the boxer too. Then Cassius would clearly understand Elijah's vindictive nature and Malcolm would not have to convince him of it. It seemed like a good plan, but Elijah didn't fall for the trap.

Angelo suspected that Malcolm was up to something but was not sure what. He seldom pried into Cassius's private life, but when outsiders stepped into *his* gym, his sanctuary, and disrupted training, he voiced his displeasure. This was no time for distractions, he told Clay. They were about a month away from the biggest fight of his career. He refused to let anyone, especially some guy named "X," cost Clay the title.

Dundee had already started losing patience with Cassius. Sometimes the boxer simply ignored his instructions. It seemed that he didn't listen to anybody except the Muslims, and now he was looking to Malcolm for training advice, financial counsel, and emotional support. It was nearly impossible to carry on an actual conversation with him. "Nobody ever talks *with* Cassius," Clay's fight doctor Ferdie Pacheco observed. "You listen *to* him. This man known all over the world for his mouth can't even converse. You don't get an exchange of ideas. He doesn't even hear you." Pacheco was wrong on one point: Clay heard who he wanted to hear.[26]

When Dundee saw Cassius talking with Malcolm, he pulled his boxer into a corner of the gym and made sure that he heard him clearly. "Get that guy out of here," he said. Clay assured him that Malcolm was leaving town the next night.[27]

What he didn't tell Angelo was that he was going with him.

On Tuesday, January 21, two days after Betty and the children departed Miami, Malcolm, Cassius, and Archie Robinson flew to New York. Malcolm was worried about going home. In Harlem, where he once ruled the streets, he now had to look over his shoulder. He was not

entirely sure who he could trust at Mosque No. 7. Searching to "find some way to defend" himself, he wrote in his journal, he had "to retaliate against those enemies without hurting [Elijah]."[28]

He knew that he was not safe around the mosque or the Rockland Palace Ballroom on 155th Street and Eighth Avenue, where the Fruit of Islam had planned a dinner. So he sent Cassius Clay to the dinner in his place. On their flight from Miami, Malcolm had tutored Cassius, outlining a speech for him and explaining that some Muslims might not approve of their friendship, and the two had continued to rehearse the speech at Malcolm's home in Long Island. Malcolm told Cassius that he wished he could go with him, but that that was not possible because he had a prior engagement.[29]

In front of about 1,200 Muslims, Clay delivered what Archie Robinson claimed was "an impromptu speech." "There wasn't anything planned," Malcolm's aide falsely insisted.[30]

"I'm a race man," Clay began, "and every time I go to a Muslim meeting I get inspired." The crowd thundered with applause as Cassius grinned with gratification. "I'm a free man, and I'm talking so much because of the [Muslims'] teachings."[31]

Sonny Liston, according to Cassius, was not a race man like him. In poetry, he attacked his opponent as a race traitor, living next door to white people.

He's not doing as he should,
Because he lives in a white neighborhood.
And because he doesn't like black,
I'm going to put him on his back!

Again, a loud burst of laughter and applause. Cassius insisted that because he was a Muslim, he was purer than Liston too. He didn't smoke, didn't drink, and had never been arrested like Sonny. "I'm training on lamb chops and that big ugly bear is training on pork chops!"[32]

Then Cassius walked into a bear trap. He announced that he'd had another advantage during training in Miami: the wisdom imparted by his brother, Malcolm X. When Cassius declared that he was proud to walk the streets with Malcolm, the mood of the evening changed. The crowd was stunned. No one in the mosque talked publicly about

Malcolm, let alone called him brother. An informant told the FBI that "the Muslims were very cold towards" Cassius for "defending Minister Malcolm," especially after "the Messenger had said to put him down."[33]

When William C. Sullivan, the assistant director of the FBI, learned about Clay's presence at the Muslims' dinner, he concluded that the boxer had joined the Nation of Islam. A few weeks earlier, Sullivan had circulated a memo among leading FBI officials encouraging a counterintelligence program (COINTELPRO) to discredit Malcolm, Elijah Muhammad, Martin Luther King, and other prominent black figures. Special agents working in the Bureau's covert program had infiltrated organizations like the Nation of Islam, disrupted their activities through wiretaps, surveillance, forged documents, and blackmail, and planted false media stories. Armed with information about Clay's affiliations, Sullivan tipped off the press and added his name to a list of NOI targets.[34]

The day after his speech, reports about Clay and the Muslims appeared in New York newspapers. The *Herald Tribune*'s Dick Schaap, who had known Cassius since his amateur boxing days, was not sure if the fighter was "a card-carrying Muslim," but he had no doubt that he sympathized with the Nation. "If Clay shares the anti-white sentiments of the Black Muslims," he wrote, "he has always disguised his feelings well." Although he had interviewed Malcolm in the past, when Schaap investigated the minister's relationship with the boxer, he learned very little. "Malcolm won't say anything publicly," an acquaintance told Schaap, "and the one subject he won't talk about even privately is Cassius Clay."[35]

While Malcolm remained in New York, Cassius returned to Miami, where reporters pressed him for details about his trip. Promoter Bill MacDonald said that Clay "swore by all that's holy" that he was not a member of the Nation. "I'm not a Black Muslim any more than you are," he told the *Miami Herald*'s Pat Putnam. The Harlem dinner was not an exclusive NOI affair, either, he claimed. Members of the NAACP and Congress of Racial Equality had attended the event too.[36]

Yet his relationship with the Nation had just deepened significantly. The truth was that he had discarded his "slave name"—Clay—and received his "X" from Chicago. In the Nation, he was now officially "Cassius X." Clearly, Malcolm was not the only Muslim betting on the heavyweight contender.

His denials fooled few reporters. They had seen him with Malcolm. While writers could not understand why he would associate with a man who had spoken so cruelly about the deceased president, Clay feigned ignorance. "If [Malcolm] said that about President Kennedy then he should be shot too," he said. "I knew he said something about chickens coming home to roost, but that's all I heard."[37]

That could not have been all he heard. Malcolm spent days in Miami and talked with Cassius for hours. He knew exactly why Malcolm had time for a vacation. While Malcolm may not have disclosed the details about his deteriorating relationship with Muhammad, Cassius had close ties with various NOI officials who talked with him regularly and would have spoken of the tensions between the suspended minister and Muhammad. Clay's ignorance about the Nation's politics was just another act. He knew that he was harboring a renegade Muslim.

Talking to reporters, Cassius tried to finesse his opinions, staking out territory between the civil rights movement and the Nation of Islam. "I don't believe in hate," he said. "I don't believe in violence; I don't believe in forced integration. I believe the important thing is knowing where you belong and where you don't belong. Then the farmers won't come out with pitchforks. The cops won't come with the clubs. And the firemen won't come out with hoses." Then he said something that sounded like it came directly from one of Malcolm's speeches. "All I know is that I'm *black* and my people are catching hell. I want some answers."[38]

The questions surrounding Cassius's relationship with Malcolm troubled MacDonald, Dundee, and the Louisville Sponsoring Group. With disappointing ticket sales, they worried that too many fans would avoid the convention center in protest of his involvement with Malcolm and the Black Muslims. To counter the bad publicity, on Saturday night, January 25, he sparred for nine rounds at the Miami Beach Auditorium to raise money for a cerebral palsy organization. It was an attempt to repair his image and remind the public that he was "just a nice, sweet kid."[39] Yet if MacDonald and the LSG urged Clay to stop speaking his mind, he wasn't listening.

Still weeks away from the championship fight, reporters needed stories to fill their columns. And they knew that Clay's conversion to the Nation was a sensational scoop. Like bloodhounds on the trail, the best writers in the country followed the scent all the way to Miami. They

needed few detective skills. Cassius was tired of running from reporters, weary of hiding the truth. "Sure, I talked to the Muslims," he admitted, "and I'm going back again. I like the Muslims."[40]

Lying on a massage table with a masseuse kneading his shoulders, Cassius relaxed while reporters asked him questions. Contrary to news reports, he was not brainwashed. He could see and think for himself. "In Cleveland, the Negroes tried to integrate and you could see what happened," he said. "The white people hit the Negroes and the Negroes hit the white people." Rising from the table, throwing wild punches and covering his face with his arms, he exclaimed, "Bam-bam, bam-bam!" The racial violence only proved what he had already learned from Muslim ministers: integration wasn't just wrong, it was dangerous.[41]

The writers peppered him with questions. Are you actually a member of the Nation of Islam? one asked. "I was born a Muslim, I'm told. My race descended from the people in Egypt [and] Africa . . . whose religion had always made them Muslim." For the first time writers heard him connect the struggles of black Americans and colonized Africans. It upset him that "the Africans are treated better in this country than the American Negro." The "Negro" was not treated like an American, he said, echoing Malcolm.[42]

Cassius denied that the Muslims preached hatred. "I'm not mad at the white people. If they like me, I like them." But a closer look at his childhood showed that he held deep suspicions toward whites. His father maintained that the Black Muslims had indoctrinated his boys ever since Cassius returned from Rome an Olympic champion, teaching them "to hate all white people; to hate women; and to hate their mother."[43]

Clay Sr. was always stirring up trouble, and some of the Muslims in his son's camp thought that he interfered too much. Sometimes he argued with them, shouting that they were a bunch of crooks robbing his family. He could not abide hearing his boys talk about the Nation, either. When they did, he erupted, "Don't talk that Muslim stuff!" He complained that the Black Muslims kept him away from his boys because the Nation feared that he would drag them "right back to church." But nothing irritated him more than when his youngest son called collect, identifying himself as "Rudolph X." "I don't know no Rudolph X!" he yelled at the operator, slamming the phone.[44]

In Miami, an FBI informant called the *Herald*'s Pat Putnam, telling him that some Muslims had threatened to kill Clay's parents. Putnam wondered if the combustible father might want to talk about it, so he arranged for an interview in a restaurant across the street from the 5th Street Gym. For nearly three hours, Clay Sr. ranted about how the Muslims had "ruined his boys," stole money from his son, and threatened to take him out on a boat and drown him. He felt shoved aside by Malcolm, replaced by a man who "sneered at him." He despised the way his sons worshipped Malcolm. "You should have seen them all," he said. "They did everything but bow and kiss his feet." Rudy's and Cassius's membership in the Nation angered him so much that he threatened to "whup" both of them and Malcolm. Cassius paid him no mind. "I don't care what my father said," he insisted. "I'm not interested. I'm not talking."[45]

Putnam learned quickly that he had better stop asking Clay Sr. about the Muslims. After the story was published, someone called his house, warning him that he and his wife were going to die. Putnam did not recognize the voice on the other end of the line, but he got the message. Late one night, he drove out to Clay's house and told him about the death threats. He had known Cassius since he first started training in Miami and had always gotten along with him. Clay reassured him, "Pat, don't worry about it; you'll never get another call." Putnam never knew what Clay did, but he received no more death threats.[46]

BY THE THIRD week in January, America's thoughts had started to tilt toward South Florida. Brutally cold winds ripped across the Midwest and Northeast. "Death and Misery Mounting," proclaimed a headline. In the worst blizzard of the year, snow drifted twelve feet and more from the Mississippi to the Atlantic Seaboard, stranding drivers, challenging walkers, and generally making life uncomfortable. Miami beckoned.

The *Miami Herald* reported that the top syndicate bosses were among the recent arrivals. Paul "the Waiter" Ricco, Sam "Mooney" Giancana, and Felix "Milwaukee Phil" Aldersino escaped the slush of Chicago for the sand of Miami. There they waited out the worst of the winter, looking forward to watching Sonny button the Louisville Lip.[47]

Liston's National Airlines flight from Las Vegas arrived in Miami shortly before noon on January 26. He stepped off the plane relaxed

and wearing a champion's smile, but neither lasted long. Waiting for Sonny, Clay shouted insults and challenges. "I'm the champ! You're the chump!" he screamed, whipping his tuxedo jacket about like a war flag. "Let's fight now. I want my title!"[48]

Liston fixed Clay with "that evil look" and told him, "Look, this clowning isn't cute, and I'm not joking."

Liston refused to give Cassius the satisfaction of another glance, but his ceremonial arrival and press conference were in tatters. To bypass the commotion, Sonny boarded a VIP golf cart and raced toward the interview room. Clay sprinted behind, screaming insults and waving an African walking stick. In a tunnel Liston told the driver to stop. "Listen, you little punk, I'll punch you in the mouth—this has gone too far!" Then, as Clay continued his taunts, Liston swung at him, missing with a wild right.

In the melee that followed, Sonny's wife, Geraldine, got whacked on the head, his manager, Jack Nilon, threatened to fight the entire mob, and the champion lost his cool.

The door to the interview room was shut and locked. Inside, Liston steamed, glaring at the door that separated him from Clay. Outside the room Cassius shouted, "It's a free country . . . you can't stop me from coming in." Brandishing his cane, he banged the locked door and continued, "Free! You think I'm jiving, chump? I'll fight you free, right here!"

Red-faced, MacDonald apologized. He told Sonny that he hoped the champion would knock out Clay in three rounds. Regaining his customary sangfroid, Liston claimed that Clay's act "didn't upset me. But it got kind of . . . you know, even iron wears out." Then, with the interview concluded, policemen escorted Liston out a back door and whisked him away in a car.

Liston said that it didn't bother him. But it did. He had traveled a long way from a sharecropper shack in Arkansas and the whippings of a cruel father. He had survived the streets, prison, and the police of Missouri and Pennsylvania. Unable to read or write, he preferred violence as his medium of expression. But as journalist Jerry Izenberg noted, "Sonny was illiterate, but he wasn't ignorant or stupid or unfeeling." There was a sort of dignity to his sullen, brutal life. He accepted who he was and the fact that people regarded him as a thug. As the heavyweight

champion of the world, he did not ask for love or popularity. Still, he thought he deserved some semblance of respect. That, of course, was precisely what Cassius Clay denied him. Socially and culturally, Cassius transformed the title fight into a contest about many things—beauty, age, law and order, and race—but dignity was not on the list.[49]

There was hardly a quiet corner of Liston's life that Cassius did not invade. For instance, Sonny designed a training program with the production qualities of a Las Vegas show. Setting up shop at the Surfside Civic Arena, overlooking the sea in North Miami Beach, he charged fifty cents to watch him train. The sessions struck George Plimpton as well worth the modest cost. They began with a twenty-minute "official" film of Liston's destruction of Patterson in Las Vegas. When the film ended, an assistant removed the screen, revealing the champion, standing still and expressionless in a ring elevated on a stage. The combination of his immobile face, massive body, and fearsome reputation sent ripples of applause through the audience. Only then did Sonny begin his workouts. He shadowboxed, gliding across the ring with a sparring partner, each throwing punches, bobbing and weaving, feinting and ducking, but never making the slightest contact during their choreographed performance. Next he punched a speed bag with a rat-a-tat-tat syncopation and the heavy bag with a thud-thud-thud demonstration of rib-breaking power. After pounding the bags, it was time for Liston to receive some punishment. His trainer, Willie Reddish, picked up a fifteen-pound medicine ball and threw it with all his considerable strength at the champion. The ball seemed to explode into Sonny's stomach, but without the slightest change in expression he trapped it on the rebound. While the exertions exhausted Reddish, they hardly seemed to interest Liston.[50]

The last exercise was the capstone of the show. To the soulful beat of "Night Train" he skipped rope, man and music in perfect harmony. "Note," an announcer said, "the champion's heels never touch the board. He does it all on his toes." It was almost too much for the spectators to contemplate—the most devastating puncher in the world, perhaps the most powerful fighter in the history of the sport, was also as graceful as a tap dancer.

It was a fine show, and after it was over its star mixed with the audience, answered a few softball questions, and posed for pictures. But

from the opening day of the Sonny Liston Revue, Clay threatened to crash the gate. Wearing jackets with "BEAR HUNTING" on the back and carrying walking sticks, members of Cassius's camp watched Sonny train, creating an uneasy feeling in the champion's quarters. Cassius also spoke often about invading Liston's plush digs. Liston wasn't amused. "This guy is some kind of nut," he said. "They had better stop him or I will. Enough is enough."[51]

But enough was never enough for Cassius. On February 7, he made his move. Dressed in a tuxedo and carrying his hand-carved cane, he led a march to the Surfside headquarters. Denied entrance, he hollered and protested, sure that some constitutional principle was at stake. "I'm ready to go to jail if I'm breaking the law," he asserted. "This is a public place and I have the right to be here."[52]

For the generation of sportswriters who had matured during the era of the two Joes—DiMaggio and Louis—Clay's performance indicated the passing of an age when dignity framed the game. None was more outraged than Jimmy Cannon, the dean of the reverential school of sports journalism. "In the year of the Beatles, it is right that Cassius Clay fights Sonny Liston for the heavyweight championship of the world," he wrote from Miami. "It is the time of the freak on earth. You see it all and watch it happen, but you can't believe it. It belongs in the territory of dreams. The next war must be between the sane and the insane." To Cannon, Clay and the Beatles were the essence of modernity—of artists "splattering canvases with gobs and streaks," of actors who "seem to be reading their lines off pieces of confetti thrown up on a windy day," of musicians "who repudiate melody," of "the bored children of the atomic age."[53]

Liston was as traditional as Cannon, lumping Clay and the Beatles in the same trash heap of modern culture. On Sunday, February 9, the Beatles changed the landscape of popular music with their appearance in New York on *The Ed Sullivan Show*. As adolescent girls screamed hysterically and an estimated 73 million television viewers looked on in amazement, they sang five songs, ending with their number-one hit single, "I Want to Hold Your Hand." The next Sunday they made their second appearance on the show, this one televised from the Deauville Hotel in Miami Beach. Liston attended the performance with Joe Louis and publicist Harold Conrad. When Sullivan introduced him, he stood

and acknowledged the smattering of cheers, but he was unimpressed with the Beatles. When they began to sing, he nudged Conrad with his elbow and asked, "Are these motherfuckers what all the people are screaming about? My dog plays drums better than that kid with the big nose."[54]

After the show Conrad arranged for the Beatles to come to the 5th Street Gym for a photo op with Cassius. It was a pitch-perfect idea, the marriage of sports and music, signaling that at the highest level it was all about entertainment and money. The Beatles were compliant, though none had any interest in boxing. George Harrison remembered, "It was all a part of being a Beatle, really; just getting lugged around and thrust into rooms full of press men taking pictures and asking questions."[55]

They had performed in some dingy, cigar-smelling clubs in Hamburg and Liverpool, so the grimy walls and dank smells of the 5th Street Gym were nothing new. But being stiffed by Clay was. "Where the fuck's Clay?" Ringo asked as they arrived. When John Lennon learned that Cassius was not in the gym, he said to the others, "Let's get the fuck out of here." But two security guards blocked their exit and pushed them into an empty dressing room.[56]

Fifteen minutes later Cassius burst through the door, his personality filling the dressing room. "He was beautiful," Lipsyte reported. "He seemed to glow. He was laughing."

"Hello there, Beatles!" he shouted. "We ought to do some road shows together, we'll get rich."

The mood of the Beatles brightened immediately. Though the musicians knew almost nothing about Clay, and he had never even heard of them, they seemed to siphon energy from each other. They performed a campy act for the cameramen—Cassius knocking down all four with a single punch, standing over them in a victory pose, grabbing Ringo and lifting him above his head. "They were all, Beatles and boxer alike, consummate showmen; they knew their roles, hit all their cues," wrote Bob Spitz.

"Clay mesmerized them," recalled photographer Harry Benson. They were captivated by Clay's looks—fresh, innocent, oddly an Americanized image of themselves. But more than that, they sensed his physical and emotional power. They were products of their manager, Brian Epstein, packaged and presented according to his uncanny commercial

It began as a publicity photo op—the Beatles, fresh from a sensational appearance on The Ed Sullivan Show, *and Cassius Clay, preparing for his heavyweight title fight against Sonny Liston. No one present in the 5th Street Gym realized that the rock group and the boxer would become the two enduring cultural icons of the 1960s.* Associated Press

instincts. But Cassius was his own man. He controlled who he was. He had manufactured himself. He lived on his own terms.

But living on his own terms came with greater risks than the Beatles realized.

ON FEBRUARY 20, after spending nearly a month in New York, Malcolm X returned to Miami. That night, in the lobby of the Hampton House, he sat on a sofa answering questions from a *Herald* reporter, a clear violation of his suspension. He could not resist a platform and he loved the attention. Malcolm may have said that he wanted to return to the Nation, but as important as Elijah had been to his development, he had grown beyond the Messenger's limited goals. He had his own ideas, his own plans, and he wanted the world to know it. What he wanted most was freedom—freedom to speak his mind, freedom to

engage politicians and foreign dignitaries, and the freedom to think for himself. At this stage he was unsure of how to achieve his ambitions. He desperately wanted to remain in the Nation, but he wanted it on his own terms.[57]

The following day, the FBI mailed an anonymous tip to various media outlets suggesting a widening rift between Malcolm and Elijah. Based on wiretap intelligence, specialists working the COINTELPRO fabricated a story, hoping to widen the gulf between Muhammad and Malcolm. The story suggested that the minister felt that "Elijah Muhammad is in his declining years and that he is slipping." Given the chance, the source claimed, Malcolm "would not hesitate one moment to take over the leadership of the Nation of Islam." Convinced that the tip came from a legitimate source, journalists began reporting that Malcolm had started a war for power against Muhammad.[58]

The news traveled fast. That same afternoon, Muhammad's personal secretary called Malcolm with a message: his request for reinstatement before the upcoming Saviours' Day Convention had been denied. She told him that Elijah refused to lift his ban because he "continued to rebel." Malcolm requested a hearing to defend himself against the charges, but again his appeal was rejected. Later that night, Muhammad delivered another message. This time, though, he made the call himself. He warned Cassius X that "all good Muslims should stay away from Malcolm" during his suspension.[59]

Four days before his title match, Cassius began contemplating the repercussions of hosting Malcolm. Muhammad reminded him that Malcolm had violated his edict and that all disobedient Muslims would suffer punishment. After speaking with Elijah, Cassius realized that he had endangered his relationship with the Supreme Minister. The failure to heed his warning, he understood, would have consequences.

BILL MACDONALD DID not like having Malcolm in Clay's camp anymore than Elijah Muhammad did. The same day that Clay spoke to Elijah, MacDonald called Clay into his office, threatening to cancel the fight if he didn't denounce the Black Muslims. MacDonald complained that his involvement with Malcolm had provoked a boycott by the Jewish community, which was large and powerful in Miami. The Muslims'

past comments about Jews exploiting blacks were hurting the gate, he insisted.[60]

Others criticized Clay's relationship with the Nation of Islam as well. Marion Jackson, a black writer for the *Atlanta Daily World*, condemned Cassius for opposing integration and promoting the views of the Nation. "Clay, through his association with Malcolm X, Muhammad, and other Black Muslims, has revealed himself as a white-hating racist at the time when intergroup progress is being made throughout the South."[61]

Yet MacDonald failed to convince Clay to rebuke the Muslims. He could not understand why Cassius would allow him to cancel the match, risking his only chance at the title. "My religion is more important to me than the fight," Clay said. Despite his sincerity, MacDonald replied that he had no choice. He was canceling the fight.[62]

Publicist Harold Conrad was stunned by the decision. He told MacDonald that it was too late. They had already sold thousands of tickets and signed contracts with closed-circuit theaters.

"The hell I can't call it off," MacDonald retorted. "You're a Northerner. You don't understand. You don't realize that Miami is the Deep South and is just as segregated as any town in Mississippi. How can I promote a fight down here with a guy who thinks we're white devils?"

Conrad pleaded with him to change his mind. "Bill, you're gonna go down in history as the guy who denied a fighter a title shot because of his religion," he said.

"Bullshit. Don't start hitting me with the Constitution." MacDonald was unsure of his next move. "It's that Malcolm X. He's responsible for all this trouble and he's practically running the kid's fight camp. That don't look good."

Conrad had an idea. If he could convince Malcolm to leave town, would MacDonald allow the fight to go on?

"Yeah, I guess so," the promoter answered.

Conrad drove out to Clay's house where he met the fighter, surrounded by somber Muslims. When he walked into the house the hostility was palpable. Cassius was in no mood to talk with him, either. Conrad turned toward Malcolm and explained that the fight was off, "but you can save it for him."

"How?" Malcolm asked.

"You have to get out of town now. You're the focal point. You're the guy the press knows."

Malcolm looked away from Conrad. He just stood there calculating. He thought about Cassius. Finally, he answered. "All right, I'll go, but I'm coming back for the fight."

Conrad offered his hand and a forced smile, but Malcolm wouldn't shake it. He simply touched the white man's wrist with his forefinger, and walked away.

The fight was back on.

Chapter Eleven

THE CRUSADE

It's widely believed that there are more people in the world who understand Einstein's Theory than think Cassius Clay has a chance.

—JIM MURRAY

Beethoven wrote some of his greatest symphonies when he was deaf. Why couldn't Cassius Clay fight when he was blind?

—FERDIE PACHECO

A hard, cold wind blew in from the west, dumping a few inches of snow in northern Florida and whipping rain across Biscayne Bay toward the resorts of Miami Beach. Sonny Liston had an ideal view of the storm. He and Geraldine were sharing a palatial sixteen-room beach house on Biscayne Bay with Joe Louis and his wife. Together, Sonny and Joe, two of the most laconic champions in the history of the division, could watch the stinging rain swirl around the hotel towers, pockmarking the sand on the beach.[1]

It was two days before the title match and Liston had finished his training and was now hunkered down with his thoughts. He never had much to say, and even less in the days before a fight. Hungry for some news from Liston's inner circle, reporters turned to Louis. Sonny would win, Joe predicted confidently. He called Clay a good amateur boxer who had never mastered professional tactics. He might last a few rounds if he ran like a rabbit, but eventually Sonny would catch him.

In 1964, Sonny Liston seemed the indestructible superman of boxing. In his three previous fights he had knocked out his opponents in the first round. He expected his match with Cassius Clay would follow the same course. He was surprised, however, to find that Cassius had the power and the skill to hurt him. Associated Press

Though it was just a short drive from Liston's quarters to Cassius Clay's tiny white house on 5th Street in a low-rent district of North Miami, the two neighborhoods were worlds apart. Clay's place had cheap louvered windows and a porch so small that only one chair could fit on it. The inside of his house matched the porch. It was tiny and crowded—a mob of men, some with the thinnest ties to his camp, slept dormitory-style three or four to a room; children slammed doors as they ran laughing and screaming in and out of the house; and the smells of cooking greens and beans soaked every room. Outside, in a dusty patch of lawn along 5th Street, men sat in cheap folding chairs under a large ficus tree talking and watching "foxes" stroll up and down the street.[2]

Often in the evenings, as soon as the moon rose over the city, an aide strung an extension cord out of a window and set up a movie projector and a white-sheet screen. Kids gathered on the lawn, pulling their knees close to their chests to make room for a capacity audience. While moths gathered in the light of the flickering film, Clay narrated a voice-over

commentary of the action on the screen. He had watched all the movies repeatedly and enjoyed preparing everyone for the plot twists.

One movie silenced even Cassius. He showed it three or four times, and on each occasion he watched in hushed, wide-eyed respect. Only the slow crawl of traffic intruded on the film, the 1956 science-fiction horror classic *Invasion of the Body Snatchers*. The story of pods from somewhere in outer space that replicate and replace humans, transforming them into mindless, soulless automatons, transfixed the fighter.

A few white sportswriters and journalists visited Clay in his 5th Street quarters. They wrote about the chaos, the cast of characters that included jesters, trainers, hangers-on, and somber, angry-eyed, intimidating men in dark suits, white shirts, and bow ties who watched the action around them and hardly had a good word to say to any white man. Other members of Clay's camp referred to them as "the brotherhood." But they looked to the white reporters like a sect of pod people. They dressed alike, acted alike, talked alike, and seemed to think alike.

Malcolm X, the physical prototype for the brotherhood, returned to Miami on February 24, the day before the fight. Once again, Cassius, along with Archie Robinson, picked him up at the airport. No sooner was Malcolm in the car than Clay inquired about his standing in the Nation. "Any word from Chicago?" he asked.[3]

Of course, there had been. Elijah's personal secretary had told Malcolm that his suspension was still in effect, and that the Supreme Minister remained deeply disturbed by his disciple's independent ways. But instead of telling the full truth, Malcolm answered deceptively, "Nothing positive," and let it go at that. He said it cheerfully, in a sort of no-news-is-good-news tone of voice, yet he knew that "nothing positive" translated to "everything negative."[4]

Outwardly, Malcolm looked as cool as ever, smiling as if he knew a secret nobody else did, as if fear were an alien concept. But that night when Cassius left him at the Hampton House, he did not visit the hotel's jazz club. He sat in his room, plotting his future. At the heart of his plan was Cassius Clay.

It all depended on Clay defeating Liston. Malcolm believed that Allah had delivered Cassius to him, and Allah would not have brought the two together in that Detroit luncheonette, shown the boxer the light of truth, and allowed him to ascend to the top of the heavyweight division

only to abandon him now. Surely, if he could talk to Elijah, he could convince him of the divine importance of the match in Miami.

Early on the day of the contest, Malcolm phoned "Chicago." Whether he talked directly with Elijah or one of the Prophet's leading aides is unclear from the FBI informant's report. But it hardly mattered—"Chicago" was Elijah Muhammad. Malcolm and Elijah engaged in a conversation, even if it traveled through a third person. Malcolm repeated his absolute belief that Clay would defeat Liston, making the boxer potentially the Nation's most important convert and marketable asset. What would the heavyweight champion be worth in terms of world prestige, propaganda, and revenues? What would be the value of his image on the pages of *Muhammad Speaks*, and how much power would it carry among young black men stifled in the ghettoes of America? Could Elijah imagine the waves of emotion that would roll across the auditorium when Malcolm, yes Malcolm, delivered Cassius and the title to the Supreme Minister at the Saviours' Day convention on February 26? It would mark a new age for the Nation of Islam and elevate Elijah to new heights. And all it would cost was Malcolm's full reinstatement.[5]

"Chicago" turned him down flat. Clearly, Elijah, Raymond Sharrieff, and the other Muslim leaders thought that was Malcolm daydreaming. They agreed with the experts that Liston would dispatch Clay in a few rounds, ending the meteoric rise of the boisterous contender. Once defeated, and possibly even humiliated, "he would be just another boxer," battered, scarred, on the road to oblivion. Malcolm, they judged, was as bad at evaluating boxers as he was sizing up political infighters. What was more, if by some chance Clay did upset Liston, the Nation was prepared to push Malcolm out of the picture and claim Cassius as their own, reaping all the rewards.

WHILE MALCOLM TRIED to barter Clay for his reinstatement, Cassius prepared for the final act in his psychological campaign against Liston. A few days before, he had told the press, "I'm tired of talking . . . I'm ready to go to war." But he had one more set piece planned before he stepped into the ring.[6]

At precisely ten thirty a.m., he burst into the Cypress Room in the Miami Convention Center for the weigh-in. Cassius wore a blue denim

jacket with "Bear Huntin'" embroidered in red, carried a bamboo cane given to him by Malcolm, and appeared highly agitated. Drew "Bundini" Brown and Sugar Ray Robinson flanked him. Sugar Ray looked a bit sheepish, like a man who had been stationed in the center stage for no apparent reason. Bundini, however, played his part in the farce with consummate professionalism. Dressed in a yellow plaid sports jacket fit for a Las Vegas showroom, he appeared wide-eyed and wild, a sweating, mumbling, shouting provocateur ready to burst with excitement. Bundini, Angelo Dundee claimed, "charged Clay's battery." Together with Cassius he exhorted: "Float like a butterfly and sting like a bee—rumble, young man, rumble—aaahhhh!—rumble, young man, rumble!" They repeated the lines again and again, admiring each other's performance and stretching out the open-mouthed "Aaaahhhh!" to remarkable lengths. Jim Murray of the *Los Angeles Times* thought Cassius acted "like Donald Duck on a bender."[7]

As Cassius ranted, his voice rose higher and then turned hoarse with strain. "I'm ready to rumble, I'm the champ, I'm ready to rumble," he kept repeating. "You can tell Sonny I'm here with Sugar Ray," he yelled. "Liston is flat-footed, and Joe Louis is flat-footed, but me and Sugar Ray are two pretty dancers." While Robinson shifted about uneasily, Cassius continued. "Round eight I'll prove I'm great." Then the "spaniel-eyed" Bundini joined in for another chorus of "float like a butterfly and sting like a bee."

William Faversham, the main representative of the Louisville Sponsoring Group, waded into the middle of the activity to restore order. He was soon in over his head—having recently suffered from heart problems, his futile, hectic efforts to pull Clay out of the mess threatened his life. When Clay and his group retired to a dressing room to strip down for the weigh-in, the exhausted Faversham turned to LSG lawyer Gordon Davidson and told him to take over. "Gordon," he instructed, "go back to the dressing room and tell Clay that if he causes a scene they're gonna fine him, and it's gonna be his money, not ours. Tell him to behave himself."[8]

Davidson pushed through the crowded room and into the dressing room. He found Clay lying on a rubdown table, relaxed and serene. "Cassius looked like he didn't have a worry in the world," he remembered. "Like it was just another day at the office." Davidson warned

Cassius that the boxing commission was going to fine him. "They're gonna hit you pretty good."

Clay brushed off the threat like it was a lone raindrop on his shoulder. "Don't worry about it. I'll take care of it." It was the cost of doing business, he figured, and not worth a second thought. Davidson's effort to domesticate Clay by threatening him with a fine was as pointless as telling Malcolm X not to express an opinion.

For half an hour, first Davidson and then Faversham talked to Cassius about proper behavior and decorum. All the while, in the Cypress Room, hundreds of reporters and cameramen jockeyed for position for the show. At 11:09, when Davidson led Clay, Bundini, and Sugar Ray out of the dressing room, it seemed like a scene from a Hollywood premiere. The place pulsated with flashes from camera bulbs. Wearing a terrycloth robe and trunks, Cassius moved through the throng toward the weigh-in platform.

Then Liston emerged from his dressing room. Cassius exploded. Excitedly, he jumped up and down screaming, "Hey, sucker, you a chump. Are you scared?" He hollered that he was the real champ, that Liston had not fought anybody, and that he would knock him out. He promised, "Somebody's gonna die at ringside tonight." Cassius was uncontrollable. One reporter commented that Sugar Ray and Bundini "patted him on the shoulders as if they were trying to calm a skittish colt" and grabbed him around the waist to keep him away from Liston, but Clay continued to rage and shout and threaten.

Liston observed the scene with cold disinterest. Once he cupped his enormous hands over his mouth and said mysteriously, "Don't let anybody know. Don't tell the world." Know what? That Cassius was crazy? That he was a fool? That he was afraid? Interpretations of his cryptic statement varied.[9]

The comment threw Clay into an even wilder rage. Watching the action, reporter Mort Sharnik thought that there was no way that the boxer could fight that night. "It looked to me like Cassius was having a seizure," he recalled. Then he witnessed something strange, something that few others saw. While five or six people in his entourage were struggling to keep Clay from attacking Liston, "he winked at Robinson." At the absolute center of the chaos, surrounded by cameras, shouting, and confusion, "Cassius was probably having a ball."[10]

Weighing 218 pounds, Liston was a few pounds heavier than expected, and at 210½ Clay was a few pounds lighter. But the numbers that seemed to matter most were 80 and 120. On the platform, where bedlam reigned, Liston's resting pulse rate registered 80 beats a minute, up slightly from his normal 72. Clay's normal rate was 54, but it had rocketed to 120. That alarmed Dr. Alexander Robbins, the attending physician. "Clay is nervous and scared and he's burning a lot of energy," he said. Later, sportswriter Jimmy Cannon pressed him to elaborate on the comment, asking, "Could it be that the kid is scared to death, Doc?" Robbins said yes and proceeded to venture well outside his professional competency: "He is hysterical. He has a fear of death . . . a fear of getting killed. He acted like a maniac. He's definitely out of control. . . . He acted like a man off the beaten path."[11]

Clay's performance at the weigh-in ticked the odds against him up from 7–1 to 8–1. Some observers ventured even odds that he would not even show up for the fight. Most of the four hundred to five hundred onlookers would have agreed with Jim Murray that Cassius looked like a man who had just seen his own ghost. Rumors circulated that he was high on "reefers," Benzedrine, or both. Most reporters agreed that Clay was too intelligent not to know that the gig was up. "No man could have seen Clay that morning at the weigh-in and believed that he could stay on his feet three minutes that night," concluded the *New Republic*'s Murray Kempton.[12]

THE MIAMI BEACH Boxing Commission fined Clay $2,500 for his conduct on the platform. Hours away from facing the most feared fighter in the world, Clay, many reporters insisted, must be nearly paralyzed with fear. Jimmy Cannon openly questioned his manhood. Cassius was "shaped for a more effete and gayer line," he wrote, speculating that "the big riddle is will he fall apart in the dressing room?"[13]

Cannon and the others were reading into Clay their own fears of Liston, rather than listening to what the challenger said. Cassius brimmed with confidence, affirming his masculinity and promising retribution against the army of journalistic naysayers. "I don't know what it feels like to be afraid," he told Leonard Koppett of the *New York Times*. "The only thing I fear is fear itself. . . . I'm going to win and be champion, and you writers better get on the bandwagon right now. If you're voting

for me, write it now. I'm keeping lists." He was reading the papers, noting the doubters, and filing the information. "Right after the fight, I'm going to have my roll-call right there in the ring."[14]

Although fifty-nine of sixty-two writers polled picked Liston to win the fight, generally by a knockout before the end of the third round, Clay was blithely confident, an attitude that Malcolm buttressed. Malcolm told him that it was the will of Allah that he would win, arguing that it was all part of a divine plan. The night before the fight he told journalist Murray Kempton that Cassius feared no man: "To be a Muslim is to know no fear."[15]

George Plimpton wanted to discover more about the source of Clay's fearlessness. After the weigh-in spectacle, he took a car ride with Archie Robinson, who asked if he would like to meet Malcolm X. Plimpton said certainly, and Robinson drove him to the Hampton House. He took a side table in the luncheonette, and soon Malcolm walked in, carefully weaving through the crowded room, tapping the floor with a walking stick identical to Clay's. Wearing horn-rimmed glasses, Malcolm stood tall, giving the appearance of a stately professor. He sat across from Plimpton, opening a package of peppermints and popping one in his mouth.[16]

He was as serene as a monk. The troubles keeping him awake at night were invisible to Plimpton. He said his problems with Elijah Muhammad were over; in fact, he would be "unmuzzled" in March, less than a week away. Speaking gently, occasionally he jotted a word or two that he wanted to emphasize on the paper tablecloth. Plimpton watched him write, noticing the red ring with a small crescent on one of his thin fingers. Malcolm was polite, repeating "Sir?" when he did not hear a question in the noisy room, but Plimpton detected a slight mocking air about his fastidious manners.

He affirmed his belief that Clay was "likely to beat Liston." Again, Malcolm stressed the importance of belonging to the Muslim faith. "[Cassius] has tremendous self-confidence," he explained. "I've never heard him mention fear. Anything you're afraid of can whip you. Fear magnifies what you're afraid of. One thing about our religion is that it removes fear. Christianity is based on fear."

Malcolm spoke respectfully, even lovingly, about Cassius, ignoring his athletic talents and concentrating on his intellectual and emotional

assets. The boxer was kind, gentle, and humble, not at all like the clown that he played for public consumption. But the minister thought his pupil's greatest gift was his political instinct. "He should be a diplomat. He has the instinct of seeing a tricky situation shaping and resolving how to sidestep it." Perhaps it was that ability, the fighter's instinct for avoiding the knockout punch, that Malcolm most admired. Malcolm had always been a magnificent debater, but maybe he was realizing that he gave too much of himself away when he talked, that he showed his weaknesses to his most observant opponents. He admired in Cassius the very quality that he lacked. Clay talked endlessly but had the ability to keep his options open.

Meanwhile, Malcolm's options were closing. Officially silenced, instructed to avoid the press and to make no public statements, he continued to pop peppermints in his mouth and discuss black rage and revolution with Plimpton. The day of reckoning would come, he emphasized. "There *must* be retribution." It was proclaimed in the Koran, chapter 20, verse 102. Later Plimpton checked the citation: "The day when the trumpet is blown. On that day we will assemble the guilty white-eyed (with terror)."

"These are the things you are teaching Cassius?" Plimpton asked.

Malcolm answered: "He will make up his own mind."

RAIN PELTED THE Miami Beach Convention Center on the day of the fight, washing away any chance William MacDonald had of seeing a profit. After paying too much ($625,000) for the rights to the live promotion alone—he had no part of the lucrative closed-circuit television rights—he had compounded the error by scaling ticket prices too high. They ranged from $250 for the Golden Circle seats located just behind the press rows to $20 for seats high up in the arena and far from the ring. High rollers, the sort who came to fights to be seen as much as to see, had quickly bought the Golden Circle seats. And the cheap seats moved briskly. But the tickets for the mid-ranged seats, those priced at $200, $150, and $100, gathered dust in the offices of the Convention Center. MacDonald refused to discount the ducats, hoping that when this inescapable fact sank in, there would be a late rush of buyers. But the hard rain combined with MacDonald's hard line thoroughly dampened the sales. In the end, MacDonald sold only 8,297 of the 15,744

seats in the arena. Altogether he lost in the neighborhood of $363,000 on the venture.[17]

The rain and ticket prices were not the only obstacles for the gate. The contest was generally judged by boxing authorities to be a gross mismatch. When Robert Lipsyte was sent to Miami, his elders at the *New York Times* had only one practical instruction: "As soon as I landed, I was to drive my rental car from the arena to the nearest hospital, mapping the quickest route. My paper didn't want me to waste any deadline time following Clay to intensive care." Lipsyte's seniors in the profession probably already knew the ambulance route. Writing columns about the fight that seemed penned in acid, Jim Murray's only hope "for Cassius Clay is that he clots easily." Offering a strategy to the challenger, Murray wrote, "If I were Cassius Clay I would fight him at such a long range he would have to reach me through Western Union."[18]

It seemed that the only people willing to go on record predicting a win by Clay were close family members and a smattering of associates of Malcolm X. Meanwhile, the stories about Clay's connections with the Nation of Islam had worked a public relations miracle: they had transformed Sonny Liston into the sentimental favorite. Long before, Liston had accepted his role as the villain in the morality plays of professional boxing. But Clay's extreme religious and political opinions had made the champion's peccadilloes seem almost quaint. In a classic understatement, sportswriter Dan Parker commented, "Liston hasn't been a popular champion but, since Clay's yen for the Black Muslim white-hating sect of fanatics was revealed, neither is Cassius a popular challenger."[19]

The rain, the ticket prices, the expected mismatch, and the unpopularity of both fighters created a perfect storm for the fight's promoters. Capping it off, just an hour or so before the fight a local radio station reported that Clay had been seen at the Miami airport purchasing a ticket for a foreign country. Jerry Izenberg, covering the fight for the *Newark Star-Ledger*, heard the news in a taxi while he was riding to the match. The bizarre twists and turns of the Liston-Clay saga had left even him dizzy. "I didn't know what was going to happen. No one did. Maybe there would be a fight. Maybe there wouldn't. Maybe Clay was in Miami. Maybe he was somewhere over the Atlantic, heading who knows where."[20]

IZENBERG HEARD HIM before he saw him. When the reporter reached his seat, a familiar voice knifed through the silence in the near-deserted arena. "Keep your left hand up! Keep your left hand up! Move to your right!" Turning around, Izenberg spotted Cassius Clay, dressed in a tight tuxedo and a white ruffled shirt, his eyes trained on the ring, where his brother Rudy was making his professional debut in a four-round preliminary bout. As he watched his brother, Cassius ducked and weaved, rolled with the punches and threw a few in return, agonizing over any blow that connected with Rudy. When the referee raised Rudy's hand at the end of the contest, Cassius slipped out of the exit and hurried to his dressing room.[21]

Rudy's victory seemed to momentarily calm Clay. Dr. Robbins made a perfunctory prefight examination, noting that Clay's pulse had dropped to sixty-four. But no sooner did he begin to relax than new concerns troubled his mind. Told repeatedly by the Muslims that he could not trust any white man, he fretted that some vast conspiracy of Caucasians was plotting his defeat. Looking at Pacheco and Angelo Dundee, his white corner men, he thought they might be part of the cabal. Angelo, according to Clay's tortured logic, was Italian, and an Italian must be associated with the mafia, which certainly had a stake in Liston's keeping the title. After all, it was no secret that the mob controlled Sonny.

"They"—whoever "they" were—were out to get him, Cassius reasoned. But how? Doping him by making him ingest some odorless, tasteless, colorless, debilitating drug seemed a logical guess. It had happened before. Fixers had doped water bottles, oranges, and towels to drug a fighter. And all day Cassius had received calls from Black Muslims warning him to beware of the "white devils." Shouldn't he at least consider the possibility? As he waited in the dressing room, weaving a web of suspicions, the water bottle assumed an ominous presence. He dumped out the water and refilled it himself, taping it shut and assigning Rudy to make sure no one got near it. But Rudy had just won his first pro fight, and his attention lagged behind his intention. When Cassius noticed this, he again emptied, filled, and taped the bottle. "He did that three or four times," recalled Pacheco.[22]

Cassius was nervous. For all he had said about his opponent being a chump, boxing authorities claimed that Sonny Liston was one of

the two or three greatest—maybe the best—heavyweight champions in history. Big, mean, and vicious, he had hurt most of his opponents, knocking out the finest boxers in the division. Even as masseur Luis Sarria rubbed Clay's shoulders, Pacheco noticed that the fighter was tight. "He was just a kid, and that night he had no idea if he could really do what he had been saying he could do all along."[23]

Almost providentially, someone knocked on the door. Malcolm X came into the dressing room, exuding a sense of cool confidence. Malcolm, Cassius, and Rudy faced east toward Mecca, bowed, and prayed, praising Allah and blessing his name. Then Malcolm repeated a variation of what he had been saying since coming to Miami. It was more a prophecy than a pep talk. "The fight is the *truth*. It's the Cross and the Crescent fighting in the prize ring—for the first time. It's a modern Crusades—a Christian and a Muslim facing each other with television to beam it off Telstar for the whole world to see what happens!" This was destined to be a historic moment. "Do you think Allah has brought about all this intending for you to leave the ring as anything but the champion?"[24]

When he had completed his mission, Malcolm walked back to his seat near ringside, stopping briefly to chat with the singer Sam Cooke, who was seated close to Malcolm in row seven.[25] He moved to seat number seven, a "lucky seat." Seven, along with twelve and twenty-one, were the three numbers that Elijah Muhammad taught were special for the Asiatic black man. The date of the fight also had significance. It was the twenty-fifth day of February. Two plus five equaled seven. And the following day would be the thirty-fourth Saviours' Day convention. Again, three plus four equaled seven. Believing fully in the power and meaning of numbers, Malcolm must have smiled, at least inwardly. "I took this to be Allah's message confirming to me that Cassius Clay was going to win," he later told Alex Haley.[26]

WHEN CASSIUS, WEARING a stylish thigh-length white robe, slipped through the ropes into the ring, the Convention Center looked as if it were an experiment in economic segregation. The Golden Circle seats were practically full, celebrities packed next to each other and to other wealthy ticket holders willing to pay top dollar just to sit close to them. And far from them, up high in the hinterlands of the arena, sat the

twenty- and fifty-dollar patrons. Between the two classes of spectators was a *cordon sanitaire*, row after row of hundred- to two-hundred-dollar seats that were so sparsely populated that they looked as if they had been designed as a physical barrier.

In his corner, Cassius was nervous, like a person who had ventured too far out on a high limb. When he met Sonny in the middle of the ring for the referee's instruction, he later admitted, "I was scared. Sonny Liston was the greatest fighter of all time . . . and he was fixing to kill me. It frightened me, just knowing how hard he hit."[27]

Meanwhile his opponent came into the ring as unfeeling as a rock. His head had been partially covered by the hood of his white robe, but when the fighters met in the center of the ring and Sonny removed the hood, he fixed Clay with a malevolent stare. In the previous three years Liston had fought four times, winning three by knockouts in the first round and once by knockout in the third round. Barry Gottehrer wrote in *Sport* magazine that Liston commanded the center of the ring: "A former convict, a onetime union goon, and a man who seemed drawn to violence, Liston . . . had assumed the aura of a superman, a destroyer who came to kill."[28]

Clay's trepidation was understandable. Most boxers know fear; the greats rise above it and execute their fight plans anyway. Cassius planned to exploit Sonny's age and overconfidence. He knew that Liston expected another short fight and had not wasted much energy training. Clay's plan was to make Liston chase him, fighting in spurts and circling constantly to his left, away from Liston's lethal left hand. Clay later recalled, "I trained to fight the first two rounds, and to protect myself from getting hit by Liston. I knew that with the third, he'd start tiring, then he'd get worse with every round. So I trained to coast the third, fourth, and fifth rounds. . . . I wanted him to wear himself out and get desperate. He would be throwing wild punches and missing. . . . And so I conditioned myself to fight full steam from the sixth through the ninth round. . . ." Cassius thought by the eighth he would have Liston: "I'd cut him up and shake him up until he would be like a bull, just blind, and missing punches until he was nearly crazy. And . . . when he had thrown some punch and left himself just right, I'd be all set, and I'd drop him."[29]

That, anyway, was the plan.

Waiting in his corner for the opening bell, Cassius danced, gracefully shifting his weight from one foot to the other. Sonny scraped his feet against the canvas like a bull digging into the dirt before charging. At the clang of the bell he attacked, moving toward Clay in a straight line as if they were fighting on a tightrope. Yet while Sonny's assault was linear, Cassius's defense was rococo. His hands at his side, he bounced tantalizing just beyond the champion's reach, slipping, ducking, side-stepping, and pulling back from punches. All the while Cassius circled left, making it difficult for Sonny to land a left jab and impossible to connect with a left hook. Liston lunged like an amateur, missing hooks by several feet. When he got too close, Clay briefly clinched and then quickly pushed him back to a safe distance.[30]

For the first half of the round Clay hardly threw a punch. He dominated simply by the artistry of his movement. Forward, backward, side to side, feinting up and down—the complexity of his defense baffled Liston. Cassius, wrote Edwin Pope of the *Miami Herald*, moved "like a kid on a pogo stick." He backed into corners and then slithered out of them so adroitly that Liston was still moving forward when Clay was already brushing by. The harder the champion tried, the more awkward he looked. Then Clay began to jab.

At first he threw snake-tongue jabs designed to gauge his distance from his prey and get a sense of Liston's reaction. Feeling safe, he tried a few harder jabs, mixing in a couple of cruel, flat-footed lead rights and left hooks that stopped Liston's forward movement. Angered, the champion charged, fighting wildly even after the bell.

Although most of the spectators reacted with a communal exhale to Liston's thunderous misses, the more discerning fight fans watched as Clay dominated the action. Between rounds color commentator Joe Louis was characteristically stingy with his observations—but also perfectly accurate. "I think this is one of the greatest rounds that we have seen in a long time. I think Clay completely outclassed Sonny Liston," he told his ringside colleague Steve Ellis. But, the Brown Bomber concluded, if Clay got too confident, Liston would knock him out.

Sonny pressed hard in the second. He threw more body punches, hoping to take some of the speed out of Cassius's legs. But he had no better luck reaching Clay's body than he had hitting his head. Cassius remained at a safe distance. "Liston came at me throwing everything,"

he later recalled. "He was going to make up for looking so bad that I had lasted *one* round."

While Clay moved, he watched Sonny's eyes, seeing in them his opponent's thoughts. "Liston eyes you up when he's about to throw a heavy punch," he said. "Some kind of way they just flicker." So Cassius watched, looking for the flicker, the warning to move out of range. But he saw something else—a soft red mouse high on Liston's left cheekbone. He knew that one or two sharp punches would split the bump wide open, proving to the experts, the spectators, and, most important, Liston himself that the champion could bleed like any other fighter. And if he could bleed, he could be defeated.

Cassius threw and landed the first punches of the third. He had planned to coast that round but saw that Liston was hurt and confused. He later explained, "I couldn't waste no time. I needed one more good shot, for some insurance with that eye." His left jabs angled off Sonny's left eye. Then a right-left combination landed with tom-tom precision. Tex Maule of *Sports Illustrated* thought Cassius worked as methodically as a bullfighter placing *banderillas*.

Suddenly it happened. A right hand split Sonny's cheek "from dark to red as cleanly as a sharp knife cutting through the rind of a watermelon."

"It didn't take but one good combination," Cassius recalled. "My left was square on his right eye, and a right under his left eye opened a deep gash. I knew it was deep, the way the blood spurted right out."

Then Cassius opened up, throwing left and right hooks. While a nearly electric shock jolted the spectators to their feet, the blow-by-blow announcer reacted excitedly. "Sonny wobbled! Sonny wobbled! Cassius has him hurt! . . . Sonny has a big mouse below the left eye! Sonny's cut below the eye! And he's getting hit with all the punches in the book!"

Cassius watched as Sonny pawed at his eye. A cut under the eye, as Jerry Izenberg commented, "doesn't mean shit. But it did to Liston when he was the one who had been cut." Seeing blood on his glove he rushed forward, throwing all of his weight into wild, wide punches. A few crashed painfully into Clay's body, but most missed, visibly tiring the champion. Jim Murray commented, "The old champ was as clumsy as a guy groping for a light switch in the dark with a hangover." But

several of the punches that missed whooshed just inches past Cassius's jaw. The thought of what might have been kept the spectators on their feet roaring.[31]

From his press row seat, Maule watched Clay dismantle the Liston legend. The champion had no answer for Cassius's speed and tactics. At one point in the third round, Maule noticed Liston "leaning heavily against the rope, peering between raised gloves. His expression was puzzled and shocked and almost frightened." His "arrogant self-confidence," the cornerstone of his awesome reputation, had vanished. And six feet away, Clay was screaming at him. "Come on! Come on, you bum!" At that moment it was clear to Maule that "Sonny Liston was no longer the heavyweight champion of the world."[32] But the fight wasn't over yet.

SONNY TRUDGED TO his corner like an aged sparring partner, collapsing hard onto his stool. His trainer, Willie Reddish, and cut man, Joe Polino, crowded in front of him. Polino immediately went to work on Liston's eye, sponging it clean and smearing Monsel's solution, a thick, caustic substance that's now illegal in boxing, on the wound. Monsel's dries quickly, leaves a black residue, and can be blinding if it gets into a fighter's eyes.

Quite possibly another blinding substance was put on Sonny's gloves. According to Jack McKinney, a Philadelphia sportswriter sitting near Liston and Polino, when Sonny returned to his corner he ordered Polino to "juice the gloves"—that is, smear some illegal substance on the them. In several previous fights Liston's opponents had complained that a painful astringent, perhaps from Sonny's gloves, had gotten into their eyes. McKinney claimed that Liston's corner men had a history of juicing his gloves and did it once again in the Clay fight. "If you look at a film of what went on in Liston's corner between the third and fourth rounds of that fight," McKinney told writer Thomas Hauser, "you'll see Polino in the ring with Willie Reddish standing behind him, blocking everyone's view. And Polino is at Sonny's knees, rubbing something on his glove."[33]

Round four belonged to Clay from start to finish. No longer was he moving in jerky, pogo-stick bursts. Still circling Liston, he maneuvered more slowly, confidently, snapping out jabs that seemed to explode in

Sonny's face. Soon Liston's right eye had an angry welt under it, and his nose and lips looked like he was having an allergic reaction to multiple bee stings. Sonny tried to respond, but his jabs consistently missed their target and his hooks mostly punished the air around Cassius's head. Once, however, Liston forced a clinch, and although he could not punish Clay with punches, he rubbed his glove across Cassius's eyes. If his gloves were juiced, this is when he did the damage.

Several sportswriters thought that Cassius's jabs connected with the Monsel's on Sonny's left eye and that then he transferred the substance to his forehead as he wiped off sweat. The "thin skin of the caustic on his forehead," wrote Maule, "washed down into his eyes between rounds when his trainer, Angelo Dundee, swabbed him with a wet sponge." The trouble with this view is that Cassius did not brush his forehead with his left, his primary punching hand, during the round. The only hand that swept across Clay's eyes and forehead was Liston's.[34]

Nor did Dundee contribute to the problem. By the time Clay reached his corner, his face was already contorted with pain. He felt like "some acid" was in his eyes. "I could just see blurry . . . it felt like fire." Blinking as if he were trying to clear grit out of his eyes, he told Dundee that something was wrong. Removing his mouthpiece, he screamed at Dundee, "Cut off the gloves. Cut off the gloves." At the time Cassius believed that someone was trying to fix the fight. "Dirty work afoot!" he told Dundee. "Dirty work afoot," he repeated to his other corner men.[35]

Dundee was not about to cut off Clay's gloves, not in a heavyweight championship contest. He quickly examined his fighter. "I put my pinky in his eyes and then mine," he recalled. "It burned like hell." While Cassius complained, Dundee tried another test. He dried Clay's eyes with a towel, sniffing and tasting it when he finished. "There was something wrong. I tasted a strange substance." Maybe it was from Liston's gloves; perhaps it was something else that had been put on Sonny's body.

Unconcerned with the cause, Dundee focused on the problem. He sponged Clay's eyes, trying to flush out whatever substance was in them. He tried to reassure him, telling Cassius that the pain would pass and that he would be fine. "If you can't see, keep away from him until your eyes clear. This is the big one. Nobody walks away from a heavyweight championship."

While Dundee was earning his wages in Clay's corner, Black Muslims at ringside had reached their own conclusions about the cause of the problem. Izenberg remembered that Captain Sam and Archie Robinson were out of their seats, watching Dundee wipe Clay's eyes while he convulsed in pain. They clearly believed that Dundee was the culprit. Seeing the rising anger of the Muslims, Chris Dundee signaled to his brother Angelo to wipe his own face with the sponge, which the trainer soon did, telling Archie and Sam, "Look! Look! Look!"

But before that demonstration, he had a fighter to motivate. When the bell rang for round five, Cassius said Angelo pushed him forward and shouted, "This is the big one, daddy. We aren't going to quit now! . . . Run until your eyes clear! RUN!"

As Clay moved forward, half blind and confused, Bundini Brown offered a piece of tactical advice: "Yardstick 'im, champ! Yardstick 'im!"[36]

It was the perfect strategy. Often in previous fights, Clay had used his left, held straight out from his shoulder, as a yardstick for measuring distance and punches, and occasionally for taunting opponents. Now he could use his straight yardstick left as a seeing-eye device. As long as Liston remained an arm's length away from him, Cassius was in safe territory.

Liston eyed Clay at the start of the fifth round "like a kid looks at a new bike on Christmas." Seeing Cassius's condition, he rushed forward with cruel intentions. Instead of maneuvering to cut off the ring and force Clay into a corner, he moved directly toward him like an aggressive street brawler stalking a frightened victim. Cassius moved backward, unable to completely avoid Sonny's bull rushes. But he could grab and hold, thereby denying Liston leverage for his most lethal punches. But in the clinches Clay absorbed frightful punishment. Liston pounded his sides and stomach with combinations. At one point, early in the fifth, Clay grabbed the back of Liston's neck and Sonny landed sixteen consecutives body blows before the referee broke the clinch.[37]

Clay had no plans for fighting blind. More than other fighters, he boxed in a head-high, wide-eyed style. At times he looked like a painter, stepping back to inspect his work before adding a final dab of color. But now he was robbed of his vision, glimpsing Liston imperfectly through "tear-fogged" eyes.

"Man, in that round, my plans were *gone*. I was just trying to keep alive, hoping the tears would wash out my eyes. I could open them just enough to get a good glimpse of Liston, and then it hurt so bad I blinked them closed again. . . . He was trying to hit me square . . . it could be over right there."[38]

There is a widely accepted myth that during the fifth, Clay's speed kept him out of harm's way. In truth, during the first ninety seconds of the round, Liston landed scores of punches, to the head as well as the body. Rather than his speed, Clay's ability to take a punch kept him in the fight. Soon after the match, Clay reflected, "He shook me with a left to the head and a lot of shots to the body. Now, I ain't too sorry it happened, because it proved I could take Liston's punching."[39]

Liston "was snorting like a horse" during his onslaught, Cassius remembered, but by the middle of the round he was breathing heavily through his mouth. Arm-weary and bone-tired, he began to slow, throwing fewer punches, and those were mostly slow, lazy, and purposeless. In the clinches, he rested rather than pulling his arms free and banging Clay's body. Now, Cassius began yardsticking him and, as his eyes cleared, stung him with sharp jabs. He began to talk. "You ain't nothing!" And to prove the point, he yardsticked Liston and then slapped him lightly five or six times in the face, almost like a teenage boy play-boxing with a five-year-old, or, wrote Tex Maule, "like a man knocking on a door."[40]

Sonny had thrown more punches in the first half of the round than he normally threw in two or three, and now his lack of conditioning showed. For Sonny, the bell that ended the round came as a relief, even though it ended his best opportunity to win the fight. Nothing was working. Cassius Clay had weathered Liston's stare, intimidation tactics, bull rushes, juiced gloves, and best punches. The arm-weary, mouth-breathing champion had nothing left—no plan B, no second wind, no chance.

Cassius had everything the champion lacked. As the result of hard conditioning and the advantages of youth, he felt the rise of a second wind as his eyes cleared and his confidence grew. "Get mad, baby!" Dundee told him. He said to go for the knockout. "No," Clay answered. "I ain't in a hurry. Maybe I'll carry him for the 15."[41]

Taking his last deep breaths before round six, Cassius knew, "I was going to make Liston look terrible."[42]

He did. Closing the distance to the champion, boxing at a slower, more deliberate pace, he started to punish Sonny. Steve Ellis described the action for the closed-circuit viewers: "We note that Sonny stands flat-footed most of the time. Easy target. EASY!" His voice rose on the second "easy" as Clay landed a punishing jab and a powerful right cross. Although Clay held his hands low, his boxing was classic. Every attack followed from his perfectly timed jab, always aimed at the cuts below Sonny's eyes. As Liston moved sluggishly forward, Clay jabbed, sometimes softly, as if he was just toying with Sonny, other times with jolting force. Depending on how Liston reacted to the jab, Clay might throw a right cross or a right-left-right combination of hooks. Then he backed away before Liston could set himself to counterpunch. "Sonny can't seem to slip or knock down that jab effectively," Ellis said. "Cassius throws it from all angles. Very tricky left lead."[43]

It was a textbook round. Clay knew that Liston had entered the pain zone, and there was nothing he could do about it. "He was gone," Clay realized.

Between rounds Cassius twisted around and called to the reporters, "I'm gonna upset the world!" "I never will forget how their faces was looking up at me like they couldn't believe it," he said later. But sitting close to the reporters was Malcolm X, and he believed it. He had prophesied it. Throughout the fight he never lost faith, not even when Cassius fought blind in the fifth. Although inwardly Malcolm rejoiced, outwardly he was the picture of tranquility. "I folded my arms and tried to appear the coolest man in the place," he wrote, "because a television camera can show you looking like a fool yelling at a prizefight."[44]

While Clay's confidence swelled, Liston's deflated like a pinpricked balloon. Willie Reddish had to convince him to sit down at the end of the sixth, and while Joe Polino labored to mend the fighter's cuts, the normally silent and undemonstrative Sonny jabbered about something. He stayed on his stool after the warning buzzer, and at the bell Reddish turned to referee Barney Felix and made a slight, low gesture with his hands, the signal that his fighter was through, the match was over. Liston remained immobile on his stool, tears mingling with the blood below his eyes.

On his feet at the buzzer, Cassius saw what was happening before Reddish's capitulation. "I happened to be looking right at Liston when the warning buzzer sounded, and I didn't believe it when he spat out his mouthpiece. . . . And then someone just told me he wasn't coming out! . . . It's a funny thing, but I wasn't even thinking about Liston—I was thinking about nothing but that hypocrite press. All of them down there had written so much about me bound to get killed by the big fists."

As Clay looked toward Liston's corner, he raised both arms high and broke into a jig, floating effortlessly in the center of the ring, before Bundini embraced him in a bear hug. Then, his mouth wide open, he wriggled loose from Bundini's arms and made a mad dash toward the reporters.

For the record, everyone in Liston's corner—and later a team of eight doctors from St. Francis Hospital in Miami—insisted Sonny had torn a tendon in his left arm early in the fight. The blood had drained into his bicep and deadened his arm, they said. Sonny had wanted to continue, his manager, Jack Nilon, claimed. "I made the decision. Before Sonny could protest, Willie and I stepped in front of him and waved the referee off. Sonny spit out his mouthpiece and cursed me and cursed Clay." "I can beat the bastard one-handed," Liston supposedly said. And perhaps, as unlikely as it seems, he did not play any role in the decision to end the fight while slumped on his stool. Still, the fact that Clay was willing to fight blind and Liston refused to continue because of a sore shoulder tells much about both boxers.[45]

But the moment Reddish signaled Felix that his fighter was done, Sonny Liston became just another bruised, bloodied, beaten ex-champion, looking older than his age, whatever that was, and sadder than any ex-mob goon ever had. Surveying Liston's face, which looked "like a melon that had fallen off the back of a truck," Murray thought "it was possible to feel sorry for this mastodon."[46]

Clay's gate-crashing sprint for the reporters, however, grabbed all the attention away from Liston's suffering. He pulled away from his handlers, dodged well-wishers, and "climbed like a squirrel onto the red velvet ropes." Perched above the multitude, he pointed with a still-gloved hand at the working press and commenced a long-repressed harangue. "I am the greatest!" he shouted. "I shook up the world! . . . You

hypocrites! You ought to hang your heads. Eat your words! Eat! Eat your words!"

At ringside, Red Smith of the *New York Herald Tribune* took a large bite. He had confidently, even humorously and arrogantly, predicted Clay's defeat, and now he heard Cassius's response. "Nobody ever had a better right" to tell reporters to eat their words, he wrote. "In a mouth still dry from the excitement of the most astonishing upset in many roaring years, the words don't taste good, but they taste better than they read. The words, written here and practically everywhere else until the impossible became the unbelievable truth, said Sonny Liston would squash Cassius Clay like a bug when the boy braggart challenged for the heavyweight championship of the world."[47]

Then, bounding off the ropes, Cassius veered toward the center of the ring, where he continued to shout his praises. "I am the greatest! I shook up the world!"

He moved from radio announcers to television commentators, saying the same thing. Trapped for a minute by Steve Ellis and Joe Louis, Cassius announced, "I'm the greatest fighter who ever lived! I'm so great I don't have a mark on my face. And I upset Sonny Liston and I'm just twenty-two years old. I must be the greatest! I told the world! I talk to God every day! With God with me can't nobody be against me!"

Ellis worked to ask a question and got a brief response, but Cassius was lost in his own world. "I'm a baaad man! I shook up the world! I shook up the world! I shook up the world!"

Standing in row seven, seat seven, Malcolm X fixed his eyes on the man who shook up the world and talked with God. His God. The black man's God. Allah. It was part of His plan and Malcolm's. No longer could the Honorable Elijah Muhammad doubt the greatness of Cassius Clay. Now, in the ebullience of Miami, Cassius had won the most important and symbolic crown in all of sports, and Malcolm's was the voice in his ear. It must have seemed, at that moment, that Malcolm's deepest dreams were on the cusp of coming true.

Chapter Twelve

FREE TO BE ME

The power of the white world is threatened whenever a black man refuses to accept the white world's definitions.
—JAMES BALDWIN

N ow everyone wanted him, not Sonny Liston. Before the match, experts and casual fans alike thought Cassius would go directly from the fight to the hospital, and that Sonny would head to his own victory celebration. But Sonny got the ride to St. Francis and Cassius, resplendent in a black tuxedo, disappeared.

Outside his dressing room, Dee Dee Sharp waited patiently with her mother. After recording "Slow Twistin'" with Chubby Checker and releasing such hit singles as "Mash Potato Time" and "Do the Bird," the attractive and coquettish Sharp was at the top of her recording career. During the previous few months she had seen Cassius off and on as their schedules permitted, but their relationship had not yet bloomed into a full-scale romance. She was just one of the "foxes" that seemed to form the wallpaper of his life. George Plimpton suspected Cassius's use of the word *foxes* was "half affectionate and half suspicious: he feels that girls can be 'sly' and 'sneaky' and are to be watched warily."[1]

Dee Dee saw herself as more than just another fox, and she had plans to spend the evening with the new heavyweight champion of the world. So she waited, crammed among the other well-wishers who claimed they knew all along that Cassius would win, and every once in a while she would call out to someone squeezing in or out of the dressing room, "Tell Cassius that Dee. . . ." She called him Cassius around the men,

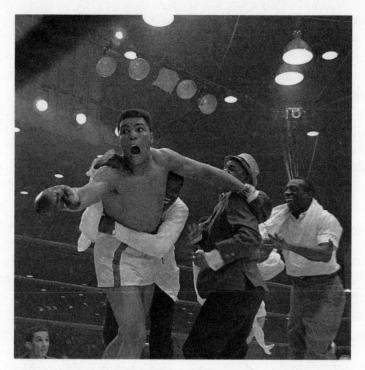

"I shook up the world!" Cassius Clay shouted after defeating Sonny Liston to win the heavyweight title. "I'm a baaad man!" Sitting near ringside, Malcolm X smiled inwardly. He believed that Cassius's victory was destiny. Associated Press

but in private she used his middle name, Marcellus. "A beautiful name. I can say it over and over," she told Plimpton.[2]

Perhaps Dee Dee thought she would go to the Fountainebleau Hotel with Cassius. Sam Cooke, friends with both Cassius and Dee Dee, was staying there, although it took a virtual sit-in by his manager for the front desk to find him a suite. Several of the members of the Louisville Sponsoring Group had even talked about a victory celebration for Cassius at the most luxurious hotel in Miami Beach. Champagne, showgirls, cakes—the celebration would be first class.[3]

The scenario, Dee Dee Sharp on his arm and champagne at a luxury hotel, conjures images of heavyweight championship style—Jack

Dempsey and Estelle Taylor, Joe Louis and Marva Trotter, and, from baseball, Joe DiMaggio and Marilyn Monroe. That was the way it was supposed to be. By fighting blind in the fifth round and battering Sonny Liston in the sixth, Cassius Clay had earned the title of champion and his share of the good life.

While Dee Dee waited, Cassius was in his dressing room holding court. He had told the reporters that he was going to win—told them loudly and often. Now that he had their full attention, he gave them another chance. After castigating them for their lack of faith, he demanded "Who's the greatest?" A few browbeaten scribes surrendered and said, "You are." Only then did the new champion smile.[4]

It was after midnight when he came out of his dressing room. Accompanied by his brother and a few friends from the Nation, he pushed through the mob of photographers and newspapermen. Standing on her toes, Dee Dee waved, calling out "Marcellus! Marcellus!" She didn't even receive a glance as he swept past her.[5]

From the arena he headed north toward the Hampton House and a small, private celebration with Malcolm X and a few other friends, including Rudy, Howard Bingham, Sam Cooke, and Archie Robinson. A joyous crowd had packed the Hampton House's luncheonette by the time Clay's party arrived. Cassius and Rudy, the two victorious boxers, sat in places of honor on the center stools at the lunch counter, surrounded by loud, talking, joking black men who had attended the fight or turned up to shake hands with the new heavyweight champion. Cassius's victory dinner was a large bowl of ice cream, which he wolfed down in a matter of seconds. While Cassius ate, Malcolm and Howard Bingham snapped photographs—Malcolm whispering in Cassius's ear, his hand resting on the champ's shoulder; Malcolm bursting with laughter while Cassius teased him; Malcolm and Cassius exchanging knowing glances. It was the happiest moment they had ever shared together.[6]

The two appeared inseparable. Malcolm seemed to take as much satisfaction from Clay's triumph and Hampton House victory party as the fighter himself. In his mind, after all, Cassius's victory was his as well. Associates had remarked that they seemed as close as brothers. During the raucous stage of the evening he called writer Alex Haley, with whom he had become close during their collaboration on Malcolm's

Immediately after defeating Sonny Liston, Cassius celebrated at the Hampton House with Malcolm X, playfully sparring with and entertaining his supporters. But behind closed doors, Cassius weighed choices that would change both of their lives. Getty Images

autobiography. Clay was like Malcolm's "little brother," Haley recalled. "[Malcolm] was very, very proud of him." During the phone call, over the loud voices in the background, "Malcolm was boasting how his little brother had done marvelously well." Showing more excitement than he had displayed at the match, he called to Cassius to holler something to Haley, which he did. It was as if the big brother called the shots and the little brother amiably went along.[7]

After a short public celebration, the inner group moved to Malcolm's bedroom for more serious conversation. The bubbly, playful banter was left behind at the lunch counter, replaced by a more somber mood. Now that Cassius was champion, Malcolm had urgent matters to discuss. He thought it was time for his friend to play a more active role in his plans. Cassius, Malcolm, and Jim Brown, the National Football League's premier running back, began talking about the future of the black man. Sympathetic to many of the Nation of Islam's goals, Brown was as respected by "race men" as he was by professional football players.

He did not believe in heroes, but he admired Malcolm's confrontational mentality. Like the combative minister, the outspoken football star insisted that blacks must demand their rights, fight for them, and defend them at all costs. Distrustful of white men, Brown questioned passive resistance and nonviolence. "I am skeptical of white men," he would later write in his autobiography, "because even the best of them want me to be patient, to follow Martin Luther King's advice and turn the other cheek until God knows when."[8]

Listening to Brown, Malcolm could tell that he was sincere in his beliefs. Malcolm clearly shared his view that famous black athletes had a responsibility to join the freedom movement. For Cassius, then, the heavyweight title was a prelude to more important accomplishments, ones that transcended sports and crossed over to politics. "Well, Brown," Malcolm asked the football player, "don't you think it's time for this young man to stop spouting off and get serious?"[9]

Brown agreed. The title was not an end in itself; it was a platform from which to advance far more urgent matters. The plan called for Cassius to use the title for his purposes, not to be used and consumed by it.

Cassius also understood that his victory over Liston marked the beginning of a new stage in his life. There was nothing left to conquer in the world of boxing. His athletic achievements now matched his worldwide fame. His actions had vindicated his boasts, certifying his incessant claims that he was the greatest. Listening to Malcolm's plans, Cassius didn't brag or rhyme. He paid attention and, as far as Malcolm could tell, agreed.

Malcolm said that they talked for several hours, which is doubtful given the time line of the evening. But they did converse long enough to hit the points that were important to both of them. Finally, exhausted from a day that had included a wild weigh-in, action-filled title fight, post-fight ring antics, and several press conferences, Cassius said he needed a nap. Stretching out on Malcolm's bed, he went to sleep.[10]

But he didn't sleep long. While Malcolm was somewhere else, Cassius awoke and had a meaningful tête-à-tête with Jim Brown. They talked about race in America, the politics of the Nation of Islam, and the feud between Malcolm and Elijah. As he listened, it was clear to Brown that there was a serious disconnect between Malcolm's plans and

Cassius's. He recalled that Clay had already made up his mind: he could no longer follow Malcolm. The Messenger would not allow it. "Elijah was a little man," Clay told Brown, "but extremely powerful, and had always supported him." Cassius "loved Malcolm, but from that day on, he would never again be his friend."[11]

Had Clay made that choice by the early morning hours of February 26? When he ate vanilla ice cream and Malcolm whispered in his ear, had he made the hard political decision that would inevitably alter both men's lives? Was it possible for Jim Brown and Malcolm X to have such different interpretations of Clay's intentions that morning? Given Cassius's avoidance of personal disagreement and his reluctance to say anything in a one-on-one personal exchange that would disappoint a friend, he might have allowed Malcolm to hear and believe what the minister desperately wanted to hear and believe. Or he may have told both Brown and Malcolm versions of the truth and kept the full truth to himself.

Huston Horn of *Sports Illustrated* reported on some of the post-fight events, though he knew nothing about Clay's conversations with Malcolm and Brown. But the thought that Malcolm was even there led to a sagacious conclusion. From Cassius's activities at the Hampton House two things were certain, Horn wrote: "His tastes are just as simple, and his thoughts on life just as murky as they have been for years."[12]

SOMETIME SHORTLY AFTER two a.m., while Cassius was nodding half-asleep in bed, someone informed him that a score of neighbors were waiting in his yard for him to return to his bungalow. "They are the people I mean something to," he said before dressing and departing the Hampton House. Once back at his house, he spent fifteen minutes or so shaking hands and signing autographs before announcing that he was calling it a night. He had another press conference in the morning and wanted to get at least a few hours of sleep.[13]

If Cassius had gotten to sleep, a doubtful proposition, he hadn't been in that state for long when a loud knock at the door disturbed everyone in the champ's bungalow. Three Los Angeles reporters—Brad Pye and Doc Young of the *Los Angeles Sentinel* and Jim Murray of the *Los Angeles Times*—just happened to be driving up in "Colored Town" and by chance saw a single bulb glowing through a frosted glass window.

All three knew Clay, and they seemed blissfully unconcerned about the propriety of the visit.[14]

Stretched out on a couch, wearing only white undershorts and gray socks, Cassius politely ignored the time and the intrusion and said, "Come in."

This was no scene out of a Hollywood boxing movie, thought Murray. In *The Champion*, the Kirk Douglas character wins the title and immediately moves uptown—the best booze, broads, and clothes that money could buy. In Cassius's low-rent dwelling, however, there were "no crowds in mink and cigar smoke, no clink of glasses, no loud music and louder sycophantry." There was just the exhausted boxer and a small circle of half-asleep friends.

Tired, occasionally rubbing his stomach, Cassius began to talk, "slowly, like a man on his first visit to a psychiatrist." He talked about Sonny—"I jes' played with him, jes' played with him, is all." About Angelo pushing him out of the corner for the fifth round—"This is for the heavyweight championship of the world. Get out there and fight." But mostly about God and his own providential journey to the title. "I'm not around rich people. I'm the champ now and God wants me to be champ." God, he believed, had a plan for him.

At two thirty Archie Robinson arrived, looking angry that a white reporter (Murray) was taking up Cassius's time. "What's this? A press conference at 3:30 in the morning?" he said without checking his watch.

"I'm the boss here," Clay said in a near whisper.

"Oh, I know, I know," Robinson responded. But the reporters departed nonetheless.

"That man sure puts a pall on a place when he comes in to see Cassius, doesn't he?" Pye said.

"For a fact," Young answered.

Around Malcolm X Cassius bubbled with life, a mixture of pleasure and mischief. But Archie Robinson prompted a wholly different vibe. It was like *The Invasion of the Body Snatchers*. Cassius seemed like one of them. One of the pod people.

THE RESULT OF the Clay-Liston match shocked reporters. Some even mused in their columns about the possibility that the fight might have been fixed. But the history of boxing is full of upsets, and Clay's

victory over Liston was no more improbable or unexpected than James J. Braddock's 1935 defeat of Max Baer. What was more startling than the result, however, was the traditional day-after press conference with the champion.

During Joe Louis's reign, such events had been relaxed affairs. Joe would show up at Mike Jacobs's Madison Square Garden office, take a seat in the large red leather chair, leaf through the morning's funny pages, eat an apple, and field reporters' questions. Joe never really said much, but he managed to give the sportswriters at least a germ of a story. As often as he tried to explain what it was like to be the most feared fighter in the world, he could never exactly convey how it felt to be Joe Louis.

There was nothing informal or cozy about Clay's late-morning press conference on February 26. Less than twelve hours before, just after defeating Liston, Cassius had enough energy left to take on the press, excoriating them repeatedly "in a rude arrogant speech" for backing the wrong fighter. In several mean, bitter tirades, he'd told the writers that they should hang their heads in shame, repent for their literary transgressions, and beg him for forgiveness. "You hypocrites," he had shouted. "What are you going to say now?"[15]

Clay's words prompted reporter Jack Kofoed to respond, "He probably never will become a great fighter because a man with his ridiculous egoism isn't likely to learn. This man is neither a credit to the game he plays nor his race."[16]

His race—it was that, even more than his words, that lent a cutting edge to the conference. That morning, in an article about Malcolm X and the Black Muslims, Mike Handler had reported in the *New York Times* that Clay was "a Muslim and a close friend of Malcolm." Printed in the journalistically conservative *Times*, a paper that prohibited its reporters from editorializing in their articles, the statement carried added weight. Although it was widely known that Cassius was sympathetic with the Nation of Islam, he had not yet admitted publicly that he had formally joined the organization.[17]

He arrived at the Veterans Room at the convention center punctually at eleven a.m., looking and acting as if he were applying for admission to Princeton University. Dressed in a tweed jacket with leather elbow patches and a white button-down Oxford shirt, he answered

questions in a singularly non–Cassius Clay manner. Instead of display-
ing his usual 150-watt eyes and P. T. Barnum mouth, he began talking
in a quiet voice, his eyes focused on his feet, speaking barely above the
sound a soft wind makes rustling through the leaves of a tree.

"Speak louder, Cassius. We can't hear you," several reporters called
out. "In the past no one had to give that sort of urging," Arthur Daley
wrote in his column. Clay's personality pivot shocked him. This was the
day for the fighter to crow and preen, to tell the world once again that
he was the greatest. Instead, Clay wore "a discernible cloak of humility,"
eschewing the sound and fury of the day before and now speaking with
a "quiet modesty."[18]

"I'm through talking," he began. "All I have to be is a nice, clean
gentleman. I've proved my point. Now I'm going to set an example for
all the nice boys and girls. I'm through talking." It was as if the Lou-
isville Lip had died, or had never existed at all. It had just been a role
Clay played, a part he created and mastered, but it was not who he was.
He did it to breathe life into his sport and to promote his career. "My
mouth overshadowed my ability," he admitted.[19]

He confessed that he did not even enjoy boxing. "I only fight to
make a living, and when I have enough money I won't fight anymore. I
don't like to fight. I don't like to get hurt. I don't like to hurt anybody."
All he wanted was to be the champion for the people, especially the dis-
possessed—"the poor folk and the drunks and the bums." "I just want
to make people happy." The reporters had heard variations of Clay's
statements before: the desire to do good, make a difference, get out of
the brutal sport before it robbed him of his senses. They were promises
other fighters had made and failed to keep.

For a while, Cassius discussed the odd twists and turns of the match.
He admitted he had wanted to quit before the fifth round and actually
felt sorry for Liston. "You people put too much load on him. You built
him up too big and now he has such a long way to fall." As he talked,
the older writers nodded their heads and smiled in agreement. "If he
sticks to this pose, he . . . can win a vast amount of popularity," Daley
wrote.[20]

Soon most of the sportswriters had what they needed and departed
the room to attend Liston's press conference or to file their stories. The
bombast and poetry was all an act, they would write, and the real Cassius

Clay was a clean-living, thoughtful young man whose only harm was playing a role too well.

When the room was less than half full, a younger reporter asked an essentially forbidden question. "Are you a card-carrying member of the Black Muslims?" For a moment Clay looked shocked, then angry. The unwritten code of the sports world ruled some questions out of bounds. Unless the athlete raised the subject, reporters did not ask questions about politics, religion, drinking, or marital infidelities. Now someone was asking Clay if he belonged to what most white Americans and some black Americans believed was an extreme religious cult.

Immediately Clay's countenance shifted from quietly respectful to pugnaciously defiant. "Card-carrying, what does that mean?" he challenged. It sounded like he was being accused of belonging to the Communist Party.

Then, without directly answering the question, he defended the Nation of Islam and addressed the expectations of white Americans. "I believe in Allah and in peace. I don't try to move into white neighborhoods. I don't want to marry a white woman. I was baptized when I was twelve, but I didn't know what I was doing. I'm not a Christian any more." As for the Nation: "I go to a Black Muslim meeting and what do I see? I see that there's no smoking and no drinking and their women wear dresses down to the floor. And then I come out on the street and you tell me I shouldn't go there. Well, there must be something in there if you don't want me to go there."[21]

Robert Lipsyte's *New York Times* report captured the moment when the worlds of sport and politics collided. "There was a trace of antagonism when [Clay] refused to play the mild and socially uninvolved sports-hero stereotype, and began to use the news conference as a platform for socio-political theory."

That was exactly what Cassius and Malcolm had discussed—using the title as a venue to address political issues, not as an accomplishment to curry favor with white America. Floyd Patterson made liberal Americans optimistic about the future when he spoke quietly of the need for peace, cooperation, and integration. He played by the existing rules of the sports world, presenting himself as an acceptable role model for black and white youths. Clay refused to play that part in the heavyweight morality play. "In the jungle, lions are with lions and tigers are

with tigers, and redbirds stay with redbirds and bluebirds with blue-birds," he said. "That's human nature too, to be with your own kind. I don't want to go where I'm not wanted."

Cobbled from the teaching of Elijah Muhammad and rhetoric of Malcolm X, Cassius had made variations of this speech before, but never as the heavyweight champion, a position of some authority. Tak-ing advantage of the moment, he spoke his mind freely and boldly. He defended Malcolm: "If he's so bad why don't they put him in jail?" He addressed his support for Malcolm's teachings: "I catch so much hell, why? Why me when I don't try to bust into schools or march around or throw bricks?"

Clay's rambling defense of the Nation of Islam and Malcolm X was an example of his main point, one that Lipsyte used in his lede the next day. Glancing at the group of mostly white reporters—some angry, oth-ers shocked, a few supportive—Clay asserted, "I don't have to be what you want me to be. I'm free to be who I want."

It was a revolutionary statement, announcing his emancipation from the prescribed role for "Negro" athletes. In a shockingly radical declaration that amounted to a manifesto, he said that he was neither a "Negro", a Christian, nor an advocate of racial integration. He was *black*, a Muslim, and a separatist.[22]

SHORTLY AFTER THE press conference ended, Rudy Clay and Sam Saxon arrived together at the Chicago Coliseum for the Saviours' Day Convention. About two thirty, the celebration began with Louis X, Malcolm's replacement as master of ceremonies, introducing a proces-sion of speakers honoring Elijah Muhammad. Rudy was not an impres-sive orator nor was he considered an important figure in the Nation, but on this day—the day after his brother became heavyweight cham-pion of the world—he found himself center stage, standing at the po-dium just a few feet away from Elijah. "Cassius sends the greetings of As-Salaam Alaikum to all his Brothers and Sisters at Saviours' Day," Rudy announced. "He said he'd like to thank each and every one for the prayers they have said for his success in winning the heavyweight title."[23]

Rudy's speech was part of Elijah Muhammad's carefully orchestrated plan. Placing Clay's brother on the dais, surrounded by the Nation's of-ficials, conveyed a clear message: Malcolm believed that he and Cassius

shared a brotherhood, but Elijah intended to make Cassius and Rudy feel like they were part of the royal family. Muhammad reminded the five thousand followers in attendance, "I have been given the keys to your salvation and I can send you to either [heaven or hell]." When he announced that Cassius belonged to the Nation of Islam, the crowd roared with cheers and applause. Elijah beamed with pride. "I'm so glad that Cassius Clay admits he is a Muslim."[24]

Before the fight, Muhammad had made no public announcement supporting Cassius. He had believed what most boxing experts believed: Liston would not only defeat Clay, he would pummel him. No one from *Muhammad Speaks* was sent to Miami to cover the fight. The last thing Elijah wanted was for the Nation to be disgraced by a follower laid out on his back. When Malcolm first asked Muhammad for permission to attend the fight in Miami, the Messenger answered, "Yes, [but] if you do go, it will be as a private person. You will not in any way be representing us, because it's impossible for Cassius Clay to win."[25]

The day after Clay won, Muhammad confessed something that no one had heard from him before. The deaf, dumb, and blind "wanted [Cassius] to get his face torn up, but Allah and myself said, 'No!'" Then he delivered a message meant for Malcolm: "Clay had confidence in Allah and in me as his *only* messenger." His faith in Allah and his inspiration from Muhammad—not Malcolm—"assured his victory and left him unscarred."[26]

AROUND EIGHT O'CLOCK the next morning, Malcolm met Cassius for breakfast at the Hampton House, where they read Muhammad's announcement in the papers. Cassius had become a pawn in a power struggle between Malcolm and Elijah, and the Supreme Minister had just made a bold move. Now it was Malcolm's turn. He realized that he had to do something to lure Cassius; he had to offer him something that Muhammad could not.[27]

Time, Malcolm realized, was running out. Elijah would not wait much longer before he made another move. At that moment, Robert Lipsyte observed, Malcolm "understood that he had not really, totally" reached Clay. When he finished reading Muhammad's statement, he folded the paper and tossed it onto the counter, knowing that he had to keep one eye on Cassius and the other on Elijah.[28]

Seeing Cassius talk with Malcolm made reporters ask the new champion if Muhammad's statement about his membership in the Nation was accurate. "That is true, and I am proud of it," he answered. "But what's all the commotion about?" The commotion was all about the country's fears—fears of a religion most Americans knew little about; fears that the Muslims were a black menace lurking in the shadows; fears that Elijah Muhammad intended to lead a violent uprising; and fears that Cassius Clay was the bogeyman in the closet.[29]

Sportswriters wanted to know why he had joined the Black Muslims. "You call it Black Muslims, I don't," he asserted. "This is a name that has been given to us by the press. Yet people brand us a hate group. They say we want to take over the country. They say we're Communists." None of it was true. The Muslims, he said, didn't carry knives or guns. They were peaceful people who avoided confrontation. He joined the Nation because the Muslims offered a sanctuary, a utopia free from racial violence. "I want peace and I do not find peace in an integrated world," he explained. "I don't want to be blown up. I don't want to be washed down sewers. I just want to be with my own kind."[30]

A childhood friend later explained to Jack Olsen that when Cassius talked "about race—when he says, 'I don't want to be bombed. I don't want to be set on fire. I don't want to be lynched or have no dogs chase me'—he's expressing a general fright more than a real racial attitude." Cassius "finds it safer to be with Negroes, his own kind. It allays his fear of all those things his father used to tell him the whites'd do to him. He keeps this tight little Negro group around him, and he's scared to death to venture away from it."[31]

Clay maintained that it was only "natural" for blacks to live among blacks and for whites to live among whites. Sounding like Malcolm's assistant minister, he said, "We believe that forced and token integration is but a temporary and not an everlasting solution to the Negro problem. It is merely a pacifier. We don't think one people should force its culture upon another." Malcolm grinned as he listened to his pupil deliver one of his favorite lines: "A rooster crows only when it sees the light. Put him in the dark and he'll never crow. I have seen the light and I'm crowing."[32]

As he listened to Clay's answers, he heard his voice grow stronger, bolder, and more defiant. There was no other athlete in America who

so audaciously challenged the politics of the sports world. "Clay is the finest Negro athlete I have ever known," Malcolm asserted, "the man who will mean more to his people than any athlete before him. He is more than Jackie Robinson was, because Robinson is the white man's hero. But Cassius is the black man's hero. Do you know why? Because the white press wanted him to lose. They wanted him to lose because he is a Muslim. You notice nobody cares about the religion of other athletes. But their prejudice against Clay blinded them to his ability."[33]

White men were not the only ones blinded by Cassius. In their private moments together, between the minister's lectures and lessons, during their conversations and laughter, Malcolm came to believe in their friendship, their brotherhood, their bond. He rarely trusted any man, and few ever visited his home for family dinners the way that Cassius did. Malcolm fell for Clay's boyish wonder, his innocence and charm. Never did he imagine that Clay would hurt him. He trusted his own eyes, seeing only what he wanted to see: a magnetic young black man full of conviction and sincerity.

But Malcolm failed to apply the key lesson from his relationship with Elijah Muhammad: things were not always what they seemed. Later that day, Malcolm and Cassius made plans to see each other again soon. They shook hands, Malcolm congratulated him once more, and then he departed for the airport.

As he waited for his flight to New York, Malcolm probably thought about Clay and how their friendship had evolved. He'd never felt closer to him than he had during the days between his suspension and Clay's title celebration. They had known each other for only a little more than a year and a half, but in the past month their relationship had matured swiftly, as swiftly, almost, as it would crumble.

After Malcolm left, Rudy and Sam Saxon returned from Chicago. They arrived with a message for Cassius. During the Saviours' Day Convention, Saxon told Captain Joseph all about Malcolm's maneuvering in Miami. Joseph shook his head in disgust, convinced that the suspended minister was trying to manipulate Clay. Elijah, he told Saxon, had already determined that Malcolm would never return to the Nation. Malcolm was an outcast, a marked man with one foot in the grave. Send word to Cassius, Joseph instructed: he better not get too close to Malcolm.[34]

Chapter Thirteen

THE SHAKEUP

Boxing is sport, not politics. But Cassius Clay, without any political experience, would immerse sport in politics.

—A. S. "DOC" YOUNG, *LOS ANGELES SENTINEL*

Cassius Clay arrived in New York on a mission. "I'm gonna shake up this town," he announced.

On March 1, around three p.m., after riding more than 1,200 miles in his bus Big Red, he and his six-man entourage checked into the Hotel Theresa. Clay stepped off the bus in no mood to celebrate. Crossing the Mason-Dixon line convinced him, once again, that he would rather live in New York than Louisville or Miami. "I'm heavyweight champion of the world, yet, for a day and a half I had to eat bologna out of a bag . . . simply because I'm black," he complained. At every southern stop white men could not have cared less that he was the heavyweight champion. No black man, they reminded him, was welcome in a white restaurant. And yet, he could not understand why his "own people," he said, "so-called Negroes," still asked him, "'Why are you a Muslim?'"[1]

Clay felt more at home on the streets of Harlem, where black fans gave him a hero's welcome. "I could be living all exclusive, downtown, in some skyscraper," he said, but he preferred being around his own people at the Theresa. His face broke into a wide smile when a crowd of black kids rushed toward him, shouting his name. For more than an hour, he signed autographs in the lobby. At a hotel with mostly black clientele, he figured that he would not find any trouble, except for the

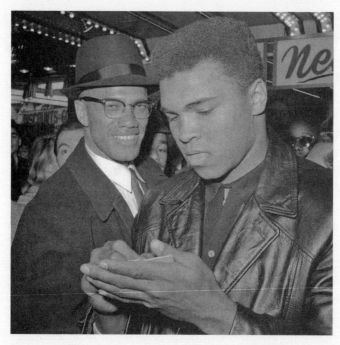

In Harlem, Malcolm's home turf, the minister smiled like he was in the catbird seat. During the first week of March 1964, Malcolm clung to the new heavyweight champion as if his life depended on him. His designs for Cassius X seemed within his grasp, but the boxer had plans for slipping away. Associated Press

women who showed up at his suite at all hours of the night, posing as Muslims.[2]

At the corner of Seventh Avenue and 125th Street, the Hotel Theresa sat at the nexus of black culture. A white terracotta building situated near Harlem's most popular nightclubs and the Apollo Theater, the Theresa was known for catering to black celebrities. Writers, actors, bandleaders, and athletes found everything that they needed inside the hotel: multiroom suites, business offices, a barbershop, beauty parlor, bar, and restaurant. Reporters looking for a scoop came to the Theresa knowing that something newsworthy was always happening. All they had to do was tip a doorman and they were bound to learn something that they could write about. Every night, it seemed, somebody

important—a diplomat or a national leader—stayed at the Theresa. Castro, Lumumba, Nasser, Nkrumah, and Khrushchev, a who's who of American critics, had all visited the "Waldorf of Harlem."[3]

Outside the thirteen-story hotel, soapbox speakers railed against the white man while paperboys sold copies of the *Amsterdam News*. Across the street, radicals held court at Lewis Michaux's African National Memorial Bookstore. Surrounded by stacks of books, pamphlets, and magazines, Michaux, a slight septuagenarian known among Nationalists as "the Professor," educated visitors about history and politics, telling old stories about his days in the United Negro Improvement Association. Malcolm became one of his most prized pupils, listening intently as the former window washer preached about Pan-Africanism and American hypocrisy. One time, as he often did, Malcolm pulled out a pocket-size notebook and a red pen, jotting down something Michaux had said about "America's chickens coming home to roost."[4]

After his banishment from Mosque No. 7, Malcolm moved into an office at the Theresa, even though the most famous "Negro" hotel in the country was no longer the popular destination it once was. In fact, it was never really the glamorous getaway writers made it out to be. "With its dimly lit hallways, drab colorless bedrooms, dingy ancient furnishing, and limited room service, the Theresa," *Ebony* magazine noted in 1946, "is anything but a first-rate hotel." In the succeeding years, the hotel's owners neglected necessary repairs, and the building began deteriorating along with the neighborhood around it. By the time Malcolm settled into Suite 128, the hotel's white brick was smeared with soot, its luster long gone.[5]

Malcolm's mezzanine office had served at one time or another as a brokerage firm and a cosmetics company, and traces of both were still present. When visitors reached his office door they could still read an old hand-painted sign: EVE NELSON COSMETICS. Inside the large conference room, sparsely furnished with two cluttered desks and a few folding chairs, Malcolm designed his future plans, pinning news clippings to a bulletin board and writing ideas on a wall-sized chalkboard. It was an unimpressive workspace, but Malcolm recognized that its proximity to his former mosque—the home that he had known for the last decade—made it an ideal place to set up his new headquarters.[6]

When Cassius checked into the hotel, he visited with Malcolm for "a secret conference," only they did not meet in his mentor's office. Instead, Malcolm came to him, knocking on Clay's suite door. Even before Cassius became champion, from the moment Malcolm set foot in Miami, their relationship fundamentally changed. Cassius, the title contender, altered Malcolm's thinking. In a moment of weakness, he exploited his friendship with Clay, manipulating him and withholding the truth about his future in the Nation. In a desperate attempt to prove his value to Elijah, he offered to deliver Clay to Chicago after the title fight, treating Cassius like some prize that could be bartered or traded. But Elijah did not have to buy Clay's loyalty. He already owned it.[7]

Reporters assumed that Clay was Malcolm's most devoted follower. One New York writer claimed that "an insider" told him that Clay was "solidly in Malcolm's corner and would" prove influential in helping "his friend to establish a cult of his own." Other writers speculated that if Cassius teamed with Malcolm, then Elijah would lose many of his followers to their rival Muslim movement.[8]

By all appearances, Cassius and Malcolm had never been tighter. After Cassius arrived, later that afternoon, they toured Times Square, parading the streets and shaking hands with strangers as if they were running for office on the same ticket. When a reporter from the *Amsterdam News* spoke to Malcolm, he gave no indication of trying to persuade Clay to leave the Nation. He was still waiting for just the right moment to tell him the truth about Elijah. Cassius, he told the writer, "dances like Sugar Ray, punches like Joe Louis, and *thinks* like Elijah Muhammad." In time, Malcolm would wish that Cassius thought more like him.[9]

LATER THAT EVENING, after watching a film of Clay's championship match at a theater, Cassius and Malcolm were surrounded by a crowd of nearly five hundred on Broadway at Times Square. While Clay signed more autographs, photographers snapped pictures of Malcolm standing beside him with a satisfied smile on his face. Seeing them together, reporters concluded, no one could doubt that they were planning a bold political initiative. Clay felt he had jumped beyond the world of sports. "I'm shaking up Times Square now," he declared. "In a few days, I'll

shake up the United Nations. I'm going to meet all the delegates." After speaking with writers and fans for about twenty-five minutes, Clay and Malcolm squeezed through the crowd, making their way toward a limousine, and disappeared.[10]

The next day, March 2, Malcolm arranged for them to visit the offices of the *Amsterdam News*, where Clay said that he would no longer acknowledge the name of "a Kentucky slave master." Now, he said, "I will be known as Cassius X." When a reporter at the *News* asked him about Elijah and Malcolm, he feigned ignorance of any rift between them. "Elijah Muhammad is the sweetest man in the world," he said. "Malcolm X? I fell in love with him after watching him on television with those educators—leaving them with their mouths wide open."[11]

Malcolm was not the only friend Cassius visited in New York. The following evening, he met Sam Cooke at a Columbia recording studio on Seventh Avenue, where they cut a snappy rendition of "Hey, Hey, the Gang's All Here." Since the previous summer, when he'd covered Ben King's hit song "Stand By Me," Cassius had become more comfortable in the studio, though he still sounded a bit tentative when he sang. On his album, *The Greatest*, he did not really sing—he mostly recited poems—but his unbridled confidence and Sam's encouragement convinced him that he could become a singer. Realizing Cassius's range was limited, Sam arranged for him to perform a simple, fun tune that accentuated his soulfulness.[12]

Later Sam and Cassius appeared on BBC's *Grandstand*. Host Harry Carpenter had met Clay in England before the Cooper fight and now detected that Cassius was "a changed man." The champ admitted that he had changed, and that he no longer needed "to talk like I used to." Yet he struggled with his identity. He was unsure how he would express his new freedom now that he was champion and the world knew that he was a Muslim. Only a few months earlier, he'd told the Louisville Sponsoring Group that he no longer wanted to be a showman. He was not interested in being a clown on television. He'd said that he wanted people to take him more seriously. But now his representatives at the William Morris Agency were in the middle of negotiating "a deal involving millions of dollars" where he would perform on television, on tour, and on more records. It was an enticing offer that made him reconsider his position. Ultimately, the negotiations broke down when booking

agents and record executives learned more about his relationship with the Black Muslims. "Malcolm X," one New York columnist learned, "has cost him a fortune in endorsements, TV shots, and disc sales."[13]

If he was not careful, Elijah warned, Malcolm might cost him much more. Captain Joseph called Elijah on March 4 and told him that Malcolm had informed a local radio station that his suspension was over and that he had been reinstated with his full responsibilities. Stunned, Elijah replied, "Well, I'll stop him." Muhammad then mailed Malcolm a letter informing him that his suspension remained indefinite. Furthermore, Elijah told Captain Joseph, Cassius should not visit the UN with Malcolm during his suspension. In the meantime, Muhammad continued to calculate his next move.[14]

The next afternoon, March 5, around one p.m., Cassius, Rudy, Archie, and Malcolm arrived at the United Nations, where they met with delegates from Africa and Asia. As the group entered the delegates' lounge, African dignitaries greeted Cassius and Malcolm with invitations to visit their countries. "We're proud of you. Come whenever you can," a Liberian ambassador said. "Thank you, sir," Cassius replied. "I have longed to go back home to Liberia." Cassius floated in a room of important men, all paying homage to him. Esteemed political figures from around the world knew his name; they knew that he was champion—the first Muslim champion of the world—and they treated him with respect. He recognized that he was becoming a global figure, "champion of the *whole* world," he emphasized. "The people are really shook up and they look at me as if I was a messenger or prophet or something."[15]

During their conversations with African leaders, Clay deferred to Malcolm. He was uncomfortable speaking, and uneducated, about the issues concerning African nations. Watching Malcolm interact with ambassadors, Cassius recognized that Malcolm's relationships with African leaders could help elevate his own standing in the world. It was "obvious," journalist Murray Robinson concluded, that Malcolm had "set out to make the heavyweight champion an international political figure."[16]

Reporters wondered if Malcolm had scripted the entire week in an effort to strengthen his bond with the champ. Malcolm's critics suggested that he was just using Clay. The champ, a writer from *Sport*

maintained, had become nothing more than a "tool in Malcolm X's feud with the Muslims."[17]

After Malcolm and Cassius made plans to travel the world together, writers speculated that Clay's visa might be withheld given his uncertain military status. When the *Louisville Courier-Journal* published a story that Cassius had failed a military intelligence test, reporters pressed him about his case. He did not know if he passed the Selective Service exam he took on January 24 in Miami, but he insisted that it was difficult. "I finished Louisville Central High School," he said, "but I wasn't very bright. I was in the Golden Gloves and didn't have time for studies."[18]

If he passed the test and was drafted, writers asked, would he oppose military service on religious grounds? Did the NOI oppose military enlistment? Would he declare himself a conscientious objector? Cassius was unaware of the Nation's opposition to the army and Elijah Muhammad's past imprisonment for draft evasion. In fact, he had no idea what it meant to be a conscientious objector. "I just want to do what's right," he said. "I don't want to go to jail, and I don't want to get into trouble."[19]

On the morning of March 6, around seven a.m., Malcolm picked up Rudy and Cassius at the Theresa in his dark blue Oldsmobile 98. During their drive back to the UN, Malcolm explained the crafty ways black men avoided military service, recounting his own experience evading the draft during World War II. In June 1943, when he was scheduled for induction, Malcolm made sure that army officials thought that he was mentally unstable. He showed up "costumed like an actor," wearing a zoot suit, his hair frazzled "into a reddish bush of conk." At the reception desk, he ran his mouth, talking nothing but jive, addressing a white officer as "daddy-o." Finally, a man in a white coat pulled him out of the induction line and sent him to see a military psychiatrist. He appeared incredibly paranoid, rambling and whipping his head around as if somebody was spying on him. Suddenly, he bolted from his seat and peered beneath the door. Then he whispered into the psychiatrist's ear, "I want to get down South. Organize them nigger soldiers, you dig? Steal us some guns, and kill us some crackers!" A few months later, Malcolm's performance earned him a 4-F classification, mentally disqualified for duty.[20]

When they arrived at the UN, Malcolm and the Clay brothers had brunch with Simeon O. Adebo, an ambassador from Nigeria. Adebo thanked Cassius for befriending Nigerian boxer Dick Tiger and invited him to visit his country. Adebo also encouraged him to accept the responsibilities that came with being champion, a champion recognized by black people all over the world. "You are not now what you were before the fight," he said. As the champion of the world, Adebo advised, he possessed cultural power, the kind of power that could unify black people "in the name of world brotherhood."[21]

As Cassius walked out of the UN, a reporter from the *New York Times* spotted him and asked a few questions. When he said that his new name was "Cassius X Clay," the writer inquired if the "X" had replaced his middle name. "X is what the slave masters used to be called," Cassius answered, making an obvious error. Malcolm clearly had more teaching to do. He elbowed Cassius, suggesting that they should end the interview.[22]

Elijah seethed when he learned that Malcolm had escorted Cassius to the UN again. He knew that his former minister "was out to destroy" him, but he refused to let Malcolm "snatch Cassius Clay" away from him. Since he called Cassius on the eve of the Liston fight, the boxer had ignored his warnings against socializing with Malcolm. Perhaps Cassius did not fully understand what was at stake, or maybe Malcolm had persuaded him that everything was fine. After Cassius returned from the UN, Elijah called him at the Theresa and made clear that he could no longer associate with the exiled minister. Cassius understood, promising that he would "stop seeing Malcolm starting today."[23]

Torn between his friendship with Malcolm and his faith in Muhammad, Cassius wavered. He admired both men, but he was confused by Malcolm's behavior. What no one knew was that Malcolm had told him something that he just could not believe. For nearly two years, he'd taught Cassius that Muhammad was Allah's Messenger, the most powerful black man in America. Nearly every lesson began with, "The Honorable Elijah Muhammad teaches us . . . " Yet on or around the day of their second visit to the UN, Malcolm told Cassius and Rudy that Elijah was a false prophet who had lied and abused his power. He probably also revealed that Muhammad had impregnated numerous secretaries.

When Rudy heard Malcolm talk such blasphemy, he wrestled him to the floor until Cassius pulled them apart. Malcolm's allegations made Cassius question his friend's motives. It made him wonder "why Malcolm was staying so close [to him] all the time."[24]

Malcolm had a good reason to attach himself to Cassius. About a week earlier, when he returned from Miami, Malcolm had learned that Captain Joseph had contacted a soldier in the FOI. During a private conversation outside the Nation's Harlem luncheonette, Joseph gave Lukman X a deadly assignment: "Plant a bomb in [Malcolm's] '63 Oldsmobile that will take care of him." Suspicious of Joseph's instructions, Lukman wondered why he did not follow the chain of command and deliver the message to one of his lieutenants as he normally did. Joseph never gave direct orders to the Fruit. The assignment made Lukman uneasy. He had long admired Malcolm for protesting police brutality. Skeptical of Joseph, he shared the assassination plot with Malcolm, forcing him to finally accept that his life with the Nation was over. "I knew they didn't intend to reinstate me as a Muslim," he said later. "You don't point a shotgun at somebody who's suspended."[25]

HOURS AFTER HE left Cassius and Rudy at the Theresa, Malcolm turned up the volume on his car radio when he heard the voice of Elijah on WWRL. Over a nationwide broadcast, Muhammad announced that the name Cassius Clay "has no divine meaning. I hope he will accept being called by a better name. Muhammad Ali is what I will give to him as long as he believes in Allah and follows me."[26]

Malcolm erupted behind the wheel, shouting to one of his aides, "That's political! That's a political move! He did it to prevent him from coming with me." In the past, the boxer had professed great admiration for his name. It was hard for him to imagine being anyone other than Cassius Clay. Knowing that there were lifelong members in the Nation who never received their "original" names from Elijah made him doubt that he had earned such an honor. But the Messenger reminded him that his "original" name meant "one who is worthy of praise," and no one was more deserving of the distinction than him.[27]

Cassius instinctively knew that the internecine fighting between Elijah and Malcolm had escalated to a critical, violent stage. He had heard stories about Muslims who crossed Muhammad and paid severely for

it. Malcolm himself had once told him, "Nobody leaves the Muslims without trouble." Now he had a choice to make. If he accepted the name Elijah gave him, would it end the brotherhood with Malcolm? If he rejected Elijah's overture, would it cost him his life? Politics, he was discovering, was more dangerous than fighting Sonny Liston.[28]

Ultimately, he submitted to Elijah. When he denounced his "slave name" and accepted the name Muhammad Ali, he symbolically broke with a heritage tied to bondage. It signified an awakening, a reclamation of freedom from the white world. But it also cut his ties with Malcolm. Instinctively more than intellectually, he understood the choice he had to make. And as he had so often before, he chose the less dangerous path.

When he was Cassius Clay, he had said, "I don't have to be what you want me to be. I'm free to be what I want to be." Yet that was never really true. There were limits to his new freedom. If he had remained friends with Malcolm, he would have fallen out of favor with Elijah and would have been forever known as Cassius Clay. But when he chose Elijah over Malcolm, Elijah determined who he wanted him to be, and that was Muhammad Ali, a devout Muslim and his loyal subject.

Once Cassius Clay became Muhammad Ali, Elijah won his political chess match with Malcolm. When Malcolm heard Elijah's radio address, Clay had not yet publicly announced that he had accepted the Muslim name, but it did not matter to Malcolm. When Malcolm lost the contest for Clay's loyalty, he had no more moves, no more pawns to sacrifice. At that moment Malcolm was expendable. At that moment his life was in jeopardy.

MALCOLM WAS SINKING fast, like a man drowning in quicksand. Hearing Elijah's announcement over the radio elevated his heartbeat. In a panic, he telephoned the boxer's suite. A voice on the other end of the line told him that Clay was not taking his calls. Elijah had already assigned members of the Fruit to guard his most prized possession. The Muslims around the boxer spoke with one voice: Malcolm was a liar and a traitor. Dejected, Malcolm hung up the phone without ever speaking to his friend.[29]

Malcolm's mistake was that he believed Cassius would see the world through his eyes. If he spent enough time with Cassius, he thought, he could prove that he had his best interests in mind, and perhaps their

brotherhood would become stronger than Clay's allegiance to Elijah. He had hoped that he could mold Clay's combative boxing instincts into fighting for black freedom outside the ring.

But unlike Malcolm, at his core, Cassius was never comfortable with the politics of confrontation. He had said again and again that he was afraid of what would happen if he joined a demonstration or a sit-in. He felt far more secure within the Nation, where he was constantly praised for simply being who he was: a boxer.

Malcolm never wielded the same power over him that Elijah Muhammad did. How could he? Clay's vision of Elijah Muhammad was a product of Malcolm's creation—part man, part prophet, all-powerful, and all-knowing. Cassius respected authority, and there was no higher authority, Malcolm said, than the Messenger. Although he admired Malcolm, he viewed him only as Muhammad's representative. When Malcolm belatedly challenged Muhammad's sovereignty, he became a castaway in a lifeboat, drifting in the wrong direction. Elijah, on the other hand, was the emperor of an entire kingdom, and now Cassius had become his shining new prince.

Elijah also offered him something that Malcolm could not: the love of a father. "The Nation," Jerry Izenberg observed, "became [Clay's] family, even to the extent that he was able to bring his brother into it. And Elijah Muhammad became his father."[30]

Yet he seldom let anyone get too close. Few ever really knew, as Malcolm thought he did, the man who became Muhammad Ali. Over the course of his career, people moved in and out of his life as if they were walking through a revolving door. Friends, promoters, hustlers, entrepreneurs, accountants, agents, lawyers, and women came and went. Cassius built a wall around himself in the form of an entourage, hiring men with fake titles whose only job was to take care of him. As long as they served his needs, as long as Cassius did not have to worry about anything or anyone, they remained in his life.[31]

He willingly allowed older men to take charge of his life. He did not need another brother or best friend. Rudy filled those roles. Searching for a father figure, he found security in the hands of patriarchs, whether a boxing trainer like Angelo Dundee, the members of the Louisville Sponsoring Group, or Elijah Muhammad. Ceding his life to Elijah, though, reveals a certain irony. "It was Clay's father who laid

the groundwork for the boy becoming a Muslim," Gordon Davidson explained. Clay Sr. frequently told his sons not to trust white men and warned them about the dangers of integration. He claimed that he had "Arabian" features and, like Elijah, prophesied about the Day of Judgment. "It's the end of times!" he often ranted. "We're in the last days! The last days!" Clay Sr., who was not a devout Christian, claimed that he read the Bible closely and that he knew that only Christians would survive the resurrection. "Those Muslims," he said, would incur God's wrath. Listening to him and Elijah, one could hardly tell them apart.[32]

THE CHAMP WAS in no mood to deal with his father. On Saturday, March 7, Cassius and Rudy arrived at Standiford Field, where nearly four hundred people, including the Louisville mayor, welcomed him home. At the airfield, he met with reporters, fans, and family, who all expected him to arrive with "a boyish grin, bold boasting, and comic attempts at poetry." The public expected an entertainer, but the champ was not interested. When his father tried to crown him with a golden papier-mâché coronet, scarlet cloak, and scepter, Cassius, looking visibly agitated, pulled away and said, "I don't want any of that stuff." His father didn't let up, pestering him again until he finally posed for photographers wearing the royal costume with a frown.[33]

Clay fidgeted throughout his press conference, appearing uncomfortable with the entire affair. Rubbing his eyes, he complained that he was tired and just wanted to go home. After answering a few questions, he signed autographs using the name that people had always recognized. Elijah Muhammad may have given him a new name, but he had not yet fully embraced it. "I plan to fight under the name Cassius Clay, unless," he said, "I'm ordered not to."[34]

During his stay in Louisville, he visited a local radio station, answering questions from listeners. A nervous boy called and addressed the champ, "Cassius?" The champ replied, "Cassius speaking." He did not correct the young fan for failing to use his Muslim name or denounce his "slave name." He did not deliver a harangue about integration or sermonize about the wisdom of Elijah Muhammad. His fans in Louisville did not want to hear him hollering about the Nation of Islam. They wanted to hear from their hometown hero. When a caller suggested that he should boast less and show more humility, Cassius surprised the man

with a clever lesson. "Well you keep this in your books," he said. "A wise man can act a fool, but a fool cannot act a wise man."[35]

Stunned, the caller did not know what he had just heard. "Uh-huh," he said.

Impressed, the show's host, Milton Metz, said, "That's pretty good. Where's that quotation from?"

"Oh, that's something I figured out," Clay replied.

"Sounds like Shakespeare."

Cassius laughed. "Might be. I heard it somewhere."[36]

He knew exactly where he had heard the maxim. He had been reciting it ever since he fought Henry Cooper in London. Now, about a week after he said that he had fallen in love with Malcolm watching him debate on television, he could not even utter his friend's name on the radio.

Chapter Fourteen

AN AMERICAN NIGHTMARE

The Negro has long since learned that his real heroes are always depicted as villains by the white world.
—*LIBERATOR*

———————

Amerca was unprepared for the name "Muhammad Ali." Seldom had a man's new name mattered so much to so many. He was not the first boxer to change his name. Countless other fighters changed their names too, many the sons of immigrants, who willingly adopted a new identity to make themselves more acceptable, more marketable, and more "American." But none, until Muhammad Ali, chose a name that was freighted with such racial and political meaning.

Fight fans, promoters, and sportswriters had no problems using the other aliases, yet for political reasons, many refused to say the name "Muhammad Ali." It sounded too foreign and too subversive. Skeptical of his sincerity, the *Chicago Tribune* printed an editorial assailing his religious beliefs: "It needs to be made quite clear that the 'Islam' which heavyweight champion Cassius Clay has adopted is a far, far cry from the religion practiced in the Arab world." Mocking Ali, columnist Jim Murray referred to him as "Abdul the Bull Bull Ameer." Sonny Liston dismissed the champ's new name too: "Ahmed Mali, Mamud Wally, who's that? I met you as Cassius Clay and I'll leave you as Cassius Clay." Recognizing the champ's Muslim name would have meant accepting Ali's freedom to define himself, a freedom that many whites—and even some blacks—were unwilling to acknowledge.[1]

Muhammad Ali worshipped Elijah Muhammad. So did his brother Rahman. Both men denounced their "slave name"—their father's surname—and embraced Elijah's paternal authority. As Muhammad Ali, the heavyweight champion became the most valuable commodity in the Nation of Islam. With Ali at Elijah's side, Malcolm X became expendable. Associated Press

For the crusty, cigar-chomping crowd of old-school reporters—Red Smith, Dan Parker, Dick Young, Arthur Daley, and Jimmy Cannon— Ali was a national disgrace, the scourge of American sports. Cannon could not hide his disgust for Ali. He wrote, "I pity Clay and abhor what he represents." The Black Muslims, he insisted, were "exploiting Clay" the same way that the "Communists used famous people" during the Great Depression. Now that Ali had become champion, boxing, Cannon feared, had reached its nadir. "The fight racket, since its rotten beginnings, has been the red light district of sports. But," he lamented, "this is the first time it has been turned into an instrument of mass hate."[2]

At a time when minorities held half of the major division boxing titles, it appeared that black and brown men dominated the entire sport. The days when boxing made "white men rich and black men cripples" were long gone. White writers and white fans lamented the loss of an

era. Whites, they said, never got a shot at the heavyweight title anymore. It seemed that the black man had taken over everything: the cities, the streets, the old neighborhoods, even sports. More blacks could be seen on television playing baseball, basketball, and football. And now the black man had taken over boxing too. "Now that the equal opportunity movement has brought such an improvement to the lot of the Negro," Dan Parker asked, "when are the white heavyweights going to start picketing the weighing-in scales at boxing commission offices for the same deal[?]"[3]

The moment Ali defeated Liston, sportswriters and politicians revived their campaign to abolish boxing. In the greatest uproar since the death of Benny Paret, moralists demanded an investigation into the sport, questioning the legitimacy of Ali's victory. "The odors of the Clay-Liston thing continue to assail the nostrils," Arthur Daley wrote. Weeks after the match, Daley and other writers were still stunned that Liston had lost. Ali had looked unimpressive during his training camp, Daley argued, but overnight "became transformed into a clever" fighter. And Liston, usually an indomitable force, was unrecognizable sitting on his stool by the end of the sixth round.[4]

Conspiracy theorists suspected that Ali had won the match for only one reason: the fight was fixed. They said that Ali had wanted to quit the fight, but his corner would not let him. They said that Liston wanted to continue, but his corner would not let him, either. That was why Liston, considered the toughest man in the game, complained that his injured shoulder prevented him from continuing. And of course, Sonny had ties to organized crime. But the most damning evidence, critics claimed, was that before the fight Ali had signed a contract with Liston's promotional agency for fifty thousand dollars, guaranteeing International Promotions the right to name the new champion's first opponent in a title defense. Ed Lassman, president of the World Boxing Association (WBA), insisted that the agreement violated their rules on return bouts, despite knowing all about the arrangement before the match. Since Liston was president of International Promotions, Lassman argued, he stood to benefit financially from a rematch with Ali, even though boxers often held a stake in promotional agencies.[5]

There was no real evidence of a betting conspiracy involving Liston or Ali. Bookmakers insisted that the "smart money" was bet on Liston,

and the gambling odds against Ali actually increased from 7–1 to 8–1 on the day of the match. If the fight was fixed for Ali to win, why did he beg Dundee to end the fight? If the fight was fixed for Liston to lose, why did he try to blind Ali? Every conspiracy theory about the fight crumbles under the weight of inconsistencies.

Despite the lack of any evidence against the champ, Lassman announced that the WBA would vacate Ali's title because his behavior as champion was "detrimental to the boxing world." Joining the Black Muslims, Lassman contended, made Ali "a very poor example for the youth of the world." The WBA's commissioner, Abe Greene, echoed his sentiment. "Clay should be given the chance to decide whether he wants to be a religious crusader or the heavyweight champion," he said.[6]

None of the most influential state athletic commissions supported the WBA's endorsement. And, after a few days of hearings in front of the Senate Subcommittee on Antitrust and Monopoly, there was still no evidence that Ali or Liston had done anything illegal. The subcommittee recommended passing a bill that would create a federal boxing czar who would oversee the sport, but the proposal never materialized. Facing strong opposition, Lassman ended his campaign against the champ. Still, Arthur Daley maintained that the WBA's abortive efforts were inconsequential. "Boxing," he wrote, "is beyond redemption. It should be abolished."[7]

For many critics, the future of the sport remained in doubt, but one thing was certain: Muhammad Ali was not the savior that Cassius Clay had been.

MUHAMMAD ALI HAD made a world of enemies. While white critics denounced his membership in the Nation of Islam, blacks debated his relationship with the Muslims. Some feared that he would exploit his position as champion to recruit young blacks into the sect. Proclaiming his belief in separatism, Ali had created "more apprehension" among middle-class, integrationist blacks "than Malcolm X." Black writers, entertainers, and activists compared his views to those espoused by the Ku Klux Klan, the White Citizens' Councils, and the Dixiecrats. "When Cassius Clay joined the Black Muslims and started calling himself Cassius X," Martin Luther King charged, "he became the champion of racial segregation—and that is what we are fighting."[8]

Joe Louis, considered the greatest heavyweight champion of all time, beloved by blacks and whites alike, declared that he would never cheer for the Muslim champ. "Clay will earn the public's hatred because of his connections with the Black Muslims," he told reporters. "The things they preach are just the opposite of what we believe." *What we believe.* Louis and many black Americans insisted that Ali no longer represented the race. He was an outsider, condemned for rejecting the ideals of the civil rights movement.[9]

Ali disappointed many blacks because he rejected the traditional responsibilities associated with being heavyweight champion. In a xenophobic outburst, Floyd Patterson condemned Ali as unfit to be a champion. He accused him of being ignorant of the Black Muslims' ideology and confused about their real goals. Ali "might just as well have joined the Ku Klux Klan," he charged.[10]

There was only one thing left for Patterson to do: save boxing from Muhammad Ali and the Nation of Islam. The good Catholic fighter challenged "Cassius X" to a holy war, announcing that he would fight him anytime, anywhere, even though the ninth-ranked heavyweight was in no position to proclaim himself a title contender. In his self-righteousness, Patterson made himself out to be more patriotic than Ali, a purer champion, and a better citizen. "I am an American," he declared, implying that Ali was not—not as long as he belonged to the Nation of Islam.[11]

Ali dismissed Patterson's challenge. If anyone was exploiting boxing, he retorted, it was Patterson: "The only reason he's decided to come out of his shell now is to try to make himself a big hero to the white man by saving the heavyweight title from being held by a Muslim." When Patterson attacked Ali's religion, the champion said that he might as well have been "attacking Cairo, Egypt, the Holy City of Mecca, Pakistan, Turkey, and 300,000" Muslim Americans. In defense of Islam, he began to see himself not just as an American but also as a global citizen, a guardian of all Muslims.[12]

The feud between Patterson and Ali demonstrated that the backlash against the Muslim champ was as much about Islamophobia as it was about race. During the Cold War, many Americans linked Islam to the Middle East and Africa, a region perceived as backward, brutal, and politically oppressive. The vitriol aimed at Ali, therefore, derived from

Americans who considered Islam a destructive alternative to Christianity, and from fears that the Middle East had succumbed to the influence of the Soviet Union.[13]

Americans' stereotypical views of the region as an endless sand trap, filled with genies, harems, sultans, sheiks, and camel-riding nomads, influenced their views of Ali. In a satirical column, Jim Murray portrayed him as "the Sheik of Araby," fighting against infidels. "I think Cassius sees himself as Lawrence of Arabia or the Red Shadow rather than a guy licking stamps for hate literature," he wrote. "Cassius has always had a lively imagination and it was only a question of time before he'd wrap a towel around his head and begin to play Saladin, the Saracen. I expect him to trade in his Cadillac for a camel any day now."[14]

Jackie Robinson did not use Ali's Muslim name, but he recognized his right to practice Islam. "Clay has just as much right to ally himself with the Muslim religion as anyone else has to be a Protestant or a Catholic," he wrote in his syndicated column. Robinson cautioned that there was no reason to think thousands of blacks would follow Ali because he had joined the Nation. Too many blacks had marched, fought, and bled for freedom to join a separatist movement, he argued.[15]

While most black Americans rejected the theology of the Nation, many identified with Ali's politics of self-determination. Young urban blacks viewed his resistance to white authority through the prism of their own struggle for empowerment and freedom. Jill Nelson, a writer who grew up in Harlem during the 1960s, recalled, "We weren't about to join the Nation, but we loved Ali for that supreme act of defiance. It was the defiance against having to be the good Negro, the good Christian waiting to be rewarded by the righteous white provider." Nelson and black youths across the country loved Ali for many reasons—his racial pride, his outspokenness, his independent attitude. But most of all, she said, they loved Ali because "he epitomized a lot of black people's emotions at the time, our anger, our sense of entitlement, the need to be better just to get to the median, the sense of standing up to the furies."[16]

Facing an onslaught of criticism, Ali stood his ground, refusing to retreat from his beliefs. When Americans challenged his religious freedom, he began to question America. He was tired of hearing that he should show more restraint and dignity. He could not understand why people hated him just for being a Muslim. "People are always telling me

what a good example I could be if I just wasn't a Muslim," he said. "I've heard it over and over, how come I couldn't be like Joe Louis and Sugar Ray. Well, they're gone now, and the black man's condition is just the same, ain't it? We're still catching hell."[17]

"It's going to be different now," Malcolm explained to *New York Times* writer Mike Handler. "I'm going to join the fight wherever Negroes ask for my help, and I suspect my activities will be on a greater and more intensive scale than in the past." The past—it's where Malcolm wanted to leave Elijah Muhammad and the Nation, but he could not break away from them, not as long as he lived. On Sunday, March 8, he drove to Handler's home and told him that he no longer represented Muhammad and the Nation. In the interest of peace, he advised all Blacks Muslims to continue following Elijah, even though a group of confidants from his old mosque had already joined him.[18]

The front page of the next day's edition of the *Times* included Handler's story, headlined, "Malcolm X Splits with Muhammad." He addressed his plans for the future: building a Black Nationalist political party, organizing a voting campaign, speaking at college campuses, and working with civil rights groups—all activities Elijah had discouraged.[19]

Around the same time, he started talking more about armed self-defense and purchased a semi-automatic rifle. If he wished to broker peace with Muhammad, he showed no restraint in blaming him for turning their dispute into a blood feud. When Handler asked why he was leaving Muhammad's side, he answered, "Envy blinds men and makes it impossible for them to think clearly. This is what happened."[20]

Malcolm, Elijah had declared, was a hypocrite, a word with a special meaning among the Black Muslims. In the Nation, a hypocrite was the "most hated by God." Elijah preached, "They are double-crossers; they come in claiming belief and then go out disbelieving." These wicked, "evil-tongued people" who deceived Allah and deviated from His Messenger would suffer Allah's wrath. A hypocrite like Malcolm was the enemy, and Allah would show him no mercy, Elijah warned.[21]

On the Sunday that Malcolm spoke to Handler, Elijah sent Louis X to preach at Mosque No. 7 in Harlem. In a subsequent phone conversation, Elijah praised Louis for his good work replacing the exiled minister, though merely mentioning Malcolm's name aroused Elijah's

anger. It was time to make an example of "that no good long-legged Malcolm," he exclaimed. Hypocrites like him could only be dealt with one way: "you . . . cut their heads off."[22]

Elijah also stayed in close contact with his son Herbert, whom he had selected to manage Ali. He told Herbert that he wanted to meet with Ali in Chicago to ensure that the boxer had severed ties with Malcolm. He also wanted to discuss Ali's upcoming trip abroad because the "young fellow" needed to learn how to behave when he met with statesmen. He worried that Ali had never been out of the country, which was untrue, revealing how little he actually knew about the boxer's career. Elijah instructed Herbert not to let Ali make any "plans with anyone until" they met. Finally, he advised, add "four more pages to [our] paper," so that the whole world could read about the famous Muslim champion.[23]

On Monday, March 9, Muhammad telephoned Captain Joseph and declared that Malcolm must give up everything that belonged to the Nation of Islam, including his home. Joseph sent word to Maceo X, the secretary of the New York mosque, to draft an eviction letter. That same day, Herbert's assistant called Malcolm to inform him that Elijah's son would now serve as Ali's manager and that Ali no longer planned to travel abroad with him.[24]

Malcolm fumed. *He* was the one who introduced Ali to African ambassadors. *He* was the one who had convinced Ali that he should embrace a larger role on the world stage and develop relationships with African leaders. *He* was the one who had strategically planned for Ali to visit Muslim countries in Africa and the Middle East, and now the Black Muslims had stolen his friend and his plan. But Malcolm was not ready to give up on Ali yet. Desperate to reach him, he telephoned Ali eight times that day, but he could not get through the men who surrounded the champ. In a phone interview, Ali told a reporter from the *Amsterdam News* that he still intended to tour Africa, but added, "I will not be traveling with Malcolm X."[25]

After Malcolm announced his official break from the Nation, more reporters called Ali to learn about his future. He said that he disagreed with Malcolm's sanguinary rhetoric. "I am against violence," the boxer said. "I am a fighter and I am religious," but "I am not going to do anything that is not right. I don't know much about what Malcolm X is doing, but I do know that Muhammad is the wisest."[26]

In front of newsmen at his Phoenix home, Muhammad wept, feigning disbelief over Malcolm's departure. "I am stunned," he professed. "I never dreamed this man would deviate from the Nation of Islam. Every one of the Muslims admired him." Muhammad's tears gave the impression that Malcolm had left the Nation under his own free will. Acting deserted and betrayed, Muhammad seemed to grieve the loss of a man whom he once considered his own flesh and blood, the same man that he had blamed for poisoning the Nation with lies about him.[27]

That same afternoon, March 10, Captain Joseph, Maceo X, and a squad from the Fruit showed up at Malcolm's East Elmhurst home on 97th Street in Queens. Joseph served Malcolm with eviction papers and demanded that he surrender some of the mosque's valuables. Malcolm handed over a few documents and securities from the Nation's treasury, but he refused to leave the house. Muhammad had once told him that the house was his, even though the deed showed that the home was the legal property of the Nation of Islam. The moment Captain Joseph showed up at his doorstep, Malcolm regretted ever taking a vow of poverty and determined that he would fight back.[28]

Malcolm knew that this was only the beginning. The war had just begun. "They've got to kill me," he told a reporter. "They can't afford to let me live."[29]

ON THURSDAY, MARCH 12, around ten a.m., a sleek black Chrysler pulled up to the curb in front of the Midtown Park Sheraton Hotel. Malcolm stepped out of the car wearing a pearl gray pinchecked suit and carrying a briefcase. A cadre of black men followed him inside, through the noisy lobby and up to the packed second-floor Tapestry Suite, where a crowd of reporters, photographers, and undercover FBI agents waited for him. Before he stepped to the podium, his aides distributed press releases announcing his split from the NOI and the creation of Muslim Mosque, Inc. (MMI), a politically oriented Nationalist group of Muslims and secularists.[30]

Malcolm looked fried after a week of sleepless nights. Before he began speaking, he managed to smile, nodding at some of the reporters he recognized. Then he offered a chilling prelude to a long, hot summer in Harlem. "Because 1964 threatens to be a very explosive year on the racial front"—in fact, it would be one of the most violent in American

history —"and because I myself intend to be very active in every phase of the Negro struggle for human rights, I have called this press conference this morning to clarify my own position in the struggle." In careful language he advised blacks to purchase guns, form rifle clubs, and defend themselves by any means necessary.[31]

Malcolm offered only a vague description about the objectives of MMI, as he was not entirely sure of his own direction. He had said that whites were welcome to support his organization, but they could not join. There could be no unity between blacks and whites until blacks had unified themselves. And although he still rejected the goals and tactics of civil rights leaders, he claimed that he wanted to cooperate with those leaders, whom he had once derided as Uncle Toms.[32]

The media focused most of its attention on Malcolm's self-defense rhetoric, characterizing his message in simple, violent terms. Malcolm had never sounded so dangerous, writers fretted. Elijah Muhammad assured a *New York Times* writer that Malcolm was not nearly as threatening as the press made him sound. His former minister had no following, no guns, and no divine authority. Malcolm's plan sounded "silly" to him. "Where are they going to get guns and arms?"[33]

In the wake of Malcolm's press conference, black Americans debated his future in the freedom struggle. Bayard Rustin suggested that most blacks would never consider creating a separate state or migrating back to Africa, but they accepted Malcolm's "analysis of the evils that are being practiced on the Negro people," and that could make him a potent leader. "In appearance, personality, and philosophical outlook," a *Sepia* writer opined, "Malcolm comes closer to being a revolutionary than any other American Negro leader." *Liberator*'s Carlos Russell agreed. He found Malcolm charismatic and persuasive, but the Nationalist minister provided more slogans than answers to the black man's problems. If Malcolm ever developed an effective program, "he would indeed become the most formidable leader black people have ever known."[34]

Freed from Elijah Muhammad's authority, many wondered if Malcolm had changed. Who was this independent Malcolm X? Was he a demagogue or revolutionary? Was he merely an orator or would he actually fight for freedom? Did he really hate white people or did he simply hate the injustices that he had witnessed?

Dick Schaap sought the answers when he visited with Malcolm at the Hotel Theresa. When the Muslim minister welcomed the Jewish reporter into his office, Schaap realized that Malcolm was nothing like the frightening agitator that he had read about. Malcolm was surprisingly friendly. "It is almost impossible, upon meeting him, not to like him," he wrote. In private, other white writers learned that Malcolm did not love the white man, but he did not necessarily hate him either. "There were two Malcolms, really," said Mike Handler, one of the few white journalists whose home Malcolm had visited. "There was the private Malcolm, a man of ineffable charm and courtesy, a born aristocrat. And there was the public Malcolm, Malcolm in combat, whose job was to frighten the white man out of his shoes."[35]

Schaap departed Malcolm's office with a new perspective, yet he remained frustrated. Malcolm had avoided most of his questions, repeating old lines and delivering verbose answers. He left wondering if Malcolm would ever lead when action was needed. "No one really knows the extent of his power because he has never put his power to any real test." But he could not dismiss Malcolm either. He was too eloquent and too intelligent to be ignored. Trying "to figure out Malcolm X," he concluded, was as difficult as cracking a secret code. "It is a game that almost every thinking person in Harlem is playing these days."[36]

ELIJAH'S PRECIOUS TREASURE finally arrived at his home. On Saturday, March 14, a day after Muhammad Ali took another army entrance exam in Louisville, the champ visited Elijah in Chicago. Before he drove to Elijah's mansion, a crowd of reporters met Ali at the airport, pestering him with questions about his relationship with Malcolm. "Muhammad taught Malcolm X everything he knows," he said. "So I couldn't go with the child, I go with the daddy."[37]

At the mansion, Ali and his brother embraced Elijah. Sitting on the living room couch with his arm around Elijah, Ali listened as the soft-spoken elder read from the Koran, lecturing about Allah. They discussed his victory over Liston, the backlash against his Muslim name, and his plans to travel abroad. Elijah told him that many Americans hated the idea of a Muslim champion because there was widespread "hatred of the Muslims and Islam in America." That is why boxing

officials wanted to vacate his title, and why so many people refused to use his Muslim name. Ali left that night convinced of Elijah's wisdom and power. "Can't nobody prove Elijah Muhammad wrong," he declared.[38]

During Ali's visit in Chicago, Elijah entrusted his third son to supervise Ali and manage his financial affairs. Herbert Muhammad spent most of his time in Chicago running various Muslim enterprises, chauffeuring his father, and editing *Muhammad Speaks*. A short, pudgy photographer with his own studio and limited formal education, Herbert knew very little about managing a boxer. When he was a boy, his father saw him punching a speed bag in the family garage and scolded him for wasting his time. "I don't want you around the ring, boxing for any little fat white man with a big cigar," he lectured. "Don't be around any sport world. Sport is the ruin of our people. Turns them into children who're used and then left broken. Stay out of it."[39]

By the time the heavyweight champion sat in his living room, though, Elijah had changed his mind about Herbert's involvement in boxing. He reminded his son that crooks ran the sport. Con men, he warned, would try to dupe Ali. "Make sure nobody robs him or takes advantage of him." Elijah told Ali that he could trust his son, and that Herbert would treat him like a brother. In time, Herbert would become Ali's financial adviser, mentor, and confidant. Most importantly, he served as Elijah's eyes and ears, following Ali everywhere.[40]

That weekend, when Ali first met Herbert at his studio, the fighter did not know much about him, except what Elijah had told him. Herbert had photographed many famous black men, including Kwame Nkrumah, Prince Faisal, Gamal Abdel Nasser, and other statesmen whom he promised Ali would meet when they visited the Middle East and Africa. But when Herbert began traveling with Ali, he refused interviews and photographs. He did not want to do anything that would raise questions about his personal life. The last time his name made headlines was in October 1962, when a white woman pressed charges against him for shattering her jaw in four places. Herbert's former mistress told police that he stalked her, broke into her apartment, and threatened to kill her if she ever left him. The Muslims adamantly denied the charges, claiming that the woman was not even white—she

was black—and that Herbert was being framed, all in an attempt to "smear and malign" the Nation of Islam.[41]

Although the story disappeared from the front page of the *Chicago Defender*, it caught the attention of the FBI. When special agents began investigating Herbert, an informant told them that he carried on extramarital affairs and was nearly "possessed" with taking nude photographs of women and making pornographic films. According to a "reliable" source, Herbert convinced women to pose for his camera in exchange for gifts of jewelry and mink coats. Of course, Ali did not know about any of this. He had only just met Herbert, after all, and Elijah had said that he could trust his son. Ali never questioned the Messenger. He simply did what he was told.[42]

MUHAMMAD ALI'S LIFE had become a daily news story, unfolding across the pages of America's newspapers. Since he took his first military entrance exam, writers had speculated that he would be drafted any day, ending America's nightmare of having a Muslim boxing champion. On March 20, the army announced that Ali had failed his second entrance exam, disqualifying him from serving in the armed forces. One report claimed that he scored 78 on an IQ test, placing him well below a passing grade. Embarrassed by his poor performance, Ali admitted that he struggled to comprehend the questions. "I said I was the greatest, not the smartest," he quipped.[43]

After returning to New York, he fielded questions from reporters at an impromptu press conference from the Hotel Theresa. Writers' repeated queries about his intellect angered him. When a reporter addressed him as Cassius, he snapped, "Don't call me Cassius Clay. My name is Muhammad Ali. It is a beautiful Arabic name." It was the first time that he insisted writers use his new name. When another reporter made the same mistake, he corrected him. "Don't call me Cassius Clay anymore. I am *Muhammad Ali*, the heavyweight champion of the whole world."[44]

Later that night, he attended a welterweight match between Luis Rodríguez and Holley Mims at Madison Square Garden. Expecting a champion's introduction, Ali was stunned when promoter Harry Markson refused to let the ring announcer use his Muslim name. Standing

near the aisle, about twenty rows away from the ring, Ali declared, "Cassius Clay is a slave name. My real name now—from now on—is Muhammad Ali. I'll be introduced as Muhammad Ali—or there'll be no introduction." Fans booed the champ until he bolted out of the arena.[45]

Many Americans were just as outraged that the army had rejected Ali as he was that they refused to use his Muslim name. Furious citizens, soldiers, and veterans grumbled that Ali was certainly smart enough to peel potatoes, scrub a ship deck, or polish boots. A real American, they complained, would certainly find a way to serve. In Philadelphia, a concerned Irish Catholic mother, whose son had been recently drafted, resented the special treatment Ali seemed to receive from the military. She could hardly believe that Ali failed the military's entrance requirements. In a letter to President Lyndon Johnson, she asked why the army did not draft the famous boxer. "Is it because he is a millionaire and pays lots of taxes? Is it because he is heavyweight champion of the world? Is it because he is colored and colored people are being handled with 'kid gloves' these days?"[46]

Those who knew Ali well were not really surprised that he had flunked the military exam. Petros Spanakos, a bantamweight teammate of Ali's during the 1960 Olympics, wrote to columnist Red Smith, explaining that he had no doubt that his old roommate could not pass the written exam. When they roomed together in Rome, Spanakos "spelled out, corrected, and finally wrote [Ali's] letters home." Louisville Sponsoring Group member William Faversham told a writer that he had also witnessed Ali struggle to read. While he could read a newspaper column in three or four minutes, it could take Ali more than twenty. Faversham recalled that in January 1963, shortly after Ali fought Charlie Powell, he suggested that Ali could schedule a match against Doug Jones in March. Uncertain if he had enough time to train, Ali asked, "How many months until March?"[47]

From every angle, Americans scrutinized Ali's intelligence. J. Edgar Hoover was so convinced that Ali had deliberately failed the test that he ordered special agents to obtain the champ's high school transcript, which only proved that Ali lacked a rigorous academic education. Critics emasculated him as simple-minded and childlike. Others reduced him to the big, dumb boxer, as ignorant as Amos Jones's friend Andy Brown, a bombastic and buffoonish black man.[48]

A few days after the army disqualified Ali, Robert Lipsyte ventured into Harlem to interview the champ, but first he dropped by Lewis Michaux's bookstore, where he interviewed Malcolm X. Accompanied by the reporter's friend, comedian and activist Dick Gregory, Lipsyte found Malcolm lounging in a back room, rapping with Michaux. Malcolm spoke "warmly" about Ali, "less like his guru than an older brother or uncle." Divulging no hard feelings, he had nothing but nice things to say about him. When the writer asked Malcolm if he had tried to persuade the champ to join MMI, Malcolm shook his head and explained that Ali would have to decide for himself how he would live his life. As Lipsyte turned toward the door, Malcolm praised his fight coverage as among the best. Lipsyte smiled and thanked him. Later, when he recounted the story to an editor at the *New York Times*, he received a flippant reply: "That's just great, we'll put it up on the [newspaper] trucks, 'Malcolm X Loves Lipsyte.'"[49]

After departing Michaux's bookstore, Lipsyte and Gregory crossed the street to the Hotel Theresa, where the champion was staying in a suite just a few floors above Malcolm's second-story office. In the most popular accounts, Ali immediately cut Malcolm out of his life and stopped seeing him after March 6, but that would be hard to believe since Ali was staying in the same building where Malcolm worked. The reality was that neither man had let go of the other. After Ali returned to Harlem in late March, a reporter from the *New York Post* interviewed Malcolm and noted that "a parade of visitors" entered his office, including Ali, who dropped by "for a swift low-voiced chat." Ali may have been "a follower of the Lost-Found Nation of Islam under Elijah Muhammad," the writer observed, "but schism has not damaged an old friendship with Malcolm X."[50]

While Elijah's lieutenants scorned his friend as a hypocrite, Ali had not yet rejected Malcolm's friendship, despite telling Elijah what he wanted to hear. Unquestionably, after Ali visited Elijah in Chicago and returned to Harlem, he and Malcolm saw each other. Most likely, they met on March 22, the same day that Malcolm held a rally at the Rockland Palace. Earlier, Malcolm had acknowledged to a television reporter that he had "a long meeting with" Ali, but he refused to discuss the details of their conversation. "We are brothers," he told the newswoman, "and we have much in common." What he did not tell her was

that they could no longer be seen together in public. Instead, Malcolm implied that he still advised Ali. However, a few hours after the WBA announced its intention to vacate Ali's title, Malcolm clearly had heard nothing about it. He no longer knew what Ali was really doing. When the reporter asked how he would counsel the champ about his career, Malcolm found himself speechless. All he could say about the matter was "no comment."[51]

Instead, Malcolm talked about Ali's potential as a cultural force, a global hero inspiring people around the world. Americans misunderstood the boxer, he explained. The champion was an ideal role model for black youths, living a clean life, avoiding alcohol and cigarettes. And, Malcolm reminded the reporter, Ali had never been involved in any legal trouble. "He's actually an all-American boy, or an all-African boy." The problem, he charged, was that the media distorted his image and attacked his religion, damaging America's reputation abroad. Malcolm had received stacks of letters from Africans who admired Ali and everything he represented. "Cassius is in a better position than anyone else to restore a sense of racial pride not only to our people in this country, but to people all over the world."

Malcolm's conversation with Ali made it difficult for the boxer to completely divorce his friend. While Ali hated the idea of disappointing Elijah Muhammad, he also wanted to avoid hurting Malcolm. In his private moments, he must have wondered if he had made the right decision. When a writer from *Jet* asked him if he would ever see Malcolm again, he answered, "Elijah Muhammad will determine my future associations." Then, in a wistful moment of sincerity, he disclosed his true sentiments. "Malcolm," he said, "is still a friend, however." It was not the kind of comment that would please the Messenger.[52]

IN THE WEEKS after he announced his independence from Elijah, Malcolm spoke at rallies, met with reporters, and began planning a trip to the Middle East and Africa. The excursion would serve two needs, one personal, the other political. When he broke from the Nation of Islam, his religious foundation cracked. As a "servant of Allah," he sought a renewed faith and a broader understanding of Islam. In a quest to fulfill his religious evolution, he prepared for the pilgrimage to Mecca, the holiest Muslim city in the world.[53]

The journey to the Middle East would also help him realize his vision for internationalizing the black freedom struggle. In Cleveland on April 3, he preached the "gospel of Black Nationalism," arguing that blacks needed to control their own communities, their own politics, and their own religion. At the Cory Methodist Church, Malcolm espoused a message fusing together electoral politics, self-defense, and Pan-Africanism, framing the civil rights movement as part of a global struggle against racial oppression. "We need to expand the civil rights struggle to a higher level—to the level of human rights," he suggested.[54]

Focusing on civil rights made blacks too dependent on the United States government, a government that had failed to protect their legal rights. Human rights differed from civil rights, he explained. Human rights were "your God-given rights," recognized by the United Nations. "And anytime anyone violates your human rights, you can take them to the world court," he promised. At the UN, "our brothers" from Africa, Asia, and Latin America would finally hear the charges against the US. "Uncle Sam's hands are dripping with blood, dripping with the blood of the black man in this country."[55]

If Uncle Sam would not defend black citizens, then they needed to defend themselves "by any means necessary." "If we don't do something soon, I think you'll have to agree that we're going to be forced either to use the ballot or the bullet," he argued. If Uncle Sam denied them the vote, they must rise up in arms. "It'll be liberty or death."

Malcolm spoke that night not as an American but as a black man. "No, I'm not an American," he declared. "I'm one of the 22 million black people who are the victims of Americanism. One of the 22 million black people who are the victims of democracy, nothing but disguised hypocrisy. So, I'm not standing here speaking to you as an American, or a patriot or a flag-saluter, or a flag-waver—no, not I. I'm speaking as a victim of the American system. And I see America through the eyes of the victim." Bristling, he concluded, "I don't see any American dream. I see an American nightmare."

Malcolm's rhetoric altered the way many blacks viewed themselves and their country. In "The Ballot or the Bullet," he spoke about what it meant to be an American. He reminded them, "Being born here in America doesn't make you an American." How could a black man call himself an American as long as he was denied basic freedoms? If black

men and women were Americans, then they would not need civil rights legislation. "You and I," he declared, are "African-Americans—that's what we are—Africans born in America."

Muhammad Ali also began to see himself as an African born in America, interpreting his title in global terms. After meeting with African ambassadors who praised him as an international hero, he began to view himself as something more than an American champion. When he changed his name and announced that he was a Muslim, critics vilified him as unpatriotic and un-American. He understood, as Malcolm had said, that being born in America did not make him an American. In his search for self-discovery, he decided to travel to Africa. When he returned, he came back a new man, one who defined himself as a global citizen, declaring, "I'm not an American. I'm a black man."[56]

Chapter Fifteen

KING OF THE WORLD

Millions of so-called Negroes in this country have a distorted image of our homeland. They think Africans eat each other and live in mud huts. They've been brainwashed by the white man—why, I'll show you muddier huts in Harlem than they've got over in Africa.

—MALCOLM X

I heard a voice once that told me one day I would be a world figure.

—MUHAMMAD ALI

———————

"The king! The king!" the crowd shouted, swarming the famous American as he sat in an open-top cream-colored convertible.

"Who's the king?" Muhammad Ali called, basking in the adulation and equatorial sunshine of Accra.

"You!" the locals assented, celebrating the arrival of the self-proclaimed "king of the world."

From the moment Ali set foot on African soil, Ghanaians treated him like royalty, showering him with praise and gifts. At the Accra airport, on May 16, 1964, the minister of foreign affairs, the director of sports, the chairman of Ghana Boxing Authority, and other state officials welcomed him. President Kwame Nkrumah, the first national leader to embrace Ali, directed the government's radio stations and newspapers to promote the American champion as an African hero, "a source of inspiration to the youth of the world." In the words of a

Muhammad Ali proclaimed that he was "the king of the world." And sometimes it seemed so. In Lagos, Nigeria, during his tour of Africa, he was the vortex of swirling humanity. Associated Press

writer from the state-owned *Daily Graphic*, "If there is one man who can assist positively to bring about [Nkrumah's] cherished aims of projecting the African personality"—an Africa freed from the vestiges of colonialism—and disprove "the superiority complex of the white man, he is Mohammed Ali (Cassius Clay)."[1]

Ali told reporters that he was "anxious to get around and see Africa and meet my own brothers and sisters." Unsure how his words would translate in a foreign land, he spoke cautiously when he explained that white slave traders had captured his ancestors from Africa and sold them into bondage in America. "We are glad to be back home to see things for ourselves, meet pretty Ghanaian girls, take pictures, and tell our people that there are more things to be seen in Africa than lions and elephants."[2]

As Ali prepared to leave the airport, children shouted his name and waved welcome signs while policemen brandishing truncheons ordered the crowd to back away from the motorcade. Driving through the paved streets of Accra, Ali marveled at what he saw: streetlights; honking buses and taxis; apartment buildings; and department stores, hotels,

nightclubs, and restaurants where blacks and whites socialized amicably. The city came alive with the sounds of Highlife music blaring from storefront windows, laughing children running through the streets, and saleswomen bartering with customers in the Makola Market. He was surprised to see that Accra had "wide streets, tall buildings, and other modern features." He explained to a local reporter that whites had so distorted the image of Africa that black Americans would not dare visit their homeland. "They never told us about your beautiful flowers, magnificent hotels, beautiful houses, beaches, great hospitals, schools, and universities."[3]

Like many Americans, Ali had imagined Africa as an exotic land, a vast jungle inhabited by wild animals, noble savages, and great white hunters. Most Americans knew very little about Africa beyond what they saw on-screen or read in magazines. In 1953, when Ali was eleven years old, *Time* published a feature article about the British Gold Coast that described the colony as "a rectangular patch of jungle, swamp, and bushland," even though deserts, forests, and rolling savanna grasslands shaped its landscape. The British colony that would eventually become Ghana was nothing more than "a sun-baked wasteland," filled with "primitive people" living "in holes in the ground; their women go naked with a tuft of leaves before and behind." According to *Time*, the "happy-go-lucky Gold Coasters" crowded "their mud huts with radios, sewing machines, bicycles, and even TV sets (though there is no TV station to tune in to)."[4]

Ali grew up in a culture saturated with myths about Africa. In 1960, during the Rome Olympics, he had compared America favorably to Africa, whose natives, he said, were still fighting alligators and living in mud huts. Unlike Muhammad Ali, Cassius Clay thought very little about Africa and cared even less. In his view, Africans were not a celebrated people; they were the butt of his jokes. In 1962, he told sportswriter Myron Cope a story about an encounter with two African men. "Man," he chuckled, "I was down at the beach with two of them Africans. They so black they almost *blue*, but they said to me, 'Cassius, we have to leave now and go put on our turbans and uniforms 'cause, if we don't, people gonna think we're Negroes.'"[5]

Yet when he accepted the name Muhammad Ali, he embraced the idea of being an African born in America. In Accra, he proudly declared,

"I am an African and my proper name is Muhammad Ali. There is greater dignity in my new name" than his slave name. In America, he explained, too many blacks "disgracefully bear the names of our masters." Echoing Malcolm, he suggested that if "Negroes" could not find justice in America, then they should migrate back to Africa.[6]

His Pan-African rhetoric pleased Elijah Muhammad. At a time when Malcolm, civil rights leaders, and the national media were criticizing the Nation of Islam, Elijah determined that Ali's trip abroad would overshadow their attacks, helping him legitimize his Muslim movement. Sending Ali on an international excursion would bring "universal recognition" to the Nation. Before the heavyweight champion left the US, he went on a tour of Black Muslim mosques, where he signed autographs, sold copies of *Muhammad Speaks*, and announced his future travels, crediting Elijah for his worldwide fame. "It is because I am a follower of The Messenger that has brought me personal invitations from Asia and African Presidents and Prime Ministers."[7]

Elijah predicted that Ali would receive a hero's welcome in Africa and the Middle East, but he reserved profound doubts about the regions. Romanticizing his own journey there in 1959, Elijah embellished the way Egyptian president Gamal Abdel Nasser graciously welcomed him into his palace. While he enjoyed meeting Arab and African statesmen and Muslim clerics, he returned to America disillusioned by the extreme poverty he saw, which he interpreted as a weakness in the people. Before his trip, he had talked about building an emigration movement to Africa, but afterward he ceased considering the plan.[8]

Years after his trek abroad, he complained that Africans still lived "a jungle life," deriding them as "savages" in need of his civilizing influence. Although he praised the emergence of independent African nations, he remained uninterested in building any genuine relationships with African leaders. Malcolm was convinced that Elijah had sent Ali to Africa solely for personal gain. "You cannot read anything that Elijah Muhammad has ever written that's pro-African," he charged. "I defy you to find one word in his direct writings that is pro-African. You can't find it."[9]

For Elijah, Ali's journey abroad served as a propaganda mission that he hoped would demonstrate his stature in the Islamic world, elevating his standing among black Americans. During his five-week trip, Ali was accompanied by Muslims and friends, including the champ's manager,

Herbert Muhammad; his brother Rudy, who had recently taken the name Rahman Ali; Archie Robinson, who now introduced himself as Osman Karriem; photographer Howard Bingham; and Ronnie King, an old friend. Herbert also hired Charles P. Howard, a United Nations correspondent, to write stories about Ali's journey for *Muhammad Speaks*.[10]

By the time Ali's motorcade reached the government-owned, six-story Ambassador Hotel, it seemed as if the entire city was trailing behind it. Countless locals camped outside the hotel, hoping to get a glimpse of him. Not wanting to disappoint them, Ali emerged into view on the terrace, shouting below, "Who's the king?"

"You are!" the crowd thundered.[11]

In Africa, Ali discovered that he was more popular abroad than at home. While most Americans refused to recognize his Muslim name, strangers, writers, and dignitaries in Ghana, Nigeria, and Egypt, showed him respect by acknowledging it. Everywhere he went people cheered his name like he was *their* champion, a black hero whose name mattered as much as his accomplishments in the ring. "Muhammad Ali is in Africa, all over Africa," he said later. "The name is in Ethiopia, Morocco, Syria, Indonesia, Pakistan, Turkey, Algiers, Saudi Arabia. Muhammad Ali [was a common name] when I traveled. Muhammad is the most common name in the world."[12]

Ali's African journey marked a pivotal moment in his life, ushering in a new era when he would become one of the most recognizable and written-about people in the world. But he had become something more than famous. His name had global meaning. During an age of rapid global change, decolonization in Africa and Asia, and the emerging political power of the Middle East, Ali became a liminal figure, quite literally a man betwixt and between cultures. More than any other athlete, he put the "world" into the title of "world champion."

In Africa, one could sense that Ali's views about himself, his country, and the world had changed. Something happened to him on that trip, something that stuck with Osman Karriem. "I'll remember that trip for as long as I live because that was where I saw Cassius Clay become Muhammad Ali."[13]

ABOUT A WEEK before Ali arrived in Accra, another famous black American checked into the Ambassador Hotel, igniting rumors that the champ

had already arrived. While Malcolm X waited to meet his hosts, he sat in the dining room, overhearing conversations about the controversial ending to the previous evening's world featherweight championship match between Cuban Ultiminio "Sugar" Ramos and Ghanaian Floyd Robertson. Perhaps people confused Malcolm with Ali because the Ghana Boxing Authority had announced that the heavyweight champion would attend the match, bringing greater attention to the first title bout ever held in Accra, but Ali did not arrive in Ghana until a week after the fight.[14]

Malcolm had had no idea that boxing was so popular in Africa and the Middle East until about a month earlier, when he arrived in Cairo. In Egypt, he "was mistaken time and again for Cassius Clay." Talking to Egyptians, he learned that theaters across the country had shown Ali's fight against Liston, and popular newspapers, like *Al Ahram*, had published pictures of them together in New York. Ali was so popular in "the Muslim World," Malcolm wrote in his diary, that "even the children know of him." When Ali defeated Liston and publicly embraced Islam, the young champion "captured the imagination and the support of the entire dark world."[15]

Throughout his five-week tour of the Middle East and Africa, Malcolm recorded his thoughts in a diary. His journal revealed that he still considered Ali his brother, even though many assumed that once Ali sided with Elijah, his brotherhood with Malcolm was over. In his mind, they remained on good terms. On April 20, he wrote that Muslims in Saudi Arabia had "mistaken" him "for Cassius Clay," but when they "learned that I am his friend, many questions [were] asked about him." Malcolm quickly recognized that Ali was the most famous Muslim-American in the world. In Egypt and Saudi Arabia, where most people spoke Arabic, locals' understanding of boxing and their recognition of Ali allowed Malcolm to communicate without speaking. Muslim men, women, and children smiled when he proudly pointed at a picture of himself with Ali. By sharing that picture and his stories about Ali, Malcolm gained friends and credibility among Muslims abroad.[16]

But Malcolm was not the same man that he was in the picture, smiling with his friend while he hid his fears about a life outside the Nation of Islam. By the time he reached Ghana, his thinking about race, religion, and politics had evolved. After making the pilgrimage to Mecca,

he completed his break from Elijah Muhammad's brand of Islam. Years earlier, in 1959, he had traveled to Egypt and Saudi Arabia as Elijah's emissary. During that trip, he witnessed orthodox Muslims of various races praying together and practicing rituals that conflicted with the Messenger's teaching. Although Elijah taught his followers that Islam was the "black man's religion" and that whites were devils, Malcolm had seen for himself that members of the *ummah* could belong to any nationality or race, as long as they performed the Five Pillars and observed other traditions. At that time he had avoided making the pilgrimage to Mecca because his "devotion to [Elijah]" made him "not want to go there ahead of him." For years, he suppressed the truth about Elijah's faith, denying the contradictions between the Messenger's parochialism and the practices he encountered in Saudi Arabia. But when he completed the hajj in 1964, he finally accepted that Elijah's orthodoxy was incompatible with the Koran.[17]

The hajj broadened his understanding of Islam and opened him to the possibility that blacks and whites could live together peacefully. When an Arab asked him what impressed him most about his experience, he answered, "The *brotherhood!* The people of all races, colors, from all over the world coming together as *one!* It has proved to me the power of the One God." Visiting the Holy City inspired him to write letters to American friends describing his spiritual transformation. During his holy pilgrimage, he ate from the same plate, drank from the same cup, slept on the same cot, and prayed on the same rug with white Muslims. For the first time in his life he did not see these men as "white" because they did not identify themselves as whites did in America. He knew that when his letter to the *New York Times* reached American readers, they would be stunned to learn that he now professed that Islam had cleansed him of his belief that all whites were devils.[18]

Yet he continued to rail against white Americans. The American white man was still his enemy. He could not absolve them of their sins against blacks; there was too much blood on their hands. Malcolm's belief that whites were not inherently evil developed gradually, but this realization did not alter his political ideology. At his core, Malcolm was a Black Nationalist, a soldier at war searching for allies in the black liberation movement.[19]

In Ghana, he hoped to find solidarity with black expatriates and state officials. As the fountainhead of Pan-Africanism, Ghana had long served as a haven for expatriates like W. E. B. Du Bois, Richard Wright, and Julian Mayfield. After Malcolm spent a night at the Ambassador Hotel, Mayfield, Leslie Lacy, Maya Angelou, Alice Windom, and other exiles welcomed him "home." As editor-in-chief of the *African Review* and one of Nkrumah's advisers, Mayfield offered the kinds of connections that Malcolm needed to build diplomatic ties with African leaders.[20]

At Mayfield's home, thirty to forty guests huddled around Malcolm as he described how the hajj had changed him. He said that he was still a Muslim but would no longer follow Elijah Muhammad, and that he intended to help unify "the various rights groups in America." Maya Angelou could not believe that this was the same Malcolm who had served as "the bombastic spokesman" for Elijah Muhammad, preaching about the white man's doom. The man sitting in Mayfield's living room smiled easily, exuding a warmth and friendliness that she had never felt before in his presence. Freed from Elijah, Malcolm radiated a renewed energy, grinning and rubbing his sandy beard as he spoke about his new outlook.[21]

Malcolm toured Accra with his camera, snapping pictures like a tourist. He absorbed the sights, sounds, and smells of the city. Immersed in Ghanaian culture, he spoke to street vendors, students, and intellectuals. He gave interviews, delivered university lectures, and attended lunches and dinners with government officials and ambassadors from various countries.[22]

Before he arrived in Ghana, Malcolm had determined that he would expose the hypocrisy of white Americans who claimed that they supported Africa. He bristled at the sight of whites "who spit in the faces of blacks" back home but "are seen throughout Africa, bowing, grinning and smiling in an effort to 'integrate' with Africans." Charging the United States as the "master of imperialism," he urged African leaders to take a strong stand against the American government for violating blacks' human rights.[23]

Many Ghanaians praised Malcolm for questioning the State Department's claims about racial progress in America. His message echoed throughout Africa at a time when the United States' image abroad

suffered from civil rights protests. As the movement escalated during the early 1960s, international news coverage of brutal discrimination against blacks took on increased significance as the United States and the Soviet Union fought over the alignment of African countries. Appealing to African leaders, the United States promoted a narrative of color-blind democracy in America, while international correspondents and photographers told a different story. In the aftermath of the Birmingham crisis, images of police dogs and fire hoses unleashed on black children were published across Africa. In Accra, the US embassy reported that the American government took "a heavy beating in Ghana over Birmingham." And after the March on Washington, a small group of Ghanaian protestors demonstrated outside the American embassy, carrying placards that read, "America, Africa is Watching You."[24]

In the mid-1950s, Kwame Nkrumah was celebrated as a symbol of hope throughout the continent. Since 1957, when Ghana became the first sub-Saharan state to gain independence from colonial rule, Nkrumah's promise of democracy had gradually deteriorated into an authoritarian regime plagued by rigged elections, mass arrests, new taxes, and prison sentences for criticizing the government. Yet during the Kennedy administration, the United States courted Nkrumah, hoping that the president's charisma would persuade him to ignore the Soviet Union's overtures.[25]

But Nkrumah's mercurial personality made him unpredictable. Dependent on foreign investment, the Ghanaian government exploited the superpowers for financial aid. Still, Nkrumah harbored fears that the CIA, acting independently of the American government, was out to get him, a fear exacerbated by two assassination attempts against him. He also suspected that some black expatriates were working as foreign agents.

In February 1964, about a month after Nkrumah survived a second attempt on his life, two hundred workers from his Convention People's Party staged a protest outside the American embassy, shouting, "Yankees, go home!" A few days later, protestors lowered the American flag in front of the embassy. The state's official newspaper, the *Ghanaian Times*, accused the US of plotting against Nkrumah "because he is the biggest thorn in their neocolonialist ambitions, [and] because he is forging the path of Socialism." In response, Undersecretary of State

W. Averell Harriman warned Nkrumah that if his government contin-
ued to criticize America, the United States would suspend funding for
the Volta River hydroelectric dam project, the centerpiece of Ghana's
industrialization.[26]

By the time Malcolm and Ali arrived in May, Nkrumah had ex-
pressed regret over the embassy protests, instructing all government me-
dia to cease disseminating anti-American propaganda. After Malcolm
reached Accra, he asked Mayfield if he could arrange a meeting with
the president, but the Ghanaian leader hesitated after US ambassador
William Mahoney warned him that Malcolm's inflammatory rhetoric
might damage the goodwill between their countries. Nkrumah made
sure that as long as Malcolm, and Ali for that matter, were in Ghana,
neither man would jeopardize his relationship with the United States. In
Accra, American diplomats reported, "anti-American statements . . . by
Malcolm X, militant former Black Muslim leader, and Cassius Clay . . .
had received little attention in the press."[27]

Nkrumah well understood the risks of engaging Malcolm. Hav-
ing met him at a Harlem rally in 1960, he was aware of the minister's
provocative image. Only after W. E. B. Du Bois's widow, Shirley, ap-
pealed to Nkrumah on Malcolm's behalf did he consent to a private
meeting at the Christiansborg Castle, an old slave fort.[28]

On May 15, at about noon, Julian Mayfield dropped Malcolm off out-
side the castle. After guards patted Malcolm down, Nkrumah, a slight
man, rose from behind his large office desk, offering a firm handshake
and a warm smile. For about an hour they sat on a couch, discussing
the plight of black Americans and the importance of Pan-Africanism.
If Malcolm asked Nkrumah to support a UN resolution charging the
United States with human rights violations, he left disappointed. The
Ghanaian leader may have sympathized with his cause, but politics pre-
vented him from considering such a proposal.[29]

Initially, the State Department viewed Malcolm's journey abroad as
a threat to American foreign policy. If he'd convinced just one Afri-
can nation to charge the US with human rights violations, he could
have damaged America's international reputation. In the end, though,
the State Department concluded that Malcolm lacked political lever-
age with the officials he met. He had nothing tangible to offer—no
bridges, no dams, no money. The fact that he did not receive "an official

endorsement" from Nkrumah minimized "his impact." "All in all," American officials surmised, "Malcolm X created less of a stir than the Embassy feared."[30]

Yet Malcolm's experience in Ghana deepened his commitment to Pan-Africanism. Talking with Africans who expressed a sincere interest in the struggle of African Americans convinced him that they all shared a common struggle against racial oppression. He left Ghana inspired. If there was a single lesson that he learned, it was that "our problems were their problems. We are all one people—Africans or of African descent. We are all blood brothers!"[31]

MALCOLM HAD PACKED his bags. Before flying back to New York, he planned four more days of traveling in Senegal, Morocco, and Algiers. On Sunday morning, May 17, Maya Angelou, Alice Windom, and Julian Mayfield met him in front of the Ambassador Hotel. They were all laughing and talking about their time together when suddenly they heard loud American voices. One voice sounded especially familiar to Malcolm. He turned around and saw the handsome face of Muhammad Ali.[32]

"The next moment froze," Angelou recalled, "as if caught on daguerreotype, and the next minutes moved as a slow montage." Malcolm brightened at the sight of him. "Brother Muhammad! Brother Muhammad!" he shouted with a crooked smile, uncertain how Ali would react with everyone watching. At that instant, Ali had to make a split-second decision. He knew that he could not publicly embrace Malcolm, not as long as Herbert stood next to him, not as long as he had professed his loyalty to Elijah. Malcolm had betrayed the Messenger and the entire Nation, and no true Muslim could maintain a friendship with him.

Ali paused in the middle of his conversation, looking quizzically at Malcolm, who appeared almost unrecognizable sporting a reddish goatee, white robe, and sandals. At first, Ali said nothing. He just kept walking, slowly moving away from his friend, leaving him behind like an old suitcase, heavy baggage he no longer wished to carry. When he and his entourage reached a row of parked cars, Malcolm rushed up to him, hoping to flag him down before he drove away. "Brother Muhammad! Brother Muhammad!" Finally, Ali stopped and faced Malcolm.

"Brother, I still love you, and you are still the greatest," Malcolm said.

Glaring, Ali shook his head. "You left the Honorable Elijah Muhammad," he said, his voice as cold as his eyes. "That was the wrong thing to do, Brother Malcolm."

Malcolm wanted to explain that he did not leave Elijah; he was forced out of the Nation. But there was no time to explain, no way to make Ali understand that he never intended to hurt him or Elijah. Ali abruptly marched away, leaving him puzzled and wounded. Malcolm had never expected his friend to treat him so harshly, not after he had shown him how much he cared for him, standing by his side in Miami when the whole world was against him, when Elijah refused to publicly claim him as one of his own. Malcolm did not have the words to convince Ali that they could remain friends. All he could do was sadly watch him walk out of his life.

Visibly shaken, Malcolm rejoined his friends, walking with his head down, his shoulders slumped. "I've lost a lot. A lot," he repeated. "Almost too much." Then, saying nothing else, he crammed his long legs into the front passenger seat of Maya's tiny Fiat, "the heavy mood destined to stay."

Ali's encounter with Malcolm convinced him that everything he had heard about his old friend was true. Malcolm had gone mad, the Black Muslims said, and now Ali had no doubt that they were right. "Man, did you get a look at him?" he asked Herbert. "Dressed in that funny white robe and wearing a beard and walking with that cane that looked like a prophet's stick? Man, he's gone. He's gone so far out he's out completely." Ali did not understand that Malcolm, like other penitents who had completed the hajj, wore traditional Muslim attire. "Doesn't that just go to show, Herbert, that Elijah is the most powerful? Nobody listens to that Malcolm anymore."[33]

If Ali hardly recognized him, Malcolm perceived that Ali had changed, too. He could see that the boxer was no longer the sweet, affable young man who had once bounced Malcolm's daughters on his knee. This man, Muhammad Ali, was Elijah's loyal subject, wearing a new mask, playing the part of the serious, vindictive Black Muslim. When Ali cut Malcolm out of his life, he revealed a new side of himself that the public had not yet seen, an angrier, crueler side that would develop

more and more in the coming years. Whenever there were other Black Muslims around, he assumed this role, conforming to the expectations of the Nation, punishing anyone who crossed them, whether it was his father, Floyd Patterson, or Malcolm X.

Yet, after their confrontation, Malcolm could not help but try to protect Ali. Before he departed Accra, he sent Ali a telegram, offering brotherly advice as he always did, reminding him of his immense cultural power. "Because a billion of our people in Africa, Arabia, and Asia love you blindly, you must now be forever aware of your tremendous responsibilities to them. You must never say or do anything that will permit your enemies to distort the beautiful image you have here among our people." When he made a vague reference to Ali's "enemies," he was really referring to his own adversaries in the Nation of Islam, those who would exploit Ali, use him up, and discard him when he was no longer valuable, just as they did to Malcolm.[34]

ALI MOVED ON as if he had never seen Malcolm. He performed his usual shtick, making outrageous pronouncements and entertaining strangers. When a local man asked him why he was going to visit Egypt, he answered that he intended to find his future wife there. Actually, he was "going to get four wives" and bring them back home, where he would build a castle. One of his wives, "Abigail," would feed him grapes. Another wife, "Susie," would rub olive oil all over his "beautiful muscles," while "Cecilia" shined his shoes. He was not sure what his fourth wife, "Peaches," would do. Perhaps, she would entertain him, singing or dancing. It was all part of his fantasy of being worshipped, being loved, being king of the world.[35]

Mesmerized by the crowds of ordinary men and women who followed him at every stop, Ali fell in love with Africa. He toured Ghana like a politician courting voters. Whenever he met government authorities, state boxing officials, or casual fans, he made sure that he won them over with his charm, endlessly praising Ghana, hugging women, and kissing babies. He claimed that he wanted to build a home and a gym in Accra so that he could train among his people. "Until I came to Ghana, I never realized that I was so popular and loved by Africans, my people," he said. "I am so overwhelmed and fascinated and I feel it is my obligation to arrange for my next championship fight to be staged

in Accra." This was one of many empty promises he uttered during his visit. He never intended to defend his title in Ghana, let alone move there. In fact, he would not return to Africa until a decade later.[36]

Soon, Kwame Nkrumah invited Ali to Ghana's presidential palace. Draped in a striped orange and blue kente cloth, Ali towered over the tiny president as they toured the Flagstaff House. Nkrumah, dressed in his signature khaki pants and open-necked shirt, a modern look befitting a man who aspired to lead Africa into the modern age, presented Ali with his two books, both promoting African nationalism.

They visited for a short time, just long enough for the state's photographers to snap pictures for the next day's newspapers. Ali told reporters that he was honored to meet Nkrumah, which translated into the headline, "Mohamed Ali Meets His Hero." The press exaggerated his reverence for Nkrumah, a propaganda ploy advancing the Ghanaian leader's agenda. Just as he did for Elijah Muhammad, Ali followed Nkrumah's party line. When they met, he said, "I humbled myself before him, a thing I rarely do, because I saw in him a dedicated man who is anxious to free Africa and bring about unity."[37]

On May 18, the same day he visited Nkrumah, Ali met with Ambassador William Mahoney at the US embassy. Less than four months after protestors demonstrated outside the embassy, the State Department feared that Ali might inflame anti-American rhetoric. Consequently, the United States Information Agency, the government's foreign affairs propaganda machine, did not publicize his tour. Even before his meeting with Mahoney, Ali understood the political implications of his trip. "Many Negro celebrities," he said, "take State Department 'goodwill tours' of Africa or Asia, but few have received the personal congratulations and invitations from so many world leaders." Promoting black athletes as symbols of American democracy, the State Department figured that famous stars like Rafer Johnson, Bill Russell, and Floyd Patterson could counter anti-American views among Africans.[38]

Yet Ali rejected the role of the State Department's goodwill ambassador. As an independent guest of the Ghanaian government, he assumed no responsibility for the embassy's agenda. During a press conference, he criticized the NAACP and derided the Civil Rights Act as a deceptive attempt to convince blacks that integration would work. The law, he charged, "won't change the hearts of the slave masters. And like the

counterfeit money it is, if the Negroes tried to spend it they would be arrested."[39]

Four years before, as an Olympic champion in Rome, he had defended America. Now he abandoned the government's official line. Emerging as a potent international symbol of anti-American defiance, he described America as a violent country where blacks who demanded freedom were "getting killed" and children were "being bombed in churches." History showed, he said, that whites and blacks could not get along because "the so-called master doesn't want his slave to be his equal. This is America."[40]

On Friday, May 22, Ali flew by private plane to Kumasi, Ghana's "Garden City," where more than five thousand people greeted him. Rivaling his welcome in Accra, locals filled the streets as his caravan meandered downtown, paralyzing traffic. Sitting atop a convertible, Ali, perspiring beneath his white shirt and loosened dark tie, led the crowd in his usual call-and-response routine. Shopkeepers, clerks, and merchants left their jobs just to see the famous American champion. Teenagers climbed trees, scrambling for a better view, while others rode bicycles alongside his car. For them, Ali was a symbol of black pride. "By returning to Africa," a *Daily Graphic* columnist wrote, "he has fulfilled a long cherished mission which the other great Afro-American champions left unaccomplished." Ali, another writer explained, "is a real specimen of the African. He thinks anything the white man can do the African can do better."[41]

At Kumasi Sports Stadium, thousands of fans watched him spar with his brother, raising money for the Kwame Nkrumah Trust Fund, a charitable organization. Throwing very few punches against Rahman, he mostly stalked his brother around the ring and chased the referee. Near the end of the match, he "feigned grogginess, then fell to the canvas, stunning the crowd." Bouncing back to his feet, the crowd roared with applause. Assuring his fans, he said, "If we had been really fighting, I would have won in one."[42]

After spending three weeks in Ghana, on June 1 Ali traveled to Lagos, Nigeria. For hours, a few thousand fans waited at the Lagos International Airport, holding signs that read, "Welcome Back Home

Mohammed Ali King of the World." Reporters, photographers, and government officials greeted the champ while fans shouted his name, convincing him that he really was the most popular man in the world. A crowd swarmed his car, pressing against it as they reached out to touch him. "They love me, they love me," he kept repeating.[43]

The ebullient mood was short-lived. Many local newsmen disapproved of his egotism, listening to him deride Joe Louis and Floyd Patterson for not being "true world champions willing to travel everywhere like me." Making matters worse, Ali angered his hosts from the National Sports Council when he informed them that he could not stay more than three days. The council had expected him to visit for a week and perform two boxing exhibitions, just as he had in Ghana. Stunned by Ali's sudden change of plans, the officials could not understand why he had reneged on their agreement. A day after he arrived, he visited the American embassy, where he explained to his hosts that he already had plans to travel to Egypt. "They got big things planned for me in Cairo. Nasser is gonna see me and it's gonna be really big. The only plane to Cairo this week [leaves on] Wednesday, so I gotta go." His hosts protested, reminding him that thousands of Nigerian fans were counting on him, but he insisted that Egypt was "more important than Nigeria."[44]

Outraged, Hogan "Kid" Bassey, former world bantamweight champion and Olympic boxing coach, scolded Ali. Egypt, he said, was not more important than Nigeria. Gripping the arms of his chair, he explained that Nigeria was the biggest country in Africa. In fact, one in five Africans lived in Nigeria. Of course, "every Nigerian schoolboy" knew that, but Ali didn't.[45]

"Well," Ali replied, "isn't Egypt the powerfulest country with all them rockets and their big army and their dam?"

"Mr. Muhammad," Bassey exclaimed, "you are a champion. You are supposed to keep your promises. We scheduled an exhibition in Ibadan. Thousands have bought tickets to see you. We organized a soccer game especially in your honor. We invited important officials to banquets. You were picked to judge the Miss Nigeria contest Saturday." His voice rising, Bassey fumed, "If you leave us now, you'll mess everything up."

At that point Bassey and Ali were no longer just talking. Now they were sparring with words, and Ali was determined to prove that he was

the better fighter. "Now look," he said, pointing his finger at Bassey, "I don't appreciate anybody telling me to do this or do that. Nobody tells me what to do or when to do it but me."

Herbert Muhammad tried to calm everyone down. Ali stood up and shook hands with his hosts, but the tension remained. Afterward, they packed into cars so that Ali would not be late for a radio interview, but along the way he ordered the driver to stop the car so that he could buy a record player. Infuriated, Bassey vented, "That clown! He wants to go shopping? He calls himself a champion?"[46]

Critics lambasted his treatment of Nigeria as a "disgrace." *Boston Globe* columnist Bud Collins suggested that Ali's "diplomatic blunder" might damage America's reputation in Africa. Ali had "insulted Sonny Liston and got away with it, so why should 36 million Nigerians concern him?" Yet a Nigerian writer defended Ali, suggesting that any criticism of his early departure was unfair. The *Daily Times*' Cee-Kay blamed his short stay on the National Sports Council for poorly planning the boxer's visit after he had already arranged his trip to Egypt. Comparing the heavyweight champion to a foreign minister, the columnist argued that Ali deserved better treatment. "Apart from being a world champion," he wrote, "Mohammed Ali is our own brother. He is even more than that. He is an ambassador of his country. And that is more reason why he should be given V.I.P. treatment."[47]

For months, Egyptians had anticipated Ali's arrival. Immediately after he defeated Sonny Liston and announced that he practiced Islam, Egypt's Supreme Islamic Council invited him to visit the United Arab Republic. His religious declaration had thrust him into the international spotlight. Yet American diplomats feared that if Ali accepted the invitation, he might embarrass the United States. Equally troubling to officials, the Arab press made no distinction between orthodox Muslims and the Black Muslims, giving Ali and the NOI "undeserved credit and status" throughout the Middle East. In advance of his visit, the State Department attempted to diminish Ali's appeal by planting articles in newspapers and magazines that exposed the "true nature of Black Muslims," making it clear that the sect was "not genuinely Islamic."[48]

On June 3, Ali finally reached Cairo International Airport, where an eager crowd nearly crushed him as he made his way through a terminal.

Scores of policemen, soldiers, and ex-boxers struggled against the people enveloping the champ. Looking at the crowd of nearly two thousand people and placards reading, "Victory to Islam," Ali realized that these people loved him not only for his boxing talents but also because he was a Muslim. "I'm fighting for Allah," he declared. "I'm proud to be a Moslem, and among you. I feel at home."[49]

In Cairo, Ali showed far greater respect for his hosts than he had in Nigeria. Elijah Muhammad had taught him that the "Asiatic black man" had descended from the rich Nile Valley region, and that ancient Egypt was once the most powerful black nation in history. Perceiving Egyptian superiority, Ali viewed his surroundings as evidence that he had reached the most advanced Muslim country in the world. From his balcony at the Nile Hilton, a gleaming twelve-story white slab replete with modern amenities and air-conditioning, a panoramic historic vista met his gaze. Overlooking the western bank of the majestic river, in the distance he saw the Citadel, ancient mosques, and the Pyramids, surrounded by desert. Looking eastward, he glimpsed Tahrir Square, Cairo's commercial district. In his reverence for Egyptian history and culture, he adopted a more dignified countenance befitting a distinguished Muslim. Studying his performance, Charles Howard observed, "Muhammad Ali is not only a boxer—he's an actor."[50]

During his twenty-day tour of Egypt, Ali met the Supreme Islamic Council; watched a boxing tournament at an athletic club; visited monuments, museums, and the Aswan Dam; and performed a few boxing exhibitions. Outside Cairo, near the Pyramids of Giza, he straddled a stubborn camel, tightly pulling the reins when the ornery bull bucked. He confidently waved off the camel's owner and steadily gained control. "I'm the champ," he announced with a grin, "and I can tame a camel just like I handled Sonny Liston." While some locals laughed at his boasts, others resented his jocular behavior. "A real king," a Cairene suggested, "would not say he is king of the world about himself. He'd leave it for others to say it about him."[51]

Egyptians also wondered if Ali really understood how to perform traditional Muslim rituals. At the Al-Hussein Mosque, he and his brother prayed barefoot on a carpet among 1,500 worshippers. Afterward, Ali was so moved by his experience that he announced he would make the pilgrimage to Mecca before returning home, though he never reached

the Holy City. He also claimed that he wanted to learn Arabic, train Egyptian boxers, marry an Egyptian woman, and live near the Great Pyramids. Watching him pray during what seemed like inappropriate moments, with his palms facing the sky, shouting, "*Allahu akbar,*" left some locals questioning his sincerity.[52]

Near the end of his stay, he met Egyptian president Gamal Abdel Nasser. A passionate boxing fan, Nasser told Ali that he had watched his victory over Liston. Afterward, Ali said they talked for nearly forty minutes "about life, boxing, different things," seemingly harmless topics. But given Nasser's friendly relationship with Soviet premier Nikita Khrushchev, State Department officials must have cringed when Ali told a reporter that everything he had read about Nasser in the United States was "nothing but lies. It is a shame how they tell lies about great people like Nasser."[53]

While the State Department considered whether Ali might make more provocative statements, they soon realized that they no longer had to worry. After five weeks of traveling, he abruptly canceled the final leg of his trip. "I'm tired," he said to a group of reporters at Kennedy International Airport. "People have been mobbing me. They've been killing me. Women and children were jumping off roofs, and people were coming straight out of the mountains to see me."[54]

But Ali wasn't embellishing when he said, "I was treated like a politician." In Africa, he discovered a whole new world, one where people respected him as a black man and as a Muslim. His experience transformed him into a global icon, an international symbol of Black Power and anticolonialism. Reflecting on his journey, he realized that his worldwide celebrity came with tremendous responsibility. "Sometimes it scares me, all this fame, the world watches me, little children know me, old ladies," he said. "Gotta set an example of good living, everybody knows me." He could easily close his eyes and imagine all the black faces smiling at him, chanting his name. "You should have seen them pour out of the hills, the villages of Africa, and they all knew me. Everybody knows me in the whole world."[55]

Chapter Sixteen

THE MUSLIM CHAMP

This hypocrite is going to get blasted clear off the face of the earth.
—ELIJAH MUHAMMAD ON MALCOLM X

Talmadge Hayer was the perfect man for the job. He had lived a life of dreams deferred, with festering sores that never healed. He came of age in the slums of Paterson, New Jersey, a depressed and broken city. By the 1960s the "Silk City" had frayed into a badland of poverty, crime, and urban decay. Walking the streets of Paterson, Hayer could see the "crumbs of civilization" all around him: broken glass scattered on the sidewalks, garbage-strewn alleys, "the burned-out shell of a tenement," abandoned redbrick buildings that were once filled with noisy looms, hustlers loitering on corners, and the vacant stares of old men sitting on stoops, passing time until they had no more time to pass.[1]

He recalled later that in his early twenties, his "life started coming apart." He committed petty crimes and eventually was arrested for disorderly conduct and possession of stolen firearms. Some of his friends who were convicted of more serious crimes went to prison and came out as converted followers of Elijah Muhammad. Curious about their transformations, he began reading about the Nation of Islam. Soon he became a regular at Mosque No. 25 in Newark. Transfixed by the rugged, uniformed soldiers standing in military formation, Hayer decided what he really wanted to be: a soldier in the Fruit of Islam. "Had their own *army*, man," he said years later. "I thought we were going to fight this white, blue-eyed devil."

The Fruit of Islam had been waiting for Malcolm X to return home from his trip abroad. Malcolm knew when he arrived at JFK International Airport on May 21, 1964, that his life was in danger. The Fruit had orders from the Supreme Captain. "Malcolm," Raymond Sharrieff promised, "will soon die out." Getty Images

After receiving his "X" in the fall of 1962, he embraced his role as a soldier in Elijah Muhammad's army. But on one occasion, when a fellow brother violated Muslim law, Talmadge X zealously took matters into his own hands, violently punishing the man. Consequently, mosque officials suspended him. In exile, he realized that he had to do something to regain their trust and prove his loyalty to the cause.

By the spring of 1964, Talmadge had returned to the Nation in good standing. In April, he unfolded the pages of *Muhammad Speaks* and found a provocative cartoon of Malcolm's decapitated head, replete with satanic horns, bouncing toward a pile of skulls that belonged to the worst

traitors in history. Talmadge read the cartoon clearly. This was a test, he realized, a challenge to the Fruit to eliminate the renegade minister who had betrayed the Messenger.[2]

On an early June afternoon, while Talmadge strolled through downtown Paterson, a black Chrysler rolled up alongside him. He recognized two young Muslim brothers from Mosque No. 25. After Ben X and Leon X opened a back door, Talmadge got in. The men began talking about how Malcolm had slandered the Messenger. Cautiously, they probed Talmadge for his attitudes about Malcolm and Muhammad. Talmadge told the men that Malcolm must be silenced. Nodding with approval, Ben and Leon had no doubt that he was committed to retaliation.[3]

When they mentioned killing Malcolm, Talmadge listened intently, assuming that Ben, an assistant secretary, was acting on orders from Minister James Shabazz. A good soldier, he acknowledged, followed orders, and he had a duty to carry out the mission. Soon, they began meeting at Ben's home, plotting Malcolm's death. According to Talmadge, Ben recruited two other men that he knew as Wilbur X and William X. Since Talmadge was familiar with guns, Ben charged him with acquiring the weapons they needed. He dutifully purchased a twelve-gauge shotgun, a Luger, and a .45 automatic. "I didn't ask a whole lot of questions as to who's giving us instructions and who's telling us what," he said later. "We just knew what had to be done."

A FEW WEEKS before Ben and Leon approached Talmadge, on May 21, Malcolm returned home after traveling for more than month. Around four thirty p.m., Betty, the kids, and a few of his lieutenants greeted him at Kennedy Airport. Following a brief respite at home, a few minutes before seven p.m., Malcolm entered the Hotel Theresa's eleventh-floor Skyline Ballroom, wearing a blue seersucker suit and a broad smile. Reporters hardly recognized the man with the reddish goatee. Some had heard that he was now using his Sunni Muslim name, El-Hajj Malik El-Shabazz, but before he stepped to the podium one of his assistants introduced him as Minister Malcolm. When a writer asked him if "Shabazz" would replace his "X," he replied with a grin, "I'll probably continue to use Malcolm X as long as the situation that produced it exists."[4]

More than fifty photographers, newswriters, and television reporters had crowded into the ballroom. After describing his journey, Malcolm

announced his intention to work with African leaders who would support his charges against the United States for violating black Americans' human rights. Immediately a writer asked him the one question everyone wanted him to answer. "Do we correctly understand that you now do not think that all whites are evil?"

"*True*, sir! My trip to Mecca has opened my eyes. I no longer subscribe to racism. I have adjusted my thinking to the point where I believe that whites are human beings," he said, pausing contemplatively, "as long as this is borne out by their humane attitude toward Negroes." He added that although he had seen Muslims of different races living in harmony in the Middle East, he remained unconvinced that such interracial brotherhood would ever exist in America.

When another writer inquired if he planned to cooperate with civil rights groups, Malcolm replied that he wanted to develop a "united front" with other organizations and that he was willing to meet various leaders. Sitting next to Alex Haley, the *New York Times*' Mike Handler could not believe what he was hearing. "Incredible! Incredible!" he kept muttering.[5]

Malcolm's willingness to work with civil rights leaders led many writers to conclude that his trip had fundamentally changed his political views. Some of his own followers, hearing him concede that he no longer considered all whites to be devils, began wondering if the minister sporting a reddish beard was an imposter. In private meetings, a few men challenged him, and sometimes the disagreements became physical. "I had to hold some brothers off Malcolm," his aide Charles Kenyatta said later. While Malcolm's perspective had changed—becoming more internationalist—he still identified himself as a minister and a teacher, a Muslim and a revolutionary. Most importantly, he still considered himself a proud black man.[6]

In the days after his return, Malcolm found himself trapped between his past and his future, struggling to convey his new position as an alternative to the status quo. If he deviated too far from his previous rhetoric, looking for a rapprochement with white liberals, he risked losing his most loyal followers, but if he failed to broaden his thinking, inviting alliances with those he had condemned in the past, then he could not build the unified movement that he envisioned. Malcolm was now convinced that brotherhood between blacks mattered more than

ideology. If a black man was willing to fight alongside him, risking his life for freedom, then that man was his brother.[7]

When fellow activists pressed him about his position, he maintained that whites were still the enemy of black Americans and that he fully intended "to fight that enemy." On May 23, during a debate with Louis Lomax at the Civic Opera House in Chicago, he explained that traveling abroad had helped him discover a wider perspective. "Separation is not the goal of the Afro-American," he told the moderator, Irv Kupcinet. "Nor is integration his goal. They are merely methods toward his real end—respect and recognition as a human being."[8]

While Malcolm debated Lomax, he looked out at the audience and noticed John Ali and a squad from the Fruit glaring at him. It was the beginning of an emerging pattern. The moment Malcolm returned home, the Black Muslims escalated threats against him, appearing everywhere he went: lecture halls, radio stations, airports, even his home. In Chicago, Raymond Sharrieff had ordered the Fruit to "get" Malcolm. In early June, the Supreme Captain visited Mosque No. 7, where he delivered a harangue against the "hypocrite," demanding vengeance. Make no mistake, he said, "Malcolm will soon die out."[9]

Malcolm could sense his enemies closing in on him. Walking the streets at night, his eyes darted in every direction while he listened for footsteps. He could imagine a squad from the Fruit sneaking up behind him. The Black Muslims, Peter Goldman wrote, "had crowded him into a corner and so had brought him to his most dangerous condition—that reckless, free-swinging, gut-punching fury in which he would use whatever weapon came to hand."[10]

His most potent weapon against the Muslims, of course, was evidence that Elijah Muhammad had carried on numerous affairs, impregnating several of his secretaries. He began retaliating by sending his chief aide, James 67X, to California to obtain signed legal documents from women who claimed that Elijah had fathered their children. Then he began working the phones, calling other women who could corroborate the former secretaries' charges. Malcolm knew that once he pursued this course, his chances of survival deteriorated. Muhammad would stop at nothing to protect his secrets. The FBI overheard Malcolm say on the phone, "Any man who will go to bed with his brother's daughter, and then turn around and make five other women

pregnant, and then accuse all these women of committing adultery, is a ruthless man."[11]

On the evening of June 7, at the Audubon Ballroom, Malcolm told nearly five hundred people that Elijah kept several concubines and was the father of six illegitimate children. This was the first time that he spoke publicly about Elijah's adultery, a move as wise as swinging a broom at a hornet's nest. The Nation's officials, he declared, "would even murder to keep it quiet." Later that night, across Harlem, the Black Muslims mobilized, preparing for war. The following morning Betty received the first of many threatening phone calls. Sometimes her tormentors dialed and hung up. Sometimes they said nothing while she pleaded for them to stop calling. And sometimes they threatened her children. But this time a man told her to deliver a message to her husband. "Just tell him he's as good as dead."[12]

MALCOLM GOT THE message. Later that day, he appeared on CBS with Mike Wallace, divulging Elijah's improprieties. Muhammad forced him out of the Nation of Islam, he charged, because when he learned about Muhammad's indiscretions he told other officials, who then made it look as if he was "stirring up things." Wallace asked him if he feared the consequences of exposing Elijah's trysts. "Oh yes," he answered. "I'm probably a dead man already."[13]

No matter how much the Black Muslims threatened him, Malcolm refused to back down. On Friday, June 12, he arrived in Boston under police escort. An anonymous caller warned a radio station dispatcher that Malcolm would be "bumped off" if he spoke on the air. Undeterred, he recited Muhammad's affairs on air and called him a fraud. Later that evening, when he appeared on another station, Malcolm said that Boston minister Louis X knew all about Muhammad's transgressions long before he did. He also claimed that National Secretary John Ali had ordered a hit on him. According to one witness, Ali had recently visited the New York mosque, trying to convince the lieutenants that Malcolm had to die. Malcolm accused Louis, John, and other officials of conspiring against him, essentially "declaring war on the entire leadership group of the Nation of Islam."[14]

In the following days, after the NYPD received several tips about an attempt on his life, Malcolm prepared for a two-day eviction trial. The

proceedings began on June 15, when thirty-two police officers and eight bodyguards escorted him into the Queens courthouse for the Civil Court of the City of New York. When he took the stand, he looked out into the courtroom and saw about fifty menacing faces from the Fruit staring back at him. That same day, the Fruit held its regularly scheduled meeting at Mosque No. 7, where more than 180 soldiers from New York and New Jersey heard one of the speakers declare, "We should destroy Malcolm." Yet one of the captains, most likely Joseph, warned that the timing was not right. "Malcolm is not to be touched, the rest is okay."[15]

On the second day of the trial, Malcolm testified for nearly two hours. At times he appeared unnerved, fidgeting and rambling. He did not have a solid legal claim on the house, even if Muhammad had told him it was his home. Near the end of his testimony, perhaps realizing that he was losing the case, Malcolm blurted that the Honorable Elijah Muhammad had taken nine wives. Dismayed, his lawyer, Percy Sutton, tried to redirect him, but Malcolm persisted. "*This* is the reason for my suspension," he said. "My mouth was closed so that I couldn't talk."[16]

With each passing day, he more viciously attacked Elijah. "Muhammad was nobody until I came to New York as his emissary," he argued. He suggested that since Muhammad broke with him, blacks had left the Nation in droves. Muhammad was so furious about the rising number of apostates that he planned to speak at a New York rally on June 28. The truth, Malcolm suggested, was that Mosque No. 7 no longer made the same kind of money it did when he was the minister there. "They haven't found anyone to do the job I have been doing in New York." Convinced that he was irreplaceable, Malcolm imagined that no one else in the Nation could excite the Black Muslims the way he once did. But he was wrong.[17]

IT WAS THE kind of heat-soaked day when the police expect trouble. On June 28, Elijah Muhammad and Malcolm X organized competing rallies, battling for the soul of Harlem. In the days leading up to Muhammad's arrival, the police had heard rumors that Malcolm's men would assassinate him at the airport. They had also heard that the Black Muslims would never allow Malcolm to preach on the same day as Muhammad. The threats became so intense that Malcolm wrote

Muhammad an open letter declaring a truce, but he knew as well as Elijah did that the war would not end without causalities.[18]

At 142nd Street and Fifth Avenue, a long line formed outside the Harlem Armory, where members of the Fruit frisked the crowd, searching for weapons and spies. Inside the building, the Fruit's security team took their positions, guarding the exits and patrolling the aisles. Two ranks stood in front of the speakers' platform, arms folded, while another squad scanned the audience from the balcony. Packing the auditorium, an estimated 7,500 followers stood up when a phalanx escorted Elijah on stage. Muhammad delivered a seventy-five minute harangue, coughing and wheezing as he strained his voice, while the audience fanned the stifling air with programs. Denouncing Malcolm without mentioning his name, he fumed, "There is some person who wants to be what I am, but that person is not able to be what I am."[19]

Sitting a few feet away from Elijah, where Malcolm once sat, the Nation's guest speaker, a handsome, enthusiastic black man, led the chorus, "Teach us! Teach us!" Reminding the faithful of his power, Elijah preached, "Maybe you won't believe it, but I am the key to everyone of you. I'm not something of myself, I'm something of a God." Nodding, the guest speaker shouted above the crowd's applause, "Yes, sir! Yes, sir!"

When Elijah finished his address, the most famous Black Muslim walked over to the podium. Dressed in a black suit, white shirt, and skinny black tie, Muhammad Ali, tight-lipped and solemn, approached the lectern. After offering the traditional Muslim greeting—"*As-Salaam-Alaikum*"—he explained that he had rushed home from Cairo at Elijah Muhammad's request. Elijah desired his presence at the Armory so that Ali could remind all of Harlem why he had chosen the Messenger over the hypocrite. Ali told the Nation that Muslims all over the world recognized the Honorable Elijah Muhammad as a legitimate spiritual leader. Clearly, with Malcolm gone, the boxer would serve as Elijah's new spokesman.[20]

Ali delivered the goods. He said exactly what Elijah wanted him to say. Everywhere he went—Ghana, Nigeria, and Egypt—Muslims asked him the same question: "'How is the Honorable Elijah Muhammad?'" If it were not for the Honorable Elijah Muhammad, he insisted, the whole world would not know his name. He owed everything to the Messenger. Graciously, he presented Elijah with a miniature golden

mosque, a gift sent from Egypt's Supreme Council of Islam. As he raised the mini mosque in the air, Louis X, Herbert Muhammad, John Ali, and Elijah Jr.—all enemies of Malcolm—crowded around him, smiling for the cameramen.[21]

That same day, Ali's recently assigned press secretary, Leon 4X, also known as Leon Ameer, attended an FOI meeting at the Armory. A lean, diminutive man standing barely five foot four, Ameer was known as a karate expert with a quick temper. He had joined Mosque No. 7 in 1956, four years after receiving an honorable discharge as a steward in the marines. According to his FBI file, Leon was diagnosed with schizophrenia after exhibiting "a sudden episode of acutely disturbed and obviously psychotic behavior." In a sudden rage, he attacked a large man with an axe during "an argument over a bedding roll." After spending a few months in a psychiatric hospital, he returned to New York, where he was arrested on separate occasions for robbery and grand larceny. But the life of a hardened criminal dissatisfied him. He missed the marines and the feeling of camaraderie that came with serving in a military unit. When a fellow veteran convinced him to attend a meeting at the local mosque, Leon embraced the Nation's code of strict discipline and became a soldier in the Fruit of Islam. Soon, he turned his life around, teaching martial arts and eventually becoming one of Malcolm's bodyguards.[22]

After Malcolm left the Nation, though, he remained loyal to Elijah Muhammad, and John Ali gave him direct orders to keep an eye on the heavyweight champion. But when he heard the Messenger's son talk at the Armory, he began questioning his decision. Elijah Jr. spoke with a viciousness that troubled him. Malcolm was a "red, no good dog," a hypocrite who deserved to die. "If we decide to kill Malcolm," he said, "no one can help him." Consumed with rage, Elijah's son berated the New York Fruit for failing to execute him. "Malcolm should have been killed by now!" If Malcolm refused to leave the Queens home deeded to the Nation, then they would make him leave. "All you have to do is go there and clap on the walls until the walls come down and then cut the nigger's tongue out and put it in an envelope and send it to me. And I'll stamp it approved and give it to the Messenger."[23]

Leon knew what he had just heard. Everyone in the room understood the implications of the tirade. Looking back, Thomas 15X, a member of

the New York Fruit, said that when the Messenger's son spoke, he spoke on behalf of his father. "Back then, that was an *order*."[24]

LATER THAT EVENING, twenty blocks away at the Audubon Ballroom, more than six hundred people listened to Malcolm announce his latest initiative: the Organization of Afro-American Unity (OAAU), a movement inspired by his trip to Africa and the limitations of Muslim Mosque, Inc. (MMI). He had not given up on MMI, but he recognized that it lacked a clearly defined focus and that its religious name turned off too many secularists. Seeking a political platform, Malcolm courted black radicals and intellectuals to join his revolutionary program. In his opening address, he outlined the OAAU's goals: voter registration campaigns, rent strikes, business boycotts, and "an all-out war on organized crime."[25]

Malcolm's speech articulated an ambitious program that he could not deliver. Facing mounting pressures, his attention fractured under too many demands. Without his salary from the Nation, Malcolm could hardly afford to feed his family, let alone fund two fledgling organizations. Continuing an extensive travel schedule, he tried raising money and building alliances abroad, but spending so much time away undermined his ability to build the OAAU. He hoped that publicizing the death threats would give him added protection from his assassins, but it also scared away potential members from attending his meetings.

On July 2, a few days after Malcolm announced the formation of the OAAU, two women filed paternity suits against Elijah Muhammad in Los Angeles. The sex scandal made sensational headlines. In large, bold letters, the *Chicago Defender* screamed: "PATERNITY SUITS AGAINST MR. MUHAMMAD DENIED." Muhammad's former secretaries were not the only ones discrediting him. His grandson Hasan told the *Defender* that he had quit the NOI because the officials, including his relatives, exploited the members. His grandfather was nothing more than "a fake and a fraud," stealing money from the poor. He could not understand why many of his grandfather's longtime followers never received their "original names," yet "Cassius Clay was blessed to receive a Holy name." Hasan's uncle Wallace echoed his nephew's charges, claiming that the Nation's officials ordered attacks against dissidents. "The leadership in Chicago is ruthless and frantic," he said, and "they will kill you."[26]

THE TIME FOR talking was over. The blood season was beginning. A day after Muhammad's mistresses filed paternity suits, Malcolm worked from home while Betty rested at the hospital, recuperating from childbirth. Around eleven thirty p.m., he told the babysitter that he needed to move his car, possibly because he did not want assassins to think that he was home. After teaching the teenage girl how to handle a shotgun, Malcolm quietly opened the front door and peeked outside. Darting toward his car, he spotted two knife-wielding men charging at him. Before they could catch him, he leapt into the sedan, turned the key, and sped away. After circling the neighborhood, he returned home, called the police, and waited for them to arrive, shotgun in hand.[27]

The following day, Boston captain Clarence X and Springfield captain John Muhammad visited the Harlem mosque. Given full authority over the East Coast Fruit, Clarence, an arrogant, stocky man built like an "ex–middleweight boxer," offered a reward to anyone who eliminated Malcolm. While he was in New York, he met with Leon Ameer. The two knew each other well because Clarence had been assigned as Muhammad Ali's bodyguard and Leon worked as the champ's press secretary. According to Leon, Clarence revealed a .38 caliber revolver that he intended to use on Malcolm and asked Leon if he could help locate a silencer. Stunned, Ameer said that he did not know where Clarence could find one, and began contemplating whether he should warn Malcolm.[28]

But Malcolm needed no warning. He already knew that his life was in danger. For his family's sake, he needed to get away from his assassins. Only Betty and a few trusted assistants knew that he planned to attend the second Organization of African Unity Conference in Cairo, tour Africa, and return in six weeks. On July 9, when he boarded TWA Flight 700, bound for London, he felt a sense of relief that he had not experienced since he last visited Africa. Escaping abroad brought him peace—a peace that would prove hard to relinquish even after a nearly twenty-week hiatus from the troubles that followed him at home.[29]

IN THE MONTHS after Muhammad Ali's return from Africa, Elijah Muhammad forbade him from staying at the Hotel Theresa. In early July, when Ali appeared on a television show, *Ladies of the Press, New York Amsterdam News* writer Sara Slack asked him if he and Malcolm had

split. Cautiously, he explained that when the Honorable Elijah Muhammad "cuts a man off, then he's automatically cut off from all of his followers." Curious, the reporter asked if the division between Elijah and Malcolm had led him to cancel his accommodations at the Theresa. Interrupting her, Ali said, "My leader told me, uh, not my leader, but various officials said it would not be nice being in the same hotel he was in, and whatever they say goes."[30]

It was clear from Ali's statement that he no longer made his own decisions. The writers mostly asked him questions about political issues, the Nation of Islam, and the civil rights movement. When one of the writers mistakenly called him "Mr. Clay," he corrected her, reminding the panel that he had a new name. Appearing serious, Ali frequently referenced the Honorable Elijah Muhammad, just as Malcolm used to do. "Our leader teaches us that we are a nation within a nation," he maintained. Confused, the moderator asked him what that really meant. Ali explained that America did not belong to the black man. The fact that whites constantly attacked blacks proved it. When the moderator asked him if he considered himself an American first and foremost, Ali definitively answered, "No, sir. No, sir. Proud to say no. First, I'm a black man. I'm an Afro-American." When the moderator pressed him again, Ali insisted, "Well, I'm not no American. I'm a black man."

After Ali returned from Africa, reporters and businessmen learned that if they wanted to meet with him privately, they had to see Herbert Muhammad. Herbert controlled everything. Following his father's orders, he began promoting Ali as a righteous and devoted follower of the Messenger, turning *Muhammad Speaks* into a photo album of the heavyweight champion. Inside the Nation's newspaper, readers found pictures of Ali learning from Elijah, meeting Nkrumah, shaking hands with Nasser, and playing with black children. Herbert also created opportunities for the Nation to profit from Ali's likeness. For only two dollars, kids could join the Muhammad Ali International Fan Club and receive a personally autographed photo of the champ, wallet-size membership card, membership button, and newsletter.[31]

As a famous black athlete, Ali proved invaluable to the Nation of Islam. Jeremiah X recalled, "People wanted to hear what he had to say, so his visibility and prominence were of great benefit to the Nation. His voice carried throughout the world, and that was a true blessing for us."

Ali's appearances at Muslim rallies, even the possibility that he *might* appear, enticed blacks to attend the Nation's meetings. "There's no doubt," Jeremiah said, "our following increased enormously, maybe a hundred percent, after he joined the Nation. When he went to a temple, there were overflowing crowds."[32]

With Malcolm out of the picture, Ali became the Nation's most visible symbol of redemption. Like Malcolm once did, he exaggerated how the Nation's moral code transformed him, crediting Elijah Muhammad for purifying his soul. "Well, before I became a Muslim, I used to drink," he said disingenuously. "Yes, I did. The truth is the truth. And after I fought and beat somebody I didn't hardly go anywhere without two big, pretty women beside me." People would be stunned to learn how much he had changed after becoming a Muslim, he said. Being a Muslim gave him the strength to resist sinful temptations, especially with so many women throwing themselves at him. "All types of women—white women, too—make passes at me. Girls find out where I live and knock at the door at one and two in the morning. They send me their pictures and phone numbers, saying, 'Please, just telephone me.'"[33]

A few weeks after Ali returned from Africa, Herbert introduced him to Sonji Roi, a beautiful cocktail waitress who spent her evenings socializing at Chicago nightclubs. During the daytime, she answered phones for Herbert at the office of *Muhammad Speaks* and occasionally posed for pictures at his photography studio. She had lived a hard life, losing both parents before she was nine years old. When she was a teenager, Sonji became pregnant, dropped out of school, and began working to support her baby. On the night she met Ali, he asked her to marry him. Stunned at his proposal, Herbert warned him that he was making a terrible mistake. Ali did not realize that Herbert had arranged for him to meet Sonji only for a night of fun. Herbert simply wanted her to show the champ a good time. "Man, you don't marry this girl," he said. "She works at a cocktail place wearing one of those little bunny things on her behind. You don't marry no girl like this."[34]

The Louisville Sponsoring Group had reached the same conclusion. When they discovered that Ali had become involved with Sonji, they conducted their own investigation and compiled a dossier. They discovered police reports charging her with solicitation. Although the group

followed a policy of never interfering with Ali's personal life, they har-
bored deep reservations about his relationship with Sonji, doubting the
wisdom of his marrying her.[35]

But Ali did not care that she was not a Muslim. He wanted her, and
that's all that mattered. On August 14, forty-one days after they met,
Ali and Sonji wed in a private ceremony in Gary, Indiana. He made
it clear that he expected her to be a submissive wife who obeyed his
rules and the Nation's. The only reason he married her, he said later,
was "because she agreed to do everything that I wanted her to do." He
told her that she could no longer wear makeup or short skirts. She had
to quit drinking alcohol, smoking cigarettes, and eating pork. Sonji
complied, accepting the Nation's religious code. When they were alone,
Ali revealed his affectionate side, singing her love songs and blowing
her kisses. Gradually, though, friction developed between them. When
Ali explained that they could not buy a house because the Mother Ship
would arrive in three years and take them away, she asked him why,
then, did Elijah Muhammad live in a mansion? Ali objected to her
questioning him and Elijah. "Woman," he scolded her, "you're too wise.
Don't be asking them questions."[36]

As time went on, Sonji noticed that when the Muslims were around,
Ali became more controlling. "When nobody was around, he'd want
one thing from me; and then in public it was another. I couldn't under-
stand his two faces." Too often, she said later, the Muslims interfered
with their marriage. "They wanted to control his entire life." Being the
wife of the Muslim champ became an isolating experience, especially
after they began renting an apartment in Chicago to be closer to the
Nation's headquarters. When she wanted to eat at a restaurant, he took
her to the Muslims' luncheonette. When she wanted to go shopping,
they visited the Muslims' department store. When she wanted to see
her old friends, he said that she had all the friends she ever needed at
the mosque. And when she thought it would be a good idea to do in-
terviews, he reminded her that she could not speak to reporters unless
Herbert had sent them from *Muhammad Speaks*.[37]

Not even the best investigative reporters knew much about her.
When Myron Cope asked if he could interview Sonji, Ali replied that
he had to make a phone call and see "if they'll give me permission." The
following day, Ali told Cope that Sonji could not talk to him because

"they" had denied the request. "They" said it was time for Ali to quit messing around with Sonji and get back in the ring.[38]

In the six months since he last fought, Ali had hardly trained and had gained nearly thirty pounds. In mid-September, after he signed a contract for a rematch against Liston that would take place at the Boston Garden, Angelo Dundee urged him to get back to work. The trainer worried that the champ was losing interest in fighting. The problem, Dundee discerned, was that Ali knew that he would fight Sonny again, but he no longer feared him.[39]

Yet Ali still had something to prove against Liston. Most observers still believed that his last victory was a fluke or, worse, a fix. Some of his friends would not admit it publicly, but even they questioned whether he could beat Sonny again. After all, Ali didn't knock Liston out, and many people still wondered how he had won the fight after being temporarily blinded. When Sonny refused to rise from his stool, Ferdie Pacheco said, "it tarnished the victory." It seemed almost too easy, like Liston had handed him the title. "All you knew for sure somehow was that this kid had survived," Pacheco reflected. "There was some doubt."[40]

ALI DIDN'T QUITE remember it that way. In his mind, there had never been any doubt that he would defeat Sonny Liston. In Miami, when he was not training at the 5th Street Gym, he liked to replay the fight film, reliving his moment of glory, round by round, blow by blow. Studying the film, he recognized that he was too fast for Sonny. He could see that Liston had become slow and predictable, planting himself before he threw a punch. Liston could only hit a man who moved forward, but Ali dodged his punches, bouncing forward and backward and side to side. The film did not lie: Liston had become a shell of himself, "a shadow on the wall—bleeding, tired, suddenly aged, an imposter."[41]

When Ali was not training, Myron Cope followed him around Miami. Since he last wrote a profile of him in 1962, Cope learned, the boxer's innocence had faded as he was hardened over time by the pressures of fame and politics. Two years after their first meeting, the "Muslim champ" sounded more like an evangelical preacher at a tent meeting than a boxer, "convinced he is a beacon of righteousness in a wicked world." Looking back on his time with the young contender in 1962,

Cope realized that even then, before any reporter knew that he had been attending the Nation's meetings, the boxer hid a part of himself. At that time, Cassius Clay had schooled the writer about the dangers of pork without explaining that his dietary views came directly from the Muslims. "Poke ninety percent maggots," he had told Cope.[42]

Upon reflection, Cope realized that the boxer had a "history of calculated deceptions," prompting sportswriters to wonder, who is the real Muhammad Ali? Harold Kaese of the *Boston Globe* asked, "Is Clay the fellow who boasts like a Viking when he has an audience, hurls venomous insults at Sonny Liston and Floyd Patterson, and makes listeners giggle with his silly little rhymes?" Or, Kaese pondered, is he "the fellow who when alone with a few friends is quiet, serious, calculating, modest, and eminently sane?" Observing Ali, one could hardly separate the man from the myth, the boxer from the actor, because he deliberately cultivated a dual identity.[43]

Although he displayed no genuine animosity toward individual whites, many writers painted him as a villainous automaton, filled with hatred. Ali's ties to the Nation, Jimmy Cannon wrote, were "the dirtiest in American sports since the Nazis were shilling for Max Schmeling as a representative of their vile theories of blood." Yet Ali was not the naive racist that Cannon, made him out to be. His feelings toward whites were more complicated. He told Cope that whites who sacrificed their lives "for colored people" were not really devils. "It's not the color that makes you a devil," he said, "just the deeds that you do."[44]

Many white writers who had known him before he joined the Nation refused to believe that he wholly accepted the Black Muslims' ideology. He may have preached separatism, but he did not articulate a sophisticated view beyond that basic principle. "People seem[ed] to believe this man was a threat to America's values because of his affiliation with the Muslims, which was seen as a racist organization," George Plimpton observed. "What they didn't seem to realize is that Ali himself wasn't going around calling whites 'devils.' He seemed to have a mind of his own on that matter."[45]

Jerry Izenberg suggested that Ali performed for everyone, including the Black Muslims. "He'd be talking with you about something, and one of the Muslims would come into the room and the conversation would change completely." Ali would do anything to please Elijah

Muhammad and gain the approval of the Muslim officials around him. "He wanted desperately to be taken seriously, to be respected, and told that he was special."[46]

Ali sounded sincere when he talked about Malcolm X. Probing for answers about their relationship, Cope asked Ali about their time together in Miami on the eve of the Liston fight. Irritated, Ali snapped, "I didn't invite him down here. He came down here on his own. He's nothing now." Under Elijah's trance, Ali assaulted Malcolm's character. Taking the well-worn Muslim line, Ali said, "Our teacher took him off the streets, a jailbird, a hoodlum, and it was Elijah Muhammad's teachings that made him able to go on any TV. But he failed. Who is he gonna represent now?" Listening to him fume, there was no doubt that Ali had buried Malcolm somewhere in Africa.[47]

After Ali was called back from Africa, he adopted a new role as the noble warrior, a Muslim mercenary defending Allah's Messenger. Whenever reporters asked him about Malcolm, Ali erupted into a scornful harangue against "that chief hypocrite." Out of the war between Elijah and Malcolm emerged the "ugly period" of Ali's life, a viciousness aimed at anyone who opposed the Honorable Elijah Muhammad. In his zealousness, Ali believed that Malcolm had crossed "The Messenger of all mighty God." And that, he prophesied, would prove a grave mistake. "Mr. Muhammad will destroy him through Allah. You just don't buck Mr. Muhammad and get away with it."[48]

BY THE TIME he arrived in Boston, Muhammad Ali looked like a new man. The champ had shed the excess weight around his stomach and looked stronger, broader, and more toned. His biceps measured seventeen inches around and his thighs twenty-seven inches, both two inches larger than before the Miami fight, though his waist remained the same size, a svelte thirty-four inches. He'd never felt better. Standing in front of a department store mirror, admiring his physique, he declared, "I'm so beautiful I should be chiseled in gold. Look at that build. It's pretty. I mean, it's ready to dance. Right now!"[49]

On Thursday, November 12, for more than an hour, he danced around the ring, jumped rope, and hit the speed bag at the Boston Arena annex. When he finished working out, he showered while Clarence X and a few other large men abruptly ordered his fans to leave. A few minutes

later, the champ reappeared for his daily news conference. Ali sat on the wooden stands, flanked by two court jesters, Bundini Brown and Lincoln Perry, better known as "Stepin Fetchit," the first black movie star of the 1920s and 1930s. No one really knows how Fetchit met the champ, but his presence in Ali's camp puzzled reporters. Once billed as "the World's Laziest Man," the tall, lanky comic had created a minstrel caricature based on the worst stereotypes of black men as lazy, shiftless, and ignorant. Writers could not comprehend how Ali, the embodiment of racial pride, could ever befriend an actor who denigrated blacks with his performances. "It would be difficult to find a more incongruous situation than the Clay-Fetchit association," one writer suggested. "The world's perhaps most famous and most arrogant Negro, Cassius Clay, has among his entourage the Negro who probably has done more than any man to label his race with all things Clay isn't."[50]

Ali didn't see any problem having Fetchit around him. In some ways, he could relate to the aging actor. For years, most Americans perceived "Lincoln Perry and Stepin Fetchit the character as one and the same," much the way people viewed Muhammad Ali and the Louisville Lip, an outrageous, loudmouthed character. Sportswriters and biographers have failed to recognize that Ali created the Louisville Lip not just for show business but also to hide his emerging political defiance. Experts in subterfuge, both Ali and Fetchit had mastered the game of "putting on ole massa," a shrewd masking tactic employed by slaves. In this tradition, Ali and Fetchit embodied the old folk tune sung by plantation slaves: "Got one mind for the white folks to see; 'nother for what I know is me."[51]

Fetchit understood that Ali's shrewdness confused people, but that was the way the champ had designed it. "People don't understand the champ, but one of these days he'll be one of the country's greatest heroes," he predicted. "He's like one of those plays where a man is the villain in the first act and then turns out to be the hero in the last act. That's the way it'll be with the champ. And that's the way he wants it, because it's better for the box office for people to misunderstand him than to understand him."[52]

The following evening, three days before the fight, Ali stretched out on his bed at the Sherry Biltmore Hotel while he watched *Little Caesar* on a sixteen-millimeter projector. After a five-mile run earlier that morning, he'd spent the day resting and visiting with friends in

his sixth-floor suite. His brother Rahman, Captain Sam, and Bundini served his every need.

Suddenly, around six fifty, he became nauseous. Ali streaked toward the bathroom and began vomiting.[53]

"Oh, something is awful wrong," he groaned. "You better do something."

"I'll call a doctor so the press won't find out!" Rahman said.

"Damn the press! Get me to a hospital, man. I'm real sick."

Within minutes, paramedics placed Ali on a stretcher and rushed him to the emergency room. When the ambulance reached the hospital, a *Boston Herald* photographer attempted to snap a few pictures, but Captain Clarence and the Fruit ran him off. "Keep away!" Louis X shouted. Then the minister gave his lieutenants strict orders: "Nobody goes through these doors. Somebody will get hurt if they try."[54]

At the hospital, doctors discovered that Ali had "a swelling the size of an egg" in his right bowel—in medical terms, an incarcerated hernia. Had Ali waited any longer to call an ambulance, the hernia could have killed him. After emergency surgery, the surgeon announced that Ali would be fine, but he would not be able to box for several months, delaying the fight. The Black Muslims suspected foul play, theorizing that someone had poisoned the champ. Patrolling the fourth floor, "the X boys"—Leon, Sam, Louis, Otis, and Clarence—guarded his recovery room. Before the police arrived, Clarence stood on a chair, giving orders. Watching the brooding Captain, Jimmy Cannon observed, "There wasn't any doubt who was in charge."[55]

Devastated, Sonny Liston mixed a screwdriver when he heard the news. He really believed that he was in the best shape of his life. All those hours of training now meant nothing. He would have to wait months until Ali could fight, which meant that he would have to start training all over again. He had no idea if he would be able to train with the same focus and the same ferocity that he had built up on the eve of the fight. All he could do now was shake his head, muttering to himself, "That damned fool. That damned fool." Then he took a long drink.[56]

ON NOVEMBER 24, four days before Ali left the Boston City Hospital, Malcolm X returned to New York after spending nearly five months abroad. During his second tour of Africa, he'd met with several heads

of state, dozens of ministers, and scores of cabinet members. Gradually, though, the trip had worn him down. Although African leaders welcomed him "with open minds, open hearts, and open doors," he must have realized that some doors closed tightly when he left. While African leaders listened politely to his proposals, he learned that most could not risk losing American foreign aid by charging the United States with international crimes. In Ghana, his old friends Julian Mayfield, Leslie Lacy, and Maya Angelou could see his fears weighing on him. Suspicious and irritable, he was certain that someone was following him. He admitted that he had extended his trip abroad because there were men in Harlem waiting for him, willing to take his life "for a dime."[57]

Malcolm knew that his time was up. Every day for nearly three months, he awoke wondering if this was the day that he would die. But dying did not scare him nearly as much as failing to help his people. He had so much work to do that hardly a night passed that he slept more than four hours. Late one evening in December, Malcolm called Claude Lewis, a reporter at the *New York Post*. Lewis could tell that something was wrong. Malcolm spoke with an urgency to "get something 'on the record'" before it was too late. Shortly thereafter, they met at a crowded Harlem coffee shop on 135th Street. Malcolm insisted that they meet in public. Sitting in a booth with Malcolm's bodyguard, Lewis asked a range of questions about his image, his new organization, his evolving politics, and the threats on his life.[58]

Listening to the fragile minister, Lewis sensed his vulnerability, that at any moment he might crack. The reporter waited to hear the old Malcolm, the fiery minister, bursting with rage and wrath. But the flame had burned out. The Malcolm he met that day looked exhausted and unraveled, beset with trepidation. Wondering how he would survive, Lewis asked about his future. Where was he headed? "I have no idea," he repeated, "I have no idea." All he knew was that he was "for the freedom of the 22 million Afro-Americans by *any means necessary*." In the past, Malcolm had spoken in absolutes. Everything was black and white. Now, he lived in a world of grays. He remained open to anything that would bring freedom to black Americans. "I'm headed in any direction that will bring us some immediate results."

By any means necessary. Those words were not just a slogan or an ideology. They conveyed the mentality of a man pushed to the edge,

desperate for survival. "Whatever I say, I'm justified," he told Lewis. "If I say the Negroes should get out of here right tomorrow and go to war, I'm *justified*. Really! It might sound *extreme*, but you can't say it's not *justified*." Speaking like a soldier on the front lines, he insisted, "If I say right now that we should go down and shoot fifteen Ku Klux Klansmen in the morning, you may say well that's insane, but you can't say I'm not justified."

Near the end of their interview, Malcolm talked about death. "I'll never get old," he said. Lewis asked him why. "Well," he explained, "I'll tell you what I mean and why I say that. When I say 'by any means necessary,' I mean it with all my heart, and my mind, and my soul." A black man, he said, should be willing to sacrifice his own life for freedom. And "he should also be willing to take the life of those who want to take his. It's reciprocal. When you really think like that, you don't have long to live."

Chapter Seventeen

WORTHY OF DEATH

The price of freedom is death.
—MALCOLM X

M
alcolm X, Elijah Muhammad foretold, would not survive Allah's wrath. In his *Muhammad Speaks* column, he warned his former minister, "Allah is sufficient as a helper. You will not be able to help yourself pretty soon." His acolytes interpreted these prophetic words as a directive. For months, since the spring of 1964, vicious men, some with criminal records, seethed, daring Malcolm to return from Africa. Condemning Malcolm as a gutless coward, his former protégé Louis X called him an "international hobo" too scared "to face the music." During Malcolm's time abroad, the Nation's avengers threatened retribution if he ever set foot in America again. At the Richmond, Virginia, mosque, Minister Nicholas condemned him: "Malcolm X really should be killed for teaching against Elijah Muhammad."[1]

Inside the pages of *Muhammad Speaks*, NOI officials published a series of cryptic articles predicting Malcolm's death. In a five-page harangue, Louis pilloried his old mentor, denouncing him as a heretic. The Boston minister also praised Muhammad Ali for resisting Malcolm's advances. True believers like Ali would never fall for Malcolm's deceptions. "Only those who wish to be led to hell, or to their doom, will follow Malcolm," he wrote. "The die is set, and Malcolm shall not escape, especially after such evil, foolish talk about his benefactor. . . . Such a man as Malcolm is worthy of death."[2]

Although there is no evidence that Elijah Muhammad sent his disciples a direct order to assassinate Malcolm, in this climate no such command was necessary. The vengeful language espoused at Muslim meetings and in the pages of *Muhammad Speaks* conveyed a clear mandate: Allah's Messenger blessed those who struck back against the most dangerous hypocrites.

The rhetoric espoused by Chicago officials contaminated the entire Nation. Muhammad Ali was convinced by their claims that Malcolm fabricated vicious lies about Elijah's infidelities. And no man, Ali declared, could slander the Messenger and get away with it: "Malcolm X and anybody else who attacks or talks about attacking Elijah Muhammad will die."[3]

CAPTAIN CLARENCE COULD smell a rat. He was not certain, but he suspected that Leon Ameer, Ali's press secretary, had been talking to Malcolm, divulging the Nation's secrets and maybe even Clarence's plot to kill the despised minister. Ameer knew that any Muslim who talked to Malcolm risked his life. He had heard the Messenger say so himself. According to Ameer, in September, Muhammad called a secret meeting, ordering about two hundred men from the Fruit to report to Chicago. For hours, Muhammad berated the sect's defectors. Anyone who left the Nation should be treated as a hypocrite, he announced. And all hypocrites should be "taken care of, either by beatings or killings, but it [must] be done carefully when there were no witnesses." As for Malcolm, "the greatest hypocrite," Muhammad demanded that the Fruit stop him "at all costs."[4]

Ameer was convinced that the Fruit would go to any length to fulfill the Messenger's order. Shaken, he left the meeting certain that Malcolm was as good as dead. Since late July, when Clarence approached him about locating a silencer, he'd begun thinking about how he might leave the Nation. He would need protection, but not even Malcolm could offer that. Malcolm could hardly protect himself.

In October, while Ali trained in Boston, the heavyweight champion complained to Ameer that the Muslims required "numerous donations." Usually, members paid monthly dues to their local mosque. In his case, he would have donated to the Miami mosque, but the Nation's officials demanded that he send all contributions directly to Chicago.

No one knows exactly how much money Ali funneled to the Nation's headquarters, but it was enough for him to grumble about it to Ameer.

Listening to Ali's complaints, Ameer thought that he might be able to persuade him to quit the Nation. The boxer "was foolish" for letting the Black Muslims exploit him, he said, and someday the Muslims would jettison him when he was no longer valuable to Muhammad. Yet Ameer's arguments failed to convince Ali. Malcolm had already told him the same thing, after all. "He's just a boy," Malcolm later said. "He doesn't know what he's doing. He's being used."[5]

Ameer should have kept quiet. Around one p.m. on Christmas Day, he received a phone call in his room at the Sherry Biltmore Hotel in Boston. He was told that four newsmen wanted to talk to him about Ali's recovery. When one of the reporters asked if they could come up to his room, Ameer became suspicious and said that he would meet them in the lobby. Stepping out of the elevator, he immediately recognized Clarence X. Puzzled, he asked the Boston captain if he had seen a group of reporters, but before Clarence could answer, a man struck him from behind. Clarence and his three henchmen kicked Leon until an off-duty detective came to his rescue.[6]

Later that night, after he received stitches above his left eye and returned to his hotel room, a group of men posing as investigators knocked on his door. When he opened it, they rushed him, swinging fists and clubs. Leon covered his face while they pummeled and kicked him, shattering his eardrum, breaking his ribs, and fracturing his skull. The following morning, a chambermaid screamed when she found him lying nearly lifeless in a tub splattered with blood.[7]

Ameer survived. Recovering from a coma, he spent fifteen days in the hospital. On January 9, 1965, at a press conference in Harlem, he told reporters that he feared assassins would come after him again and that Ali's life was in jeopardy too. Ali would not admit it, but he had expressed "grave doubts about the integrity of certain powerful Muslims." He knew all too well what could happen to him if he so much as thought about leaving the Nation.[8]

Siding with Malcolm, Ameer began meeting with reporters, publicizing the violent threats the Nation made against him. In an interview with the *Amsterdam News*, he divulged Chicago's order to beat and kill any member who joined Malcolm. Clarence X and the Muslims who

attacked him were convinced that he was trying to drive a wedge between Ali and Elijah. And they were certain that only a man working for Malcolm would have told Ali to quit the Nation.[9]

Three days after Ameer's press conference, on January 12, Raymond Sharrieff and other high-ranking officials attended the annual Fruit of Islam banquet, an evening of dinner, music, dancing, and a guest appearance from the heavyweight champion. The *Amsterdam News* reported that more than two thousand members from the East Coast packed the Audubon Ballroom, the same location where Malcolm held his weekly meetings. Located between Broadway and St. Nicholas Avenue on the south side of West 166th Street, the two-story building served as a dance hall and lodge for local organizations. What no one suspected, however, was that the Fruit's party at the Audubon was just a ruse for planning an attack on Malcolm. Over the next month, members from the Fruit would hold several meetings at the Audubon in which they plotted Malcolm's murder. On this night, though, Ali enraptured the angry young men seeking vengeance against hypocrites, denouncing Malcolm as jealous and attention-starved. "Malcolm believed the white press, which referred to him as the 'number two man' and became disillusioned," he said, sounding more and more like the Nation's ministers. Ali did not know it, but he had become a puppet in the assassination plot against Malcolm.[10]

The following day, he became agitated when Robert Lipsyte asked about his relationship with Ameer. Feigning ignorance, he replied, "Ahmeer? Little fellow? I think I remember a little fellow who hung around camp, a little fellow who liked to go downstairs and get me papers." Scribbling his answers in a notepad, Lipsyte encouraged Ali to keep talking. "Now I hear he's telling lies, saying he was my press secretary."[11]

Ali shrugged, but when Lipsyte persisted, the champ burst into a tirade. "Any fool Negro got the nerve to buck us, you want to make him a star. Jim Brown said something about the Muslims and they made him a movie star." The truth, Ali ranted, was that Ameer cheated on his wife with a young girl and stole money from the Nation. Ameer was nothing but a hypocrite. "He got what he deserved."

Stunned, Lipsyte had never heard Ali speak so cruelly. When the *New York Times* columnist inquired if Ameer should really fear for his life, Ali snapped, revealing the depths of his disgust for Ameer—and

Malcolm. "They think everyone out to kill them because they know they deserve to be killed for what they did."

TALMADGE X HAD put his guns away. During the months Malcolm traveled abroad, he had not heard from any of the New Jersey men who plotted against Malcolm. He figured that maybe his partners had cooled to the idea of killing the minister. "Nothing was happening," he recalled. "So I thought that maybe things were going to get better, man." But when Malcolm returned home, the cadre began meeting again. Sometimes they drove around Paterson, planning the perfect crime. Other times they canvassed New York, looking for Malcolm outside the Audubon. One evening they drove out to his home in Queens, planning an ambush, but when armed guards appeared they sped away.[12]

The New Jersey hit men were not the only ones stalking Malcolm. Around eleven fifteen p.m. on Friday, January 22, three Muslims rushed toward him when he stepped outside his front door. He quickly slammed the door, locked it, and called the police. By the time officers arrived, his attackers had disappeared. Betty lived in fear of his assassins knocking on the door at any moment. Late at night, she watched Malcolm stand near the front window holding a double-clip automatic carbine rifle, his eyes scanning the shadows for the slightest movement. While he protected their home, Betty cried herself to sleep, fearing that her worst nightmare would come true by the time she awoke.[13]

Every time Malcolm left the house, she agonized that he would not return. On January 28 he flew to Los Angeles to meet with attorney Gladys Towles Root and the two secretaries involved in the paternity suit against Elijah Muhammad. His cousin Hakim Jamal and his friend Edmund Bradley arrived at the gate about an hour before his plane was scheduled to land. While they waited for TWA Flight 9, Jamal noticed a heavyset black man with a familiar face. At first, Jamal was certain that he had seen the man at the Nation's meetings, but when the stranger bought a pack of cigarettes he began doubting whether he was truly a Muslim. Later, after Malcolm checked into the Statler Hilton Hotel, Jamal saw the man from the airport again. Walking through the lobby, Malcolm noticed Minister John Shabazz, Captain Edward, and a half dozen other men from Mosque No. 27. Spotting Malcolm, no one from the Fruit moved. "They absolutely froze," Jamal recalled. When they

hesitated, Malcolm and his hosts slipped out of the hotel and drove away.[14]

How could the Fruit have known when Malcolm would be in Los Angeles and where he was staying? "An official must be in town—someone from Chicago," Malcolm surmised. "There were a lot them [in the lobby]. . . . I wonder if it could be Raymond [Sharrieff] or John Ali?" When he mentioned John's name, Jamal immediately realized that he was "the brother at the airport—the cat who was buying the cigarettes."[15]

Malcolm was right; John Ali was in town. But there was no way, he thought, that Ali and the Black Muslims had the resources to track him from New York to Los Angeles. He knew their operations too well. Besides his wife, cousin, two aides, the two secretaries, and their attorney, no one knew about his flight to Los Angeles. Only the FBI could have known that he would be in California—and they did. About two weeks earlier, an informant had notified special agents that Malcolm planned to visit Los Angeles. Somehow that information fell into the hands of John Ali.[16]

It was Malcolm's belief that John Ali had turned FBI informant. Nor was he the only one. Journalist Louis Lomax also suspected that Ali was working for the FBI. In 1963, when he published *When the Word Is Given*, a study of the rise of the Nation of Islam, Lomax referred to Ali as "a former FBI agent." According to FBI documents, Lomax's book threatened the anonymity of a highly placed informant inside the Nation. In a series of memos, FBI officials considered telling Lomax about Ali's "true status," though it's unclear if the Bureau ever approached Lomax about Ali. Nonetheless, Malcolm was convinced that the Muslims had a chain of informants working with the FBI and that the Bureau's agents gave the Black Muslims his itinerary.[17]

After his meeting with Gladys Root and the two secretaries, Malcolm returned to the Statler Hilton. Surrounded by the Fruit's soldiers, he darted through the lobby, their angry stares piercing his body like daggers. He safely made it to his suite, but he hardly slept. His phone rang constantly throughout the night. One caller in particular rattled him. "You are dead," an unfamiliar voice whispered. "You are a dead nigger."[18]

Malcolm dreaded leaving the hotel in the morning, knowing that the Fruit was camped outside. Holed up in his room, he waited for

sunrise like a prisoner on death row. Around nine thirty a.m. Edmund Bradley arrived to take him to the airport. Driving down the Hollywood Freeway, two cars chased them. Accelerating to seventy miles per hour, Bradley zigzagged through traffic, shaking one of the pursuing vehicles. When the other car inched closer, Malcolm reached into the backseat and pulled out an old walking cane. Aiming it like a rifle, he pointed the cane out the window, scaring the other driver enough to hit the brakes, allowing Bradley to race away.[19]

Eventually, after the Los Angeles police intercepted two more Muslim men at the airport, Malcolm boarded TWA Flight 26 for Chicago. For three days, the Chicago police guarded him. Somehow, he orchestrated a surreptitious meeting with Wallace Muhammad. Malcolm told Elijah's son that he had also met with the Illinois attorney general's office, offering his testimony in a case involving a Black Muslim prisoner who was suing the state for denying him the right to practice Islam behind bars. In exchange for protection, Malcolm had said that he would testify that the Nation of Islam was not a legitimate religious group and therefore Black Muslim ministers should not receive access to state prisons. More importantly, if he testified, he could cost the Nation its tax-exempt status and, potentially, millions of dollars.[20]

On Saturday, January 30, Malcolm taped a television interview with *Chicago Sun-Times* columnist and popular television personality Irv Kupcinet. Noticing that he had arrived under heavy police detail and with personal bodyguards, Kupcinet asked if his life was in danger. "*They* are trying to kill me," Malcolm said. "Who?" the writer asked. "You know who," he answered vaguely.[21]

After the interview, he left the television studio in an unmarked police car with two detectives and two state attorneys. Driving toward his hotel, a van swerved in front of them, cutting off the police car. About a dozen Muslims swarmed them. Malcolm must have thought that this was it. There was no way two policeman could protect him from this mob. They were clearly outnumbered until six more officers who had tailed behind them rushed to their rescue. Later, when the police escorted him to his hotel room, Malcolm recognized about fifteen Black Muslims loitering in the lobby. He told a detective, "It's only going to be a matter of time before they catch up with me."[22]

THE TIME HAD come for Malcolm to head south and join forces with grassroots civil rights activists. On Thursday, February 4, a day after he lectured at the Tuskegee Institute, he traveled to Selma, Alabama, where Martin Luther King and the Southern Christian Leadership Conference had organized a voting rights campaign. Facing a court injunction against demonstrations and relentless harassment from police, King led a march, landing himself in jail with more than seven hundred other protestors.[23]

While King sat behind bars, student activists from the Student Nonviolent Coordinating Committee invited Malcolm to join a rally at the Brown Chapel American Methodist Episcopal Church. From the Christian pulpit, he exhorted the audience "to use whatever means are necessary to gain the vote." He praised King's commitment to peace, but he reminded the congregation that he did not believe in nonviolence. "The white man should thank God that Dr. King is holding his people in check, because there are other ways to obtain their ends." When he finished speaking, he visited with King's wife, Coretta. He regretted that he did not visit Martin in jail, but he wanted her to know that he came to Selma to help him. "If the white people realize what the alternative is," he said, "perhaps they will be more willing to hear Dr. King."[24]

A day after returning home from Alabama, he flew to London for the first Congress of the Council of African Organizations. Three days later, on February 9, he traveled to Paris, but when he stepped off the plane customs agents detained him. The ministry of the interior claimed that he threatened to disturb "the public order," and therefore his presence was "undesirable in France." Malcolm could not understand why he was being sent back to London. Three months earlier, he had been welcomed in France. What had changed? Some writers have suggested that the French had learned that the CIA intended to kill Malcolm, and the government "didn't want his blood spilled on its soil." Although there is no substantiated evidence supporting this theory, the episode in Paris made Malcolm reconsider who it was that truly wanted him dead.[25]

MALCOLM COULD NO longer rest comfortably at home. On February 13, hours after he returned to the United States, he took a sleeping pill and dozed off. At two forty-five a.m. he woke to a startling

sound: *Whoom!* A Molotov cocktail smashed through his living room window, torching the floor and the furniture. *Whoom!* A second fire-bomb shattered another window, scattering glass everywhere. Malcolm shook Betty awake, leapt from the bed, and darted across the hallway to grab his four daughters from their smoking bedrooms. Blinded by the smoke, Betty winced as she stumbled into the hallway. *Bam!* Another firebomb bounced off the back door, landing in the frosty yard, where it died. Rushing the screaming children and Betty through the kitchen, Malcolm swung open the back door and yelled at Betty, "Stay here!"[26]

Frightened, she and the children shivered outside, watching the brick bungalow burn. Malcolm hurried back into the five-room house to re-trieve a few belongings, some coats, and a .25 caliber pistol. Quickly, he reemerged, coughing, in a singed topcoat. Five minutes later, the Queens fire department arrived, sirens blaring. Incensed, he paced bare-foot, holding the gun at his side, while firefighters extinguished the flames. He could not believe that the Muslims would bomb a house containing four little girls, ages seven months to six years. His assassins had sent a clear message. They would kill him by any means necessary, even if it meant murdering his wife and children. Malcolm increasingly sensed his murder was inescapable. "I won't burn to death," he said to the fire inspector. "I'll probably be shot to death in the street one day. Or maybe while I'm speaking."[27]

The following day, the press reported that the fire department had found a whiskey bottle filled with gasoline on his daughters' dresser. Harlem minister James 3X suggested that Malcolm planted the jug on his own, staging the fire for publicity. Why, James asked, would the Muslims torch a house that they owned? "He is obsessed with the idea that we're after him," he told the *New York Daily News*. Later, Malcolm secretly met with a fireman who said that he had seen "a man wearing a police uniform" walk into the house carrying the jug. He had no doubt that someone was trying to frame him.[28]

In the days after the bombing, the Black Muslims dismissed claims that they were trying to kill Malcolm. Muhammad Ali joined the cam-paign, discrediting the minister on the Irv Kupcinet show. Malcolm was no better than a criminal, he charged, "a jail bird who could neither read nor write until Muhammad educated him." No one should trust anything Malcolm said, he maintained.[29]

Shortly thereafter, in the Hotel Theresa lobby, Ali ran into Betty. Scolding him, she said, "You see what you're doing to my husband, don't you?" Raising his hands in the air, Ali pleaded innocence, "I haven't done anything. I'm not doing anything to him." Yet Ali was not innocent. He had joined the chorus of violent ringleaders who raged about punishing Malcolm. As the most visible figure in the Nation, his malicious attacks echoed throughout the country, further convincing Elijah's followers that they had to silence Malcolm. Without throwing a punch or raising a hand, Ali managed to hound the man he had once called his brother.[30]

Under siege, Malcolm threw a bomb of his own. On Monday evening, February 15, he held a meeting at the Audubon Ballroom. More than five hundred people gathered to hear him talk about his political agenda. Instead, he revealed another secret of Elijah Muhammad's, one that threatened to ruin his reputation as a defender of black citizens. In December 1960, Elijah had dispatched him to Atlanta along with Minister Jeremiah X to negotiate an agreement with the Ku Klux Klan. At the time, Muhammad had wanted to purchase farmland in the South, but he'd needed assurances that if the Nation organized there, the Klan would let them live peacefully. As Muhammad's emissary, Malcolm had made it clear that the Nation and the Klan both wanted the same thing: complete separation between blacks and whites. Malcolm regretted meeting with the Klansmen, he said, but the public had to know why it was that Muhammad never criticized or challenged the white supremacists.[31]

It was a risky revelation, but no more so than the insufficient security measures that he'd imposed. Earlier, Malcolm had instructed his security to cease frisking people who attended his rallies. He realized that he could not build a movement if people were too scared to attend his meetings. His lieutenants argued that he was risking his life, but he overruled them. "We don't want people feeling uneasy," he said. "We must create an image that makes people feel at home."[32]

During his speech, a commotion between two men in the audience drew Malcolm's security away from the rostrum, leaving him vulnerable to an attack. "Get your hand out of my pocket!" a man shouted. "Just sit down and be cool," Malcolm implored the brothers. When a young man wearing a blue suit, white shirt, and red bow tie got up and

started walking down the middle aisle, Gene Roberts, one of Malcolm's chief security guards, approached the stranger until the man ducked into a second-row seat. Everything seemed fine, so Malcolm continued speaking, but the incident made Roberts nervous. Certain that he had witnessed "a dry run on Malcolm's life," he went home and wrote a description of the events. The details were essential if his real supervisors were going to do anything to protect Malcolm.[33]

In 1964, officials from the NYPD's intelligence agency, the Bureau of Special Services (BOSS), had directed Roberts, a twenty-five-year-old detective, to infiltrate Malcolm's organization and get as close to the minister as possible. Gradually, he gained Malcolm's confidence and became one of his most trusted bodyguards. As soon as he thought that he saw the rehearsal of Malcolm's murder, he called his superiors. In response to the growing threats against Malcolm, the police offered the minister twenty-four-hour protection, but he turned it down, insisting that his men were security enough.[34]

But Malcolm never had enough security. For more than a year, the Black Muslims had stalked him, following his every move. In his private moments, he could not help replaying all the times that they had tried to kill him. Morbidly, he imagined how his life would end. He had dodged death too often to live much longer. When a friend called him to meet the following Tuesday, Malcolm somberly replied, "I'll be *dead* by Tuesday."[35]

ON FRIDAY, FEBRUARY 19, Malcolm met with *Life* magazine photographer Gordon Parks. The photographer asked Malcolm if he really believed that his life was in danger. "It's as true as we are standing here," he answered. "They've tried it twice in the last two weeks." Perhaps, Parks suggested, the police would protect him. "Brother," Malcolm chuckled, "nobody can protect you from a Muslim but a Muslim—or someone trained in Muslim tactics. I know. I invented many of those tactics." Did Malcolm have any protection? He laughed again. "Oh, there are hunters and there are those who hunt the hunters. But the odds are certainly with those who are most skilled at the game."[36]

That same afternoon, John Ali checked into the Americana Hotel in Midtown Manhattan. In recent weeks, the official from Chicago had demonstrated an uncanny ability for being in the same city as Malcolm.

The following evening in Harlem, Talmadge X and his accomplices attended a dance at the Audubon Ballroom, inspecting the windows and exits one last time. According to one witness, later that night, Talmadge met with Ali, finalizing their plans. Everything was set. They were ready to kill for the Messenger.[37]

Two blocks away from the Americana, Malcolm checked into a room on the twelfth floor of the Hilton Hotel at Rockefeller Center. Soon, a group of black men began asking the bellmen about Malcolm, probing for his room number. Someone notified the head of security, a former policeman who knew that Malcolm had received numerous death threats. After escorting the men out of the hotel, the security chief added extra protection on the twelfth floor. The next morning, February 21, at eight a.m., Malcolm's phone rang. An unfamiliar voice—a voice that sounded like it belonged to a white man—said, "Wake up, brother."[38]

Before he could even think of a response the caller hung up. Hardly a moment passed when he was not reminded that someone wanted him dead. And yet, despite the constant danger, he called Betty about an hour later, inviting her and the children to his afternoon rally at the Audubon Ballroom. Initially, he had told her that it was unsafe for her to attend his public meetings. For some reason, this time he changed his mind.[39]

That morning, Talmadge X and the brothers from New Jersey left Paterson in a blue Cadillac. Driving across the George Washington Bridge, they reviewed their assignments. After parking a few blocks away from the Audubon, the men scouted the building's perimeter. They confidently strode past Malcolm's security, concealing their weapons under long overcoats. They knew that no one would frisk them since Malcolm had called off body searches at previous meetings. What they could not have known was that Malcolm had also directed his security to arrive unarmed, though at least one man disobeyed him: his bodyguard, Reuben Francis.[40]

The New Jersey group drifted into the second-floor ballroom unmolested. Arriving earlier than most guests, the five men made sure that they found seats near the stage. With a .45 tucked into his pants, Talmadge sat in the front row next to Leon, who carried a Luger beneath his coat. Behind them sat William, hiding a shotgun, and Ben,

the Newark secretary. Wilbur, the getaway driver, sat somewhere in the middle of the hall's four hundred folding chairs.[41]

At one o'clock, around the same time the armed men headed for the Audubon, Malcolm drove his blue Oldsmobile uptown to Harlem, parking it at the southeast corner of Broadway and West 146th Street, twenty blocks away from the ballroom. He walked alone for a few blocks, perhaps, an aide suggested later, so that if his assassins tried to kill him no one else would be harmed. Standing at a corner near a movie theater, he waited for a bus when a white Cadillac with New Jersey plates slowly pulled up beside him. Malcolm did not recognize the driver waving at him. Cautiously, he peered into the backseat and noticed one of his security guards, Charles X. Grinning with relief, Malcolm entered the backseat next to Charles, who then introduced him to his friends sitting up front.[42]

Around two o'clock, Malcolm arrived at the Audubon. As he approached the entrance, he passed a single police officer, patrolman Thomas Hoy. Typically, four or five officers guarded the entrance, but someone from Malcolm's camp, supposedly acting on the minister's authority, asked the duty officer to reduce the police presence. Two uniformed officers took positions inside the Rose Ballroom, adjacent to the main hall. Curiously, the police had discreetly assigned another twenty officers across the street at the Columbia-Presbyterian Medical Center. When Malcolm's aide, Charles Kenyatta, arrived at the Audubon, he could not understand why people were not being searched. Reuben Francis insisted that he was just following Malcolm's orders. "That's bullshit!" Charles exclaimed. "You know he don't know what he sayin' or doin'. Y'all know better."[43]

Malcolm slowly climbed the stairs up to the main ballroom, taking long, heavy steps. By the time he reached the second floor, he looked exhausted, "harried," an OAAU member recalled, "not fearful . . . but just [like] somebody who had a lot on their mind." Backstage, Malcolm sank into a metal folding chair and rested his elbow on a counter in front of an old vanity mirror. From the anteroom, he could hear the noisy crowd filling the ballroom. When he learned that the guest speakers had not arrived and that no one had printed his official program, he snapped at his assistants, "Get out! Everybody! Get out!"[44]

Restless, he bounded from the chair and began pacing, occasionally peeking out at the audience. "He was more tense than I'd ever seen him," Benjamin 2X remembered. Without an official platform or a guest speaker, he sent Benjamin to give the introduction. "Make it plain," Malcolm instructed. A few moments later, he apologized to the aides who had returned to the green room. Anxious, he admitted, "I don't feel right about this meeting. I feel that I should not be here. Something is wrong, brothers."[45]

After improvising for more than twenty minutes, around three o'clock, Benjamin brought Malcolm on stage. Wearing a dark brown suit and a solemn expression, Malcolm stood behind the plywood lectern, a few feet away from an old white grand piano, a drum set, and a row of folding chairs. For more than a minute the audience gave him a standing ovation. Right before he began, Gene Roberts retreated from his position near the stage and headed toward the back of the ballroom, leaving only two bodyguards standing in front of the rostrum. As the crowd continued clapping, Malcolm cracked a crooked smile. When the audience quieted down, he greeted them. "*As-Salaam-Alaikum*," he announced. "*Wa-Alaikum-Salaam*," the crowd rejoined.[46]

Taking a long deep breath, like a boxer moving out of his corner before the first round, Malcolm began, "Brothers and sisters . . ." Then it happened.

A man in a black overcoat jumped from his seat, tossed a homemade smoke bomb, and shouted, "Get your hand out of my pocket!" Suddenly, two men in the middle of the audience were on their feet, entangled in a shoving match. Startled and confused, the spectators began yelling. Immediately, the two rostrum guards dashed toward the commotion, leaving Malcolm unprotected. Gene Roberts and several other security guards standing in the rear left their posts too.[47]

"Now, now, brothers," Malcolm urged, "break it up. Be cool, be calm."

At that moment a large black man stepped into the aisle and raised a sawed-off double-barreled shotgun. "Hold it!" Malcolm pleaded, extending his arm in the air. "Hold it!"

Boom! The gunman pulled the trigger, blasting shotgun pellets through the plywood lectern, cutting a crater of holes in the center of Malcolm's chest.

Malcolm staggered, rocking back on his heels. His body swayed backward, crashing into two empty chairs. His head slammed onto the hardwood, making a loud thud.

The gunman fired again into his jerking body. Two more shooters, Talmadge and Leon, streaked toward the stage and sprayed him with bullets.[48]

Within seconds, it was over. Fleeing, the man with the shotgun fired above the crowd. "Get out of the goddamn way!" one of them yelled. Screaming and cursing, people ran for the exits, colliding into each other. Others helplessly dove onto the floor, tossing chairs aside. Covering her girls, Betty tried to shield them from the horror. "They're killing my husband!" she cried.[49]

Hurdling chairs, Talmadge ran right at Gene Roberts, firing a shot at the undercover agent, grazing his coat. Roberts flung a chair at his legs, knocking Talmadge down. Rising from the floor, he sprinted toward the exit. Just as he reached the top of the stairwell, Reuben Francis fired three shots, clipping him in the left thigh. "Oh!" Talmadge screamed. Writhing in pain, he tumbled down the stairs. When he reached the bottom, a mob seized him. "Kill him! Kill him!" the horde shouted.

Rushing toward the crowd, patrolman Hoy grabbed on to the suspect's arm, yanking it "like the rope in tug-o'-war." "They were trying to pull him apart the way you pull a drumstick off a turkey," one witness recalled.[50]

Moments later, two more patrolmen emerged from a squad car. When one of the officers realized that the crowd was winning the tug-of-war, he fired his revolver into the air, ordering them to disperse. Quickly, the patrolmen shoved Talmadge into the back of the cruiser. The suspect, identified in the press as "Thomas Hagan," was the only assassin caught at the scene.[51]

Inside the ballroom, Malcolm lay on the stage, his heartbeat still pulsing. The screaming had subsided, but people were still crying and moaning. "The whole room was a wailing woman," one writer recalled. A half dozen people bent over him while Malcolm's men paced furiously, regretting that they had not done enough to protect their brother. One fumed, "There ain't no goddam hope for our people in this lousy country. You got to fight them lousy whites and fight the stupid niggahs too. There ain't no goddam hope!"[52]

Frantic, Betty kneeled beside her husband, his white shirt ripped open and soaked with blood. Gene Roberts had tried to revive him, but by then it was too late. Betty attempted to resuscitate him too, frantically pumping his chest. Suddenly, she began digging through his pockets, searching for a paper that included the names of five men Malcolm believed would be responsible for his murder, a list that Betty never revealed. Clinging to the bloodstained paper, friends pulled her away while a stretcher rolled into the dance hall. "Oh, Muriel," she sobbed to a friend, "he's gone! And I'm *pregnant!*"[53]

Police investigators knew very little except that Malcolm was dead and that a wounded suspect was already being interrogated. Beyond those facts, they had more questions than answers. Why hadn't Malcolm's guards been armed? Why weren't the spectators searched? Why wasn't there tighter security near the stage? Was this an inside job? "He was definitely set up for it," an investigator later told *Newsweek* writer Peter Goldman. "To us, it was all so—*perfect*. Nobody would have walked in there to shoot him unless you know nobody has a gun and unless you know you've got one key man in your pocket."

Malcolm's men had questions of their own. The police knew that his life was in danger, and yet on the day of the murder, they deployed only two officers inside the Audubon and one outside the entrance. Why did the police hide twenty officers inside the hospital across the street? Did the police look the other way? Was the FBI involved? Malcolm had told his most trusted assistants that the FBI had agents working inside the Nation—agents who deliberately exacerbated the feud between him and Elijah, knowing that it would lead to a bloody war. Malcolm's men did not doubt that Talmadge X and his accomplices belonged to the Nation of Islam. The real question, the one that has lingered for decades, was much simpler: who sent them?

MALCOLM'S MURDER ENRAGED his followers, setting in motion a vendetta against Elijah Muhammad and the Nation's most prominent members. After the FBI warned the Chicago police that Malcolm's avengers were headed to their city, the department placed heavy details at bus stations, train stations, and airports. Police cruisers and unmarked cars parked outside Muhammad's mansion, Mosque No. 2, and the offices of *Muhammad Speaks*. Under police protection, Elijah seemed safe, but

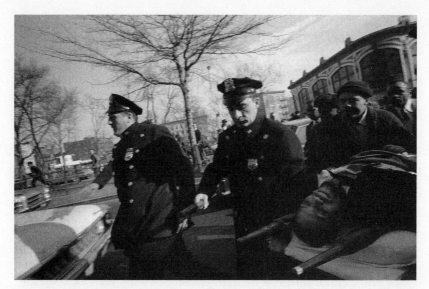

There was little hope that Malcolm would survive the massive gunshot wounds that ripped open his chest. Emergency room doctors tried to revive him at Columbia-Presbyterian Medical Center, but it was too late. Shortly before three thirty p.m., a surgeon delivered the tragic news to the fallen minister's friends and loved ones: "The gentleman you knew as Malcolm X is dead." Associated Press

around ten p.m., a call went out over police scanners: a fire had broken out at a South Side apartment on Cregier Avenue. While the fire burned for more than an hour, the police interviewed a resident who lived on the second floor. At first they suspected arson because Muhammad Ali had an apartment on the third floor. Perhaps, the police surmised, Malcolm's men had planned to immolate the boxer while he slept. But after interviewing Ali's drunk neighbor, the man admitted that he had started the fire when he fell asleep on a sofa with a cigarette in his hand.[54]

Fortunately for Ali, when the fire occurred, he and Sonji were out dining after attending religious services. Earlier that evening at the mosque, one of the ministers announced that Malcolm had been murdered. Immediately, Sonji feared that her husband might be next. No one knew that they were eating dinner at the Arabian Sands Motel, but somehow John Ali, who had already returned from New York, called

to tell the champ that his apartment had caught fire. Arriving at his apartment with the national secretary, the boxer told writers that he was "shocked and surprised" that someone had killed Malcolm. The Nation, he insisted, had nothing to do with the murder. It was just a coincidence that the fire occurred on the same day that Malcolm was killed, he said. Privately, though, Ali told Sonji that "somebody started it on purpose."[55]

The following day, Elijah held a press conference from his living room. He spoke impassively, denying any knowledge about Malcolm's murder. According to his grandson, Elijah was sitting in his office when he heard the news on the radio. "Oh my God!" he exclaimed. Speechless, he sat quietly for about thirty minutes until he said that he wanted to go home. When reporters asked him if he had ever heard of the suspect, "Thomas Hagan," he answered, "he is a stranger to us."[56]

In the days leading up to the annual Saviours' Day Convention, officers escorted Ali everywhere he went. The police figured that if Malcolm's avengers could not get their hands on Elijah, they most certainly would try to kill Ali. On Tuesday, February 23, the morning after a firebomb exploded at Mosque No. 7, completely gutting the Harlem temple, reporters hounded Ali. Anticipating open warfare, writers asked him if he feared death. "I'm with God. If I'm gonna die for truth, I'm ready to die. I ain't afraid. I ain't afraid of nothing."[57]

Facing death threats, he remained defiant, professing his faith in the Honorable Elijah Muhammad. Publicly, he maintained a loyal front, but his mother sensed that her son wavered about being in the Nation. "I heard he wants to quit [the Muslims]," Odessa said. "I hope he does." In her heart, though, she doubted that her son would actually leave Elijah. Ali never seriously considered breaking with him. He was in too deep. And now, as a spokesman of the Nation, he could show no remorse for the deceased. "Malcolm X was my friend and he was the friend of everybody as long as he was a member of Islam," he said. "Now I don't want to talk about him no more."[58]

On Friday, February 26, Muhammad preached for more than two hours at the Coliseum. Outside the old stadium on Wabash Avenue, the police set up a tight perimeter comparable to that for a presidential visit. Two days earlier, they had received a phone call from a man who claimed that he had planted a bomb inside the stadium. Undeterred,

Muhammad stepped to the podium. Surrounded by a phalanx of "grim-faced" troopers standing shoulder to shoulder, the Fruit created a bulwark around the Messenger.[59]

"Malcolm was a hypocrite who got what he was preaching," he declared, his voice cracking between coughing spells. "If he had not been a hypocrite, we could have given him a glorious burial," but Malcolm "went around the country trying to slander me."

Standing on the dais next to Louis X, Ali endorsed Elijah, clapping enthusiastically and repeatedly shouting, "Amen!' and "Yes, sir!" Muhammad's frail voice hardly carried in the cavernous arena, but the crowd followed Ali's cues, showering him with praise: "Sweet words! That's right! That's right!" If Malcolm had not turned his back "on me," Elijah preached, "we would have stood over his body and prayed with tears of grief in our eyes." But no one on the stage, not Louis, not Ali, not Elijah, not even Malcolm's own brothers, Philbert and Wilfred, shed a tear. "It's wrong," Muhammad reminded his followers, "to even stand beside the grave of a hypocrite."

SATURDAY, FEBRUARY 27, felt like the coldest day of winter. Just before sunrise, mourners began lining up outside Faith Temple Church of God in Christ on Amsterdam Avenue. Braving the bitter chill, grievers quietly huddled together, their hands jammed into their pockets and coat collars pulled up to their ears. As the sun climbed the morning sky, the temperature rose to fourteen degrees. Emerging from the subway, people extended the line, four abreast, down the block and around the corner onto 147th Street. Police barricades could hardly contain the overflowing crowd, estimated at 2,500. Earlier in the week, more than twenty thousand people had viewed Malcolm in his copper casket at the Unity Funeral Chapel on Eighth Avenue. Now, around nine thirty a.m., cameramen from WNBC began filming the funeral procession, capturing images of old women weeping and people hanging out of tenement windows watching the action below. Police squads patrolled the sidewalks while officers stationed on rooftops searched for signs of trouble.[60]

Inside the church, an old renovated movie house, Malcolm's glass-covered coffin lay beneath two murals of Jesus. Despite the Christian setting, Sheikh Ahmed Hassoun made sure that Malcolm received a proper Muslim funeral. At nine forty-five, Betty arrived, dressed in

black, her face hidden behind a veil. Bomb threats— "We'll cremate Malcolm with firebombs"—frightened the pregnant widow out of bringing her four daughters to the service. Escorted by Malcolm's security team and a group of policemen, she walked steadily toward the casket, tears streaming down her face, her upper lip quivering. When she reached the casket, she leaned toward Malcolm, who was wrapped in a white burial sheet, and kissed the glass that separated them. Surrounded by friends, family, newsmen, and photographers, Betty sat in a second-row pew, "looking terribly beautiful and alone." Some of the most notable figures in black America joined her, including Bayard Rustin, Andrew Young, John Lewis, and Dick Gregory.[61]

During his former friend's funeral, Muhammad Ali spent the day in Chicago performing a boxing exhibition at the Nation's Unity Bazaar. Bounding around the ring in a white T-shirt, the champ looked overweight and sluggish, not yet fully recovered from his hernia surgery. The Muslims had expected a large crowd, but less than ten percent of the Coliseum's 7,500 seats were filled. Ali did not seem too worried that the police and the FBI were watching him. It was no secret that there were men who had loved Malcolm more than he did, vengeful men who were willing to kill the champ. "Shoot Clay too," one of them said. "Why not? Why shouldn't we shoot him? Right in the ring in front of all his people."[62]

If the death threats scared Ali, he showed no fear. Instead, he clowned for five rounds, playfully contorting his face while he taunted his brother and tossed a few jabs. When Rahman hit him in the fifth, he pretended that he was hurt and took a dive, provoking laughter from the crowd. On a day of mourning, columnist Jimmy Breslin could not understand how Ali could act so flippant, entertaining the same men who reveled in Malcolm's death. The champ had surrounded himself with "the dull-minded, dangerous fanatics who will kill for this cult, just as they ran into the Audubon auditorium in broad daylight and killed Malcolm X last Sunday." Watching the scene unfold, Breslin wondered if Ali ever really loved Malcolm at all.[63]

In New York, Malcolm's friend, playwright and actor Ossie Davis, delivered a powerful eulogy. Looking out at the black faces in the packed church, Davis was reminded that Harlem truly loved Malcolm. The actor wanted the world to know that Malcolm was not a "fanatic, a racist,"

or a violent demagogue. Those who cast Malcolm as evil never really knew him, he said. To Malcolm's critics, he asked, "Did you ever talk to Brother Malcolm? Did you ever touch him, or have him smile at you? Did you ever really listen to him?"[64]

Those who really knew Malcolm understood why the congregation honored him. Malcolm spoke for the powerless, the downtrodden, the voiceless black man. He was an authentic symbol of black pride, strength, and redemption, and he spoke the truth without cowering from whites. A champion of self-determination, he probed America's deepest wound, the gulf between the country's democratic ideals and its inequalities. Ultimately, he died in the struggle for Black Power; he died so that other blacks could live without fear, so that they could realize their dreams of freedom. Malcolm, Davis declared, was one of Harlem's "brightest hopes," he was "our manhood, our living black manhood! This was his meaning to his people. And in honoring him, we honor the best in ourselves."[65]

When Davis finished speaking, the pallbearers loaded Malcolm's casket into a silver-blue hearse. For twenty miles, a police escort led the fifty-car procession out of the city, through Yonkers and Westchester, to the Ferncliff Cemetery in Hartsdale, a hamlet in the town of Greenburgh. Around eleven thirty-five, the convoy passed through the cemetery gates. In the Pinewood section of the graveyard, two hundred mourners gathered around plot 150, which was marked with a bronze plaque that read, "EL-HAJJ MALIK EL-SHABAZZ."[66]

After reciting the final Muslim prayers, a group of cemetery workers lowered the casket into the bottom of the cold, muddy grave. When the white workers grabbed shovels, a few of the brothers interjected. The undertaker told them that their caravan was already leaving. If they stayed behind, they would have no way to get home. "We'll walk," one of the mourners replied. When the brothers started tossing handfuls of dirt into the grave, the white men backed away, surrendering their shovels. The brothers picked up the tools, scooped the dirt, and filled the grave while the last mourners watched in silence. "No white man," one of them said, "is going to bury Malcolm."[67]

Epilogue

ONCE THE HATE IS GONE

Cassius Clay will be the first heavyweight champion in history to train in a bullet-proof ring.

—DAVID GORDON, *BOSTON GLOBE*, FEBRUARY 23, 1965

A poisonous mood pervaded Muhammad Ali's camp as he prepared for his rematch against Sonny Liston. "The atmosphere surrounding the fight was ugly," Jerry Izenberg recalled. "Malcolm was dead, and there were rumors Ali was going to be killed, maybe in the ring, in retaliation." At one point, a week or so before the fight, while Ali was getting a rubdown after a workout, a reporter asked him if he had heard the stories about Malcolm's people coming after him. He lifted his head angrily, a cruel note in his voice. "What people? Malcolm ain't got no people."[1]

In the days leading up to the fight, the rumors intensified. Supposedly, carloads of heavily armed men—Malcolm's men—had left New York headed for Ali's camp. There were other tales too. One story held that the Nation of Islam had threatened to kill Liston unless he took a dive. Other scuttlebutt suggested that the Nation would discard the champ if he lost, but Ali refused to believe a word of it. "LIES, ALL LIES," he shouted during a news conference. "The hell with Malcolm's boys!" he erupted, pounding a table with his fist. "Who are they?"[2]

Paranoia swept through the St. Dominic's Arena in Lewiston, Maine. On May 25, 1965, security guards scrutinized every black man who walked through the turnstiles. Officers searched purses, briefcases, and coat pockets. Hours before the contest they combed the old hockey

stadium, searching for "poison gas bombs." The match was originally scheduled to take place in Boston, but a few weeks before the fight Massachusetts authorities refused to sanction it, claiming that the promoter had ties to organized crime. The fight moved to Lewiston, an impoverished textile town and unlikely site for a heavyweight title match, leaving the Muslims increasingly suspicious that Ali was being set up. Unconvinced that the police had thoroughly searched St. Dominic's, Clarence X inspected the air vents in Ali's dressing room, "afraid poison gas would be shot into it."[3]

All the talk about a murder in the ring contributed to the pathetic turnout. Officially, the ring announcer declared the evening's attendance to be 4,280, but *Sports Illustrated*'s Tex Maule reported that there could not have been more than 1,200 fans present. And even fewer of them actually saw how the fight ended.[4]

It all happened in the blink of an eye. After the opening bell rang, Ali stormed toward Liston, hitting him with a hard right cross. For about a minute they danced as Ali moved clockwise, his head high and his gloves low. He moved cautiously, looking for an opening. Plodding toward Ali, Liston tried to cut off the ring, pawing at the champ. Liston tossed a few amateurish jabs, lunged forward, and lost his balance. At that moment, Ali leaned back, dodging Liston's punch. Quickly, he planted his left foot, and snapped a short, chopping right flush on Liston's chin. Sonny collapsed as if a sniper had shot him. But only his reputation died that night.[5]

A chorus of boos rained from the stunned fans. "Fake! Fake!" the crowd shouted. Few ringside observers could believe that Ali's single whipping punch had knocked Liston down. Sportswriters labeled the final blow "the phantom punch," implying that Ali never actually hit Liston, or at least, he had not hit him hard enough to end the fight.[6]

Upon review of the fight film, and with the benefit of slow-motion technology, writers determined that Ali "perfectly delivered" a hard, blurring right. He threw the final punch at precisely the right instant—the moment Liston lost his balance and fell toward him, exposing his chin. Sonny never saw it coming. Sprawled across the canvas, Ali loomed over him, his right hand cocked, muscles flexed, shouting, "Get up and fight, sucker!" Neil Leifer, a young photographer from *Sports Illustrated*,

snapped an iconic picture of Ali towering above Liston, taunting the fallen fighter. That photograph would become the most recognizable and enduring image of him during the sixties, capturing Ali's essence: his strength and beauty, his arrogance and boldness, everything that made Americans love and hate him.[7]

"THE ATHLETE OF the decade," Jimmy Cannon opined in 1970, "has to be Cassius Clay, who is now Muhammad Ali. He is all that the sixties were. It is as though he were created to represent them." In many ways, Ali personified the cultural changes of his times. During the decade he became the most important athlete in America, a controversial figure who transcended sports, shaping cultural debates about race, war, and religion. More than any other athlete, his life fused the political upheavals of the age. His entire boxing career was defined by the social and political movements of the decade.[8]

This became more evident in early 1966. The United States military had lowered its threshold for intelligence exam scores, leaving him eligible for service. On February 17, after the Louisville draft board denied his request for deferment on numerous procedural grounds, Ali received dozens of phone calls from reporters. Confused, he could not understand why the government suddenly wanted to send him to Vietnam. The Muslim brothers hanging around his Miami house tormented him with frightful predictions that Uncle Sam would soon tighten the noose around his neck. One of them said, "Some cracker sergeant is gonna drop a grenade down your pants and blow your balls off." Flustered by the television crews gathering in his lawn and the calls, Ali became agitated. When a reporter asked him for what seemed like the hundredth time what he thought about the Vietcong, he finally snapped. "Man, I ain't got no quarrel with them Vietcong!"[9]

Ali's memorable line splashed across the front pages of the nation's newspapers. His defensive outburst made many Americans despise him even more than they already did. Critics excoriated him as an unpatriotic coward, calling for boycotts of his matches. Amidst an escalating antiwar movement, establishment writers portrayed him as a spoiled brat, no better than the draft dodgers on college campuses. "Squealing over the possibility that the military may call him up," Red Smith

charged, "Cassius makes himself as sorry a spectacle as those unwashed punks who picket and demonstrate against the war."[10]

While Ali's draft status threatened his boxing career, his personal life unraveled. When his contract with the Louisville Sponsoring Group expired that year, Herbert Muhammad became his exclusive business manager, gaining greater control over his life. Herbert strongly disapproved of Ali's wife because Sonji frequently questioned the directives Muslim authorities gave her husband. Her disobedience, Herbert claimed, made her an unfit wife.

About a month before his military reclassification, Ali divorced Sonji, claiming that she had not adhered to the tenets of the Nation of Islam as she promised. Sonji contended that Herbert had pressured him into the divorce. Facing alimony payments, Ali had filed an appeal on the grounds of financial hardship. Now, after his draft status had changed, he protested that his previous purses were tied up in litigation, and therefore he could not afford to pay alimony unless he continued boxing.[11]

On the same day that the Selective Service announced his appeal, a New York judge sentenced Talmadge Hayer and two other men to life for Malcolm's murder. Hayer confessed his involvement in the assassination but insisted that the other defendants, Norman 3X Butler and Thomas 15X Johnson, were innocent. "I just want the truth to be known that Butler and Johnson didn't have anything to do with this crime," he said, "because I was there, I know what happened, I know the people that did take part in it." During the trial, Hayer never disclosed who ordered the hit on Malcolm. More than a decade later, though, he filed affidavits naming four other alleged accomplices. New York authorities, however, refused to reopen the case.[12]

Muhammad Ali never talked about the murder trial. He had other problems on his mind. On March 22, 1967, a few weeks after he received military orders for induction, he anxiously sat in his hotel bed, unable to sleep, his eyes downcast, contemplating his uncertain future. Around two a.m., Sugar Ray Robinson knocked at the door. Robinson worried that the draft pressure was taking its toll on him. He reminded Ali that he needed sleep if he was going to defeat Zora Folley later that evening.[13]

"What's wrong champ?" he asked.

"The army," Ali answered with trepidation. "They're gonna want me soon. But I can't go."

"But you have to go," Robinson argued, without mentioning that he had been accused of desertion during World War II. "What's this can't?"

"Elijah Muhammad told me that I can't go." The Nation's separatist principles would never allow him to serve alongside whites.

"You won't see a gun," Robinson maintained. Ali would just have to fight some exhibitions like he and Joe Louis had. "It'll be a snap. If you don't, they'll send you to jail, pick up your license." Ali risked everything if he refused to serve—his title, his career, his income—everything.

"Well, Elijah Muhammad told me," he said, conceding his future to the Messenger's wishes.

"Forget the old man," Robinson urged. "Is Elijah going to go to jail, and all those other Muslims?"

"But I'm afraid, Ray," he admitted with tears in his eyes. "I'm really afraid."

"Afraid of what? Of the Muslims if you don't do what they told you?"

Ali would not answer. Robinson pressed, but the champ remained silent. When Robinson recalled the story for a writer, he said, "If you ask me, he wasn't afraid of jail. He was scared of being killed by the Muslims."

MUHAMMAD ALI WOULD not give boxing exhibitions for the army, nor would he fight the Vietcong. "Why should they ask me to put on a uniform and go ten thousand miles from home and drop bombs and bullets on brown people in Vietnam while so-called Negro people in Louisville are treated like dogs?" he asked a reporter from *Sports Illustrated*. "If I thought going to war would bring freedom and equality to twenty-two million of my people, they wouldn't have to draft me. I'd join tomorrow. But I either have to obey the laws of the land or the laws of Allah. I have nothing to lose by standing up and following my beliefs. We've been in jail for four hundred years."[14]

On April 20, 1967, Ali refused induction at the US Armed Forces Examining and Entrance Station in Houston. He proclaimed that he was a conscientious objector, opposing all wars undeclared by Allah. Immediately after he refused induction—before he had been charged

with a crime—the New York State Athletic Commission suspended his boxing license and withdrew his heavyweight title for conduct "detrimental to the best interests of boxing." Athletic commissions across the country followed New York's lead, forbidding his presence in the ring. On June 20, a federal court convicted him of draft evasion, sentencing him to the maximum five-year imprisonment and ten-thousand-dollar fine. For the next three and a half years, during his appeal and the prime of his boxing career, he was banished from the ring. Although he never went to prison, his fans believed that the government and the boxing authorities that banned him from the ring had already shackled him.[15]

Without boxing, Ali fell on hard times. In early 1969, during a paid television interview on ABC's *Wide World of Sports*, he complained to Howard Cosell that he was nearly broke and that he would return to boxing if the price was right. Infuriated, Elijah Muhammad immediately suspended him for failing to follow his teachings of prudence. In the pages of *Muhammad Speaks*, the Messenger announced that Ali was barred from all NOI meetings and speaking with its members. The Nation would no longer recognize him as a Muslim. Giving him back his slave name, Elijah declared, "We will call him Cassius Clay."[16]

In Elijah's view, Ali had made a grave mistake, placing "his hopes and trust in the enemy of Allah for survival." When the twenty-seven-year-old boxer suggested that he would sacrifice his religious principles for "the white man's money," Elijah decided to make an example out of him for those "who are weak in the faith."[17]

Ali's experience in the Nation now mirrored Malcolm's. Like Malcolm, he outwardly worshipped Elijah. When Elijah suspended him, Ali was crushed. He hoped that the Messenger would eventually forgive him and welcome him back into the movement. Yet without boxing, Ali had lost his value. Without the ring, without that world stage, he was just another acolyte. In his weakest moment, when he could not raise money or generate good publicity for the Nation, Elijah disowned him, casting him outside the Nation as he had done to Malcolm before him.

In exile, Ali remained loyal to Muhammad, refusing to blame him or the Nation for his troubles. Dick Schaap, who had known Ali since 1960, never understood his fealty to the Messenger. Often, when the writer asked him why he sided with Muhammad instead of Malcolm,

Ali refused to answer. He had no words, no explanation. "His expressive face has turned blank," Schaap wrote in 1971. "His enthusiasm turned to dullness. Maybe he is embarrassed. He should be."[18]

The truth, George Plimpton thought, was that Ali was afraid. He did not dare cross Elijah Muhammad. Once, when Plimpton visited Ali in Chicago, they drove around the South Side. When the writer asked him to see "the leader's mansion," Ali agreed, but he drove so fast that Plimpton only got a fleeting look at it. Plimpton urged him to turn around so that he could take another look. Accelerating past the mansion at fifty miles per hour, Ali made another pass, insisting Plimpton slouch out of sight. "He didn't want to be spotted," the writer recalled. "I think he understood what they could do. They were intimidating. And because he did fear them, he was malleable."[19]

MALCOLM'S GHOST HAUNTED Ali. In early November 1974, three years after the Supreme Court overturned his draft evasion conviction on a technicality, he returned to Louisville for a celebration. He had just regained the heavyweight title from George Foreman in Kinshasa, Zaire. More than seven thousand fans greeted him outside the Belvedere, a riverfront plaza of parks, trees, and fountains overlooking the Ohio River.[20]

At the reception inside the Galt House, Ali enjoyed the singularity of being champion again. Sitting with white reporters from the *Louisville Courier-Journal*, he boasted about his comeback. Suddenly, his mood changed when two stone-faced men from the Fruit told Ali that it was time for him to go. "No, leave us alone," he snapped. "These are my people . . . these are my Louisville men. They can stay as long as they want. Don't bother us again."[21]

After his security team disappeared, Ali told the writers that the guards were just doing their job, but he did not appreciate being told with whom he could talk. "They always got somebody watching," he said.

"Who are 'they'?" reporter Dave Kindred asked.

"I would have gotten out of this a long time ago," Ali whispered. "But you saw what they did to Malcolm X. I ain't gonna end up like Malcolm X."

Kindred sensed that Ali feared what would happen if he left the Nation. Controlled by Elijah Muhammad for more than a decade, he lived

in a straitjacket, trapped by the Nation's officials. He could not eat, sleep, or breathe without worrying about the wrath of the Black Muslim leaders. "I can't leave the Muslims," Ali said, his voice foreboding. "They'd shoot me, too."

About four months later the Messenger died, signaling a turning point in Ali's life. Wallace Muhammad took the helm of the Nation, renouncing his father's divine claims, tempering the Nation's racial rhetoric, and embracing orthodox Islam. In 1976, the sect's new imam renamed Mosque No. 7 in honor of Malcolm X, acknowledging that Malcolm had told the truth about his father's paternity scandals. "What we should see in Malcolm," he declared, "is a turn for the Nation of Islam from fear and isolation to openness, courage."[22]

Freed from Elijah Muhammad's influence, Ali embraced a more universal attitude about race and Islam. "I don't hate whites," he announced after Elijah's death. "That was history, but it's coming to an end. We're in a new phase, a resurrection." Deep down he believed "that the devil is in the mind and heart, not the skin. We Muslims hate injustice and evil, but we don't have time to hate people."[23]

"I IMAGINE ONE of the reasons people cling to their hates so stubbornly," James Baldwin suggested, "is because they sense, once their hate is gone, they will be forced to deal with the pain." When Malcolm died, Ali hid the pain behind a mask of contempt, heartlessly asserting that the fallen minister "got what he deserved." Ali lived to regret those words. For years, he suffered under the burden of guilt, knowing that he had hurt Malcolm, his friend, his brother. But time softened him. Gradually, he became more humane, and more forgiving.[24]

"I wish I'd been able to tell Malcolm I was sorry, that he was right about so many things," Ali said more than forty years after Malcolm died. "Malcolm X was a great thinker and even greater friend," he reflected. "I might never have become a Muslim if it hadn't been for Malcolm. If I could go back and do it over again, I would never have turned my back on him."[25]

It was the wisdom of decades speaking—years spent fighting in the ring and evolving outside it. By the time he retired from boxing, he was nearly forty years old, his body and face ravaged by ring wars with Joe Frazier, George Foreman, and Ken Norton. By then he had become an

American icon, more than fulfilling his youthful assertions that he was "the greatest." As an athlete and man he was in a class of his own, and it is unlikely that any sportsman will ever duplicate his worldwide fame and importance. But after all the matches won and lost, all the honors received and forgotten, how many times must he have returned to those days in the early years of his career, when his body was as lithe as a dancer's and his face unmarked in its innocence, remembering the wise man who spoke with such confidence and passion, telling him about Allah's plan for his life. For about two years, Malcolm X counseled and spiritually guided the young boxer, instructing him on the evil ways of the world but also, more importantly, convincing him to love himself and his people. They were like blood brothers then, Malcolm X and Cassius Clay, and briefly it must have seemed as if the world was theirs. That it ended violently and tragically does not diminish what they once had.

From the first, theirs was an improbable relationship. The brash Olympic champion who spoke in rhymes and the ex-con disinterested in sports appeared to have nothing in common, save ego and an attraction to center stage. But perhaps they sensed some deeper kindred spirit—or some void that the other filled. Cassius loved magic and needed a powerful friend and mentor. Tall, strong, articulate, Malcolm talked of dreams and Armageddon, trafficking in the supernatural and the spiritual, promising a topsy-turvy new world where the racial order would be reversed. All he asked for in return—at least at first—was faith. It appealed to the dreamer in Cassius and validated the stories and fantasies he had heard from his father.

But what attracted Malcolm to Clay? In the early 1960s, the media treated the boxer as an adolescent clown, a bloviating athlete who lacked modesty, propriety, and dignity, the very traits that characterized Malcolm. Yet Malcolm knew that a wise man could play a clown. He looked behind the façade, seeing that even if Clay acted like a clown, he never behaved like a subservient one. He defined himself, asserting strength and pride, proclaiming his worth as a boxer and a black man. And most crucially, he attracted an audience whenever he spoke. If Malcolm did not immediately recognize Clay's political potential, if he did not sense right away that he could mobilize his unique celebrity, he soon grasped that fundamental reality. At a time when Malcolm's

ties to Elijah Muhammad were dissolving, Cassius, with the media he commanded and the followers he attracted, was a prize to be won.

In the year and a half before Cassius won the heavyweight crown, Malcolm consciously molded him into Muhammad Ali. Cassius adopted Malcolm's rhetoric, mimicked his delivery, and copied his cool, regal pose. He became, as a few journalists dimly sensed, a clone of his mentor. Always adept at imitation, Clay could slide into his Cassius X persona at a moment's notice, dispensing Malcolm's ideas and words like a seasoned actor. But after Cassius defeated Sonny Liston for the title, at the instant when his political value to Malcolm was the highest, the preacher lost his convert. Malcolm may have shaped Muhammad Ali, but Elijah Muhammad anointed Cassius *as* Muhammad Ali.

Ali followed Elijah for a decade, but their relationship was never as intimate as the one he shared with Malcolm. Malcolm, Ali came to realize, anticipated the course of the future. And although it took him ten years, Ali eventually followed the political and religious path that Malcolm had just begun to pioneer when he was assassinated.

In time, Ali understood that who he was and who he became were the results of his friendship with Malcolm. He knew that without Malcolm X, he would never have become Muhammad Ali.

POSTSCRIPT:
THE SECOND ACT

HORATIO: He was a goodly king.
HAMLET: He was a man, take him for all in all, I shall not look
upon his like again.

—*Hamlet*, Act I, Scene II

For at least three years, the media reported that Muhammad Ali was close to death. His brother Rahman Ali commented in February 2013 that Muhammad had lost the ability to speak and might die any day. But he struggled along, shedding weight, lapsing into long periods of silence, and sometimes drifting in and out of consciousness. Though he was only in his early seventies, Parkinson's disease made him seem decades older. He was in and out of the hospital—a bout of pneumonia here, a urinary tract infection there, and a steady routine of examinations and tests. The Louisville Lip, the persona that had made him the most famous athlete in the world, had been gone since the 1980s.

So it was no surprise when on June 2, 2016, he entered a Scottsdale, Arizona, hospital suffering from a respiratory illness. Although the initial diagnosis was not dire, Ali's condition rapidly worsened. He contracted septic shock, and his organs began to shut down. His family gathered near him in a death watch. "All of us were around him hugging and kissing him and holding his hands, chanting the Islamic prayer," said his daughter Hana Ali. "All of his organs failed but his HEART

wouldn't stop beating. For 30 minutes . . . his heart just kept beating. No one had ever seen anything like it. A true testament to the strength of his Spirit and Will."[1]

Then it stopped. Late in the night on June 3, Muhammad Ali died.

He was mourned around the globe, and in the age of the twenty-four hour news cycle and new digital media mourned in a way that no athlete, no celebrity, no world leader ever had been. Perhaps this was because no other person had so blurred the lines between sports, entertainment, and politics. President Barack Obama asserted, "Muhammad Ali was The Greatest. Period." Adding, "If you just asked him, he'd tell you. . . . But what made The Champ the greatest—what truly separated him from everyone else—is that everyone else would tell you pretty much the same thing."[2]

For President Obama, what made Ali the greatest was what he stood for outside the ring, not what he accomplished inside it. Ali told his countrymen, "I am America. I am the part you won't recognize. But get used to me—black, confident, cocky; my name, not yours; my religion, not yours; my goals, my own. Get used to me."[3]

The president's sentiments were echoed by others. Virtually all of the tributes to Ali emphasized what he did for his race, his religion, and the world—how he battled racism at home, imperialism abroad, and discrimination and intolerance everywhere. The idea that he was a symbol of peace, tolerance, and brotherhood was bandied about endlessly on television specials and in commemorative publications. Obama even avowed that Ali "stood with King and Mandela." Often lost in the tributes was the Muhammad Ali who abandoned Malcolm X for Elijah Muhammad, propagated the notion of "blue-eyed devils," and affirmed the tenets of racial separatism. Yet it was *that* Muhammad Ali who made the hardest choices, took the most controversial stands, and risked the greatest punishments.

"THERE ARE NO second acts in American lives," F. Scott Fitzgerald wrote in *The Last Tycoon*. Yet Muhammad Ali's life defies that notion. On December 10, 1974, about a month after his triumph over George Foreman in Kinshasa, Zaire (now Democratic Republic of the Congo), his second act began when President Gerald Ford invited the two-time champion to the White House. By then most Americans viewed the

Vietnam War as unjustified, and Ali's antiwar stance, therefore, had become linked to the larger struggle for peace. He drew the scorn of conservative critics, who derided him as unpatriotic and un-American. He would have never received an invitation from Ford's predecessor, Richard Nixon, who had relished his loss against Joe Frazier three years earlier. Nixon, rapturously jumping up and down, had celebrated Frazier's victory over "that draft dodger asshole."[4]

But Ford, confronting a fractured country reeling from the Vietnam War, Watergate, and racial divisions, aimed to unify America. Three months before Ali visited with Ford, the president issued a proclamation offering amnesty for anyone who evaded the draft during the war. Seven years after the United States government tried Ali for refusing induction into the military, Ford—and by extension the government—embraced him, marking the beginning of his transformation into an American hero, a process that culminated in 2005 when George W. Bush awarded him the Presidential Medal of Freedom for promoting world peace.[5]

Over the course of three decades, six presidents courted Ali and appropriated his worldwide popularity. Ford, Jimmy Carter, Ronald Reagan, George H. W. Bush, Bill Clinton, and George W. Bush all employed Ali in various political platforms. It's no coincidence that Ali became a voice for white politicians the moment he no longer threatened the Establishment. In 1980, after the Soviets invaded Afghanistan, he traveled to five African countries on behalf of the State Department to fortify support for Jimmy Carter's boycott of the Moscow Olympics. No longer a radical critic of the American government, Ali appeared as he once did as a young Olympic champion in Rome, a Cold Warrior promoting American foreign policy. In his support of Carter's boycott, one writer commented, Ali had become "a good anti-Communist Muslim."[6]

America's embrace of Ali as one of the "good Muslims" occurred only after he rejected Elijah Muhammad's unorthodox theology and embraced Sunni Islam. If he had followed Louis Farrakhan's revitalization of the Nation of Islam under Elijah's racist ideology, he would have never become a universal hero. But when he rejected his past racial beliefs, spoke about a universal Muslim brotherhood, and publicly denounced Farrakhan, he turned into a more acceptable black hero. Criticizing Farrakhan in 1984, he said, "What he teaches is not at all what we believe in." That same year he endorsed Ronald Reagan's bid

for reelection. Ali either forgave or forgot that in 1970, when the California State Athletic Commission voted to reinstate his boxing license, the governor intervened. "Forget it," Reagan said. "That draft dodger will never fight in my state." Stunned, black Americans could not understand how he would support a president who opposed the 1964 Civil Rights Act, the 1965 Voting Rights Act, and affirmative action. Backing Reagan meant stepping away from the Black Nationalist principles that had once defined him as a race man and moving closer to the center of mainstream America.[7]

After 1996, when he lit the Olympic torch in Atlanta, Ali's past became increasingly sanitized, his once controversial image repackaged for commercial purposes. The Muhammad Ali Americans came to know in the last two decades of his life was far removed from the man who had once followed Elijah Muhammad and befriended Malcolm X. For example, Michael Mann's biopic *Ali* (2001) misrepresented the Nation of Islam's doctrine as consistent with Islam as it is practiced by billions of people around the world. In a simplistic narrative, Mann's film portrayed Ali in heroic terms without acknowledging that many Americans despised him because they believed that he belonged to a racist cult. Thus, the rebranding of Ali and his beliefs made him safer for public consumption, a familiar exercise that has shaped the way Americans distort and remember black heroes.[8]

"To become a Black hero," *Ebony*'s Michael Harriot wrote after Ali died, "one must first undergo a ceremony of whitewashing. It is the same process that made Martin Luther King a fighter for 'justice and equality' instead of Black people. It is what made Jackie Robinson an 'icon' instead of the Black man who forced the United States army to accept a class of Black officers, desegregate military transportation, and changed American sports forever. Only when they are rendered breathless and toothless are they celebrated."[9]

DURING HIS FUNERAL the speakers celebrated a man most wouldn't have recognized in the 1960s. No one mentioned the Nation of Islam or Elijah Muhammad. However, Malcolm X's daughter Attallah Shabazz spoke about her relationship with him, one that grew long after her father died. Sometime in her late teens or early twenties she reconnected with Ali. "From the very moment we found each other," she said, "it

was as if no time passed at all, despite the presumptions of division. Despite the efforts at separation. Despite all the organized distancing." The veiled reference to the Nation of Islam suggests that she understood the burden Ali carried as a loyal disciple of Elijah Muhammad.[10]

But in the late 1960s Ali himself decided that Malcolm's memory was unworthy of tribute. After Malcolm died, he bashed him as nothing more than a martyr created by white people who wanted to turn blacks against Elijah Muhammad. In 1968, when Ali appeared on *Firing Line* with William Buckley Jr., he praised Elijah for making him into a prominent world figure. "Everything I got come from him," he said. "He taught me who I was. He made me proud [to be Black]. He made me fearless." Malcolm, he insisted, "was nothing until the Honorable Elijah Muhammad made him great. Now you seem to try to make it look like he was a leader and he was powerful." Ali no longer cared that Malcolm had mentored him, prayed with him, and loved him.[11]

When Buckley pressed him about his break with Malcolm, Ali became indignant. White people were to blame for Malcolm's demise, not the Nation of Islam. Whites made Malcolm believe that he was more important than Elijah Muhammad, that he should have been the leader of the Nation. If Malcolm had stayed with Elijah, he suggested, Malcolm "would have been"—he paused, searching for the right words, until he awkwardly settled on "big, big, big." Tired of hearing Buckley talk about Malcolm, he snapped, "Whites destroyed Malcolm X!"

"He's dead now," he added. "And we don't talk about dead people."

Yet Attallah Shabazz reminded us that the final chapter between Ali and her father did not end in the 1960s. Her presence at Ali's funeral made clear that he regretted speaking cruelly about her father, a man they both truly loved. Listening to her speak stirred images of January 1964, when Malcolm, his wife Betty, and their children visited Ali in Miami. Ali played with Attallah and her sisters, clowning and teasing them with affection. Malcolm said later, "I liked him. Betty liked him. Our children were crazy about him." They were like family then, and that bond stood the test of time, a credit to Betty Shabazz, who raised her daughters to forgive those who condemned their father.[12]

The relationship that Ali and Attallah forged after Malcolm died also demonstrates that Ali sought forgiveness and that she helped him find "the light of understanding," as her father would have liked. In

their shared grief, he and Attallah cried together and laughed together. Her eulogy revealed that Malcolm forgave Ali for not speaking to him. Ali helped Attallah better understand her father, and in return Attallah helped relieve Ali of the deep pain that he had buried years after Malcolm died.[13]

Attalah's eulogy demonstrated that Muhammad Ali's relationship with Malcolm X had come full circle. An odyssey that had begun with Malcolm ended with his daughter. It was a journey of accusations and incriminations, enlightenment and heartache, pain and healing. Over the course of his life Muhammad Ali regarded Malcolm X as his blood brother, as well as his enemy. But in the end love had overcome the bitterness.

ACKNOWLEDGMENTS

From start to finish, researching and writing *Blood Brothers* was a fulfilling and enjoyable collaborative journey. We, the authors, have our names on the title page, but we are also acutely aware of all the people that helped us along the way. At Fletcher & Company, Don Lamm, Sylvie Greenberg, and Christy Fletcher helped shape the book by offering wise advice and endless support. The team at Fletcher & Company helped us find the perfect home at Basic Books. Everyone at Basic Books has been incredibly enthusiastic. Publisher Lara Heimert had a clear vision of the book and gave us a brilliant critique of the draft. Asking crucial questions, Lara challenged us to sharpen our ideas and wisely encouraged us to tighten the narrative. Line editor Brandon Proia was an invaluable reader who improved every page. Copy editor Erin Granville and production editor Sandra Beris refined the manuscript and kept us on pace. And associate editor Leah Stecher fielded our countless questions deftly and (we think) with a smile. We couldn't imagine a better team.

People close to the fight game gave us the benefit of their decades of experience. Jerry Izenberg and Robert Lipsyte were there—sitting at ringside; talking to Sonny Liston, Malcolm X, and Muhammad Ali; writing the first drafts of history. Tom Hauser may not have been there, but he knows everyone who was and graciously shared his considerable knowledge of Muhammad Ali and boxing. Several academic friends read all or parts of early drafts. Aram Goudsouzian commented insightfully on an early version, and David Welky and Eric Hall read parts. They all contributed to the final book.

Our thanks also go out to those who aided us during our research: Casey Harden at the Muhammad Ali Center, George Rugg at the University of Notre Dame Special Collections, Carrie Hintz at the Columbia University Rare Book & Manuscript Library, Heather Stone at the Filson Historical Society in Louisville; and librarians and researchers at the National Archives, the Schomburg Center for Research in Black Culture, the University of Oregon Special Collections, the Library of Congress Manuscript Division, and our home base, the Library of Congress Newspaper Reading Room. Amber Paranick at the Library of Congress has been helping us for years, and we appreciate her tireless aid. We are also grateful for the research assistants who helped us track down key sources. Thanks to Kyle Larson, Shandi Sigler, Cy Hill, and Ansel Beacham.

Our home institutions have facilitated our work. At Purdue University, history department head Doug Hurt set an example of commitment to scholarship and did his best to support Randy Roberts's work. The School of Liberal Arts at Purdue supported his research with a Humanistic Fellowship Center grant. At Georgia Tech, the Ivan Allen College of Liberal Arts and the School of History and Sociology provided research and travel aid to Johnny Smith. He is especially thankful for the unwavering support from John Tone, Steve Usselman, and Jacqueline Royster.

BIBLIOGRAPHY

Abbreviations Used in Notes

AHP	Alex Haley Papers, Schomburg Center for Research in Black Culture, New York
AMX	*The Autobiography of Malcolm X*
AP	Associated Press
BAA	*Baltimore Afro-American*
BG	*Boston Globe*
BI	*Boxing Illustrated*
CA	*Chicago American*
CD	*Chicago Defender*
CDN	*Chicago Daily News*
CST	*Chicago Sun-Times*
CT	*Chicago Tribune*
DG	*Daily Graphic* (Accra, Ghana)
DT	*Daily Times* (Lagos, Nigeria)
EG	*Egyptian Gazette*
EYES	*Eyes on the Prize* Interview Transcripts, Washington University Libraries, Film and Media Archive, Henry Hampton Collection
FBIEM	Elijah Muhammad FBI File
FBIHM	Herbert Muhammad FBI File
FBILA	Leon Ameer FBI File
FBIMX	Malcolm X FBI File, Headquarters
FBIMXNY	Malcolm X FBI File, New York Office
FBIRS	Raymond Sharrieff FBI File
GBB	George Barry Bingham Papers, Filson Historical Society, Louisville, Kentucky
GT	*Ghanaian Times*

JOP	Jack Olsen Papers, University of Oregon Special Collections and Archives
LAHE	*Los Angeles Herald Examiner*
LAS	*Los Angeles Sentinel*
LAT	*Los Angeles Times*
LCJ	*Louisville Courier-Journal*
LDM	*London Daily Mirror*
LDTMP	*London Daily Telegram and Morning Post*
LT	*London Times*
LVS	*Las Vegas Sun*
MC	*Michigan Chronicle*
MH	*Miami Herald*
MN	*Miami News*
MS	*Muhammad Speaks*
MXP	Malcolm X Papers, Schomburg Center for Research in Black Culture, New York
NYAN	*New York Amsterdam News*
NYDN	*New York Daily News*
NYHT	*New York Herald Tribune*
NYJA	*New York Journal-American*
NYP	*New York Post*
NYT	*New York Times*
NYTM	*New York Times Magazine*
OT	*Oakland Tribune*
PC	*Pittsburgh Courier*
PT	*Philadelphia Tribune*
SEP	*Saturday Evening Post*
SI	*Sports Illustrated*
TBP	Taylor Branch Papers, University of North Carolina, Chapel Hill, Special Collections
WP	*Washington Post*

Books

Adams, Luther. *Way Up North in Louisville: African American Migration in the Urban South, 1930–1970.* Chapel Hill: University of North Carolina Press, 2010.

Ali, Muhammad, with Hana Yasmeen Ali. *The Soul of a Butterfly.* New York: Simon & Schuster, 2004.

Ali, Muhammad, with Richard Durham. *The Greatest: My Own Story.* New York: Random House, 1975.

Altschuler, Glenn. *All Shook Up: How Rock 'N' Roll Changed America*. New York: Oxford University Press, 2003.

Anderson, Dave. *In the Corner: Great Boxing Trainers Talk About Their Art*. New York: Morrow, 1991.

Angelou, Maya. *All God's Children Need Traveling Shoes*. New York: Vintage, 1991.

Atyeo, Don, and Felix Dennis. *Muhammad Ali: The Holy Warrior*. New York: Simon & Schuster, 1975.

Baldwin, James. *Notes of a Native Son*. Boston: Beacon Press, 1957.

———. *The Fire Next Time*. New York: Vintage International, 1993. First published 1963 by Dial Press.

The Beatles, *The Beatles Anthology*. San Francisco: Chronicle Books, 2000.

Bingham, Howard, and Max Wallace. *Muhammad Ali's Greatest Fight: Cassius Clay vs. The United States of America*. New York: M. Evans and Company, Inc., 2000.

Boyd, Herb, and Ilyasah Al-Shabazz, eds. *The Diary of Malcolm X (El-Hajj Malik El-Shabazz): 1964*. New York: Third World Press, 2013.

Branch, Taylor. *Parting the Waters: America in the King Years, 1954–1963*. New York: Simon & Schuster, 1989.

———. *Pillar of Fire: America in the King Years, 1963–1965*. New York: Simon & Schuster, 1998.

Breitman, George. *The Last Year of Malcolm X: The Evolution of a Revolutionary*. 1967. Reprint, New York: Pathfinder, 1992.

———, ed. *Malcolm X Speaks: Selected Speeches and Statements*. New York: First Grove, 1990.

Brooks, Tim, and Earle Marsh. *The Complete Directory to Prime Time Network TV Shows: 1946–Present*. 5th ed. New York: Ballantine Books, 1992.

Brown, Jim, with Steve Delsohn. *Out of Bounds*. New York: Zebra Books, 1989.

———, with Myron Cope. *Off My Chest*. New York: Doubleday & Company, 1964.

Butin, John. *L.A. Noir: The Struggle for the Soul of America's Most Seductive City*. New York: Crown, 2009.

Carson, Clayborne. *Malcolm X: The FBI File*. New York: Carrol & Graf Publishers, Inc., 1991.

Clark, Kenneth B. *The Negro Protest*. Boston: Beacon Press, 1963.

Clark, Steve, ed. *February 1965: The Final Speeches*. By Malcolm X. New York and London: Pathfinder, 1997.

Cleaver, Eldridge. *Soul on Ice*. 1968. Reprint, New York: Dell Publishing, 1992.

Clegg, Claude Andrew. *An Original Man: The Life and Times of Elijah Muhammad*. New York: St. Martin's Press, 1997.

Collings, Mark, ed. *Muhammad Ali: Through the Eyes of the World*. London: Sanctuary Publishing, 2001.

Cone, James H. *Martin & Malcolm & America: A Dream or a Nightmare.* Maryknoll, NY: Orbis Books, 1993.

Cottrell, John. *Man of Destiny: The Story of Muhammad Ali, Formerly Cassius Clay.* London: The Garden City Press, 1967.

DeCaro, Louis. *On the Side of My People: A Religious Life of Malcolm X.* New York: New York University Press, 1996.

Deford, Frank. *Over Time: My Life as a Sportswriter.* New York: Atlantic Monthly Press, 2012.

Dudziak, Mary. *Cold War Civil Rights: Race and the Image of American Democracy.* Princeton, NJ: Princeton University Press, 2002.

Dundee, Angelo, with Bert Randolph Sugar. *My View from the Corner: A Life in Boxing.* New York: McGraw-Hill, 2008.

———, with Mike Winters. *I Only Talk Winning.* Chicago: Contemporary Books, 1985.

Dunn, Marvin. *Black Miami in the Twentieth Century.* Gainesville: University Press of Florida, 1997.

Dunphy, Don. *Don Dunphy at Ringside.* New York: Henry Holt & Company, 1988.

Early, Gerald. *This Is Where I Came In: Black America in the 1960s.* Lincoln: University of Nebraska Press, 2003.

———, ed. *The Muhammad Ali Reader.* New York: Robert Weisbach Books, 1998.

Edwards, Harry. *The Revolt of the Black Athlete.* New York: Free Press, 1969.

Essien-Udom, E. U. *Black Nationalism: A Search for Identity in America.* Chicago: University of Chicago Press, 1962.

Evanzz, Karl. *The Messenger: The Rise and Fall of Elijah Muhammad.* New York: Pantheon Books, 1999.

———. *The Judas Factor: The Plot to Kill Malcolm X.* New York: Thunder's Mouth Press, 1992.

Ezra, Michael. *Muhammad Ali: The Making of an Icon.* Philadelphia: Temple University Press, 2009.

Fairclough, Adam. *Better Day Coming: Blacks and Equality, 1890–2000.* New York: Penguin Books, 2001.

Farmer, James. *Lay Bare the Heart: An Autobiography of the Civil Rights Movement.* New York: Arbor House, 1985.

Fitzgerald, Mike. *The Ageless Warrior: The Life of Boxing Legend Archie Moore.* Champaign, IL: Sports Publishing, LLC, 2004.

Fleischer, Nat. *Training for Boxers.* 11th ed. New York: Ring Athletic Library, 1960.

Fosl, Catherine, and Tracy K'Meyer. *Freedom on the Border: An Oral History of the Civil Rights Movement in Kentucky.* Lexington: University Press of Kentucky, 2009.

Fried, Ronald K. *Corner Men: Great Boxing Trainers.* New York: Four Walls Eight Windows, 1991.

Friedly, Michael. *Malcolm X: The Assassination.* New York: Carrol & Graf Publishers, 1992.

Gaines, Kevin. *American Africans in Ghana: Black Expatriates and the Civil Rights Era.* Chapel Hill: University of North Carolina Press, 2006.

Gallen, David. *Malcolm X: As They Knew Him.* New York: Carrol & Graf Publishers, 1992.

Goldman, Peter. *The Death and Life of Malcolm X.* 2nd ed. Urbana and Chicago: University of Illinois Press, 1979.

Gorn, Elliot, ed. *Muhammad Ali: The People's Champ.* Urbana and Chicago: University of Illinois Press, 1995.

Guralnick, Peter. *Dream Boogie: The Triumph of Sam Cooke.* New York: Back Bay Books/Little, Brown and Company, 2005.

Hampton, Henry, and Steve Fayer, eds. *Voices of Freedom: An Oral History of the Civil Rights Movement from the 1950s through the 1980s.* New York: Bantam Books, 1991.

Hauser, Thomas. *The Lost Legacy of Muhammad Ali.* Wilmington, DE: Sport-Classic Books, 2005.

———. *Muhammad Ali: His Life and Times.* New York: Simon & Schuster, 1991.

Hughes, Langston. *The Collected Poems of Langston Hughes.* Edited by Arnold Rampersad. New York: Vintage Classics, 1995.

Jamal, Hakim. *On the Dead Level: Malcolm and Me.* New York: Random House, 1972.

Joseph, Peniel. *Dark Days, Bright Nights: From Black Power to Barack Obama,* New York: Basic Civitas Books, 2010.

———. *Waiting 'Til the Midnight Hour: A Narrative History of the Black Power Movement.* New York: Henry Holt and Company, 2006.

Karim, Benjamin, with Peter Skutchens and David Gallen. *Remembering Malcolm.* New York: Carroll & Graf Publishers, Inc., 1992.

Kimball, George, and John Schulian. *At the Fights: American Writers on Boxing.* New York: Library of America, 2012.

Kindred, Dave. *Sound and Fury: Two Powerful Lives, One Fateful Friendship.* New York: Free Press, 2006.

Kram, Mark. *Ghosts of Manila: The Fateful Blood Feud Between Muhammad Ali and Joe Frazier.* New York: HarperCollins, 2002.

Lewis, Andrew B. *The Shadows of Youth: The Remarkable Journey of the Civil Rights Generation.* New York: Hill and Wang, 2010.

Lewisohn, Mark. *The Complete Beatles Chronicle.* New York: Harmony Books, 1992.

Lincoln, C. Eric. *The Black Muslims in America.* Boston: Beacon Press, 1963.

Lipsyte, Robert. *An Accidental Sportswriter: A Memoir*. New York: HarperCollins, 2011.

————. *Free to Be Muhammad Ali*. New York: Harper & Row Publishers, 1978.

————. *SportsWorld: An American Dreamland*. New York: Quadrangle/The New York Times Book, Co., 1975.

Little, Douglas. *American Orientalism: The United States and the Middle East Since 1945*. 3rd ed. Chapel Hill: University of North Carolina Press, 2008.

Lomax, Louis E. *To Kill a Black Man*. Los Angeles: Holloway House, 1968.

————. *When the Word Is Given: A Report on Elijah Muhammad, Malcolm X, and the Black Muslim World*. New York: The New American Library, 1964.

Marable, Manning. *Malcolm X: A Life of Reinvention*. New York: Viking, 2011.

Marable, Manning, and Garret Felber, eds. *The Portable Malcolm X Reader*. New York: Penguin Books, 2013.

Maraniss, David. *Rome 1960: The Olympics That Changed the World*. New York: Simon & Schuster, 2008.

Marqusee, Mike. *Redemption Song: Muhammad Ali and the Spirit of the Sixties*. London and New York: Verso, 2000.

Mee, Bob. *Liston & Ali: The Ugly Bear and the Boy Who Would Be King*. New York: Skyhorse Publishing, 2011.

Muehlenbeck, Philip E. *Betting on the Africans: John F. Kennedy's Courting of African Nationalist Leaders*. New York: Oxford University Press, 2014.

Muhammad, Elijah. *Message to the Blackman in America*. 1965. Reprint, Maryland Heights, MO: Secretarius MEMPS Ministries, 1997.

Nagler, Barney. *James Norris and the Decline of Boxing*. Indianapolis: Bobbs-Merrill, 1964.

Norwood, Christopher. *About Paterson: The Making and Unmaking of a City*. New York: Saturday Review Press, 1974.

Ogbar, Jeffrey O. G. *Black Power: Radical Politics and African American Identity*. Baltimore: Johns Hopkins University Press, 2004.

Olsen, Jack. *Black Is Best: The Riddle of Cassius Clay*. New York: Dell Publishing Co., Inc., 1967.

Pacheco, Ferdie. *Tales from the 5th Street Gym: Ali, the Dundees, and the Golden Age of Boxing*. Gainesville: University Press of Florida, 2010.

————. *Muhammad Ali: A View from the Corner*. New York: Carol Publishing Group, 1992.

————. *Fight Doctor*. London: Stanley Paul, 1978.

Perry, Bruce, ed. *Malcolm X: The Last Speeches*. New York and London: Pathfinder, 1990.

————. *Malcolm: The Life of a Man Who Changed Black America*. Barrytown, NY: Station Hill, Press, 1992.

Plimpton, George. *Shadow Box: An Amateur in the Ring*. Guilford, CT: The Lyons Press, 2003.

Rampersad, Arnold. *Jackie Robinson: A Biography*. New York: Ballantine Books, 1998.

Remnick, David. *King of the World: Muhammad Ali and the Rise of an American Hero*. New York: Viking, 1998.

Rickford, Russell J. *Betty Shabazz: A Remarkable Story of Survival and Faith Before and After Malcolm X*. Naperville, IL: Sourcebooks, Inc., 2003.

Roberts, Gene, and Hank Klibanoff. *The Race Beat: The Press, the Civil Rights Struggle, and the Awakening of a Nation*. New York: Vintage, 2006.

Roberts, Randy. *Joe Louis: Hard Times Man*. New Haven, CT: Yale University Press, 2010.

Roberts, Randy, and James Olsen. *Winning Is the Only Thing: Sports in America Since 1945*. Baltimore: Johns Hopkins University Press, 1989.

Rondinone, Troy. *Friday Night Fighter: Gaspar "Indio" Ortega and the Golden Age of Television Boxing*. Urbana and Chicago: University of Illinois Press, 2013.

Sales, William W., Jr. *From Civil Rights to Black Liberation: Malcolm X and the Organization of Afro-American Unity*. Boston: South End Press, 1994.

Schaap, Dick. *Flashing Before My Eyes: 50 Years of Headlines, Deadlines, and Punchlines*. New York: William Morrow, 2001.

Schulke, Flip, with Matt Schudel, *Muhammad Ali: The Birth of A Legend, Miami, 1961–1964*. New York: St. Martin's Press, 1999.

Sheed, Wilfrid. *Muhammad Ali: A Portrait in Words and Photographs*. New York: Crowell, 1975.

Shell-Weiss, Melanie. *Coming to Miami: A Social History*. Gainesville: University Press of Florida, 1997.

Spitz, Bob. *The Beatles: The Biography*. New York: Back Bay Books, 2005.

Stratton, W. K. *Floyd Patterson: The Fighting Life of Boxing's Invisible Champion*. New York: Houghton Mifflin Harcourt, 2012.

Strickland, William. *Malcolm X: Make It Plain*. New York: Viking, 1994.

Sugrue, Thomas. *Sweet Land of Liberty: The Forgotten Struggle for Civil Rights in the North*. New York: Random House, 2008.

Sullivan, George. *The Cassius Clay Story*. New York: Fleet Publishing Corporation, 1964.

Tanner, Michael. *Ali in Britain*. Edinburgh: Mainstream, 1995.

Thomas, Damion. *Globetrotting: African American Athletes and Cold War Politics*. Urbana: University of Illinois Press, 2012.

Torres, José. *Sting Like a Bee: The Muhammad Ali Story*. New York and London: Abelard Schuman, 1971.

Tosches, Nick. *The Devil and Sonny Liston*. Boston: Little, Brown and Company, 2000.

Von Eschen, Penny. *Satchmo Blows Up the World: Jazz Ambassadors Play the Cold War*. Cambridge, MA: Harvard University Press, 2004.

Warren, Robert Penn. *Who Speaks for the Negro?* New York: Random House, 1965.

Watkins, Mel. *Stepin Fetchit: The Life and Times of Lincoln Perry*. New York: Pantheon Books, 2005.

Weisbrot, Robert. *Freedom Bound: A History of America's Civil Rights Movement*. New York: W. W. Norton & Company, 1990.

Whitfield, Stephen J. *A Death in the Delta: The Story of Emmett Till*. New York: The Free Press, 1988.

Wilson, Sondra Kathryn. *Meet Me at the Theresa: The Story of Harlem's Most Famous Hotel*. New York: Atria Books, 2004.

X, Malcolm, as told to Alex Haley. *The Autobiography of Malcolm X*. 1965. Reprint, New York: Ballantine Books, 1992.

NOTES

Preface

1. Hughes, *The Collected Poems of Langston Hughes*, 426.

2. Ezra, *Muhammad Ali*, 1.

3. Olsen, *Black Is Best*, 93–94.

4. Huston Horn, "'Who Made Me—Is Me!'" *SI*, September 25, 1961, 42; *LCJ*, August 26, 1960.

5. *NYT*, February 27, 1964; Ferdie Pacheco interview with Jack Olsen, JOP; Olsen, *Black Is Best*, 94.

6. Olsen, *Black Is Best*, jacket copy.

7. For an interpretation of Malcolm's "multiple masks," see Marable, *Malcolm X*, 10–11.

8. Marable, *Malcolm X*, 10.

9. *AMX*, 421.

10. *AMX*, 447; "Playboy Interview: Cassius Clay," *Playboy*, October 1964; Hans J. Massaquoi, "Mystery of Malcolm X," *Ebony*, September 1964, 42.

11. "Fragments/Notes," Box 2, Folder 3, AHP. Numerous historians and writers have mistakenly used the Ali quote cited by Haley. See Remnick, *King of the World*, 214; Branch, *Pillar of Fire*, 259; Marable, *Malcolm X*, 293; Marqusee, *Redemption Song*, 88; Kindred, *Sound and Fury*, 75.

12. *AMX*, 448 (emphasis ours).

13. Marable, *Malcolm X*, 351. Literary critic Arnold Rampersad has argued, "Haley understood that autobiographies are almost by definition projects in fiction, in which the autobiographer selects from memory such material as seems to him or her most alluringly totemic." See Rampersad, "The Color of His Eyes: Bruce Perry's *Malcolm* and Malcolm's Malcolm," in *Malcolm X: In Our Own Image*, ed. Joe Wood (New York: St. Martin's Press, 1992), 119.

14. Floyd Patterson with Gay Talese, "In Defense of Cassius Clay," in *The Muhammad Ali Reader*, ed. Gerald Early (New York: Robert Weisbach Books, 1998), 65.

15. Cleaver, *Soul on Ice*, 117.

16. Edwards, *The Revolt of the Black Athlete*, 89–90.

Prologue

1. Joseph Martin interview with Jack Olsen, JOP; William Faversham interview with Jack Olsen, JOP; Gordon Davidson interview with Jack Olsen, JOP; Olsen, *Black Is Best*, 39.

2. For the confrontation between Cassius and his father, see Officer Kalbfleisch interview with Jack Olsen, JOP; Olsen, *Black Is Best*, 49–50.

3. Bob Coleman interview with author.

4. Olsen, *Black Is Best*, 106; Cassius Clay Sr. interview with Jack Olsen, JOP.

5. Baldwin, *The Fire Next Time*, 98.

6. Ibid., 68.

7. Cassius Clay Sr. interview with Jack Olsen, JOP.

8. Adams, *Way Up North in Louisville*, 115–117; Fosl and K'Meyer, *Freedom on the Border*, 126–127, 131–133.

9. *NYP*, February 27, 1964.

10. Whitfield, *A Death in the Delta*, 42.

11. Ali with Durham, *The Greatest*, 35; Hauser, *Muhammad Ali*, 89.

12. Goldman, *The Death and Life*, 26–27.

13. Ibid.

14. Ibid., 9. On a few occasions, Malcolm suggested that his father was not actually murdered but rather died accidentally. See Marable, *Malcolm X*, 32.

Chapter 1

1. Cottrell, *Man of Destiny*, 1–2.

2. For details of Angelo Dundee's life, see: Dundee, *My View from the Corner*, 17–56; Dundee, *I Only Talk Winning*, 21–117; Anderson, *In the Corner*, 53–84; Fried, *Corner Men*, 1–28.

3. Huston Horn, "Who Made Me—Is Me!," *SI*, September 25, 1961, 45; Dundee, *My View from the Corner*, 60–61.

4. Dundee, *My View from the Corner*, 62; Anderson, *In the Corner*, 61–62.

5. Pacheco, *Fight Doctor*, 22–23.

6. Horn, "Who Made Me—Is Me!," 47.

7. For the 5th Street Gym, see: Pacheco, *Tales from the 5th St. Gym*, 1–48; Dundee, *My View from the Corner*, 47–50.

8. Dundee, *My View from the Corner*, 49.

9. Myron Cope, "Feats of Clay," in *Great Sports Reporting*, ed. Allen Kirschner (New York: Dell, 1969), 163.

10. Fried, *Corner Men*, 9.

11. Horn, "Who Made Me—Is Me!," 51.

12. Fried, *Corner Men*, 15.

13. Dundee, *My View from the Corner*, 63–64.

14. Michael Brennan, "Ali and His Educators," *SI*, September 22, 1980, accessed at http://www.si.com/vault/1980/09/22/824976/ali-and-his-educators; *LCJ*, December 27, 1960, and December 28, 1960; *MH*, December 28, 1960.

15. For Clay-Johansson, see: Hauser, *Muhammad Ali*, 37–38; *MH*, February 5, 1961, and February 7, 1961; *LCJ*, February 7, 1961; *BG*, February 7, 1961; *NYT*, February 7, 1961.

16. *LCJ*, April 20, 1961; *PC*, April 29, 1961; *NYT*, May 14, 1961.

17. Horn, "Who Made Me—Is Me!," 40.

18. Schulke with Schudel, *Muhammad Ali*, 10.

19. Horn, "Who Made Me—Is Me!," 40; Dunn, *Black Miami in the Twentieth Century*, 143–156.

20. Shell-Weiss, *Coming to Miami*, 149; Raymond Mohl, "'South of the South?' Jews, Blacks, and the Civil Rights Movement in Miami, 1945–1960," *Journal of American Ethnic History* 18 (Winter 1999): 20–23.

21. Schulke with Schudel, *Muhammad Ali*, 26–28; *Muhammad Ali: Made in Miami*, DVD, produced by Gaspar Gonzalez and Alan Tomlinson (PBS, 2008).

22. Abdul Rahman Muhammad (Sam Saxon) interview with author; Jack Olsen, "A Case of Conscience," *SI*, April 11, 1966, n.p.; Hauser, *Muhammad Ali*, 89–90.

23. Hauser, *Muhammad Ali*, 89–90.

24. Lincoln, *The Black Muslims in America*, 71, 115–116.

25. Hauser, *Muhammad Ali*, 90; Pacheco, *Muhammad Ali*, 37–38; Lincoln, *The Black Muslims in America*, 68–69; Goldman, *The Death and Life*, 69–70.

26. Hauser, *Muhammad Ali*, 90–91.

27. Olsen, *Black Is Best*, 134–136, 138–139.

28. Bingham and Wallace, *Muhammad Ali's Greatest Fight*, 63; Robert Lipsyte, "Cassius Clay, Cassius X, Muhammad Ali," *NYTM*, October 25, 1964, 140; Sullivan, *The Cassius Clay Story*, 92; *NYT*, March 24, 1964; Branch, *Parting the Waters*, 914–915.

29. Bingham and Wallace, *Muhammad Ali's Greatest Fight*, 63; *Atlanta Journal*, October 10, 1958.

30. Olsen, *Black Is Best*, 134; Essien-Udom, *Black Nationalism*, 188.

31. Horn, "Who Made Me—Is *Me!*," 39.

32. Alex Haley, "The Implications of Cassius X," 1964, Box Two, Folder 1, AHP; Sullivan, *The Cassius Clay Story*, 90; Bingham and Wallace, *Muhammad Ali's Greatest Fight*, 63.

33. Hauser, *Muhammad Ali*, 91.

34. Ibid.; *AMX*, 177–178.

35. Isaac Sutton, "Intimate Look at the Champ," *Ebony*, November 1966, 154.

36. Monroe Berger, "The Black Muslims," *Horizon*, Winter 1964, 57.

37. Clegg, *An Original Man*, 6–17.

38. Essien-Udom, *Black Nationalism*, 43–44; Lincoln, *The Black Muslims in America*, 10–15; Clegg, *An Original Man*, 20–33.

39. Lincoln, *The Black Muslims in America*, 75–76; Essien-Udom, *Black Nationalism*, 131–132; Marable, *Malcolm X*, 85.

40. *AMX*, 179–80; Clegg, *An Original Man*, 48–52; Lincoln, *The Black Muslims in America*, 76–77; Essien-Udom, *Black Nationalism*, 134.

41. Clegg, *An Original Man*, 64–65; Muhammad, *Message to the Blackman in America*, 290–293.

42. Pacheco, *Muhammad Ali*, 40–41.

43. Olsen, *Black Is Best*, 139–140.

44. Lincoln, *The Black Muslims in America*, 80.

45. Essien-Udom, *Black Nationalism*, 15, 207; Lincoln, *The Black Muslims in America*, 81.

46. Hauser, *Muhammad Ali*, 91–97.

47. *MS*, October 15, 1962.

48. Marqusee, *Redemption Song*, 59; David K. Wiggins, "Victory for Allah: Muhammad Ali, the Nation of Islam, and American Society," in *Muhammad Ali: The People's Champ*, ed. Elliot Gorn (Urbana and Chicago: University of Illinois Press, 1995), 90.

Chapter 2

1. Lomax, *When the Word Is Given*, 27–28.

2. Ibid.; *NYAN*, May 4, 1957.

3. Ralph Ellison, "Harlem Is Nowhere," in John Callahan, ed., *The Collected Essays of Ralph Ellison* (New York: Modern Library, 2003), 321–322.

4. *NYAN*, May 4, 1957; Lincoln, *The Black Muslims in America*, 199–203; Taylor Branch interview with Yusuf Shah (aka Captain Joseph Gravitt), October 17, 1991, TBP; Essien-Udom, *Black Nationalism*, 153–156.

5. *AMX*, 254–255.

6. Essien-Udom, *Black Nationalism*, 267.

7. *NYAN*, April 29, 1957.

8. Marable, *Malcolm X*, 128.

9. *NYAN*, April 29, 1957.

10. *AMX*, 256; DeCaro, *On the Side of My People*, 113–116; FBIMX-4.

11. Karim, *Remembering Malcolm*, 23–44.

12. Herbert Krosney, "America's Black Supremacists," *The Nation*, May 6, 1961, 391; Karim, *Remembering Malcolm*, 50–51.

13. Karim, *Remembering Malcolm*, 51–52.

14. Ibid., 54.

15. Ibid., 56; Goldman, *The Death and Life*, 60.

16. Karim, *Remembering Malcolm*, 56–57; Lomax, *When the Word Is Given*, 25.

17. Lincoln, *The Black Muslims in America*, 108–110.

18. Clegg, *An Original Man*, 27; Goldman, *The Death and Life*, 46.

19. Karim, *Remembering Malcolm*, 97–98.

20. Ibid., 39–52; *AMX*, 53–55.

21. *AMX*, 166–167; Goldman, *The Death and Life*, 32–33.

22. *AMX*, 172–175.

23. Ibid.

24. Ibid., 176–177; Marable, *Malcolm X*, 77.

25. *AMX*, 208–217.

26. *NYAN*, April 20, 1957 (emphasis ours).

27. *AMX*, 199.

28. Perry, *Malcolm*, 145; Lomax, *When the Word Is Given*, 51.

29. Gallen, *Malcolm X*, 33.

30. Perry, *Malcolm*, 162–163; Essien-Udom, *Black Nationalism*, 177.

31. Perry, *Malcolm*, 146.

32. Goldman, *The Death and Life*, 47; Essien-Udom, *Black Nationalism*, 101.

33. FBIMX-4.

34. Transcript of *The Hate That Hate Produced* (1959) in FBIMX-4.

35. Clegg, *An Original Man*, 125–129.

36. *AMX*, 289.

37. Ibid.; Marable, *Malcolm X*, 140.

38. FBIEM-6; Clegg, *An Original Man*, 104, 131, 176; Marable, *Malcolm X*, 124, 162–163.

39. William Worthy, "The Angriest Negroes," *Esquire*, February 1961, 105.

40. Sugrue, *Sweet Land of Liberty*, 288; Joseph, *Waiting 'Til the Midnight Hour*, 50–52.

41. *NYAN*, June 4, 1960; Malcolm X, "Harlem Freedom Rally, 1960," Box 5, Folder 1, MXP (emphasis ours).

42. Malcolm X, "Harlem Freedom Rally, 1960"; FBIMX-3; Cone, *Martin & Malcolm & America*, 98–99.

43. Goldman, *The Death and Life*, 15–16; Alex Haley, "Alex Haley Remembers Malcolm X," *Essence*, November 1983, 54.

44. Gallen, *Malcolm X*, 49, 58–60.

45. Branch, *Parting the Waters*, 168–172, 323–324; Goldman, *The Death and Life*, 14.

46. Goldman, *The Death and Life of Malcolm X*, 14.

47. *AMX*, 316–17. Note: In February 1960, shortly after Elijah Muhammad returned from his trip to the Middle East, he declared that all NOI temples would be called *mosques*.

48. Elijah Muhammad to Mr. Malcolm Shabazz, February 15, 1962, MXP.

49. Malcolm X and James Farmer, "Separation or Integration: A Debate," *Dialogue Magazine*, May 1962, 14–18.

50. Farmer, *Lay Bare the Heart*, 224–225.

Chapter 3

1. *LVS*, June 22, 1961, and June 23, 1961.

2. For Clay's version of the story, see Hauser, *Muhammad Ali*, 39.

3. For Gorgeous George's background, see Roberts and Olson, *Winning Is the Only Thing*, 99–100.

4. For Clay and George, see: Hauser, *Muhammad Ali*, 39; Peter Carlson, "Gorgeous George Tutors Cassius Clay," *American History*, December 2011, 24–25.

5. *LVS*, June 26, 1961.

6. *LVS*, June 27, 1961; Michael Brennan, "Ali and His Educators," *SI*, September 22, 1980, accessed at http://www.si.com/vault/1980/09/22/824976/ali-and-his-educators.

7. Remnick, *King of the World*, 120; Carlson, "Gorgeous George Tutors Cassius Clay," 25.

8. Myron Cope, "Feats of Clay," in *Great Sports Reporting*, ed. Allen Kirschner (New York: Dell, 1969), 157–158.

9. Ibid.

10. Gilbert Rogin, "Cautious Comes of Age," *SI*, October 16, 1961, 22; Cope, "Feats of Clay," 160; Huston Horn, "Fast Talk and a Slow Fight," *SI*, July 31, 1961, 44.

11. Horn, "Fast Talk and a Slow Fight," 44.

12. Roberts, *Joe Louis*, 71–72.

13. Huston Horn, "Who Made Me—Is *Me!*," *SI*, September 25, 1961, 39–40; Cope, "Feats of Clay," 161.

14. Horn, "Who Made Me—Is *Me!*," 40–41.

15. Ibid., 41.

16. Rogin, "Cautious Comes of Age," 22.

17. Ibid., 33–55.

18. "A Wet Way to Train for a Fight," *Life*, September 8, 1961, 123.

19. Baldwin, *The Fire Next Time*, 23–24.

20. Howard Tuckner, "'Man, It's Great to Be Great,'" *NYTM*, December 9, 1962.

21. *LCJ*, July 23, 1961.

22. Joseph T. Friscia, "The RISE and Fall of a Heavyweight Contender," *BI*, October 1961, 64.

23. *LCJ*, October 8, 1961; *NYT*, October 8, 1961; Rogin, "Cautious Comes of Age," 22.

24. Atyeo and Dennis, *Muhammad Ali*, 24.

25. Olsen, *Black Is Best*, 186–187.

26. For the Clay-Besmanoff fight, see: *NYT*, November 30, 1961; *LCJ*, November 30, 1961; Cope, "Feats of Clay," 161–162.

27. Lew Eskin, "Bonus Boy of Boxing," *The Ring*, October 1961, 17; Dundee, *My View from the Corner*, 70.

28. "Cassius Clay Says: 'I'm Tired of Fighting Unrated Bums!!'" *The Ring*, February 1962, 54.

29. "Annual World Rankings," *The Ring*, February 1962, 42; Dundee, *My View from the Corner*, 71.

30. *NYT*, February 7, 1962; *NYP*, February 7, 1962.

31. A. J. Liebling, "Poet and Pedagogue," *The New Yorker*, March 3, 1962, 104.

32. Ibid.,106–111.

33. Ibid.,108.

34. Unless otherwise noted, for the Clay-Banks fight, see: Liebling, "Poet and Pedagogue,"114–117; *NYT*, February 11, 1962; *NYP*, February 11, 1962, and February 12, 1962; "Clay-Banks," *BI*, May 1962, 13.

35. Liebling, "Poet and Pedagogue," 117.

36. *NYT*, February 11, 1961; *NYP*, February 12, 1962.

37. *BI*, March 1962, 7, and May 1962, 6; *The Ring*, March 1962, 18.

38. *LAT*, April 8, 1962, April 10, 1962, and April 14, 1962; *LAS*, April 12, 1962.

39. *LAT*, April 20, 1962, and April 25, 1962.

40. Ibid., April 17, 1962, and April 23, 1962.

41. *LAT*, April 20, 1962.

42. For the Clay-Logan match, see: *LAT*, April 24, 1962, and April 25, 1962; *NYT*, April 24, 1962.

43. *LAT*, April 23, 1962.

44. Cope, "Feats of Clay," 163–164; *LAT*, April 17, 1962.

Chapter 4

1. Abdul Rahman Muhammad (Sam Saxon) interview with author.

2. *MS*, July 1962; Alex Haley, "The Implications of Cassius X," 1964, Box Two, Folder 1, AHP.

3. *AMX*, 332.

4. Fairclough, *Better Day Coming*, 308; Goldman, *The Death and Life*, 96.

5. Branch, *Pillar of Fire*, 3–13; Marable, *Malcolm X*, 207; *LAT* April 28–29, 1962.

6. *LAT*, April 28–29, 1962; Goldman, *The Death and Life*, 97.

7. Marable, *Malcolm X*, 207–208; FBIMX-9.

8. *LAT*, May 5, 1962; FBIMX-8; Butin, *L.A. Noir*, 252; "It Did Happen Here!" (press release), Box 12, Folder 1, MXP.

9. *LAT*, May 6, 1962.

10. Perry, *Malcolm*, 192.

11. Ibid.

12. Ibid.

13. Ibid.

14. Marable, *Malcolm X*, 208; Branch, *Pillar of Fire*, 13.

15. *AMX*, 317; Goldman, *The Death and Life*, 93–94.

16. Branch, *Pillar of Fire*, 14.

17. Ibid., 15.

18. FBIEM-6/7.

19. Essien-Udom, *Black Nationalism*, 207; Lincoln, *The Black Muslims in America*, 80.

20. Clegg, *An Original Man*, 101–102.

21. Ibid., 184–185.

22. FBIEM-7.

23. *AMX*, 322–324.

24. Ibid.

25. Goldman, *The Death and Life*, 115.

26. Clegg, *An Original Man*, 176.

27. *CD*, July 7, 1964; FBIEM-7; Perry, *Malcolm*, 223.

28. Marable and Felber, eds., *The Portable Malcolm X Reader*, xxxii; Marable, *Malcolm X*, 174.

29. Marable, *Malcolm X*, 205; Perry, *Malcolm*, 189.

30. Gallen, *Malcolm X*, 63.

31. *LAT*, June 7, 1962; FBIMX-8.

32. Branch, *Pillar of Fire*, 14; *LAT*, June 16, 1962.

33. *MC*, June 16, 1962; *MS*, July 1962.

34. *MC*, June 16, 1962.

35. *PC*, June 23, 1962; *AMX*, 332.

36. *MS*, July 1962.

37. Ibid.

38. Goldman, *The Death and Life*, 23.

39. Sam Pollard and Judy Richardson interview with Muhammad Ali, February 16, 1989, EYES.

40. FBIMX-9.

41. Clegg, *An Original Man*, 159–160, 322 (footnote 51).

42. FBIMX-8; Photocopy from *Muhammad Speaks*, "Boston, 1962," Box 12, Folder 1, MXP; Malcolm X, "An Open Letter to America's Five Negro Congressmen," n.d., Box 12, Folder 1, MXP.

43. Perry, *Malcolm*, 223; Aubrey Barnette with Edward Linn, "The Black Muslims Are a Fraud," *SEP*, February 27, 1965, 24, 29.

44. Barnette with Linn, "The Black Muslims Are a Fraud," 28–29.

45. Ibid., 23–24.

46. Lomax, *To Kill a Black Man*, 98.

47. "The Muslim Message: All White Men Devils, All Negroes Divine," *Newsweek*, August 27, 1962, 26; FBIMX-8; Marable, *Malcolm X*, 218–219; Elijah Muhammad to Malcolm X, September 21, 1962, Box 3, Folder 8, MXP.

48. *AMX*, 319–321.

49. Ibid., 310; Perry, *Malcolm*, 186; Clegg, *An Original Man*, 117.

50. *LAT*, August 15, 1962.

51. *NYAN*, August 25, 1962.

52. *MS*, September 15, 1962.

Chapter 5

1. *NYT*, May 17, 1962; *NYJA*, May 18, 1962.

2. *NYJA*, May 20, 1962; *NYT*, May 20, 1962; *NYAN*, May 26, 1962.

3. Nat Fleischer, "Alejandro Lavorante New Heavyweight Threat," *The Ring*, November 1961, 28–29, 54–55; *LAT*, April 7, 1964.

4. *LAT*, March 31, 1962, April 2, 1962, and April 7, 1962.

5. *LAT*, July 10, 1962.

6. *LAT*, July 21, 1962.

7. Ibid., July 20, 1962, and July 21, 1962.

8. Ibid., September 22, 1962, September 23, 1962, October 27, 1962, October 23, 1962, and January 24, 1963.

9. Ibid., September 23, 1962, September 24, 1962, January 24, 1963, September 28, 1962, September 27, 1962, October 19, 1962, January 19, 1963, September 30, 1962, April 18, 1963, May 5, 1963, September 19, 1963, April 2, 1964, and April 7, 1964; Randy Roberts, "The Demise of a Contender," *The Ring*, January 2015, 82–85.

10. Roberts and Olson, *Winning Is the Only Thing*, 92.

11. For the Griffith-Paret weigh-in controversy, see: Gilbert Rogin, "The Deadly Insult," *SI*, April 2, 1962, 14; *NYT*, March 25, 1962; *Ring of Fire: The Emile Griffith Story*, produced by Dan Klores and Ron Berger (2005); Norman Mailer, "Ten Thousand Words a Minute," *Esquire*, February 1963, 115; Rondinone, *Friday Night Fighter*, 193; Gene Smith, "The Shadow Boxer," *SI*, April 18, 2005, accessed at http://sportsillustrated.cnn.com/vault/.

12. *NYT*, March 25, 1962.

13. Ibid., 116.

14. Dunphy, *Don Dunphy at Ringside*, 145–146, 163; Rondinone, *Friday Night Fighter*, 196–197.

15. *NYT*, March 25, 1962, March 27, 1962, March 28, 1962, April 1, 1962, and April 4, 1962.

16. Ibid., March 26, 1962, March 27, 1962, March 28, 1962, March 30, 1962, March 31, 1962, April 1, 1962, and April 7, 1962.

17. Brooks and Marsh, *The Complete Directory to Prime Time Network TV Shows*, 112–114.

18. Randy Roberts, "The Wide World of Muhammad Ali: The Politics and Economics of Televised Boxing," in *Muhammad Ali: The People's Champ*, ed. Elliot Gorn (Urbana and Chicago: University of Illinois Press, 1995), 25–39.

19. Harry Markson, "TV Loss Not Fatal," *The Ring*, November 1964, 16–17; "The End of an Era in Garden Boxing," *The Ring*, November 1964, 7–15.

20. William Nack, "O Unlucky Man," *SI*, February 14, 1994, 156.

21. Gilbert Rogin and Morton Sharnik, "Can't a Fellow Make a Mistake?," *SI*, July 17, 1961; Jerry Izenberg interview with author.

22. Rogin and Sharnik, "Can't a Fellow Make a Mistake?," 27–28; Tosches, *The Devil and Sonny Liston*, 37–49; Jerry Izenberg interview with author.

23. Nack, "O Unlucky Man," 158; Stratton, *Floyd Patterson*, 153; Rogin and Sharnik, "Can't a Fellow Make a Mistake?," 27, 50.

24. "Professional Boxing," Part 2: Frankie Carbo, *Hearings Before the Subcommittee on Antitrust and Monopoly of the Committee on the Judiciary*, United States Senate, 68th Congress, 2nd Session (1960), 645.

25. Rogin and Sharnik, "Can't a Fellow Make a Mistake?," 24; Tosches, *The Devil and Sonny Liston*, 46; Leroi Jones, "In the Ring (2)," *The Nation*, June 1964, 661.

26. Rogin and Sharnik, "Can't a Fellow Make a Mistake?," 29, 48; Tosches, *The Devil and Sonny Liston*, 92–96.

27. Tosches, *The Devil and Sonny Liston*, 99.

28. "World Rankings," *The Ring*, July 1960, 10; "Professional Boxing," 790.

29. Steven A. Riess, "Only the Ring Was Square: Frankie Carbo and the Underworld Control of American Boxing," *International Journal of the History of Sport* 5, no. 1 (May 1988): 41–42; Nagler, *James Norris and the Decline of Boxing*, 141–152.

30. Stratton, *Floyd Patterson*, 139–140.

31. Ibid., 141.

32. Gilbert Rogin, "The Facts About the Big Fight," *SI*, October 8, 1962, 20–21; A. J. Liebling, "The Morest," in *A Neutral Corner: Boxing Essays*, eds. Fred Warner and James Barbour (New York: Fireside, 1990), 188.

33. *NYT*, September 26, 1962; Rogin, "The Facts About the Big Fight," 20.

34. Liebling, "The Morest," 186; Gay Talese, "The Loser," in *The Silent Season of a Hero: The Sports Writing of Gay Talese*, ed. Michael Rosenwald (New York: Walker & Company, 2010), 159–160.

35. *NYT*, September 27, 1962, and September 26, 1962; James Baldwin, "The Fight: Patterson vs. Liston," in *At the Fights: American Writers on Boxing*, eds. George Kimball and John Schulian (New York: Library of America, 2012), 153.

36. Baldwin, "The Fight," 153; Mailer, "Ten Thousand Words a Minute," 117.

37. *NYT*, September 27, 1962; *LAT*, November 1, 1962.

38. James J. Doherty, "Fears and Hopes of a Heavyweight Contender," *BI*, November 1962, 8; Fitzgerald, *The Ageless Warrior*, 191.

39. Hauser, *Muhammad Ali*, 49.

40. *NYT*, October 23, 1962.

41. Ibid.; Gilbert Rogin, "Campaign's End for an Ancient Warrior," *SI*, November 26, 1962, 20.

42. Rogin, "Campaign's End for an Ancient Warrior," 20; *LAT*, November 8, 1962; Ezra, *Muhammad Ali*, 42; *NYT*, November 17, 1962; *BG*, November 17, 1962.

43. For the Clay-Moore fight, see: Rogin, "Campaign's End for an Ancient Warrior," 20–21; *NYJA*, November 18, 1962; Hauser, *Muhammad Ali*, 49; *LJC*, November 16, 1962; *LAT*, November 16, 1962; *NYP*, November 16, 1962; *NYT*, November 16, 1962.

44. *LAT*, November 16, 1962.

45. Ibid., December 23, 1962.

46. *PC*, January 12, 1963, January 31, 1963, and February 2, 1963; *CT*, January 18, 1963, and January 25, 1963; *NYT*, January 26, 1963.

47. Hauser, *Muhammad Ali*, 51.

Chapter 6

1. Clegg, *An Original Man*, 190; telegram from Elijah Muhammad to Minister Malcolm Shabazz, c/o Raymond Sharrieff, February 26, 1963, Box 3, Folder 8, MXP.

2. Ibid., 17–18.

3. Branch, *Pillar of Fire*, 18; FBIMX-8.

4. FBIMX-8; Branch, *Pillar of Fire*, 19; *AMX*, 325.

5. FBIMX-8.

6. *AMX*, 325.

7. Ibid.

8. *AMX*, 27.

9. George Plimpton, "Miami Notebook: Cassius Clay and Malcolm X," *Harper's Magazine*, June 1964, 58.

10. *Ed Sullivan Show*, February 2, 1963. "Cassius Clay (Muhammad Ali) talks with Ed Sullivan," accessed at YouTube.com, https://www.youtube.com/watch?v=TUKF_GageY8.

11. Torres, *Sting Like a Bee*, 39.

12. *NYT*, February 5, 1963; *LCJ*, February 5, 1963.

13. *NYT*, February 5, 1963; *LCJ*, February 5, 1963; A. J. Liebling, "Anti-Poetry Night," *The New Yorker*, March 30, 1963, 122.

14. Liebling, "Anti-Poetry Night," 122.

15. Frank Deford, *Over Time*, e-book.

16. Ibid.; Kindred, *Sound and Fury*, 46.

17. For the Liston-Clay meeting, see: *LCJ*, February 9, 1963, and February 10, 1963.

18. "The Dream," *Time*, March 22, 1963, accessed at http://content.time.com/time/magazine/article/0,9171,896687,00.html.

19. *BG*, March 7, 1963.

20. Scott Sherman, "The Long Good-Bye," *Vanity Fair*, November 30, 2012, accessed at http://www.vanityfair.com/culture/2012/11/1963-newspaper-strike-bertram-powers.

21. "The Dream."

22. Sherman, "The Long Good-Bye."

23. Sullivan, *The Cassius Clay Story*, 55.

24. For Clay's visit to the Bitter End, see *NYP*, March 8, 1963; *NYT*, March 8, 1963; *CT*, March 2, 1963; "Prophet's Margin," *Newsweek*, March 25, 1963, 93.

25. Clay's poetry recital quoted from *NYP*, March 8, 1963.

26. Ibid.

27. Liebling, "Anti-Poetry Night," 122.

28. Ibid., 132; Plimpton, *Shadow Box*, 113; *BG*, March 10, 1963.

29. Sullivan, *The Cassius Clay Story*, 55; "The Dream;" *NYP*, March 13, 1963.

30. *NYT*, March 13, 1963, and March 14, 1963.

31. For Clay's first meeting with Drew "Bundini" Brown, see Plimpton, *Shadow Box*, 112–113.

32. Liebling, "Anti-Poetry Night," 124, 127.

33. Ibid.; *LCJ*, March 12, 1963.

34. *NYAN*, March 23, 1963.

35. *NYAN*, March 23, 1963; *NYP*, March 13, 1963; *BG*, March 12, 1963, and March 13, 1963; *NYT*, March 13, 1963.

36. Liebling, "Anti-Poetry Night," 132, 134; "The Dream"; Huston Horn, "A Comeuppance for the Cocksure Cassius," *SI*, March 25, 1963, accessed at http://www.si.com/vault/1963/03/25/606262/a-comeuppance-for-the-cocksure-cassius.

37. In addition to the film of the contest, for the Clay-Jones fight, see: Liebling, "Anti-Poetry Night," 36–42; "Prophet's Margin," *Newsweek*, March 25, 1963, 96; *NYP*, March 14, 1963; *NYT*, March 14, 1963; *BG*, March 14, 1963; "The Night They Filled the Garden," *BI*, June 1963, 42–45; Horn, "A Comeuppance for the Cocksure Cassius."

38. Horn, "A Comeuppance for the Cocksure Cassius."

39. Plimpton, *Shadow Box*, 113.

40. *NYP*, March 14, 1963.

41. "Prophet's Margin," *Newsweek*, March 25, 1963, 96; *LCJ*, March 14, 1963; *BG*, March 14, 1963.

42. "The Dream."

Chapter 7

1. *NYAN*, March 16, 1963; *LCJ*, March 24, 1963.

2. Altschuler, *All Shook Up*, 121–125.

3. Lewis, *The Shadows of Youth*, 40–41.

4. William Nack, "Young Cassius Clay," *SI*, January 12, 1992, 80.

5. "The Dream," *Time*, March 22, 1963; Ezra, *Muhammad Ali*, 72; Alex Poinsett, "A Look at Cassius Clay: Biggest Mouth in Boxing," *Ebony*, March 1963, 36.

6. Poinsett, "A Look at Cassius Clay: Biggest Mouth in Boxing," 36 (emphasis ours).

7. Ibid. For Malcolm's retelling of his hair conking, see *AMX*, 59–61.

8. Poinsett, "A Look at Cassius Clay, Biggest Mouth in Boxing," 36.

9. *PC*, February 2, 1963.

10. Pete Hamill, "The Man Who Filled the Garden," *New York Post Magazine*, March 17, 1963, 2.

11. Ibid.

12. Ibid.

13. *PC*, March 30, 1963; *BAA*, April 6, 1963.

14. Dr. Maurice F. Rabb to Morris M. DeLisser, March 25, 1963, Box III: A35, Folder "Ali, Muhammad, 1963–1964," National Association for the Advancement of Colored People Administrative Files, 1909–1969, Library of Congress.

15. Ibid.

16. Ibid.

17. Olsen, *Black Is Best*, 136; Poinsett, "A Look at Cassius Clay: Biggest Mouth in Boxing," 36.

18. *AMX*, 324.

19. Branch, *Pillar of Fire*, 18.

20. *AMX*, 326–327.

21. Ibid.

22. Evanzz, *The Messenger*, 262.

23. Goldman, *The Death and Life*, 112–113.

24. *NYT*, May 11, 1963, and May 12, 1963.

25. Gertrude Samuels, "Two Ways: Black Muslim and N.A.A.C.P.," *NYTM*, May 12, 1963, SM14; *NYT*, May 19, 1963; *CD*, June 1, 1963.

26. *NYHT*, May 15, 1963; FBIMX-9; *NYT*, May 11, 1963; *NYAN*, May 25, 1963.

27. Ibid.

28. Gilbert Rogin and Morton Sharnik, "Can't a Fellow Make a Mistake?," *SI*, July 17, 1961, 49–50; William Nack, "Oh Unlucky Man," *SI*, February 14, 1994, 154.

29. Branch, *Parting the Waters*, 801; *NYAN*, May 18, 1963.

30. *NYAN*, March 30, 1963, and November 16, 1963; Rampersad, *Jackie Robinson*, 373.

31. *NYAN*, December 14, 1963.

32. Ibid.

33. Goldman, *The Death and Life*, 126n.

34. Interview with Alex Haley, October 24, 1988, EYES; Alex Haley, "Playboy Interview: Malcolm X," *Playboy*, May 1963, 53.

35. Haley, "Playboy Interview: Malcolm X," 56.

36. *AMX*, 421; Haley, "Playboy Interview: Malcolm X," 60.

37. *AMX*, 421–423.

38. Marable, *Malcolm X*, 247.

39. Ibid., 238–239.

40. *NYT*, June 25, 1963; Transcripts of *The Negro and the American Promise* can be found in Kenneth B. Clark, *The Negro Protest* (Boston: Beacon Press, 1963), 17–26, 35–39.

41. Profile of James Baldwin drawn from the *New York Post Magazine*'s six-part series, January 13–17 and 19, 1964; Clark, *The Negro Protest*, 8, 10, 12.

42. Baldwin, *The Fire Next Time*, 73.

43. Ibid., 62–64; Clegg, *An Original Man*, 6–9.

44. Baldwin, *The Fire Next Time*, 65–78; Clark, *The Negro Protest*, 11.

45. Baldwin, *The Fire Next Time*, 103.

Chapter 8

1. For the early meeting between Clay and McHugh, see *Pittsburgh Post-Gazette*, May 31, 1998; Roy McHugh, "Cassius Clay—He Talks So Big," *Sport*, December 1962, 35, 70–72; Roy McHugh, "Can Cassius Clay Win His Big Gamble?," *Sport*, October 1963, 15–16, 69–71.

2. Olsen, *Black Is Best*, 152.

3. Gordon Davidson interview with author; Gordon Davidson interview with Jack Olsen, JOP; *NYP*, March 17, 1963.

4. William Faversham Jr. interview with Jack Olsen, JOP.

5. *CT*, April 11, 1963.

6. Ibid., 12–13; *BG*, May 29, 1963; *NYT*, June 2, 1963.

7. *LDM*, May 28, 1963; Tanner, *Ali in Britain*, 15–16; *BG*, May 28, 1963.

8. *NYT*, June 2, 1963.

9. *NYT*, June 13, 1963.

10. Ibid.

11. *LDM*, June 15, 1963, and June 17, 1963; *NYT*, June 14, 1963; Huston Horn, "'E Said 'E Would and 'E Did," *SI*, July 1, 1963, 43; Tanner, *Ali in Britain*, 22.

12. *LDM*, June 18, 1963.

13. Horn, "'E Said 'E Would and 'E Did," 43. Attendance figures vary between 17,000 and 55,000. Horn's number is probably on the high side, but not by much.

14. *NYJA*, June 19, 1963; *LDM*, June 19, 1963; *LCJ*, June 19, 1963.

15. *NYJA*, June 19, 1963.

16. For the Clay-Cooper match, see Horn, "'E Said'E Would and 'E Did," 43–45; Tanner, *Ali in Britain*, 25–32; *LDM*, June 19, 1963; *NYT*, June 19, 1963; *LCJ*, June 19, 1963; *LT*, June 19, 1963; *LDTMP*, June 19, 1963; John S. Sharp, "Clay's Prediction—True," *Ring*, September 1963, 18–19, 44; "Number 19 for Cassius," *BI*, September 1963, 21–23; "Murder on the BBC," *Time*, June 28, 1963, n.p.

17. "Murder on the BBC."

18. *LDM*, June 19, 1963; Tanner, *Ali in Britain*, 32.

19. Horn, "'E Said 'E Would and 'E Did," 45.

20. Dundee, *My View from the Corner*, 84–85.

21. *LDM*, June 19, 1963; *NYJA*, September 19, 1963.

22. *LCJ*, June 19, 1963

23. *LDTMP*, June 20, 1963; *NYJA*, June 19, 1963.

24. *NYT*, June 20, 1963; *LCJ*, June 20, 1963.

25. Gordon Davidson to W. S. Cutchins, July 23, 1963, Box MSSA B613a, Folder 1657, GBB; Bill Faversham to Louisville Sponsoring Group, April 26, 1963, Box MSSA B613a, Folder 1660, GBB.

26. Davidson to Cutchins, July 23, 1963, GBB; *LCJ*, April 9, 1963.

27. Tom Wolfe, "The Marvelous Mouth," *Esquire*, October 1963, 192.

28. Alex Haley, "The Implications of Cassius X," Box Two, Folder 1, AHP.

29. Wolfe, "The Marvelous Mouth," 192.

30. *LCJ*, June 26, 1963.

31. *CST*, July 3, 1963; *BAA*, July 13, 1963; *PC*, July 3, 1963.

32. *LCJ*, July 5, 1963.

33. Marable, *Malcolm X*, 252–253.

34. For the exchange between Malcolm and Robert Lipsyte, see *NYT*, July 23, 1963; Lipsyte, *SportsWorld*, 85–86; Lipsyte, *An Accidental Sportswriter*, 65–66; Robert Lipsyte interview with author.

35. Wolfe, "The Marvelous Mouth," 196.

36. For the Las Vegas encounter between Liston and Clay, see *NYT*, July 19, 1963; Hauser, *Muhammad Ali*, 58–59; Jerry Izenberg interview with author.

37. *NYT*, July 25, 1963; Hauser, *Muhammad Ali*, 58–59.

38. Hauser, *Muhammad Ali*, 58–59.

39. Gordon Davidson to W. S. Cutchins, July 23, 1963, Box MSSA B613a, Folder 1657, GBB; *LCJ* July 23, 1963; "The Man, the Rabbit and the Boy," *Time*, August 2, 1963, 52.

40. *LAT*, July 24, 1963; *NYT*, July 24, 1963; Robert H. Boyle, "This Is What Clay Says He Wants," *SI*, August 5, 1963, 22.

41. *NYT*, July 23, 1963, and July 25, 1963.

42. Wolfe, "The Marvelous Mouth," 148–149.

43. "I Am the Greatest," compact disc, produced by Gary Belkin, Columbia Records (album 1963; reissued 1999); Kindred, *Sound and Fury*, 51–52, 336; *NYP*, November 6, 1963; *NYT*, April 1, 1963.

44. Marable, *Malcolm X*, 254; FBIMX-9.

45. Commanding Officer, Bureau of Special Services to Chief Inspector, August 13, 1963, Malcolm X BOSS File.

46. Roberts and Klibanoff, *The Race Beat*, 346–348.

47. *LAT*, August 26, 1963; Marable, *Malcolm X*, 242.

48. Marable, *Malcolm X*, 256; Goldman, *The Death and Life*, 103–105.

49. *NYAN*, September 7, 1963; Malcolm X, "The Farce on Washington," Box Five, Folder Five, MXP; FBIMXNY-51.

50. C. Eric Lincoln, "A Visit with Muhammad: On the Eve of Birmingham," *Negro Digest*, April 1964, 77, 79–80.

51. Ibid., 80; FBIMXNY-50.

52. Cone, *Martin & Malcolm & America*, 113.

53. *LAS*, August 29, 1963; *OT*, September 28, 1963.

54. *OT*, September 29, 1963.

55. *OT*, September 28, 1963.

56. *Philadelphia Daily News*, September 30, 1963; *PT*, October 1, 1963; Marable, *Malcolm X*, 258.

57. *PT*, October 1, 1963.

58. *PT*, October 1, 1963.

59. *AMX*, 321.

Chapter 9

1. "The Negro in America," *Newsweek*, July 29, 1963, 15–16.

2. Ibid.; *CD*, November 21, 1963; Joseph, *Waiting 'Til the Midnight Hour*, 54–55; Marable, *Malcolm X*, 263–264.

3. *CD*, November 21, 1963.

4. Malcolm X, "Message to the Grassroots," in *Malcolm X Speaks*, ed. Breitman, 8–9.

5. Ibid.

6. Ibid.

7. Goldman, *The Death and Life*, 117–118.

8. *NYJA*, November 20, 1963; *NYT*, November 22, 1963; Memorandum agreement between Louisville Sponsoring Group and Cassius M. Clay Jr., October 15, 1963, in Professional Boxing Hearings Before the Subcommittee on Antitrust and Monopoly of the Committee on

the Judiciary, United States Senate, 88th Cong., 2d Sess., Part 4: Liston-Clay Fight (1964), 1819.

9. Hauser, *Muhammad Ali*, 98.

10. *AMX*, 332; George Plimpton, "Miami Notebook: Cassius Clay and Malcolm X," *Harper's Magazine*, June 1964, 58.

11. *AMX*, 332; "Muhammad Ali on the Jack Paar Show," YouTube, https://www.youtube.com/watch?v=w0J4cN-V_l8.

12. Clay's poetry recital quoted from *The Jack Paar Tonight Show* footage, November 29, 1963. See "Muhammad Ali on the Jack Paar Show," YouTube.

13. *NYJA*, November 20, 1963.

14. W. S. Cutchins to Louisville Sponsoring Group, September 24, 1963, Box MSSA B613a, Folder 1658, GBB.

15. Ibid.; Gordon Davidson interview with author.

16. W. S. Cutchins to Louisville Sponsoring Group, September 24, 1963.

17. Hauser, *Muhammad Ali*, 99.

18. Ibid.

19. *NYT*, February 23, 1964.

20. *NYJA*, November 20, 1963; *NYT*, June 2, 1963.

21. *NYJA*, November 20, 1963.

22. FBIEM—JUNE File.

23. *MS*, October 11, 1963.

24. *Malcolm X: Make It Plain*, PBS Video, produced and directed by Orlando Blackwell (1997).

25. Ibid.

26. ABC Radio recording of Don Gardiner, November 22, 1963, accessed at http://www.radiotapes.com/JFK/ABC_JFK_03.mp3; *Malcolm X: Make It Plain*.

27. Clegg, *An Original Man*, 200.

28. Branch, *Pillar of Fire*, 184; *NYT*, December 2, 1963.

29. Branch, *Pillar of Fire*, 184.

30. *AMX*, 329–330.

31. FBIEM-8.

32. *NYT*, December 6, 1963; *NYP*, December 5, 1963; *PC*, December 14, 1963; FBIMXNY-55.

33. FBIEM-8.

34. Goldman, *The Death and Life*, 119; Lomax, *When the Word Is Given*, 177 (emphasis ours).

35. *AMX*, 331.

36. Clegg, *An Original Man*, 203–204.

37. Branch, *Pillar of Fire*, 200; FBIMXNY-56.

38. Branch, *Pillar of Fire*, 200–201.

39. This exchange between Malcolm and Elijah is drawn from FBIEM-8 and Evanzz, *The Judas Factor*, 168–170.

40. Marable, *Malcolm X*, 125–126; Goldman, *The Death and Life*, 110; *PC*, April 4, 1964.

41. Branch, *Pillar of Fire*, 201–202.

42. Ibid.

43. *AMX*, 331.

44. Goldman, *The Death and Life*, 91, 126.

45. *AMX*, 331.

46. Evanzz, *The Judas Factor*, 173–175.

47. Marable, *Malcolm X*, 282.

Chapter 10

1. Lipsyte, *An Accidental Sportswriter*, 66; Robert Lipsyte interview with author.

2. Pacheco, *Muhammad Ali*, 5–6; Fleischer, *Training for Boxers*, chapter 19.

3. Huston Horn, "A Rueful Dream Come True," *SI*, November 18, 1963, 26–27.

4. For the bus story, see: *NYT*, November 6, 1963; *LCJ*, November 6, 1963; Horn, "A Rueful Dream Come True," 26–27; Hauser, *Muhammad Ali*, 59–60; Remnick, *King of the World*, 142–143; "Playboy Interview: Cassius Clay," *Playboy*, October 1964, 72–73.

5. *NYT*, November 6, 1963; *LCJ*, November 6, 1963; Horn, "A Rueful Dream Come True," 26–27.

6. Gilbert Rogin and Morton Sharnik, "Can't a Fellow Make a Mistake?," *SI*, July 17, 1961, 24.

7. *MH*, February 9, 1964; *NYT*, December 7, 1963.

8. Gilbert Rogin, "The Many Faces of Mr. Mac," *SI*, February 17, 1964, 56; *MH*, February 27, 1964.

9. *MH*, February 9, 1964.

10. Evanzz, *The Judas Factor*, 176.

11. Ibid., 176–177.

12. Ibid.; FBIMXNY-56.

13. Evanzz, *The Judas Factor*, 177; FBIMX-10.

14. *AMX*, 331; Abdul Rahman Muhammad (Sam Saxon) interview with author.

15. Kathy Hersh, "High Cotton: Jazzing It Up at the Hampton House," in *Miami: Modern Metropolis: Paradise and Paradox in Midcentury Architecture and Planning*, ed. Allen T. Shulman (New York: Princeton Architectural Press: 2009), 335–337.

16. *AMX*, 332; Hauser, *Muhammad Ali*, 98.

17. Malcolm X, Florida Vacation Notebook, Box 1, Folder 4, MXP; FBIMXNY-56.

18. George Plimpton, "Miami Notebook: Cassius Clay and Malcolm X," *Harper's Magazine*, June 1964, 58.

19. Ibid.

20. Ibid.; *AMX*, 335.

21. *AMX*, 444.

22. Ibid., 333.

23. Marable, *Malcolm X*, 281–282.

24. Barry Gottehrer, "How Cassius Clay Tricked the World," *Sport*, June 1964, 84.

25. Abdul Rahman Muhammad (Sam Saxon) interview with author.

26. Olsen, *Black Is Best*, 94.

27. Gottehrer, "How Cassius Clay Tricked the World," 84.

28. Marable, *Malcolm X*, 282.

29. FBIMXNY-56; Evanzz, *The Judas Factor*, 182.

30. Evanzz, *The Judas Factor*, 181; *MH*, January 23, 1964.

31. *NYAN*, January 25, 1964.

32. Ibid.

33. Ibid.; FBIMXNY-56.

34. Evanzz, *The Judas Factor*, 172, 179.

35. *NYHT*, January 23, 1964.

36. *MH*, January 23, 1964; Robert Lipsyte, "Cassius Clay, Cassius X, Muhammad Ali," *NYTM*, October 25, 1964, n.p.; Abdul Rahman Muhammad (Sam Saxon) interview with author.

37. *MH*, January 24, 1964.

38. Ibid.

39. *NYT*, January 25, 1964; *MH*, January 23, 1964, January 25, 1964, and January 26, 1964.

40. *MH*, February 3, 1964.

41. Ibid.

42. *LCJ*, February 3, 1964.

43. Ibid.; *MH*, February 8, 1964.

44. Olsen, *Black Is* Best, 133–134.

45. *MH*, February 8, 1964; Hauser, *Muhammad Ali*, 65.

46. Hauser, *Muhammad Ali*, 65.

47. *NYT*, January 27, 1964.

48. For the Clay-Liston encounter at the Miami airport, see: *MH*, January 26, 1964, and January 27, 1964; *NYT*, January 27, 1964; "Playboy Interview: Cassius Clay," 74.

49. Jerry Izenberg interview with author.

50. For Liston's training routine, see: Plimpton, *Shadow Box*, 87–91; *MH*, January 29, 1964, January 20, 1964, and February 5, 1964.

51. *MH*, February 7, 1964.

52. *NYT*, February 8, 1964; *MH*, February 9, 1964.

53. Lipsyte, *SportsWorld*, 175–179; *MH*, February 13, 1964.

54. Lewisohn, *The Complete Beatles Chronicle*, 146–147; Hauser, *Muhammad Ali*, 63.

55. The Beatles, *The Beatles Anthology*, 123.

56. For the Clay-Beatles meeting, see: *NYT*, February 19, 1964; *NYP*, February 19, 1964; Lipsyte, *An Accidental Sportswriter*, 62–64; Spitz, *The Beatles*, 483–484.

57. *NYT*, February 21, 1964.

58. FBIMX-10; *NYT*, February 26, 1964.

59. Evanzz, *The Judas Factor*, 186; FBIMX-57.

60. Bingham and Wallace, *Muhammad Ali's Greatest Fight*, 78.

61. *Atlanta Daily World*, February 22, 1964.

62. For Conrad's encounter with MacDonald, see Hauser, *Muhammad Ali*, 66–67; Remnick, *King of the World*, 170–171.

Chapter 11

1. *CT*, February 24, 1964.

2. For descriptions of activities in Clay's Miami house, see: Plimpton, *Shadow Box*, 106–109, and "Miami Notebook: Cassius Clay and Malcolm X," *Harper's Magazine*, June 1964, 60–61.

3. Evanzz, *The Judas Factor*, 186.

4. Ibid.

5. *NYP*, March 3, 1964; Goldman, *The Death and Life*, 128–129; Evanzz, *Judas Factor*, 211; Marqusee, *Redemption Song*, 77; Marable, *Malcolm X*, 286.

6. *NYT*, February 22, 1964.

7. For the weigh-in, see: *NYJA.* February 25, 1964; *NYT*, February 26, 1964; *LAT*, February 26, 1964; *MH*, February 26, 1964; Murray Kempton, "Cassius Clay: 'I Whipped Him and I'm Still Pretty,'" *New Republic*, March 7, 1964, 9; Dundee, *My View from the Corner*, 95.

8. Gordon Davidson interview with author; William Faversham interview with Jack Olsen, JOP; Gordon Davidson interview with Jack Olsen, JOP; Olsen, *Black Is Best*, 111–115.

9. Jerry Izenberg interview with author.

10. Hauser, *Muhammad Ali*, 70.

11. *NYJA*, February 25, 1964; Pacheco, *Fight Doctor*, 63.

12. Kempton, "Cassius Clay," 9.

13. *MH*, February 22, 1964.

14. *NYT*, February 23, 1964.

15. Mee, *Liston & Ali*, 186; Remnick, *King of the World*, 186.

16. For Plimpton's meeting with Malcolm, see his "Miami Notebook," 58, and *Shadow Box*, 94–99.

17. "Welcome, Sportsman," *SI*, February 24, 1964, 8; Tex Maule, "Yes, It Was Good and Honest," *SI*, March 9, 1964, 20–25; *MH*, February 26, 1964.

18. Lipsyte, *An Accidental Sportswriter*, 62; *LAT*, February 23, 1964; *MH*, February 23, 1964.

19. *MH*, February 23, 1964; *NYJA*, February 24, 1964; *NYHT*, February 25, 1964; *LCJ*, February 22, 1964, and February 23, 1964; *NYJA*, February 24, 1964.

20. Jerry Izenberg interview with author.

21. Ibid.

22. Hauser, *Muhammad Ali*, 72–73; Pacheco, *Fight Doctor*, 65–66.

23. Remnick, *King of the World*, 187.

24. *AMX*, 335; Evanzz, *The Judas Factor*, 187.

25. Guralnick, *Dream Boogie*, 557; Evanzz, *The Judas Factor*, 188.

26. Evanzz, *The Judas Factor*, 188; *AMX*, 336.

27. Hauser, *Muhammad Ali*, 74.

28. Barry Gottehrer, "How Cassius Clay Tricked the World," *Sport*, June, 1964, 85.

29. For Clay's thoughts during the fight, see: "Playboy Interview: Cassius Clay," *Playboy*, October 1964, 78–80.

30. Descriptions of the fight are from the TNT production "Sonny Liston vs Cassius Clay (Muhammad Ali) Boxing Match," YouTube, http://www.youtube.com/watch?v=OezriPEepZs. For coverage also see: *MH*, February 26, 1964; *NYT*, February 26, 1964; *LCJ*, February 26, 1964; *NYHT*, February 26, 1964; Tex Maule, "Yes, It Was Good and Honest," *SI*, March 9, 1964, 20–25.

31. Jerry Izenberg interview with author; *LAT*, February 26, 1964.

32. Maule, "Yes, It Was Good and Honest," 22.

33. Jerry Izenberg interview with author; Hauser, *The Lost Legacy of Muhammad Ali*, 138–139; Thomas Hauser interview with author; Mike Silver, "Foul Play in Philly?," Boxing.com, April 30, 2014, http://www.boxing.com/foul_play_in_philly.html.

34. Maule, "Yes, It Was Good and Honest," 23; Jerry Izenberg also discounted the "juiced gloves" story based on his view that Joe Polino was an "honorable man." Izenberg interview with author.

35. For the story in the corner, see: Anderson, *In the Corner*, 66–67; Dundee, *I Only Talk Winning*, 194; Fried, *Corner Men*, 4; Dundee, *My View from the Corner*, 101–102; Pacheco, *Fight Doctor*, 67–69.

36. Remnick, *King of the World*, 196.

37. Dundee, *My View from the Corner*, 103.

38. "Playboy Interview: Cassius Clay," 80.

39. Ibid.

40. Maule, "Yes, It Was Good and Honest," 24.

41. Ibid., 23.

42. "Playboy Interview: Cassius Clay," 80.

43. *LAT*, February 26, 1964.

44. Ibid.; *AMX*, 336.

45. Maule, "Yes, It Was Good and Honest," 24.

46. *LAT*, February 26, 1964.

47. Red Smith, "I'm the Greatest," in *American Pastimes: The Very Best of Red Smith*, ed. Daniel Okrent (New York: Library of America, 2013), 364.

Chapter 12

1. George Plimpton, "Miami Notebook: Cassius Clay and Malcolm X," *Harper's Magazine*, June 1964, 60.

2. Ibid.

3. Hauser, *Muhammad Ali*, 106; Gordon Davidson interview with author.

4. *MH*, February 26, 1964.

5. Plimpton, "Miami Notebook: Cassius Clay and Malcolm X," 60.

6. *MH*, May 23, 2013.

7. Interview with Alex Haley, "Eyes on the Prize Interviews," October 24, 1988, EYES.

8. Jim Brown with Steve Delsohn, *Out of Bounds*, 187; Jim Brown with Myron Cope, *Off My Chest*, 162–166.

9. Hauser, *Muhammad Ali*, 106.

10. *AMX*, 337.

11. Brown, *Out of Bounds*, 189.

12. Huston Horn, "The First Days in the New Life of the Champion of the World," *SI*, March 9, 1964, 26.

13. Ibid., 26.

14. For the story of the reporters' visit, see: *LAT*, February 27, 1964; Horn, "The First Days in the New Life of the Champion of the World," 26–27.

15. *MH*, February 26, 1964; *NYT*, February 26, 1964; Horn, "The First Days in the New Life of the Champion of the World," 27.

16. *MH*, February 27, 1964.

17. *NYT*, February 27, 1964.

18. Ibid.

19. Unless otherwise cited, for Clay's press conference, see: *NYT*, February 27, 1964; *MH*, February 27, 1964; Lipsyte, *An Accidental Sportswriter*, 68–69; Hauser, *Muhammad Ali*, 81–84; Remnick, *King of the World*, 205–209.

20. *NYT*, February 27, 1964.

21. Ibid.

22. Hauser, *Muhammad Ali*, 84.

23. Abdul Rahman Muhammad (Sam Saxon) interview with author; *NYT*, February 27, 1964; *CT*, February 27, 1964; *MS*, March 13, 1964.

24. *CT*, February 27, 1964.

25. Hauser, *Muhammad Ali*, 100.

26. *MS*, March 13, 1964.

27. Horn, "The First Days in the New Life of the Champion of the World," 54.

28. Collings, ed., *Muhammad Ali*, 266–267.

29. *MH*, February 28, 1964.

30. Horn, "The First Days in the New Life of the Champion of the World," 57; *MH*, February 28, 1964.

31. Olsen, *Black Is Best*, 93.

32. *NYT*, February 28, 1964.

33. Horn, "The First Days in the New Life of the Champion of the World," 57.

34. Abdul Rahman Muhammad (Sam Saxon) interview with author.

Chapter 13

1. "Prizefighting: Cassius X," *Time*, March 13, 1964, 78; *NYDN*, March 2, 1964; *NYT*, March 2, 1964; Bobbie E. Barbee, "Will Link with Malcolm X Harm Clay's Career?," *Jet*, March 26, 1964, 50.

2. "Playboy Interview: Cassius Clay," *Playboy*, October 1964, 190.

3. Wilson, *Meet Me at the Theresa*, 1–7, 77, 164; "The Waldorf of Harlem," *Ebony*, April 1946, 8.

4. Goldman, *The Death and Life*, 51–53; "The Professor," *The New Yorker*, September 3, 1966, 28–29.

5. "The Waldorf of Harlem," 8.

6. Goldman, *The Death and Life*, 146; Robert Penn Warren, *Who Speaks for the Negro?*, 244–245.

7. *CT*, March 2, 1964.

8. *CD*, March 2, 1964.

9. *NYAN*, March 7, 1964 (emphasis ours).

10. *NYP*, March 2, 1964; *NYHT*, March 2, 1964.

11. *NYAN*, March 7, 1964.

12. *NYT*, March 4, 1964; Guralnick, *Dream Boogie*, 561; Barry Gottehrer, "How Cassius Clay Tricked the World," *Sport*, June 1964, 15; Cottrell, *Man of Destiny*, 175.

13. Guralnick, *Dream Boogie*, 561; Cottrell, *Man of Destiny*, 175–176; United Press International, March 4, 1964; *NYJA*, March 8, 1964.

14. FBIMXNY-57; Branch, *Pillar of Fire*, 255.

15. *NYT*, March 5, 1964; "Prizefighting: Cassius X," 78; "Cassius X," *Newsweek*, March 16, 1964, 74.

16. *NYJA*, March 6, 1964.

17. "Prizefighting: Cassius X," 78; Gottehrer, "How Cassius Clay Tricked the World," 86.

18. *LCJ*, March 4, 1964; *NYJA*, March 5, 1964; *NYHT*, March 6, 1964.

19. *NYHT*, March 6, 1964; FBIMXNY-57.

20. Evanzz, *The Judas Factor*, 193; *AMX*, 116–118; Carson, *Malcolm X*, 108.

21. *NYT*, March 7, 1964.

22. Ibid.; Marqusee, *Redemption Song*, 84.

23. Yusuf Shah (aka Captain Joseph Gravitt) interview with Taylor Branch, October 17, 1991, TBP; FBIMXNY-57.

24. Cottrell, *Man of Destiny*, 176; Abdul Rahman Muhammad (Sam Saxon) interview with author; FBIMXNY-57.

25. Marable, *Malcolm X*, 290–291; Goldman, *The Death and Life*, 130–131.

26. Branch, *Pillar of Fire*, 251.

27. Ibid.

28. Kram, *Ghosts of Manila*, 42.

29. Bingham and Wallace, *Muhammad Ali's Greatest Fight*, 86.

30. Hauser, *Muhammad Ali*, 123. A "close relative" of Ali's also told Jack Olsen in 1966, "Cassius was searching for a father, and Elijah Muhammad is it. If Elijah tell him, 'Don't go to war, go to jail,' he'll go to jail. That man have Cassius by the nose." See Olsen, *Black Is Best*, 33.

31. Collings, ed., *Muhammad Ali: Through the Eyes of the World*, 267–268; Hauser, *Muhammad Ali*, 306–307; Gary Smith, "Ali and His Entourage," *SI*, April 25, 1988, accessed at http://www.si.com/vault/1988/04/25/117552/ali-and-his-entourage-the-champ-and-his-followers-were-the-greatest-show-on-earth-and-then-the-show-ended-but-life-went-on.

32. Collings, ed., *Muhammad Ali*, 265; Jack Olsen, "Learning Elijah's Advanced Lesson in Hate," *SI*, May 2, 1966, n.p.; Olsen, *Black Is Best*, 30, 74–75, 105–106, 133, 141.

33. *LCJ*, March 8, 1964.

34. Ibid.

35. Kindred, *Sound and Fury*, 75–78.

36. Ibid.

Chapter 14

1. *CT*, March 14, 1964; *LAT*, March 26, 1964; Robert Lipsyte, "Cassius Clay, Cassius X, Muhammad Ali," *NYTM*, October 25, 1964, 141.

2. Hauser, *Muhammad Ali*, 83; *NYJA*, March 24, 1964.

3. Clayton Riley, "Boxing: Black Hope, White Cop-Out," *Liberator*, July 1964, 12–13; *NYJA*, March 10, 1964.

4. *NYT*, March 29, 1964.

5. Mee, *Liston & Ali*, 203–206; Cottrell, *Man of Destiny*, 180–181.

6. "Prizefighting: Cassius X," *Time*, March 13, 1964, 78; *NYJA*, March 23, 1964; *WP*, March 24, 1964; Professional Boxing Hearings Before the Subcommittee on Antitrust and Monopoly of the Committee on the Judiciary, United States Senate, 88th Cong., 2d Sess., Part 4: Liston-Clay Fight, (March 24–26, 30–31, 1964); *NYT*, March 29, 1964. According to a recent report, an FBI memo dated May 24, 1966, reveals that the Bureau suspected that Las Vegas gambler Irving "Ash" Resnick arranged for Liston to take a dive against Clay. An informant provided hearsay evidence to the FBI that Resnick and Liston both made over one million dollars betting against Sonny, though there has never been any concrete evidence to support this claim. See *Washington Times*, February 24, 2014.

7. *NYT*, March 29, 1964.

8. *NYT*, February 29, 1964, and March 7, 1964; Shelby Sankore, "Letter to Muhammad Ali," *Liberator*, May 1964, 6; *LAS*, March 12, 1964, and March 26, 1964; *CD*, March 12, 1964.

9. Remnick, *King of the World*, 228.

10. *NYHT*, March 8, 1964; Floyd Patterson with Milton Gross, "I Want to Destroy Clay," *SI*, October 19, 1964, 43–44.

11. *NYT*, March 22, 1964; Patterson with Gross, "I Want to Destroy Clay," 43–44.

12. "Playboy Interview: Cassius Clay," *Playboy*, October 1964, 192; *LCJ*, March 9, 1964; *NYT*, March 23, 1964.

13. Little, *American Orientalism*, 9–33.

14. *LAT*, March 12, 1964.

15. *NYAN*, March 14, 1964.

16. Remnick, *King of the World*, 212.

17. "Playboy Interview: Cassius Clay," 190.

18. *NYT*, March 9, 1964; *NYP*, March 9, 1964.

19. *NYT*, March 9, 1964.

20. Ibid.

21. Muhammad, *Message to the Blackman in America*, 255–257.

22. FBIMX-10.

23. FBIEM-8.

24. Branch, *Pillar of Fire*, 256.

25. Evanzz, *The Judas Factor*, 215.

26. *NYJA*, March 10, 1964.

27. *NYP*, March 10, 1964.

28. Branch, *Pillar of Fire*, 256.

29. Allan Morrison, "Who Killed Malcolm X?," *Ebony*, October 1965, 136.

30. Goldman, *The Death and Life*, 133; "Why Malcolm X Quit the Black Muslims," *Sepia*, May 1964, 58; "Malcolm's Brand X," *Newsweek*, March 23, 1964, 32.

31. *NYJA*, March 12, 1964; "Malcolm's Brand X," 32.

32. *NYHT*, March 13, 1964; *NYT*, March 15, 1964.

33. Joseph, *Dark Days, Bright Nights*, 78; *CD*, March 14, 1964; "Boxing's Feet of Clay," *SEP*, April 18, 1964, 86; "The Pied Piper of Harlem," *Christian Century*, April 1, 1964, 422; Gertrude Samuels, "Feud Within the Black Muslims," *NYTM*, March 22, 1964, 105.

34. *NYT*, March 15, 1964; "Malcolm X: Self-Defense vs. Submission," *Liberator*, April 1964, 3; "Why Malcolm X Quit the Black Muslims," 58; Carlos E. Russell, "Exclusive Interview with Brother Malcolm X," *Liberator*, May 1964, 16.

35. *NYHT*, March 22, 1964; Goldman, *The Death and Life*, 13.

36. *NYHT*, March 22, 1964.

37. *CA*, March 14, 1964; *NYJA*, March 14, 1964.

38. *CA*, March 14, 1964; *MS*, April 10, 1964, and April 24, 1964.

39. Mark Kram, "On the Throne Behind the Power," *SI*, September 27, 1976, n.p.

40. Hauser, *Muhammad Ali*, 377.

41. Robert H. Boyle, "Champ in the Jug?," *SI*, April 10, 1967, n.p.; *CD*, October 13, 1962, and October 20, 1962.

42. FBIHM, Summary Report, Chicago Office, January 18, 1966.

43. *NYT*, March 21, 1964, and March 22, 1964.

44. *NYJA*, March 20, 1964.

45. *NYJA*, March 21, 1964.

46. *NYT*, March 21, 1964, and April 3, 1964; Mrs. Edward Monahan to the President, March 19, 1964 (letter in authors' possession).

47. Olsen, *Black Is Best*, 22–23.

48. Bingham and Wallace, *Muhammad Ali's Greatest Fight*, 98–99.

49. Lipsyte, *SportsWorld*, 89.

50. Ibid.; *NYT*, March 24, 1964; Bobbie E. Barbee, "Will Link with Malcolm X Harm Clay's Career?," *Jet*, March 26, 1964, 50; Helen Dudar, "The Muslims and Black Nationalism," *New York Post Magazine*, April 10, 1964, 1.

51. On March 22, 1964, the WBA announced that it intended to vacate Clay's heavyweight title. On that same day, an unknown newswoman asked Malcolm if he would help Cassius respond to the WBA's threat. Malcolm replied that they had met earlier that day, but he clearly knew very little about the WBA's most recent announcement. For Malcolm's interview, see "Malcolm X on Black Nationalism & Cassius Clay," YouTube, http://www.youtube.com/watch?v=LoyrSO9Ko08.

52. *PC*, March 21, 1964; Barbee, "Will Link with Malcolm X Harm Clay's Career?," 52.

53. *NYT*, March 23, 1964; DeCaro, *On the Side of My People*, 199.

54. Unless otherwise cited, all quotes from Malcolm's speech come from Malcolm X, "The Ballot or the Bullet," in *Malcolm X Speaks: Selected Speeches and Statements*, ed. George Breitman (New York: First Grove, 1990), 23–44.

55. Joseph, *Waiting 'Til the Midnight Hour*, 102.

56. Robert Lipsyte, "Cassius Clay, Cassius X, Muhammad Ali," *NYTM*, October 25, 1964, 29.

Chapter 15

1. "Muhammad Ali in Africa," *SI*, June 1, 1964, 20; *NYT*, May 17, 1964; *GT*, May 18, 1964; *DG*, May 21, 1964, and May 22, 1964.

2. *GT*, May 18, 1964.

3. "Muhammad Ali in Africa," 25; *MS*, June 19, 1964; *GT*, May 20, 1964.

4. "Sunrise on the Gold Coast," *Time*, February 9, 1953, 22–23.

5. Myron Cope, "Feats of Clay," in *Great Sports Reporting*, ed. Allen Kirschner (New York: Dell, 1969), 163.

6. *DG*, May 20, 1964.

7. *MS*, April 24, 1964, and May 22, 1964; *NYHT*, May 7, 1964.

8. Essien-Udom, *Black Nationalism*, 275; Clegg, *An Original Man*, 135–144.

9. Clegg, *An Original Man*, 239–241; Sales, *From Civil Rights to Black Liberation*, 63.

10. Marqusee, *Redemption Song*, 124; "Muhammad Ali (Cassius Clay) Visits Africa," *Sepia*, November 1964, 10; *MS*, May 8, 1964.

11. *NYT*, May 18, 1964.

12. Sam Pollard and Judy Richardson interview with Muhammad Ali, February 16, 1989, EYES.

13. Hauser, *Muhammad Ali*, 112.

14. Boyd and Al-Shabazz, *The Diary of Malcolm X*, 46.

15. Ibid., 14, 37; *AMX*, 374.

16. Boyd and Al-Shabazz, *The Diary of Malcolm X*, 14, 35–36.

17. Ibid.,10; Marable, *Malcolm X*, 165–168.

18. *AMX*, 369; *NYT*, May 8, 1964; *CD*, May 14, 1964.

19. Goldman, *The Death and Life*, 171–172.

20. Gaines, *American Africans in Ghana*, 164–168.

21. Alice Windom to "Christine," May 29, 1964, Box 24, Folder 33, John Henrik Clarke Papers, Schomburg Center for Research in Black Culture, New York; Angelou, *All God's Children Need Traveling Shoes*, 128–130; Gaines, *American Africans in Ghana*, 180.

22. Goldman, *The Death and Life*, 173.

23. *AMX*, 376; Malcolm X, letter from Accra, Ghana, May 11, 1964, in *Malcolm X Speaks: Selected Speeches and Statements*, ed. George Breitman (New York: First Grove, 1990), 62; *DG*, May 13, 1964; Accra Embassy to Department of State, May 24, 1964, Record Group 59, Central Foreign Policy File, 1964–1966, POL 6 US, National Archives, College Park, Maryland.

24. Dudziak, *Cold War Civil Rights*, 169–170, 192.

25. Muehlenbeck, *Betting on the Africans*, 73, 78–79; Henry Tanner, "Nkrumah Steps Up Nkrumahism," *NYTM*, January 14, 1962, 23.

26. Muehlenbeck, *Betting on the Africans*, 73, 77, 90–92; Lloyd Garrison, "Portrait of Nkrumah as Dictator," *NYTM*, May 3, 1963, 17–18; Gaines, *American Africans in Ghana*, 164–165,

177, 188–90; "Ghana: Fighting Fantasy," *Newsweek*, February 17, 1964, 54; *NYT*, February 5, 1964, February 6, 1964, and May 1, 1964.

27. "Ghana and the USA," *West Africa*, May 9, 1964, 529; Gaines, *American Africans in Ghana*, 190, 194; Accra Embassy to Department of State, May 24, 1964; *NYT*, May 21, 1964.

28. Gaines, *American Africans in Ghana*, 194; Strickland, *Malcolm X*, 104.

29. *AMX*, 389; Boyd and Al-Shabazz, *The Diary of Malcolm X*, 52; Goldman, *The Death and Life*, 177.

30. Accra Embassy to Department of State, May 24, 1964.

31. Malcolm X, letter from Accra, Ghana, May 11, 1964, in *Malcolm X Speaks: Selected Speeches and Statements*, ed. George Breitman (New York: First Grove, 1990), 62; Malcolm X, "We Are All Blood Brothers," *Liberator*, July 1964, 6.

32. Unless otherwise cited, this section is drawn from Angelou, *All God's Children Need Traveling Shoes*, 143–144; *AMX*, 391–392.

33. *NYT*, May 18, 1964.

34. Ibid.

35. Ibid.

36. "Champ's African 'Love Affair,'" *Ebony*, September 1964, 92; *NYT*, May 19, 1964; *DT*, May 26, 1964.

37. *DG*, May 19, 1964; *GT*, May 19, 1964, and May 20, 1964; Early, *This Is Where I Came In*, 14.

38. *NYT*, May 19, 1964; Joint State Department/USIA Message, June 3, 1964, Record Group 59, Central Files, 1964–1966, TRV–Clay, Cassius, National Archives, College Park, Maryland; *MS*, May 22, 1964. For the history of black athletes as global ambassadors, see Thomas, *Globetrotting*.

39. *NYT*, May 20, 1964.

40. Ibid.

41. "Champ's African 'Love Affair,'" 85; *GT*, May 23, 1964; *MS*, June 19, 1964; *DG*, May 21, 1964, and May 22, 1964.

42. *DG*, May 20, 1964; *NYT*, May 24, 1964, and May 25, 1964; *MS*, June 19, 1964; "Muhammad Ali in Africa," 24.

43. *NYT*, June 4, 1964; *DT*, June 2, 1964.

44. *BG*, June 3, 1964; *NYT*, June 3, 1964.

45. For the Ali-Bassey exchange, see *NYT*, June 3, 1964.

46. *NYT*, June 4, 1964.

47. *CT*, June 25, 1964; *BG*, June 3, 1964; *DT*, June 8, 1964.

48. *CT*, March 1, 1964; *MS*, April 24, 1964; AP, February 29, 1964; From Cairo Embassy to Sec. of State, March 9, 1964, Record Group 59, Central Files, 1964–1966, TRV–Clay, Cassius; *NYT*, June 15, 1964; From Cairo Embassy to Department of State, April 25, 1964, Record Group 50, Central Files, 1964–1966, POL 13–10 US, National Archives, College Park, Maryland.

49. AP, June 4, 1964; *BG*, June 4, 1964; "Champ's African 'Love Affair,'" 88.

50. "Champ's African 'Love Affair,'" 90; *MS*, July 3, 1964.

51. "Boxing's 'King' in Cairo," *Arab Observer* (Cairo), June 15, 1964, 43; *EG*, June 8, 1964, and June 16, 1964; *NYT*, June 6, 1964, and June 7, 1964; "Champ's African 'Love Affair,'" 89.

52. *EG*, June 9, 1964.

53. *BG*, June 18, 1964.

54. *NYT*, June 24, 1964.

55. Ibid., June 27, 1964.

Chapter 16

1. Norwood, *About Paterson,* 12. Unless otherwise noted, our sketch of Hayer is drawn from Friedly, *Malcolm X,* 99–107, 214–217, and Goldman, *The Death and Life,* 414–417.

2. *MS,* April 10, 1964.

3. In a sworn affidavit signed February 25, 1978, Hayer identified his accomplices only as Ben X, Leon X, Wilbur X, and William X.

4. Unless otherwise noted, the press conference is drawn from: *AMX,* 393, 450–451; *CDN,* May 22, 1964; "Malcolm X's Famous Speech After Returning from Mecca," YouTube.com, http://www.youtube.com/watch?v=tuHYZdf-ad0. Unlike Muhammad Ali, Malcolm never insisted that people recognize his Muslim name. He preferred that his followers call him "Minister Malcolm" or "Brother Malcolm."

5. *NYP,* May 22, 1964.

6. Goldman, *The Death and Life,* 184.

7. Ibid., 183–184.

8. DeCaro, *On the Side of My People,* 250; *NYT,* May 24, 1964.

9. Lomax, *To Kill a Black Man,* 198; FBIRS, Summary Report, Chicago Office, August 27, 1964.

10. Goldman, *The Death and Life,* 193.

11. George E. Curry, "The Last Days of Malcolm X: Part I," *Emerge,* February 1995, n.p.

12. FBIMX-14; Rickford, *Betty Shabazz,* 200–201.

13. FBIMX-14; Perry, *Malcolm,* 288.

14. Branch, *Pillar of Fire,* 346; FBIMX-14; Marable, *Malcolm X,* 344, 426. In an interview with Manning Marable, Thomas 15X Johnson, one of the three men convicted of murdering Malcolm, claimed that John Ali ordered the hit on Malcolm.

15. Branch, *Pillar of Fire,* 348; Perry, *Malcolm,* 291; FBIMX-14. Thomas 15X Johnson also recalled that one of the captains said to leave Malcolm alone.

16. Goldman, *The Death and Life,* 198.

17. *NYHT,* June 16, 1964; Evanzz, *The Judas Factor,* 240; *PC,* May 30, 1964.

18. *NYP,* June 26, 1964.

19. Unless otherwise cited, the NOI rally is drawn from *NYT,* June 29, 1964; *CT,* June 29, 1964.

20. Ali's speech is drawn from "Elijah Muhammad and Muhammad Ali @ Harlem, June 28, 1964," YouTube, https://www.youtube.com/watch?v=R0-GGR17tG4.

21. *MS,* July 17, 1964.

22. Leon Phillips FBI File, Summary Report, New York Office, January 5, 1965, FBILP; Phillips FBI File, Summary Report, New Haven Office, January 19, 1965, FBILP; Lipsyte, *SportsWorld,* 92, 99.

23. *NYAN,* January 16, 1965; Evanzz, *The Messenger,* 300; Leon Ameer interview with FBI special agents, Boston Office, February 17, 1965, FBILA.

24. Goldman, *The Death and Life,* 414.

25. Ibid., 189–190; Joseph, *Dark Days, Bright Nights,* 90–91; "Statement of Basic Aims and Objectives," Organization of Afro-American Unity, June 28, 1964, in Breitman, *The Last Year of Malcolm X,* 105–113.

26. *CD,* July 6, 1964, and July 8, 1964; Clegg, *An Original Man,* 223–224; Evanzz, *The Messenger,* 303.

27. There are conflicting accounts about the details of Malcolm's escape from his assailants. See Goldman, *The Death and Life*, 204; Rickford, *Betty Shabazz*, 199–200; Marable, *Malcolm X*, 358; Perry, *Malcolm*, 307–308; FBIMX-14; *NYDN*, February 15, 1965.

28. Evanzz, *The Messenger*, 301; Leon Ameer interview with FBI agents, February 17, 1965, FBILA; Aubrey Barnette with Edward Linn, "The Black Muslims Are a Fraud," *SEP*, February 27, 1965, 27; Perry, ed., *Malcolm X*, 136.

29. Marable, *Malcolm X*, 359.

30. *LAS*, July 23, 1964; *Bridgeport (CT) Telegram*, July 8, 1964. For the Ali-Slack interaction, see "The Ladies of the Press: Guest Muhammad Ali," YouTube, https://www.youtube.com/watch?v=JsFgoB3fBbU.

31. Olsen, *Black Is Best*, 130; *MS*, June 5, 1964, June 19, 1964, July 3, 1964, July 17, 1964, January 15, 1965, March 19, 1965, April 9, 1965, and April 16, 1965.

32. Hauser, *Muhammad Ali*, 135.

33. "Playboy Interview: Cassius Clay," *Playboy*, October 1964, 82.

34. Olsen, *Black Is Best*, 152; Hauser, *Muhammad Ali*, 114–116; Remnick, *King of the World*, 231.

35. Source withheld by request.

36. *NYT*, August 15, 1964; Olsen, *Black Is Best*, 152; Hauser, *Muhammad Ali*, 130–131.

37. Olsen, *Black Is Best*, 153; Hauser, *Muhammad Ali*, 131.

38. Myron Cope, "Muslim Champ," *SEP*, November 14, 1964, 36; *BG*, October 28, 1964.

39. Cope, "Muslim Champ," 33, 37; *NYT*, September 15, 1964; Gilbert Rogin, "Still Hurt and Lost," *SI*, November 16, 1964, accessed at http://www.si.com/vault/1964/11/16/606303/still-hurt-and-lost.

40. Remnick, *King of the World*, 233.

41. Rogin, "Still Hurt and Lost."

42. Cope, "Muslim Champ," 33.

43. Ibid., 37; *BG*, November 5, 1964, and November 12, 1964; "Prizefighting: Playing Grownups," *Time*, November 13, 1964, 104.

44. Hauser, *Muhammad Ali*, 120; Cope, "Muslim Champ," 34.

45. Bingham and Wallace, *Muhammad Ali's Greatest Fight*, 89.

46. Hauser, *Muhammad Ali*, 122–123.

47. Cope, "Muslim Champ," 34.

48. *NYT*, February 23, 1965; Hauser, *Muhammad Ali*, 121; *Muhammad Ali: Made in Miami*, DVD, produced by Gaspar Gonzalez and Alan Tomlinson (PBS, 2008); Hans J. Massaquoi, "Mystery of Malcolm X," *Ebony*, September 1964, 42.

49. Rogin, "Still Hurt and Lost."

50. *NYT*, November 13, 1964; *BG*, November 12, 1964; Watkins, *Stepin Fetchit*, 266.

51. Watkins, *Stepin Fetchit*, 10, 263.

52. Remnick, *King of the World*, 246.

53. Huston Horn, "The $400,000 Bellyache," *SI*, November 23, 1964, accessed at http://www.si.com/vault/1964/11/23/614111/the-400000-bellyache; *NYT*, November 14, 1964.

54. Remnick, *King of the World*, 238.

55. Ibid.; *BG*, November 15, 1964; *NYT*, November 15, 1964; *NYJA*, February 25, 1965.

56. Remnick, *King of the World*, 239.

57. Goldman, *The Death and Life*, 217–220.

58. Malcolm's interview with Claude Lewis is drawn from Gallen, *Malcolm X*, 165–178; Goldman, *The Death and Life*, 236–238.

Chapter 17

1. *MS*, April 10, 1964, and December 4, 1964; Marable, *Malcolm X*, 347.

2. Marable, *Malcolm X*, 397–398.

3. *Muhammad Ali: Made in Miami*, DVD, produced by Gaspar Gonzalez and Alan Tomlinson (PBS, 2008).

4. Leon Ameer interview with FBI agents, February 17, 1965, FBILA.

5. Ibid; *BG*, February 22, 1965.

6. Leon Ameer, interview by Barry Gray, *Barry Gray Show*, WMCA, January 14, 1965, FBILA.

7. Ibid.; *NYAN*, January 16, 1965.

8. *WP*, January 10, 1965.

9. *NYAN*, January 16, 1965.

10. Ibid., January 9, 1965, and January 16, 1965; Evanzz, *The Messenger*, 315.

11. For Ali's quotes about Leon Ameer, see: *NYT*, January 14, 1965; Lipsyte, *SportsWorld*, 97–98.

12. Friedly, *Malcolm X*, 105; Goldman, *The Death and Life*, 417.

13. Perry, *Malcolm X*, 118; *NYAN*, February 6, 1965; Rickford, *Betty Shabazz*, 218.

14. Jamal, *On the Dead Level*, 239–256.

15. Ibid., 257–259.

16. FBIMX-13.

17. Lomax, *When the Word Is Given*, 82; Evanzz, *The Judas Factor*, 197–198; Lomax, *To Kill a Black Man*, 198–199.

18. Friedly, *Malcolm X*, 155.

19. *NYJA*, February 28, 1965.

20. Marable, *Malcolm X*, 409–410; Branch, *Pillar of Fire*, 573–574.

21. Goldman, *The Death and Life*, 251.

22. Ibid.; FBIMX-15; Branch, *Pillar of Fire*, 574–575; *AMX*, 464.

23. Weisbrot, *Freedom Bound*, 133–134.

24. Ibid., 134.

25. FBIMX-15; Goldman, *The Death and Life*, 253–254; Rickford, *Betty Shabazz*, 222.

26. Goldman, *The Death and Life*, 262; Rickford, *Betty Shabazz*, 222–223.

27. Goldman, *The Death and Life*, 262; Branch, *Pillar of Fire*, 590.

28. *NYDN*, February 15, 1965; Evanzz, *The Judas Factor*, 291; *NYT*, February 17, 1965.

29. *CST*, February 22, 1965.

30. Hauser, *Muhammad Ali*, 110.

31. For Malcolm's comments at the February 15 OAAU rally, see Perry, *Malcolm X*, 109–149. According to Manning Marable, Malcolm and Jeremiah X met with the Klan in January 1961. See Marable, *Malcolm X*, 178–179.

32. Gordon Parks, "'I Was a Zombie Then—Like All Muslims, I Was Hypnotized,'" *Life*, March 5, 1965, 28.

33. Evanzz, *The Judas Factor*, 292–293; *Newsday*, July 23, 1989; George Curry, "The Last Days of Malcolm X: Part II," *Emerge*, March 1995, n.p.; Clark, ed., *February 1965: The Final Speeches*, 123.

34. Curry, "The Last Days of Malcolm X: Part II"; Goldman, *The Death and Life*, 259–262.

35. Goldman, *The Death and Life*, 266.

36. Parks, "'I Was a Zombie Then—Like All Muslims, I Was Hypnotized,'" 28.

37. FBIMX-18. Unless otherwise noted, this section on the assassination of Malcolm X is drawn from Goldman, *The Death and Life*, 268–278, 314–315, 418.

38. George Curry, "The Last Days of Malcolm X," *Emerge*, February 1995, n.p.

39. *AMX*, 469–470.

40. Friedly, *Malcolm X*, 96–97, 216; Karim with Skutches and Gallen, *Remembering Malcolm*, 187.

41. Friedly, *Malcolm X*, 97.

42. Curry, "The Last Days of Malcolm X," n.p.

43. Rickford, *Betty Shabazz*, 228.

44. Marable, *Malcolm X*, 434; *AMX*, 471; Karim with Skutches and Gallen, *Remembering Malcolm*, 188.

45. Karim with Skutches and Gallen, *Remembering Malcolm*, 189; Curry, "The Last Days of Malcolm X," n.p.

46. Rickford, *Betty Shabazz*, 227; Marable, *Malcolm X*, 436.

47. *NYDN*, February 22, 1965; Marable, *Malcolm X*, 436.

48. *NYP*, February 22, 1965; *NYHT*, February 22, 1965.

49. *NYHT*, February 22, 1965; *CD*, February 22, 1965.

50. Rickford, *Betty Shabazz*, 230.

51. Marable, *Malcolm X*, 437–438; *NYP*, February 22, 1965.

52. "The Violent End of the Man Called Malcolm," *Life*, March 5, 1965, 26–27; *NYHT*, February 22, 1965; Rickford, *Betty Shabazz*, 231.

53. Rickford, *Betty Shabazz*, 238; Marable, *Malcolm X*, 439; Parks, "'I Was a Zombie Then—Like All Muslims, I Was Hypnotized,'" 30.

54. *CA*, February 22, 1965; *CST*, February 22, 1965; *CD*, February 23, 1965; FBIMX-15.

55. Ali with Durham, *The Greatest*, 191–192; *CA*, February 22, 1965.

56. *NYT*, February 23, 1965; *CA*, February 23, 1965; Clegg, *An Original Man*, 228.

57. *CA*, February 24, 1965; *NYP*, February 23, 1965.

58. *CA*, February 24, 1965; *CDN*, February 24, 1965; *LAS*, February 25, 1965; *BG*, February 24, 1965.

59. For quotes from the 1965 Saviours' Day Convention, see *CT*, February 24, 1965, and February 27, 1965; *BG*, February 27, 1965; *NYT*, February 27, 1965; Goldman, *The Death and Life*, 301–302.

60. *NYHT*, February 28, 1965; *NYP*, February 28, 1965; Goldman, *The Death and Life*, 302–303; Carson, *Malcolm X*, 394–395.

61. *NYHT*, February 28, 1965; Rickford, *Betty Shabazz*, 244–246, 252–253.

62. *NYHT*, February 28, 1965; *NYT*, February 28, 1965; *NYJA*, February 28, 1965.

63. *NYHT*, February 28, 1965.

64. Hampton and Fayer, eds., *Voices of Freedom*, 262–263.

65. Ibid.

66. Carson, *Malcolm X*, 396; *NYHT*, February 28, 1965.

67. Goldman, *The Death and Life*, 302–303.

Epilogue

1. Hauser, *Muhammad Ali*, 125.

2. *LAT*, May 23, 1965; Lipsyte, *SportsWorld*, 93; *NYDN*, May 23, 1965.

3. Lipsyte, *SportsWorld*, 105; *NYJA*, May 26, 1965.

4. Tex Maule, "A Quick, Hard Right and a Needless Storm of Protest," *SI*, June 7, 1965, accessed online at http://www.si.com/vault/1965/06/07/607743/a-quick-hard-right-and-a-needless-storm-of-protest.

5. Ibid.; *NYHT*, May 26, 1965.

6. *NYHT*, May 26, 1965; *NYJA*, May 26, 1965.

7. Maule, "A Quick, Hard Right and a Needless Storm of Protest."

8. Jimmy Cannon, "Cassius Clay Is the Sixties," in *The Muhammad Ali Reader*, ed. Gerald Early (New York: Robert Weisbach Books, 1998), 81–82.

9. Hauser, *Muhammad Ali*, 144–145; Robert Lipsyte interview with author.

10. Hauser, *Muhammad Ali*, 145–147.

11. Ibid., 129–132; *NYT*, April 15, 1966, and April 27, 1966.

12. Branch, *Pillar of Fire*, 602–604; Goldman, *The Death and Life*, 349–351.

13. Lipsyte, *SportsWorld*, 119. For the Ali-Robinson encounter, see Kram, *Ghosts of Manila*, 35, 38, 41.

14. Remnick, *King of the World*, 289–290.

15. Hauser, *Muhammad Ali*, 142–147, 154, 166–173; Irwin Shaw, "Muhammad Ali and the Little People," *Esquire*, November 1969, 124–125; Bingham and Wallace, *Muhammad Ali's Greatest Fight*, 160.

16. *MS*, April 4, 1969.

17. Hauser, *Muhammad Ali*, 194; *MS*, April 11, 1969.

18. Dick Schaap, "Muhammad Ali: Then and Now," in *At the Fights: American Writers on Boxing*, ed. Kimball and Schulian (New York: Library of America, 2012), 215.

19. Plimpton, *Shadow Box*, 137; Devin Gordon, "True Believer," *Newsweek*, December 23, 2001, accessed at http://www.newsweek.com/true-believer-148423.

20. *NYT*, November 9, 1974.

21. For the exchange between Ali and his security team, see Kindred, *Sound and Fury*, 204.

22. Branch, *Pillar of Fire*, 603.

23. Hauser, *Muhammad Ali*, 295.

24. Baldwin, *Notes of a Native Son*, 101; Lipsyte, *An Accidental Sportswriter*, 71.

25. Ali with Ali, *The Soul of a Butterfly*, 84–85.

Postscript

1. "Ali: The Tributes," *SI*, June 13, 2016, 49.

2. Ibid., 48.

3. Ibid.

4. Jeffrey Sammons, "Rebel with a Cause: Muhammad Ali as Sixties Protest Symbol," in *Muhammad Ali: The People's Champ*, ed. Elliott Gorn (Urbana and Chicago: University of Illinois Press, 1995), 171–172; Bingham and Wallace, *Muhammad Ali's Greatest Fight*, 234.

5. Hauser, *Muhammad Ali: His Life and Times*, 281–282.

6. Stephen R. Wenn and Jeffrey P. Wenn, "Muhammad Ali and the Convergence of Olympic Sport and U.S. Diplomacy in 1980: A Reassessment from Behind the Scenes at the U.S. State Department," *OLYMPIKA: The International Journal of Olympic Studies* II (1993): 45–66; Leah Wright Rigueur, "When Muhammad Ali Endorsed Ronald Reagan," *WP*, June 10, 2016, accessed at https://www.washingtonpost.com/posteverything/wp/2016/06/10/when-muhammad-ali-endorsed-ronald-reagan/; Doug Rossinow, "It's Time We Face the Fact That Ronald Reagan Was Hostile to Civil Rights," *History News Network*, April 20, 2015, accessed at http://historynewsnetwork.org/article/158887.

7. Gerald Early, "Introduction: Tales of the Wonderboy," in *The Muhammad Ali Reader*, ed. Gerald Early (New York: Robert Weisbach Books, 1998), xii-xiii; David K. Wiggins, "Victory for Allah: Muhammad Ali, the Nation of Islam, and American Society," in *Muhammad Ali: The People's Champ*, ed. Gorn, 108–110; Riguer, "When Muhammad Ali Endorsed Ronald Reagan."

8. Thomas Hauser, *Muhammad Ali: A Tribute to the Greatest* (New York: Pegasus Books, 2016), 210–213.

9. Michael Harriot, "No, Muhammad Ali Did NOT Transcend Race, He Was Unapologetically BLACK," *Ebony*, June 6, 2016, accessed at http://www.ebony.com/black-history /muhammad-ali-race#axzz4E2TM4Hpr.

10. Dave Zirin, "Read What Malcolm X's Daughter Said at Muhammad Ali's Funeral," *The Nation*, June 17, 2016, accessed at https://www.thenation.com/article/the-words-of-malcolm -xs-daughter-attalah-shabazz-at-muhammad-alis-funeral/.

11. *Firing Line with William Buckley, Jr.*, December 12, 1968.

12. *AMX*, 332.

13. This section is adapted from a message written by Johnny Smith to Dave Zirin. See Zirin, "Read What Malcolm X's Daughter Said at Muhammad Ali's Funeral."

INDEX